Erich Fromm's Revolutionary Hope

IMAGINATION AND PRAXIS: CRITICALITY AND CREATIVITY IN EDUCATION AND
EDUCATIONAL RESEARCH

VOLUME 4

SCOPE
Current educational reform rhetoric around the globe repeatedly invokes the language of 21st century learning and innovative thinking while contrarily re-enforcing, through government policy, high stakes testing and international competition, standardization of education that is exceedingly reminiscent of 19th century Taylorism and scientific management. Yet, as the steam engines of educational "progress" continue down an increasingly narrow, linear, and unified track, it is becoming increasingly apparent that the students in our classrooms are inheriting real world problems of economic instability, ecological damage, social inequality, and human suffering. If young people are to address these social problems, they will need to activate complex, interconnected, empathetic and multiple ways of thinking about the ways in which peoples of the world are interconnected as a global community in the living ecosystem of the world. Seeing the world as simultaneously local, global, political, economic, ecological, cultural and interconnected is far removed from the Enlightenment's objectivist and mechanistic legacy that presently saturates the status quo of contemporary schooling. If we are to derail this positivist educational train and teach our students to see and be in the world differently, the educational community needs a serious dose of imagination. The goal of this book series is to assist students, practitioners, leaders, and researchers in looking beyond what they take for granted, questioning the normal, and amplifying our multiplicities of knowing, seeing, being and feeling to, ultimately, envision and create possibilities for positive social and educational change. The books featured in this series will explore ways of seeing, knowing, being, and learning that are frequently excluded in this global climate of standardized practices in the field of education. In particular, they will illuminate the ways in which imagination permeates every aspect of life and helps develop personal and political awareness. Featured works will be written in forms that range from academic to artistic, including original research in traditional scholarly format that addresses unconventional topics (e.g., play, gaming, ecopedagogy, aesthetics), as well as works that approach traditional and unconventional topics in unconventional formats (e.g., graphic novels, fiction, narrative forms, and multi-genre texts). Inspired by the work of Maxine Greene, this series will showcase works that "break through the limits of the conventional" and provoke readers to continue arousing themselves and their students to "begin again" (Greene, *Releasing the Imagination*, 1995, p. 109).

Erich Fromm's Revolutionary Hope

Prophetic Messianism as a Critical Theory of the Future

Joan Braune
Mount Mary University, Milwaukee, Wisconsin, USA

SENSE PUBLISHERS
ROTTERDAM/BOSTON/TAIPEI

A C.I.P. record for this book is available from the Library of Congress.

ISBN: 978-94-6209-810-7 (paperback)
ISBN: 978-94-6209-811-4 (hardback)
ISBN: 978-94-6209-812-1 (e-book)

Published by: Sense Publishers,
P.O. Box 21858,
3001 AW Rotterdam,
The Netherlands
https://www.sensepublishers.com/

Printed on acid-free paper

With love and solidarity,
To my parents, Nick and Linda Braune,
And to my grandmother Yvonne Braune.

TABLE OF CONTENTS

FOREWORD

We are pleased to present this book on the work of Erich Fromm by Joan Braune during these crucial and dark times of perpetual war, economic uncertainty and the relentless drumbeats toward standardization in education. Joan's outstanding scholarship came to our attention when we were researching the intersections between the lives of Erich Fromm and Paulo Freire. We were thrilled to discover that these two men spent time together, but more than that held similar views on the role we play in creating hope as active, dynamic, and forward-looking. For Fromm, hope that is not acted upon is not hope at all. And for Freire, hope is so essential to what it means to be human that he describes it as an "ontological need". Both Fromm and Freire saw hope as active and productive, and a necessary driving force for social change. Dr. Braune's innovative reading and elaboration of Fromm's "prophetic messianism" fits precisely into this critical view of radical hope that refuses to accept the present order while actively imagining and engaging in transformative praxis in present local and global contexts. We present this book as a beacon of active and persistent hope in the midst of prevailing and often hopeless conditions in education. It is our hope that in the spirit of Fromm and Freire, this book will both inform and inspire teachers, students and cultural workers everywhere to imagine and transform schools, neighborhoods, cities and countries into dynamic places of sustainable life, radical love and the undiminished light of humanity at its best.

—*Tricia Kress and Robert Lake*

ACKNOWLEDGMENTS

This exhilarating and consuming project could not have come to fruition without feedback from and fruitful dialogue with many people. I would like to thank my dissertation committee, especially my advisor, Arnold Farr, along with the rest of the committee: Christopher Zurn, Richard Wolin, Ronald Bruzina and Theodore Schatzki. Arnold Farr was incredibly insightful and supportive throughout the dissertation process, and it has been a pleasure to work with him and to join in the Marcuse Society conferences. Oliver Leaman also provided helpful feedback.

I would also like to thank Robert Lake, co-editor of this series with Tricia Kress, both of whom have done much fine work in bringing Critical Theory into wider circles of education, including among emancipatory educators. I am publishing through this series at Bob's invitation, and I am eager to do so, not least because I think the material is timely for the left today, as well as for Critical Theory and critical pedagogy. I am very pleased that this book will form part of the series on "Imagination and Praxis: Creativity and Criticality in Educational Research."

My parents, Nick Braune and Linda Braune, were immensely helpful. I am incredibly fortunate that my parents were very interested in my research and had many ideas to offer and discuss. My father in particular was a dialogue partner, and we have presented on Fromm together at a range of conferences. Both my parents offered more proofreading help than anyone ought to ever do for free. I am immensely grateful.

My grandmother Yvonne Braune, besides knowing a slew of labor history and being in other ways equally awesome, deserves tremendous thanks for her financial assistance in helping me through both undergraduate and graduate education.

Rainer Funk, the director of the Erich Fromm archive in Tübingen, Germany and director of the International Erich Fromm Society helped to answer some questions, including sharing with me some of Fromm's correspondence via e-mail, and it has been an honor to participate in two of the European conferences he helped to organize on Fromm's work. I am also grateful to the Thomas Merton Center at Bellarmine University, where I was able to study the original correspondence between Thomas Merton and Erich Fromm. (I also viewed documents by Fromm at the New York Public Library and University of Kentucky Special Collections Library.)

I would also like to thank Beth Rosdatter, John Connell, Tiffany Rogers, Kimberly Goard, and Craig Slaven for their proofreading assistance or related feedback at different stages of the writing process. I would also like to acknowledge the encouragement of strong networks of graduate student friends, including a writers group and an online goal-setting group.

It is a pleasure to thank all those who helped me bring this work to fruition, not all of whom can be listed here. Naturally, all weaknesses of the book are my responsibility and not that of anyone mentioned here.

* * *

This is a book about a radical tradition, and my life is partly the product of radical traditions, although anyone who chooses to be part of such traditions is part of them. When my mother's grandmother Ida Solowey fled czarist Russia for New York City, after having gotten into some trouble over illegally redistributing grain to peasants, I imagine she expected the revolution would come soon. When my paternal grandfather Paul Braune left behind a Catholic seminary when the reality of the Great Depression shattered his political complacency, and when he later went to work as a lawyer for draft dodgers and Black Panthers, there must have been times when he also expected the revolution to come soon. So too, probably, did my parents in the 1960s. I, too, want to choose for the revolution, and I too expect the revolution soon. When I look back and realize how many before us felt the same way, I see it not as evidence that we will fail but as a promise to live in and if necessary (though I want to win), to pass on. Thank you, to all who have gone before in the struggle.

INTRODUCTION

Messianism is a central, recurring theme in the work of Erich Fromm (1900–1980).[1] As an idea, a theme that captured the spirit of the times, and a movement taking a variety of political, religious, and cultural forms, messianism was in the air throughout Fromm's youth, while he was deciding his position on the debates raging amongst left-wing Jewish intellectuals. He returned to the messianism question in the 1950s, grappling with it continually from the time of his 1955 book *The Sane Society* to his late, posthumously published manuscript, "Marx and Meister Eckhart on Having and Being," on which he was working in the 1970s (OBH 113).

As Michael Löwy, Eduardo Mendieta, Rudolf Siebert, and others have pointed out, Fromm's thought, like that of many other Frankfurt School thinkers, was partly motivated by a partially secularized messianism, a theoretical adaptation of the traditional Jewish hope and enthusiasm for the coming of the messianic age (Löwy, Redemption and Utopia 151-8; Mendieta 142-3; Siebert *passim*). While the concept of messianism was initially developed by Jewish theologians, not by political theorists, it has proven to be a useful tool for understanding revolutionary change, and strains of its influence can be found throughout the work of the Frankfurt School, from Walter Benjamin's "Theses on the Philosophy of History" to T. W. Adorno's *Minima Moralia* (Adorno 247).

Fromm distinguishes between two types of messianism, "prophetic" messianism (which he defends) and "catastrophic or apocalyptic" messianism (which he critiques). Prophetic messianism works for and hopes for a future "messianic age" or utopia, which will be characterized by justice, fulfillment, peace, harmony, and redemption, and it believes that this future will be brought about by human effort in history. Prophetic messianism is characterized by a "horizontal longing"; it looks ahead to the future with hope (YSB 133). It sees the future fulfillment of its hopes not as a dramatic "rupture" with history but as a result of human action in history.

Despite its bold vision of a coming time of justice and peace, prophetic messianism is not a version of historical determinism (YSB 88, 154-5). Although prophetic messianism involves a "certainty based on inner experience" (a certainty grounded in hope, not in empirical proof), this certainty is "paradoxical" and does not see the future fulfillment of its hopes as inevitable (156-7). Rather, messianism is a version of what Fromm calls "alternativism." According to Fromm, the Hebrew prophets presented people with "alternatives" to choose between and explained the likely consequences that would follow from each choice. Rosa Luxemburg, a modern-day "prophet" of socialism, presented a similar alternative when she spoke of the need for humanity to choose either "socialism or barbarism," a decision that Fromm saw as no less crucial for his time (133). The prophet never forces the people to choose one alternative over another—the people are free to choose—but the prophet communicates to the people that each choice will carry certain inevitable consequences, not only for society as a whole but for the individuals who compose it.

Catastrophic (or apocalyptic) messianism, the type of messianism that Fromm criticizes and rejects, holds that radical change can occur only through a catastrophe that creates a dramatic break from all preceding history. According to a prominent version of this type of messianism, in a time of catastrophe—in fact, at the moment of humanity's greatest corruption and failure—some kind of external force will rescue humanity and inaugurate a utopian-like future. This salvation could come in any of several forms: a political leader, a pre-determined law of history according to which crises must produce their own resolutions, a self-declared party vanguard, a deity, a small excluded minority, or an intellectual or artistic elite. Whichever form it takes, this saving force is perceived as entering society from the outside. In contrast to the horizontal longing of prophetic messianism, catastrophic messianism is characterized by a "vertical longing," a longing for forces or authorities to descend from outside the usual pattern of human affairs, as a *force majeure*, to redeem a fallen and helpless humanity (YSB 133).

According to catastrophic messianism, the vertical intervention into history by the messianic event creates a dramatic "rupture," severing the messianic future from all preceding history. Scholar of Jewish mysticism Gershom Scholem was one of the leading exponents of catastrophic messianism, and the concept of rupture is central to his understanding of messianism (OBH 142). Scholem posits a "lack of transition between history and redemption" (The Messianic Idea 10). In an oft-quoted passage, he explains,

> Redemption is not a product of immanent development such as we find it in modern Western interpretations of messianism since the Enlightenment where, secularized as the belief in progress, messianism still displayed unbroken and immense vigor. *It is rather transcendence breaking in on history, an intrusion in which history itself perishes, transformed in its ruin because it is struck by a beam of light shining into it from an outside source.* (10, Scholem's italics)

The image of the coming of the messianic age as a bolt of lightning from above differs profoundly from Fromm's prophetic messianism, which conceives the messianic age as a product of ongoing human action in (horizontal) history.

According to Fromm, catastrophic messianism has dangerous psychological and social consequences. Although catastrophic messianism may appear hopeful in its expectation of dramatic change, it is actually based upon a form of despair that gives the false appearance of hope (ROH 8). At its most benign, it is characterized by an illusory hope that manifests itself as passive, inactive waiting, sometimes combined with busy consumption of consumer goods and mass entertainment, as the depressed and socially isolated individual fills up her time while expecting to be rescued by some authority figure (ROH 6-12). At its most malignant, the illusory hope of catastrophic messianism generates attempts to "force the Messiah," such as violently instigating catastrophes in order to force revolutionary change to occur without first gaining the committed involvement of the masses.

Fromm's distinction between prophetic messianism and catastrophic messianism is also a distinction between two historical trajectories. According to Fromm, prophetic messianism originated with the Hebrew prophets, as he explains at length in his "radical interpretation of the Old Testament," *You Shall Be as Gods* (1966). After its origin among the prophets, the prophetic-messianic idea continued to play a pivotal role in a range of history-shaping movements—in certain radical forces and elements in early Christianity (Adoptionism, Montanism) and the Middle Ages (Meister Eckhart, Joachim of Fiore, and others); in Renaissance humanism; in the proto-Enlightenment pantheism of Spinoza; in the Enlightenment and the French Revolution, in the German philosophies of Lessing, Fichte, Hegel, and Goethe; in the utopian socialism of Saint-Simon; in the Young Hegelian radicalism of Moses Hess, Heinrich Heine, and Karl Marx[2] and in the philosophies of early socialist and anarchist thinkers after Marx, including Rosa Luxemburg and Gustav Landauer (MCM 54; OBH 144-5; SS 236). In interpreting socialism as the contemporary heir of the prophetic messianic tradition, Fromm knew that he was aligning himself with a particular camp of thinkers, offering allegiance to the messianism of Hermann Cohen, Ernst Bloch, and others, while differentiating himself from others, including Gershom Scholem, Walter Benjamin, and Herbert Marcuse (TB 126).

Fromm's claim that Marx's thought and that of certain figures in the socialist movement were influenced by prophetic messianism is controversial, and the claim has faced critiques both from the left and the right. The claim that Marxism was "messianic" raises warning flags for some Marxists, especially those who classify religion as mere ideology and are thus wary of language tainted by fraternization with theology. Fromm's interpretation of the Enlightenment as messianic is sometimes met with a similar alarm. Consequently, some might prefer to replace the term messianism with some less "loaded" term, like utopianism or political hope. However, it will become apparent as the book proceeds that the concept of "messianism" cannot be abandoned and that its meaning is rooted in twentieth century historical developments.

Fromm believed that prophetic messianism was under threat in his times, endangered by a catastrophic messianism that had dealt it near-deadly blows in the twentieth century through the capitulation of the Second International to nationalism before the First World War, the degeneration of the Soviet experiment into bureaucratic "state capitalism," the rise of fascism, the collapse of the Zionist movement into militarized nationalism, the destructive psychological forces unleashed by the nuclear arms race, and the despair of the waning 1960s protest movement (SS 239; MMP *passim*). What Fromm calls catastrophic messianism was prevalent in 1920s Germany and influenced the emerging Frankfurt School, at a time when, according to Fromm, humanity had yet to recover from the outbreak of catastrophic messianism that emerged with the First World War.

Prior to World War I, Jewish thinkers in the Enlightenment tradition, such as Hermann Cohen and Leo Baeck, had theorized Judaism in Kantian terms as the "religion of reason." At the time when Cohen was developing this philosophy, the prophetic messianic spirit still held considerable sway over socialist and anarchist movements. Cosmopolitan, humanist, socialist, and calmly rational, Cohen's messianism influenced a generation of German-Jewish intellectuals. But the rational, universalist messianism of the likes of Cohen and Leo Baeck stands in sharp contrast to the later, cataclysmic, semi-Romantic messianism of some German-Jewish intellectuals of the 1920s. Cohen thus came to represent a mainstay of Enlightenment optimism and Kantian rationalism that the young radicals of the 1920s repudiated as outmoded.

Before joining the Institute for Social Research, Fromm participated in the *Freies Jüdisches Lehrhaus* in Frankfurt. The *Lehrhaus* was a hub of leftwing Jewish intellectual life in 1920s Germany; its many famous participants included Martin Buber, Gershom Scholem, Franz Rosenzweig, Leo Löwenthal, Ernst Simon, Leo Baeck, and Abraham Heschel. During this time, Fromm was influenced by Hermann Cohen's work—he later called Cohen "the last great Jewish philosopher" and praised him for grasping the connection between "messianism and socialism" (OBH 143). Yet Buber, Rosenzweig, and many others in the *Lehrhaus* circle who were initially drawn to Cohen's ideas eventually broke away from Cohen's thought (Löwy, Redemption and Utopia 59). A new messianism—romantic, nihilistic, anarchic, and catastrophic—envisioned a messianic future that would arrive not as a product of human progress or planning but suddenly, in a time of disorder and despair, through a dramatic "rupture" with all prior history. Fromm stands, sometimes isolated, as a prominent Marxist theorist who continued to defend the pre-war universalistic messianism well into the 1960s and who saw it as true to Marx's vision. His commitment to this ideal set him apart from many of his contemporaries, including his colleagues in the Frankfurt School.

THE FUTURE AS A CONTEMPORARY PROBLEM

Today the questions raised by Fromm's messianism are more relevant and vital than ever. The twentieth century was plagued by the problem of the future, and the current century appears likely to remain troubled by the same problem. Nearly all ways of thinking about the future are enmeshed in dangers, which become ever more evident in light of the tragedies of the twentieth century. On the one hand, determinism with regard to the end of history can foster quietism, whether of a blindly optimistic or cynically pessimistic sort. If the determinist acts at all, she is likely to act with destructive nihilism, viewing her action as essentially meaningless. On the other hand, despite the dangers of determinism, political hope might seem to lack all foundation or justification without the certainty that historical determinism provides, and hope for a better future seems to be a necessary component of any effort to improve society. Nearly all the empirical evidence appears to suggest that humanity is faced with an uncertain future, and if things end at all, they will likely end badly, so what could possibly—one might rhetorically ask—provide a basis for hope, save a blind, deterministic faith? Yet Fromm provides us with a real alternative.

Humanity is wrestling with the future, seeking an understanding of the future that grounds political hope without encouraging quietism or nihilism. According to Anson Rabinbach, the apocalyptic/catastrophic messianism that predominated in post-World War I Germany was characterized by an "ethical ambivalence" arising from the conflicting views between the "idea of liberation" and the "absolute superfluity of any action" (Shadow of Catastrophe 33-4). Within this tradition, Rabinbach claims, "passivity and amoral violence are often coupled" (34). But there is a way out of this ambivalence, without abandoning messianism; the way forward lies in the "paradoxical" prophetic messianism Fromm describes, as I will argue. Fromm's prophetic messianism provides a basis for political hope while eschewing determinism; it couples a certainty rooted in faith with the fundamental uncertainty of empirical reality.

Compounding the difficulty of dodging the Scylla and Charybdis of quietism and nihilism is the near-pathological fear of messianic hope instilled by the events of the past century. To some, the failure of the Soviet experiment was proof positive that messianism or utopianism could end only in totalitarian violence and oppression. Allegedly a product of Marxist hope for a new messianic time before which all preceding events would be mere "pre-history," the Soviet Union turned out to be a disastrous failure in the struggle for universal human emancipation. Although I argue that rejecting messianism wholesale is not the best response to the failure of the Soviet experiment, that failure undeniably demonstrated the danger of trying to force the messianic age onto the uninvolved, unsupportive masses (under Stalin), as well as the danger of claiming that the messianic age has arrived ("real, existing communism") when it clearly has not.

Compared only with the atrocities of Stalin's regime, quietist withdrawal looks appealing. Yet quietism also holds its horrors. Whether one attempts to avoid political decisions or not, one still makes them, wittingly or unwittingly, and at some moments in history inaction resolves itself into acquiescence to injustice, silence into complicity. Of course, this criticism is often offered against Germans under the Nazi regime, but such tragic quietism occurs more frequently than one would like to admit. As bureaucratic forms of organization and technological means of destruction reached new heights, the twentieth century more than any other era demonstrated the catastrophic consequences of blind obedience, one of the manifestations of quietism.

Into the fraught twentieth century—born, in fact, in 1900—Erich Fromm emerged as a defender of Enlightenment-style messianic hope, which was anything but a popular political position throughout most of his long career as a philosopher and public intellectual. Although the brief utopian moment of the 1960s was partly an exception, even in that milieu Fromm was a dissenter from some major currents of the left, as we will see. Between acquiescence and the attempt to forcibly incarnate a utopia without the action of the masses, Fromm sought an alternative, a way to maintain humanity's long-time hope for an end to the horrors of history, while avoiding the horrors of a desperate, merely destructive nihilism. His solution was to defend hope and a way of conceiving the future that he believed society had lost around the time of World War I.

THE REDISCOVERY OF ERICH FROMM AND MESSIANISM

Messianism remains an important, contested theme in Critical Theory and in Marxism. After remaining buried for much of the twentieth century, from the 1930s to the 1990s, discussions of messianism were brought to the fore again in the 1990s by Jacques Derrida's *Specters of Marx*, which revisited Marxist messianism in the wake of the fall of the Soviet Union, and by Jürgen Habermas's increasing interest in religion, as he grappled with the Frankfurt School's current of messianism and attempted to find his place in the Frankfurt School in relation to it.[3] Since then, messianism has practically spawned a cottage industry, from the historical exegeses of Pierre Bouretz's *Witnesses for the Future: Philosophy and Messianism* (2010) and Benjamin Lazier's *God Interrupted: Heresy and the European Imagination Between the World Wars* (2008), to the recent or contemporary philosophies of Jacques Derrida, Judith Butler, Giorgio Agamben, Cornel West, Julia Kristeva, and Slavoj Žižek, all of whom, whether or not they employ the term, respond to the theme.[4]

Perhaps more than any other member of the Frankfurt School (with the possible exception of Walter Benjamin), Erich Fromm engaged directly and publicly with the question of messianism throughout his career.[5] In fact, as I will demonstrate, his approach differs greatly from the prevailing version of messianism discussed by historians and Critical Theorists today. Despite his engagement with messianism and the uniqueness of his approach, research on Fromm's messianism is still minimal,[6] a lack that this book seeks to remedy.

Until fairly recently, Fromm was largely missing or downplayed in accounts of the history of the Frankfurt School. For example, as outlined in the following chapter, one of the canonical books on the history of the Frankfurt School, Martin Jay's *The Dialectical Imagination*, dismisses Fromm too quickly for being excessively "optimistic," while Rolf Wiggershaus's important *Frankfurt School: Its History, Theories, and Political Significance*, is laced with inaccuracies and *ad hominems* about Fromm, as is David Held's *Introduction to Critical Theory*. But the recent rebirth of interest in Walter Benjamin and Herbert Marcuse, both of whom have tended to be marginalized in the history of the Frankfurt School, bodes well for Fromm scholarship, and a rediscovery of Fromm himself is occurring as well. While the reputations of Max Horkheimer, T. W. Adorno, and, lately, Benjamin and Marcuse have tended to overshadow Fromm's contribution to Critical Theory— Fromm has even been called a "forgotten intellectual"—Fromm is now making a comeback (McLaughlin, "Forgotten Intellectual").

Recently, Fromm's work has been highlighted by Lawrence Wilde, who defends Fromm's interpretation of Marxism as a humanist, normative, and deeply Aristotelian philosophical system,[7] and by Kevin Anderson, who edited a book on Fromm's critical criminology and has written some important papers on Fromm. Stephen Eric Bronner's chapter on Fromm in *Of Critical Theory and Its Theorists* (1994) was an early indication that Fromm's reputation was being revived, and Michael Löwy has recently drawn attention to Fromm as well.[8] Although it erroneously presents Fromm as positivist, Thomas Wheatland's book *The Frankfurt School in Exile* (2009) is one of a number of texts offering a necessary corrective to the official histories of Fromm's contribution to the Frankfurt School, demonstrating the extent of Fromm's involvement in shaping the Institute's early research program. An anthology of essays on Fromm's thought has recently been published through the same series as this book and is entitled *Reclaiming the Sane Society: Essays in Erich Fromm's Thought* (ed., Seyed Javad Miri, Robert Lake, Tricia M. Kress, Sense Publishers, 2014). Rainer Funk, who worked with Fromm while he was alive and serves as the executor of Fromm's literary estate, is also an important figure in Fromm studies and has written numerous books on Fromm. He has compiled useful anthologies of Fromm's writings, in addition to operating a useful website on Fromm. A number of other authors have recently explored the uses of Fromm's thought in relation to a range of fields of study.[9] Responding to the renewed attention on Fromm, publishers have produced new editions of some of Fromm's important works, for example with Continuum Press contributing the long-out-of-print masterpiece *Beyond the Chains of Illusion: My Encounter with Marx and Freud* and Harper printing a new (abridged) edition of *On Disobedience*. Several of Fromm's books have also been republished as Routledge Classics. Two new volumes of previously unpublished works by Fromm were also released in 2010 (*Beyond Freud: From Individual to Social Psychoanalysis* and *The Pathology of Normalcy*).

Due to the rediscovery of Fromm's role in Critical Theory and the rediscovery of the influence of messianism on the Frankfurt School and Marxism, an exploration Fromm's messianism is important and timely. The neglect of Fromm's brand of messianism has been nothing short of devastating for studies of the cultural climate of German Jewish intellectual circles at the opening of the twentieth century and for understanding some of the crucial events that have unfolded since that time. Practically all the scholarship on messianism and its political implications over the past two decades recognizes only the apocalyptic/catastrophic variant. This even goes for the otherwise excellent scholarship of Michael Löwy, Anson Rabinbach, Richard Wolin, Nitzan Lebovic, and Eduardo Mendieta.[10] There are many reasons why this restriction in definition of messianism has occurred, and some of the reasons will become evident in subsequent chapters. The influence of Gershom Scholem's studies of messianism definitely played a role, but more importantly, a widespread rise in pessimism contributed to the shift.

This book is a contribution both to the ongoing rediscovery of Fromm—I demonstrate that Fromm was and remains important to Critical Theory—as well as to the debate on messianism, by showing that Fromm's messianism presents a novel and defensible approach to the messianism question. Further, I demonstrate the necessity of bringing Fromm back into the conversation, to avoid losing the messianic tradition for which he so compellingly argues. More generally, this text is a contribution to the history of philosophy and to the philosophy of history, and especially to the question of the "end of history" that has so troubled contemporary political philosophy, particularly in relation to Marxism.

* * *

In the following pages, I outline Fromm's development of a messianic theory of history and the future that speaks to the concerns of his time. Once the historical framework of the first two chapters has been established, a thorough examination of Fromm's concepts of hope and messianism becomes possible. Part I (Chapters 1 and 2) is heavily historical in focus, while Part II (Chapters 3 and 4) switches gears and is more interpretive.

The opening two chapters tell the story of a forgotten idea, the motivating force of a forgotten generation of revolutionaries and avant-garde intellectuals. It was at least partly Fromm's fidelity to this forgotten idea that caused him to be largely written out of the official histories of the many movements in which he had played a central role, in Critical Theory, psychoanalysis, and Marxism. In Chapter 1, I respond to this rewriting of history by returning to the beginning of Fromm's life and re-evaluating his contribution to the Frankfurt Institute for Social Research. I begin by addressing the ways in which Fromm has been mischaracterized by some canonical accounts of the history of the Frankfurt School, including David Held's *Introduction to Critical Theory: Horkheimer to Habermas* (1980), Rolf Wiggershaus's *The Frankfurt School: Its History, Theories, and Political Significance* (1986), and Martin Jay's *The Dialectical Imagination: A History of the Frankfurt School and the Institute of Social Research, 1923–1950* (1973). I then address some themes of Fromm's life and work prior to his membership in the Institute, in large part to demonstrate how much of his work with the Institute came out of his prior ideas, work, and experiences and that the profound insights he brought to the early Institute were his own, not products of other members. The chapter then traces Fromm's work while a formal member of the Institute and evaluates some possible reasons for his eventual departure. A final interlude forms a bridge from his work as a member of the Institute to his later work, through a brief overview of his contribution in two areas: psychoanalysis and the left.

Understanding Fromm's messianism also requires engaging the philosophical, historical, and political contexts in which it emerged theoretically and practically as a possible solution to urgent questions of the time. Therefore, in Chapter 2, I explore the meaning of messianism for several thinkers who influenced Fromm, both predecessors and contemporaries, and situate Fromm's messianism within the context of the lively debates and dialogues about revolution, utopia, esoteric knowledge, national identity, and other topics in which he was engaged, and in response to which his theory of messianism took shape. Using the themes of Gnosticism, *Lebensphilosophie*, and the rejection of the masses-as-reason entailed in the cultural evolution from *Geist* to *Seele*, I explore the evolution of messianism in early-twentieth-century Germany. Beginning with anarchist revolutionary Gustav Landauer and neo-Kantian philosopher Hermann Cohen, the chapter then addresses three philosophers of the *Lehrhaus*—Martin Buber, Gershom Scholem, and Franz Rosenzweig—and two young thinkers in Heidelberg before a parting of ways, Ernst

Bloch and Georg Lukács. Finally, the chapter touches upon the peculiar affinities of the Stefan George circle to Critical Theory.

In Part II of the book, I turn towards a theoretical and interpretive approach to Fromm. Fromm's account of messianic hope and his philosophical defense of it are explored in light of both historically situated and perennial concerns. Chapter 3 focuses upon hope, examining Fromm's negative and positive definitions of it, his philosophical defense of hope, and the phenomenological experience of hope. The three negative definitions of hope are explained at length: (1) hope is not mere desiring or wishing, (2) hope is not passive or inactive "waiting," and (3) hope does not attempt to "force the Messiah." Although he holds that less can be said positively and propositionally about hope, Fromm connects hope with "life" and "growth" and provisionally defines it as an "awareness of [the] pregnancy" of the present. Fromm argues for an ethical obligation to anticipate the future with hope, including an obligation to seek out signs of potential in the present, as opposed to finding only evidence suggesting that humanity is doomed. Responding to the obligation to hope reveals the crucial choice of alternatives with which humanity is faced, and without hope (a hope that is far from politically neutral), the alternative remains hidden. The idea of what one might call an epistemologically privileged subject is also found in Lukács's assertion of the privileged standpoint of the class-conscious proletariat, and specifically on the topic of hope, in Catholic existentialist philosopher Gabriel Marcel's essay in *Homo Viator*. I draw upon Marcel in order to uncover something that Fromm appears to be trying to say but does not articulate as fully or as clearly as does Marcel's account.

Chapter 4 focuses at length upon Fromm's messianism and argues that Fromm's messianism is indeed (despite some evidence that could be interpreted to the contrary) faithful to the pre-war messianic model of Hermann Cohen, not the later, more apocalyptic or catastrophic model. Arguing against Eduardo Mendieta's and Rainer Funk's interpretations of Fromm's messianism, which reflect a widespread mis-categorization of Fromm's messianism, I suggest that a lack of understanding of Fromm's uniqueness in relation to the rest of the Frankfurt School has caused him to be incorrectly categorized with the apocalyptic/catastrophic camp of messianism. In the process, Fromm's sort of messianism has been nearly forgotten, or is often discounted as not truly messianic.

Most of Chapter 4 is structured around a response to a summation offered by Eduardo Mendieta of the collective messianic outlook of the Frankfurt School, a list that Mendieta draws and builds upon from the criteria outlined by Anson Rabinbach's book *In the Shadow of Catastrophe: German Intellectuals between Apocalypse and Enlightenment*. I break down these criteria into a list of five themes: (1) Rupture, (2) Historical Golden Age and Anamnesis, (3) the Enlightenment, (4) Progress and Catastrophe, and (5) Utopia and Imagining/Conceiving the Future. I demonstrate that on each of these five themes, Fromm's messianism differs significantly from the account offered by Mendieta/Rabinbach. This exploration is followed by a daring reply to Rainer Funk's account of Fromm's messianism, wherein I argue that Funk incorrectly portrays Fromm's messianism as a kind of esoteric "Gnosticism."

A concluding, experimental epilogue comments upon the continuing relevance of Fromm's messianism for contemporary society. In politics and popular culture, the search for a Messiah figure or magic helper, rather than actively constructing a better society, is perhaps the norm in mainstream American society. However, the protest of public employees in Wisconsin and the subsequent Occupy Wall Street movement, sparked in part by the Arab Spring, have begun to renew the prophetic messianic ideal, among a wide array of intersecting liberation struggles, including current struggles for a living wage and against mass incarceration. The resurgence of class as an organizing principle and the reemergence of populist activism in the Occupy movement are still transforming the American political landscape, despite the formidable challenges that lay ahead.

Without the prophetic messianic hope articulated and defended by Fromm, it becomes impossible to bridge the divide between the real and the ideal. This book is not only about the recovery of a lost past—it is about the construction of a different future. In Critical Theory and in theory broadly, loss of prophetic messianic hope has caused the abandonment of utopian projects and has severed the ties of theory and practice. If Critical Theorists want to make theory radical again, a firm philosophical basis for hope in the political future needs to be established, and much can be learned from the strange history of its previous rise and fall.

NOTES

[1] Most of the books Fromm published during his life directly addressed the theme of messianism, as did a range of his articles and posthumously published manuscripts. The books that directly discuss messianism include: *The Sane Society* (1955), *Let Man Prevail: A Socialist Manifesto and Program* (1960), *Marx's Concept of Man* (1961), *May Man Prevail? An Inquiry into the Facts and Fictions of Foreign Policy* (1961), *Beyond the Chains of Illusion: My Encounter with Marx and Freud* (1962), *You Shall Be as Gods: A Radical Interpretation of the Old Testament* (1966), *The Revolution of Hope* (1968), *To Have or To Be?* (1976) and his unfinished, posthumously published manuscript "Marx and Meister Eckhart on Having and Being" (in *On Being Human*).

[2] The clearest summation of Fromm's position on Marx can be found in the introductory chapter to his *Marx's Concept of Man*:

> I shall try to demonstrate that...[Marx's] theory does not assume that the main motive of man is one of material gain; that, furthermore, the very aim of Marx is to liberate man from the pressure of economic needs, so that he can be fully human; that Marx is primarily concerned with the emancipation of man as an individual, the overcoming of alienation, the restoration of his capacity to relate himself fully to man and to nature; that Marx's philosophy constitutes a spiritual existentialism in secular language and because of this spiritual quality is opposed to the materialistic practice and thinly disguised materialistic philosophy of our age. Marx's aim, socialism, based on this theory of man, is essentially prophetic Messianism in the language of the nineteenth century. (MCM 3)

[3] E.g., cf. Jürgen Habermas, *Religion and Rationality: Essays on Reason, Religion, and Modernity* (Cambridge, Massachusetts: MIT Press, 2002).

[4] Jacques Derrida, of course, employs the term "messianism" and revitalizes it; the key text is *Specters of Marx*. On Judith Butler, see her essay "Prophetic Religion and the Future of Capitalist Civilization" in *The Power of Religion in the Public Sphere*, ed. Eduardo Mendieta and Jonathan Vanantwerpen

(Columbia, 2011). For Agamben on messianism, see *The Time that Remains: A Commentary on the Letter to the Romans* (Stanford University Press, 2005). Cornel West is noteworthy in this regard for his defense of hope and the prophetic, although he is not heavily engaged in postmodern debates about "messianism." For Kristeva, cf. *Strangers to Ourselves* (Columbia University Press, 1994). Žižek's frequent talk of the "Holy Spirit" as a loving community or "emancipatory collective" bears ties, historically and theoretically, to messianism. For texts that can be read as a Žižekian account of messianism, see *First as Tragedy, Then as Farce* (Verso, 2009), especially the concluding chapter, and *In Defense of Lost Causes* (AK Press, 2011), as well as *God in Pain: Inversions of Apocalypse* (Seven Stories Press, 2012).

[5] Although Walter Benjamin was never a formal member of the Frankfurt Institute for Social Research, he is generally classed among the members of the broader category of "Frankfurt School" thinkers.

[6] For example, Svante Lundgren's *The Fight Against Idols: Erich Fromm on Religion, Judaism and the Bible* offers a helpful overview of Fromm's thought on various religious matters, and the question of messianism is treated, although Lundgren seems to miss its significance for his thought and the important historical context surrounding the issue. Rudolf Siebert's *The Critical Theory of Religion* grasps the importance of messianism for Fromm's thought, but Siebert does not seem to differentiate Fromm's messianism much from that of other members of the Frankfurt School, while I argue that Fromm's messianism is of a very different sort and somewhat a critique of the messianism of the rest of the Frankfurt School.

[7] Cf. Lawrence Wilde, *Erich Fromm and the Quest for Solidarity* (New York: Palgrave MacMillan, 2004), and Lawrence Wilde, "Against Idolatry: The Humanistic Ethics of Erich Fromm" in *Marxism's Ethical Thinkers*, Ed. Lawrence Wilde (Houndmills, U.K.: Palgrave, 2001).

[8] *Redemption and Utopia: Jewish Libertarian Thought in Central Europe: A Study in Elective Affinity.* Trans. Hope Heaney. (Stanford, California: Stanford University Press, 1992); "Anticapitalist Readings of Weber's Protestant Ethic: Ernst Bloch, Walter Benjamin, Georg Lukacs, Erich Fromm" *Logos Journal* (http://logosjournal.com/2010/lowy/).

[9] Several examples of note:
  • Education: Rafael Pangilinan, Robert Lake
  • Ethics: In addition to Lawrence Wilde, there is Francisco Illescas, *Reflexiones Éticas a partir de Erich Fromm: Una propuesta para el humanismo del siglo XXI.*
  • Sociology: Neil McLaughlin, Anderson and Quinney
  • Psychology: *Towards Psychologies of Liberation* by Mary Watkins and Helene Shulman.
  • Jewish Studies: *Material Culture and Jewish Thought in America* by Ken Koltun-Fromm (Indiana University Press, 2010)
  • Jewish theology: Rabbi David Hartman
  • Sociology of Religion: Seyed Javad Miri, in Iran ("Rereading Fromm's Conditions of the Human Situation" Volume 11. December 2010; *Transcendent Philosophy: An International Journal for Comparative Philosophy and Mysticism*; "Religion and Social Theory in the Frommesque Discourse" *Islamic Perspective*. No. 4. 2010).

[10] Michael Löwy is one of the best contemporary scholars of this cultural milieu and of the theme of messianism, but he defines the prophetic tradition out of messianism from the start, and he writes that Scholem is "universally recognized as the greatest authority in this area [Jewish messianism and political implications]" ("Jewish Messianism" 106).
    Although Wolin, Rabinbach, and Lebovic offer a compelling critique of apocalyptic messianism and a defense of the Enlightenment as a radical project, they tend to use the term "messianism" to refer only to its apocalyptic variant. For Rabinbach, for example, see Rabinbach's four criteria of messianism in Chapter 4 below. For Wolin, cf. the chapter on messianism in *Labyrinths: Explorations in the Critical History of Ideas*, which proved exceedingly useful for this book but is problematic in certain respects, perhaps largely due to its reliance on Gershom Scholem's account of messianism. Wolin has been wary of messianism, treating it partly as a nostalgic, restorative enterprise and seeing it as reliant on an undialectical intervention of transcendence into history, an account of messianism that Fromm rejects, as we shall see (Wolin, Labyrinths 49–50).

PART I

EARLY FROMM AND WEIMAR GERMANY

CHAPTER 1

ERICH FROMM'S LEGACY AND CONTRIBUTION TO THE EARLY FRANKFURT SCHOOL

Understanding Erich Fromm's messianism requires a preliminary exploration of his early life and work, since his contributions have been widely misrepresented, and since he was not an isolated scholar but an activist and a public intellectual. It is also necessary to respond to some widespread myths about Fromm's role in the Frankfurt School[1] in order to show that Fromm was a central figure in the Frankfurt School and a radical, serious, and original thinker. This examination of Fromm's early work will establish some of the themes that reappear throughout his later work, addressed in following chapters. Finally, this chapter concludes with an overview of Fromm's later life with regard to two themes: psychoanalysis and the left.

Fromm played a seminal role in Critical Theory, but until recently his dramatic impact has been downplayed in the canonical accounts of the history of Critical Theory, often because his ideas were too radical or unorthodox. Although Fromm was central to the Frankfurt School's early work, until the 1990s he was virtually written out of the history of Critical Theory. When he is discussed in the canonical accounts, he is often dismissed as a peripheral figure, and his work is often shunned as overly "optimistic" ("Pollyannaish"), unserious, not radical, or mere popularizing. And although his work was catalytic for many on the activist left, he has often been presented by histories of the sixties as a feel-good pop psychologist, a kind of Oprah-for-the-left (or a Norman Vincent Peale, to use his contemporary Herbert Marcuse's example) (*Eros and Civilization* 262). For a time Fromm became what Neil McLaughlin termed a "forgotten intellectual" (McLaughlin, "Forgotten Intellectual"). I will not dwell at length upon the reasons for Fromm's loss of popularity in these spheres, though I will posit some possible explanations; for a more detailed account, I would refer the reader to McLaughlin's article, "How to Become a Forgotten Intellectual: Intellectual Movements and the Rise and Fall of Erich Fromm" in *Sociological Forum* (1998). In this chapter, I explore Fromm's early life and work, up to his break with the Frankfurt School in 1939, which was shortly before his first major publication in English, his best-selling book *Escape from Freedom* (1941). The relevance of Fromm's early work to his later ideas will become clearer in later chapters. Fortunately, since Fromm's ideas remain as timely as ever, he is now beginning to make a comeback. This chapter is a contribution to the ongoing rediscovery of Fromm's early work.

After exploring some common myths about Erich Fromm's role in the Frankfurt Institute, I examine his work prior to joining the Institute. This will set the stage for Fromm's later work on messianism, explored at length in later chapters, and will establish that he brought his own, original ideas with him to the Institute. Following an overview of Fromm's pre-Institute work, I offer an exploration of Fromm's work during the approximately ten years of his membership in the Institute. Fromm contributed significantly to the development of the Institute's early research program. Far from being a mere product of the Institute, Fromm was one of its leading architects.

1.1   THE AIRBRUSHING OF FROMM FROM THE HISTORY OF THE INSTITUTE

Although Fromm was one of the earliest members of the Frankfurt Institute for Social Research—he became a formal, tenured member in 1930, before both Herbert Marcuse (in 1933) and T. W. Adorno (in 1938)—and although he played a central role in the Institute's early years, Fromm was virtually written out of the history of the Frankfurt School until recently. His legacy in Critical Theory has fallen victim to an "origin myth"—as McLaughlin puts it, drawing upon the sociology of knowledge—that accords him a marginal role (McLaughlin, "Origin Myths"). Over the past two decades a renaissance has occurred with regard to Fromm's work and the history of Fromm's role in Critical Theory through the work of Stephen Eric Bronner, Lawrence Wilde, Kevin Anderson, Michael Löwy, Neil McLaughlin, and Thomas Wheatland, among others. The old origin myth of the Frankfurt School, however, continues to exert its influence over some current scholarship, and this myth fundamentally mislocates Fromm's contribution. It ignores that Fromm was an early member of the Frankfurt School's core circle and that his theoretical and empirical work were central to the Institute's program. The myth also downplays or fails to properly credit Fromm's tremendously important synthesis of the psychoanalytic and Marxist methods and his related development of the theory of the authoritarian personality, which formed the basis for much of the Institute's later work.

Fromm's marginalization was not the result of mere scholarly error, nor the consequence of some historically contingent series of events that rendered his ideas less serviceable or less noticeable. On the contrary, Fromm's role as a persistent gadfly in every institution and tradition to which he belonged did not ingratiate him to Critical Theorists, some Marxists, or orthodox psychoanalysts, and his marginalization from canonical historical accounts of these fields was often intentional and systematic. After the 1960s protest movement faded, Fromm was also unintentionally sidelined because his messianic hope was out of sync with the prevailing, pessimistic Zeitgeist, as we will see in later chapters. His refusal to confine his work to a single academic discipline or to obediently toe the line of any "school" of thought also had much to do with his marginalization during the 1970s and 80s.

In many works surveying the history or main ideas of the Institute, Fromm is barely mentioned. For example, Trent Schroyer's *The Critique of Domination: The Origins and Development of Critical Theory* (1973) and Zoltán Tar's *The Frankfurt School: The Critical Theories of Max Horkheimer and Theodor W. Adorno* (1985) say almost nothing about Fromm (McLaughlin, "Origin Myths" 113n7). Schroyer's book only mentions Fromm once in passing (Schroyer 203). To be fair, the book is not so much a history of the Frankfurt School as an exploration of certain themes, with a heavy focus on Marx and Habermas, but its lack of engagement with Fromm is symptomatic of the problems of the genre. Tar's book, meanwhile, is closer to an historical account of the Frankfurt School, yet it equates the early Frankfurt School with Horkheimer, ignoring the contributions of Fromm and others to the early Frankfurt School. The title of the book alone perpetuates the myth that the Frankfurt School was essentially a product of Max Horkheimer and T. W. Adorno.[2] And the most important recent book on Horkheimer, John Abromeit's 2011 *Max Horkheimer and the Foundations of the Frankfurt School*, while it gives Fromm more attention than some of the older texts, still treats Fromm's role in the early study of the German working class as confined mainly to gathering empirical data and supplying psychoanalytic categories, with Horkheimer as the theoretical mastermind (Abromeit 219).

Nor does Fromm fare better in bland and supposedly unbiased reference works. Despite the rediscovery of Fromm, even some recent reference works still play into the origin myth. For example, the German Library (Continuum) volume on the Frankfurt School includes selections from Horkheimer, Adorno, Walter Benjamin, Herbert Marcuse, and Leo Löwenthal, but nothing from Fromm. Likewise, *The Cambridge Companion to Critical Theory* (2004) does not contain an essay devoted to Fromm, and Fromm is mentioned only twice in the volume. He is mentioned only once and quite briefly in the essay on the "marriage of Marxism and psychoanalysis"—the very project for which Fromm was hired by the Institute!— and he is mentioned once more in Raymond Guess's contribution, which classifies Fromm with Franz Neumann and Walter Benjamin as having had a "perhaps more distanced and idiosyncratic relation to the central group" of the Institute (Whitebook 75; Guess 105). That Fromm's role in the Institute was anything but "distanced" or peripheral will become clear shortly.

When Fromm is not summarily dismissed, he is often gravely misrepresented. Three of the earliest, most important works on the history of the Institute for Social Research gravely misconstrue Fromm's contribution: David Held's *Introduction to Critical Theory: Horkheimer to Habermas* (1980), Rolf Wiggershaus's *The Frankfurt School: Its History, Theories, and Political Significance* (1986), and Martin Jay's *The Dialectical Imagination: A History of the Frankfurt School and the Institute of Social Research, 1923–1950* (1973). In this section, I examine the weaknesses of Held's, Wiggershaus's, and Jay's accounts of Fromm as presented in these three books. I am not concerned here with the merit of any of these books as a whole—each constitutes an important contribution to the study of the Frankfurt School—but only with their role in establishing the "origin myth" about Fromm's role in the Institute.

First, David Held's *Introduction to Critical Theory* offers a small number of scattered comments on Fromm, in the course of which Held distances Fromm from the early Institute. Held treats Fromm as a merely marginal member and sometimes not even as a member at all. In fact, Held incorrectly claims that Fromm did not become a formal member until after the Institute's exile to the United States, though in fact Fromm had become a member three years earlier and had helped facilitate the group's transition to the United States (Held 111). Held even contrasts Fromm with "the Institute" and "the Institute's members," while referring to times when Fromm was still a formal member of the Institute (119). He also misconstrues the reasons for Fromm's later removal from the Institute, writing that Fromm "left the Institute…in order to spend more time on clinical work and to develop a psychology that was more explicitly sociological and less Freudian," while in fact Horkheimer decided to cut Fromm's salary, and Fromm believed that he was being fired for being too Marxist and demanded a hefty severance package—more about that shortly (111). Held's tone towards Fromm is dogmatic and "priestly" in the bureaucratic, gate-keeping sense.[3] To socialists, the claim that Fromm left the Institute because he wanted to develop some other theoretical approach may sound alarmingly reminiscent of the typical excuses of some socialist party that has just kicked out a perceived troublemaker: "We didn't purge him; he abandoned our line, so in effect he'd already split from the Party anyway."

When it does not airbrush Fromm from the history of the Institute as completely as Held's book does, the origin myth often makes Fromm perform a magical vanishing act after leaving the Institute. On the rare occasions when it must be mentioned, Fromm's post-Institute work is dismissed in the literature as unserious, not radical, or excessively optimistic. A typical example of the first two of these charges against Fromm's later work can be found in Wiggershaus's book, while the last charge ("optimism") is made in Jay's book.

Compared to David Held, Wiggershaus has a fairly significant amount to say about Fromm. However, Wiggershaus presents Fromm as an unserious, flaky thinker who abandoned radicalism. According to Wiggershaus, Fromm's early thought was mired in insoluble contradictions that eventually led him to irrational escapism. Since Wiggershaus does not want to make the Frankfurt School itself look flaky, he seeks to demonstrate that Fromm abandoned some early, more sensible standpoint after leaving the Institute. Thus, following a relatively useful summary of Fromm's contribution to the early Frankfurt School, he sums up by exposing a dubious contradiction in Fromm's early thought, followed by an odd dismissal of Fromm's later work:

> First, it was shown [by Fromm] that the tight functioning of society would not permit any radical change in the conditions of life; then it was said that only a radical change in the conditions of life would be able to change the behaviour of the masses. But even this sort of change in the conditions of life would only lead to the creation of the new ideological superstructure which the "economic and social base would require." With views such as these, it was only a matter of time before someone like Fromm, who was convinced that fulfillment in life was possible for everyone, turned resolutely towards a messianic humanism which offered an ever-present escape from the endless chain of being and consciousness. (Wiggershaus 60)

Wiggershaus's perceived contradiction in Fromm's thought builds upon a reductionist reading of three texts: Fromm's empirical study of the German working class, his lengthy essay on early Christianity ("The Dogma of Christ"), and his article "Politics and Psychoanalysis" (58-9). The apparent contradiction concerns the classic, often oversimplified Marxist distinction between base and superstructure. Wiggershaus erroneously interprets "The Dogma of Christ" and the study of the German working class as saying that the ideological superstructure completely controls the economic base, to the point of freezing it in stasis. In "The Dogma of Christ," Fromm argued that the power of the Roman Empire was reinforced by a conservative theological turn in early Christianity away from radical eschatological expectation and towards a passive acceptance of earthly misfortunes. Fromm's study on the German working class, which Wiggershaus also references, had revealed that the German working class had too great an attraction to authoritarianism to be prepared to launch a truly emancipatory revolution or to effectively resist the rise of fascism. Wiggershaus concludes that both studies meant that the superstructural authoritarian beliefs of the masses *entirely control* the economic base, preventing changes to the economic system.

Wiggershaus then interprets Fromm's essay on "Politics and Psychoanalysis" to be saying the opposite, i.e., *that the economic base mechanically generates the ideological superstructure*, a view that Fromm also rejected. In fact, the "Politics and Psychoanalysis" essay was an argument against the idea that psychoanalysis could substitute for political struggle, "curing" society purely through simply making people aware of their irrational motivations. Although the essay does assert that ideologies *depend* in some way upon economic conditions, nowhere does it assert that economic conditions are the *sole* cause of ideologies or that their process of causation is unidirectional (PP 216). Finally, Wiggershaus compares his interpretations of "Politics and Psychoanalysis," "The Dogma of Christ," and the study of the German working class and concludes that the pieces amount to a "contradictory" way of saying that society cannot possibly change: the base completely controls the superstructure, and the superstructure completely controls the base. Apparently Fromm was unwilling to accept this depressing conclusion, Wiggershaus suggests, so Fromm flew off into an irrational flight of fancy. The paradigmatic example of such escapism for Wiggershaus is Fromm's messianism, which I argue is anything but irrational escapism.

Wiggershaus misrepresents Fromm's approach to the base/superstructure problem, and he vastly underestimates how dialectical a thinker Fromm was. Fromm always rejected such narrow reductionism, and his work grew even less reductionist over time, to the point that he influenced the left on this question—no one did more to circulate the views of Marx's *Economic and Philosophical Manuscripts* than Fromm, presenting a Marx who was clearly not a mechanical materialist. Contra Wiggershaus, Fromm's later work was based upon a model that recognized an interplay between economic and other social structures, with neither mechanically producing the other. Fromm's early work on the "character structure" and his later development in the early 1960s of the idea of "social character" explicitly provided an interactive intermediary between base and superstructure allowing for reciprocal influence and transformation. Nor was Fromm a pessimist (a "gloomy" thinker, in Wiggershaus's terms); Fromm never held that "society would not permit any radical change" (Wiggershaus 55, 60).

Along with disparaging Fromm's work as self-contradictory and flaky, Wiggershaus's book provides a prime example of another common charge logged against Fromm: the charge that Fromm was not radical. Wiggershaus sets out to argue both that Fromm abandoned the radicalism of his early work after being fired from the Institute, and that Fromm's later alleged conservatism was already nascent while he was a member of the Institute. Wiggershaus offers three specious arguments that Fromm abandoned radicalism:

1. The first argument is little more than a flawed exercise in guilt-by-association. Wiggershaus writes, "[Fromm] seemed to be closer to circles of psychoanalysts and sociologists that would have nothing to do with an antagonistic social theory than he was to the Horkheimer circle" (Wiggershaus 271). Wiggershaus conveniently ignores that all of the members of Horkheimer's circle in New York had friends and intellectual collaborators who were dubiously radical. In fact, some in the Institute were a great deal closer to the "New York intellectuals," such as Dwight MacDonald and Sidney Hook, who later became leaders in the U.S.'s cultural Cold War, though in fairness the Horkheimer circle could not have been expected to guess their later affiliations (cf. Saunders, Wheatland). Wiggershaus's claim is made even more unconvincing by his failure to mention any of these non-antagonistic thinkers by name. Fromm himself claimed that he was removed from the Institute because he was too far to the left, and his friend Robert Lynd was outraged by his firing and condemned Horkheimer's circle with the charge that it had fired Fromm for being too Marxist (Wheatland 85).

2. Wiggershaus buttresses his claim of Fromm's lack of radicalism by repeating the popular claims that Fromm was "traditional" and "idealist," a very common—and equivocal—critique of Fromm (Wiggershaus 270). Although there are possible interpretations under which the claim is true, the intended interpretation is quite different from these. For example, it is certainly true that Fromm employed ideas from a variety of Western and Eastern philosophical and religious "traditions," and it is certainly true that Fromm was an "idealist" in the informal sense of the term, i.e., a person strongly committed to ideals, who believes that those ideals can transform society. Perhaps one could make an argument that he was a philosophical idealist in the tradition of Fichte or Hegel, but Fromm never worked out a metaphysics or a thorough-going phenomenology. While I am not convinced that Fromm should be (or would want to be) classified as an idealist in the Fichtean or Hegelian senses, many have argued that Marxism has close affinities to German idealism that have been too often ignored. (Marxism may be Hegel *turned right-side up*, but it is also *Hegel* turned right-side up.)

No matter how much truth there may be in the claims that Fromm is "traditional" or "idealist" when these claims are properly qualified, the lack of adequate explanation typically accompanying these claims encourages a different reading. The implied meaning is that Fromm was *not revolutionary* (i.e., that he favored "tradition" over transformation), and that Fromm was "idealist" *as opposed to materialist*, and ergo, according to the prevailing wisdom, *not Marxist*. I argue elsewhere in this book that Fromm was a revolutionary (not a reformist) and was certainly Marxist—in fact, Fromm's exile from the Institute probably had more to do with him being *too* Marxist and with his desire to be involved in left-wing activism.

3. Finally, Wiggershaus bases his claim of Fromm's conservatism on the premise that Fromm believed that the solution to contemporary problems was found in the "individual" and "spontaneity" (Wiggershaus 270). Here Wiggershaus appears to take the line of Adorno, who, in a letter to Horkheimer, opined that Fromm was not a Marxist but either a social democrat or an anarchist, and that Fromm ought to "read Lenin"—more on that letter shortly (McLaughlin, "Origin Myths" 118). Although there are anarchist influences on Fromm—his *The Sane Society* engages with several anarchist thinkers, and the thought of anarchist revolutionary Gustav Landauer was an enduring influence on Fromm—it is also the case that others in the Frankfurt School were similarly influenced by anarchism and some more so than Fromm. Fromm's philosophy may be called "communitarian socialism," or to use his more common term, socialist humanism (SS 283). His anarchist affinities are definitely not of Max Stirner's individualistic type, critiqued by Marx and Engels in *The Germany Ideology*. Furthermore, Fromm's interpretation of Marx, especially by the 1960s after Fromm had studied Marx's early writings, held that Marx placed great value on the individual, and Fromm's enduring appreciation for Marxist revolutionary Rosa Luxemburg could explain his openness to the idea of spontaneous revolt (the "mass strike"), a concept Luxemburg also believed was rooted in Marx. Fromm's concern with the individual and with spontaneity was chiefly a Marxist critique of Stalinism, not a call for anarchism.

If Wiggershaus's book provides an archetypal example of the common charges that Fromm was not a serious thinker and that he abandoned his early radicalism, it is to Martin Jay that one can turn for a look at the common claim that Fromm was excessively optimistic. Martin Jay's *The Dialectical Imagination*, the last of the three early canonical books on the history of the Frankfurt School to be examined here, provides a useful and detailed summary of Fromm's early work. Although it focuses upon Fromm's theory and does not discuss his directorship of empirical studies very much,[4] Jay's account of Fromm's early theoretical work is relatively unproblematic. It is when describing Fromm's post-Institute work that Jay's narrative becomes ambiguous and weak.

Jay prefers Herbert Marcuse's theories to Fromm's on the topic of psychoanalysis, and he also views Marcuse as the most Marxist member of the Frankfurt School. Jay occasionally allows this position to distort his scholarly objectivity: for example, he claims that "only Marcuse attempted to articulate a positive anthropology at any time in his career," which is clearly false, as Jay should know, since he himself discusses Fromm's main book on human nature, *Man for Himself* (56).

Echoing a charge by Marcuse against Fromm, Jay's main complaint about Fromm's post-Institute work is that it is too "optimistic." He ties this complaint to the common claims (seen above in Wiggershaus) that Fromm was unserious and not radical, although unlike Wiggershaus, he only makes these claims with regard to Fromm's work *after* parting with the Institute (*Dialectical Imagination* 98ff). Obliquely noting that Fromm later incorporated ethics into his account of Marxism and drew from Eastern thought, especially Zen, Jay insinuates that Fromm's post-Institute work was not serious and not legitimately Marxist (100). But "to be fair to Fromm" (as though any ethical approach to Marxism or engagement with Zen Buddhism is *de facto* suspect!), Jay continues, Fromm's optimism was "not an absolute transformation of his [early] position" (100). He then cites a letter from Fromm to Jay, in which Fromm refers Jay to his response to the charge of excessive optimism in *The Art of Loving* (about which response more will be said in Chapters 3 and 4). It is disappointing that Jay simply quotes Fromm's letter as opposed to quoting *The Art of Loving*, which responds articulately to the concern about Fromm's "optimism." Jay then concludes, without explaining why a greater degree of optimism is undesirable but implying it:

> It is difficult, however, to read [Fromm's] later works without coming to the conclusion that in comparison with Horkheimer and other members of the Institut's inner circle, who were abandoning their tentative hopes of the twenties and thirties, Fromm was defending a more optimistic position. (100)

Jay's tone clearly implies that this "optimism" is a strike against Fromm, but he stops there and does not proceed to discuss Fromm's argument for hope.

In addition to his rejection of Fromm's "optimism" as either conservative or eccentric, Jay rejects Fromm's psychoanalysis as insufficiently Freudian. But Jay never seems to question the Institute's line, beginning in the 1940s, that orthodox Freudianism is naturally allied to political radicalism. Unlike Neil McLaughlin, for example, who interprets the Horkheimer circle's apologetics for orthodox Freudianism through the lens of the sociology of knowledge, Jay has no detectable suspicion towards the Horkheimer circle's sudden zeal for orthodox Freudianism. Never does he ask what *extra-theoretical* motives a group of leftist Jewish exiles in McCarthy-era America (certainly potential targets for reactionary, xenophobic, or anti-Semitic aggression) might have had for wanting to align themselves with Freudian orthodoxy against "revisionist" Freudianism. By that time, Freudian psychoanalysis was established in the U.S. and had lost its fringe, avant-garde appeal; it was safe. It was the "humanistic" camp of psychoanalysis (Fromm, Karen Horney, Harry Stack Sullivan, et. al.) who were the non-conformists on the scene. The Institute's defense of Freudian orthodoxy really came to the fore around 1946, when Horkheimer and Adorno began to publicly condemn Fromm's "revisionism."

As McLaughlin points out, to those who were accustomed to hearing the word in a different context, this sounded like a charge that Fromm was a "Marxist revisionist" (Bernsteinian reformist/social democrat as opposed to revolutionary Marxist) and thus insufficiently radical. Jay cites a personal interview with Fromm in which Fromm supposedly commented that Horkheimer had discovered a "more revolutionary Freud"—a quote that Jay almost certainly took out of context, since it is entirely inconsistent with the rest of Fromm's oeuvre (*Dialectical Imagination* 101). Fromm always sought the revolutionary implications of Freud's work, but he also excoriated Freud for his authoritarianism, nationalism, and sexism, reiterating throughout his work that Freud was limited by his bourgeois, Victorian context. From Fromm's standpoint, the revolutionary implications of Freud's thought could be found only through the method that Marcuse, Horkheimer, and Adorno rejected as an unjustified "revisionism."

Held's, Jay's, and Wiggershaus's dismissals of Fromm helped to cement until recently the common charges that Fromm was a marginal member of the Institute, that he was excessively optimistic and conservative, and that he was a flaky, unserious thinker. In concluding this overview of the "origin myth" concerning Fromm's role, it is worth noting that often what is most problematic about the canonical interpretations of Fromm's role in Critical Theory is not the interpretations themselves but the blithely presumptive way in which they are asserted. These writers and many other writers on Critical Theory seem to feel no need to justify the assumptions that "optimism" is undesirable, that drawing upon classic concepts of philosophical or religious traditions constitutes *de facto* conservatism, that orthodox Freudianism is more radical than "revisionist" Freudianism, and so forth. Fromm's marginalization has been so total that, until recently, scholars of the Frankfurt School typically have felt obliged to justify neither their rejection of his later work nor their casual swipes at his early work. The story told about the Frankfurt School by Horkheimer, Adorno, to some extent Marcuse, and sometimes Habermas has been taken at face value for decades. What has resulted is a peculiarly ideological, gate-keeping defense of the Frankfurt School "line" that has, until the mid- to late 1990s, remained uncontested.

1.2   THE LEHRHAUS TO THE THERAPEUTICUM

In order to understand Fromm's contribution to the Frankfurt School, it is necessary to examine the work that Fromm did before he joined the Institute. In particular, we need to understand that Fromm brought his socialist radicalism with him to the Institute and that his interest in Marx and Freud preceded his involvement in the Institute. Later chapters will revisit the background information provided here, in order to clarify the uniqueness of Fromm's adherence to certain ideas in the midst of a strange, apocalyptic moment in history and culture.

A psychoanalyst and a Marxist sociologist, Fromm was hired by the Frankfurt Institute for Social Research for his work on the development of a social psychology, one of the earliest goals of the Institute. (He was the Institute's only trained psychoanalyst.) Under Max Horkheimer's directorship, the early Frankfurt School was committed to studying the totality of society through interdisciplinary methods and drawing connections between theory and practice, while steering clear of orthodox Marxist reductionism. Fromm's social psychology, melding the insights of Freud and Marx, sought to avoid reducing social phenomena to purely libidinal or economic causes, instead offering multi-layered explanations, as we shall see. His early work on Freud and Marx led him to novel explanations of the role of family, political power, religion, and other social structures in shaping the psychological character of individuals and the pervasive psychological character orientations within societies. Before joining the Institute, however, Fromm's thought was shaped by his early experiences in left-wing Jewish intellectual circles in Germany, by his doctoral studies in Sociology in Heidelberg under Alfred Weber, and by his study and practice of psychoanalysis.

Fromm had more exposure to Jewish religious observance in his upbringing than others of his generation of the Frankfurt School.[5] His father was descended from a long line of Talmudic scholars and was embarrassed to be a businessman; he had probably hoped that Erich would become a rabbi. Fromm later wrote that he felt himself to have grown up in the feudal world, not the modern world, and that in his childhood he looked upon business careers as shameful (Funk, *Life and Ideas* 6, 8). In the late 1910s and early 1920s, he split his time between university study in Heidelberg, where he completed a doctorate in Sociology, and social life in Frankfurt, where he studied Judaism under prominent rabbis and Talmudic scholars and was active in left-wing Jewish intellectual circles.

In Heidelberg, Fromm completed a dissertation in Sociology under Alfred Weber, Max Weber's brother, who authored an important history of philosophy with a strong emphasis on Spinoza, Kant, and Hegel, and became famous for pioneering studies in economic geography.[6] "I had only one non-Jewish teacher whom I really admired and who deeply influenced me," Fromm later wrote, "and that was Alfred Weber, the brother of Max, also a sociologist, but in contrast to Max, a humanist, not a nationalist and a man of outstanding courage and integrity" (AS 251). Fromm also took courses from Heinrich Rickert (who also had a profound influence upon Walter Benjamin) and Karl Jaspers (Jay, *Dialectical Imagination* 202; Löwy, *Redemption and Utopia* 152). His 1922 dissertation was entitled *Jewish Law: A Contribution to the Study of Diaspora Judaism* and explored the way that the Jewish law was interpreted by the Karaite, Hasidic, and Reform Jewish communities (Lundgren 86). Like many young left-wing German Jews of the time, Fromm rebelled against the status quo by becoming interested in Hasidism. Martin Buber had embraced Hasidism for his project of utopian "renewal," and it seemed to Fromm's generation like a plausible alternative to the staid, bourgeois Orthodoxy of their parents' generation. Fromm's dissertation also employed Hermann Cohen's thought and Max Weber's work on the Protestant ethic to discuss how the Jewish perspective on labor differed from the perspective of the Puritans (Lundgren 101, 83). The distinction between meaningful and alienating dimensions of labor is an ongoing theme throughout all periods of Fromm's work.

Meanwhile, in Frankfurt, Fromm was active in the loosely socialist Jewish youth movement, the *Blau-Weiss*. A Jewish alternative to the German youth movement (which was unfriendly to Jewish membership), the *Blau-Weiss* took hikes in the countryside and sang songs about their unique Jewish identity. Fromm was still a member of the *Blau-Weiss* for a couple of years after 1922, when the organization formally declared its commitment to Zionism and began urging its members to emigrate to the newly forming kibbutzim in Palestine. But under the influence of Hermann Cohen, who was one of the leading Jewish opponents of Zionism, and the influence of Fromm's mentor and Talmud teacher, the socialist Russian exile Salman Rabinkow, Fromm soon came to see Zionism as just another of the pernicious nationalisms to which he was opposed (Funk, *Life and Ideas* 40).

Like Cohen, about whom more will be said in Chapter 2, Salman Rabinkow was an interesting figure with a circle of close students. Fromm met with Rabinkow nearly daily for five years, studying philosophy and sociology in addition to the Talmud and discussing Fromm's thesis work (AS 251). Rabinkow was remembered by his students as a humanistic and gentle person, an opponent of religious fanaticism. He differed from similar teachers in Frankfurt in that he employed the less formalistic "Lithuanian" method of Talmudic study, which "stressed psychological depth, deeper comprehension of the spirit of Jewish law, and the organization of unified points of view" (Schacter 98). Studying from morning to night with great enthusiasm, Rabinkow refused to confine himself to a particular academic discipline, refused to take payment from his students, and never sought a professorial or rabbinical position. His many students, from Ernst Simon to Nahum Goldmann, later spoke of him with tremendous admiration (Schacter).

Along with studying under Rabinkow and coming into contact with Cohen, Fromm was also part of a circle around the Rabbi Nehemiah Nobel, a highly respected Conservative[7] rabbi who was rooted firmly in the progressive tradition of the Jewish Enlightenment (the Haskalah). Nobel took an interest in Fromm's studies, and the two used to take long walks together, including on the Sabbath when it was forbidden, a precursor to Fromm's eventual break from Orthodoxy (Funk, *Life and Ideas* 39; Löwenthal 19). The circle around Nobel was radical, heavily influenced by both socialism and Jewish mysticism (Löwenthal 19). In circles such as these in early 1900s Germany, becoming aware of one's Jewish identity was a process that was often intimately tied to revolutionary politics.

In 1920, Fromm helped to found the *Freies Jüdisches Lehrhaus* (Free Jewish Study-House) out of the circle around Nobel. The *Lehrhaus* became a hotbed of left-wing German-Jewish intellectual life.[8] It would be difficult to over-estimate the environment of electric intellectual excitement that surrounded the *Lehrhaus*, whose many famous participants included Martin Buber, Gershom Scholem, Franz Rosenzweig, Leo Löwenthal, Ernst Simon, Leo Baeck, and Abraham Heschel. It is safe to say that already, approximately seven years before joining the Institute for Social Research, Fromm was developing some of his own ideas about the type of messianism that he wished to promote; messianism was a topic of heated debate at the *Lehrhaus*. Fromm taught a course on the Book of Exodus there, while Gershom Scholem (the nemesis of Fromm's messianism) taught a course on the Book of Daniel. Fromm later used Exodus as a paradigm of the struggle for liberation, and he rejected "apocalyptic" versions of messianism presented in texts like Daniel (Funk, *Life and Ideas* 42; YSB 90-116; ROH 18).

In 1924, Fromm became interested in psychoanalysis and was trained and psychoanalyzed by Frieda Reichmann, whom he married in 1926. He had first met her in the early 1920s at the expensive sanitarium near Dresden where she was serving wealthy clients while seeking donations from them to treat—or rather, to build a sort of commune out of—the members of the *Blau-Weiss*, including Fromm (Hornstein 29, 53).[9] She was a mother figure for these Jewish youth, bringing them food and allowing them to hang around and socialize in her living quarters during the daytime while she was treating wealthy clients (53-4). Rejecting assimilation, she supported the burgeoning Zionist youth movement as a rediscovery of a separate Jewish identity (63). "For close to four years," Reichmann's biographer writes, "this sanitarium within a sanitarium functioned as a model community...Patients helped each other in whatever ways they could: one would give Hebrew lessons, and another would mend his socks in return" (54). Reichmann moved to Heidelberg in 1924 to set up her own sanitarium, the "Therapeuticum," with plainly religious and utopian motivations. The principle was that "ritual practices didn't have to be compulsions performed in a rote way out of fear of punishment by God; they could be the basis for deep spirituality" (64). As Reichmann later explained,

> We thought we would first analyze the people, and second, make them aware of their tradition and live in this tradition, not because the Lord has said so, but because that meant becoming aware of our past in big style. Then we would do something not only for the individuals but also for the Jewish people. (Silver 20)

The point of communes like the Therapeuticum was a rediscovery of Judaism as a unique identity that stood outside the mainstream of German society. Although the anti-assimilationist Jewish youth did not always define their commitment in such terms, according to Leo Löwenthal this revolt against assimilation was often motivated by opposition to capitalism more than by a defense of an ethnic or religious identity (Löwenthal 19).

Founded together with Fromm, Reichmann's "Therapeuticum" was so heavily influenced by Jewish thought and spirituality that it became known as practicing a "Torah-peutic" method, serving kosher meals and celebrating Jewish holidays (Kellner "Erich Fromm, Judaism" 3, Löwenthal 26). The clientele were primarily Jewish intellectuals, including Leo Löwenthal, Ernst Simon, and Rabinkow (Funk, *Life and Ideas* 61). It was seen as radical and cutting edge; psychoanalysis was not yet popular and was still viewed with suspicion. Löwenthal later credited the Therapeuticum with influencing the Frankfurt School project of melding psychoanalysis and Marxism (Löwenthal 26). By that time, it should be noted, Fromm was becoming increasingly politically radicalized, probably largely through his experiences at the *Lehrhaus* and through the influence of Rabinkow. Gershom Scholem described Fromm in 1926 as an "enthusiastic Trotskyite" who "now pitied me for my petit-bourgeois parochialism" (by which "parochialism" he probably meant Zionism) (*From Berlin* 156).[10]

Reichmann, approximately ten years Fromm's senior, employed a therapeutic method based upon the Jewish idea of *tikkun* (redemption, making-whole) and the Hasidic messianic proverb that "to redeem one person is to redeem the world." There were no neutral actions: every moment and every encounter with another person was an opportunity to release the divine "sparks" hidden within creation (Hornstein 28, 42). (The belief in these hidden sparks was a product of the Lurianic Kabbalah, which influenced Hasidism as well as some interesting revolutionary moments in Jewish history.)

At the time that Reichmann met Fromm, both were still steadfastly Orthodox in accord with their upbringing; Reichmann had kept kosher through medical school and had refused to work on the Sabbath throughout her time as a doctor treating brain-injured soldiers during the war (Hornstein 53). Under the influence of psychoanalytic ideas, however, Fromm and Reichmann drifted away from their earlier religious assumptions. Fromm's decisive break with Orthodox Judaism came in 1928. For Fromm, the stage had already been set for his break from Orthodoxy by the contacts he had made through the *Lehrhaus*, and his walks with Rabbi Nobel on the Sabbath, which broke the rules of the Sabbath observance, would have already raised the question in Fromm's mind.

Reichmann's biographer Gail Hornstein states that Fromm's and Reichmann's 1927 articles psychoanalyzing the Sabbath ritual and kosher laws, published in Freud's journal *Imago*, already marked their initial, public break from Orthodoxy. Reichmann later said of the publications, "That's how we announced we were through [with Orthodoxy], in big style, like two real Jewish intellectuals!" (Hornstein 66). A more complete break followed in 1928, when they went to a park during Passover (feast of unleavened bread) and ceremoniously and silently shared a loaf of leavened bread (66). Perhaps with a tinge of sadness, Reichmann later joked that they were afraid at the time about the folk belief that Jews who abandoned Orthodoxy were cursed to die childless; neither of them believed in the curse, of course, but neither Reichmann nor Fromm ever did have children (Silver 22).

Reichmann later became renowned as an extraordinarily gifted and humane psychoanalyst, famous for refusing to give up hope on even the most challenging cases. Fromm and Reichmann separated in 1930, after which Fromm had romantic relationships with Karen Horney (from around 1933 to 1943) and with African American dance artist and anthropologist Katherine Dunham in the early 1940s, before marrying Henny Gurland in 1944, and Annis Freeman in 1953 after Gurland's death (Hornstein 68). (Regrettably little research has been done upon the relationship with Dunham, whose pioneering work on Caribbean dance and connection to the négritude movement merit study in their own right. Lawrence Friedman's new biography of Fromm is one of the first works on Fromm to discuss Dunham in the context of U.S. culture; Rainer Funk's "illustrated biography" of Fromm mentions the relationship but does not mention that Dunham was African American. Dunham speaks highly of Fromm as a humanist in her 1969 memoir of her time in Haiti, *Island Possessed.*)

With Fromm's help after their separation, Reichmann obtained a position at an important mental hospital in the U.S., which she directed for many years. In a feat that Freud had considered impossible, she famously used psychoanalysis to cure a patient of schizophrenia, as memorialized in the famous book and film *I Never Promised You a Rose Garden*. Fromm and Reichmann kept in touch a bit over the years after their separation and were amiable in their later years (Silver 21).

Despite some weaknesses, Fromm's 1927 article on the Sabbath was significant for his later work; it was Fromm's first formal attempt to apply psychoanalytic theory to a concrete sociological phenomenon. The article was a bit reductionist, concluding that the Sabbath was a ritual of repentance for the Oedipal desire for the mother and the killing of the father (Funk, *Life and Ideas* 61).[11] It was Fromm's first published text dealing with messianism, though it lacked the complexity of his later work on the theme. Nature and the earth, symbolically associated with the mother ("Mother Earth"), were not to be violated upon the Sabbath; the Sabbath sought to restore the harmony and oneness experienced in the womb, symbolized in Jewish thought by Paradise (Löwy, *Redemption and Utopia* 152). According to Michael Löwy, the article demonstrated a brief brush by Fromm with "restorative" messianism (153). Fromm's mature writings interpreted Jewish messianism not as a restoration of a prelapserian golden age but rather as a dialectical synthesis of history and pre-history.

Fromm's dissertation on the Jewish law and his article on the Sabbath both examine the nature of labor and point towards radical transformation of working conditions. Both express hope for a messianic future free of misery and toil (Löwy, *Redemption and Utopia* 153). In the Sabbath article, Fromm speaks of a total absence of work in the messianic age, harking back to Marx's and other early socialists' calls for an "abolition [*Aufhebung*] of labor" (Löwy, *Redemption and Utopia* 153; Zilbersheid).[12] Fromm's dissertation speaks similarly, though not of an abolition of labor but of the transformation of labor into something pleasurable. He rejected the asceticism of the Protestant work ethic and urged a return to the Jewish view of work as something good though not an end in itself (Lundgren 83).

In concluding this overview of Fromm's life and work prior to joining the Institute, it seems that there is abundant evidence that Fromm *brought* his socialist radicalism with him to the Frankfurt School and that Fromm's radicalism was not due chiefly to his involvement in the Institute. Through his dissertation on the Jewish law and his article on the Sabbath, Fromm was exploring the nature of labor and envisioning a messianic future in which labor would be liberated and leisure would be increased. The general milieu of young enthusiastic Jewish socialists in which Fromm found himself before joining the Institute, along with the influence of Rabinkow, Hermann Cohen, and Rabbi Nobel, would have encouraged him to interpret his religious background in a radical, socialist light, as would the radical excitement of the rising psychoanalytic movement and the experience of Reichmann's commune-like "sanitarium within a sanitarium" near Dresden and the Heidelberg Therapeuticum. Scholem's claim that Fromm was a Trotskyist in 1926, while spoken with derision, provides further evidence that Fromm was drawn to Marxism. In the following section, we will explore how Fromm came into contact with the Institute for Social Research, the work he did while allied with it, and the reasons for his parting from the Institute approximately ten years later.

1.3   FROMM AND THE INSTITUTE FOR SOCIAL RESEARCH

Now that Fromm's pre-Institute work has been examined, the reader has a sense of the ideas and experiences that Fromm brought with him to the Institute. Fromm's collaboration with the Institute for Social Research began in 1928 or 1929 when Fromm began working with Max Horkheimer, before Horkheimer took over as director (Abromeit 194). Fromm's friend Leo Löwenthal, whom Fromm had once introduced to the *Lehrhaus* circle, returned the favor by introducing Fromm to Horkheimer (Funk, *Life and Ideas* 72). In 1930, shortly after Horkheimer took over from Friedrich Pollock as director of the Institute, Horkheimer hired Fromm as a tenured member to head the Institute's social psychology division (Bronner 79). This was before Marcuse and Adorno joined the Institute. At this time, Fromm was a core member of the Institute, though Horkheimer later downplayed his centrality to the Institute's history (Funk, *Courage* 296-7).

Despite the Institute's heritage of a "dictatorship of the director" (as earlier director Carl Grünberg had approvingly quipped), one must not overstate the extent to which Horkheimer set the agenda for the early Institute. It is true that Horkheimer saw the need for bringing psychoanalysis into conversation with Marxism, and his interest in psychoanalysis had been stimulated by Löwenthal's stories about being psychoanalyzed at Fromm and Reichmann's Therapeuticum (Jay, *Dialectical Imagination* 87). As was popular among intellectuals of the time, Horkheimer had also undergone psychoanalysis himself (under Karl Landauer, who was also one of Fromm's analysts) (Abromeit 188; Roazen, "Exclusion" 3). However, the mere fact that Fromm was already in touch with Horkheimer in 1928 or 1929, before Horkheimer became director of the Institute, casts some doubt on the standard narrative. According to that narrative, Horkheimer's famous opening lecture as director of the Institute was a solitarily-conceived blueprint for the Institute's future work, and Fromm's effort to synthesize Freud and Marx conveniently *just happened to be* what the early Institute was seeking. But it is more likely that Horkheimer stated this commitment in his opening lecture because he was fully aware that Fromm was already engaged in this project, and because he intended to hire Fromm. The same goes for Horkheimer's articulation in the speech of plans for an upcoming empirical study of the German working class, which Fromm later led.

In his opening lecture, Horkheimer also expressed his commitment to an interdisciplinary research program that would seek to understand the social totality. In the tradition of Karl Korsch and Georg Lukács, both of whom had challenged Marxist orthodoxy in favor of a Hegelian emphasis on historical totality, Horkheimer sought to foster a radical, loosely Marxist social theory that drew upon Hegel and steered clear of economic reductionism and positivism. He also was wary of philosophical "systems" from the outset. He hoped to link theory with practice, exploring concrete examples of socio-historical phenomena while avoiding scientism and positivism (Jay, *Dialectical Imagination* 41).

By drawing upon Freud, Fromm would forge a path for Critical Theory *avant la lettre* that avoided narrow reductionism and explored multiple social phenomena, such as the family, religion, and law. Much of his work shortly before joining the Frankfurt School and while a member of the Frankfurt School in the 1930s was devoted to creating a theoretical synthesis of Freud and Marx and exploring its applications to concrete institutions and practices, such as the legal system, early Christianity, and the politics of the German working class. Fromm was intimately involved in the Frankfurt School's early project of doing theory in a way that spoke to contemporary problems and that discovered the intersections of the socio-economic totality within the lives of individuals.

Fromm's early work, however, may already have been in tension with some of Horkheimer's aims. Fromm's humanism, manifesting itself by the 1940s in the assertion that, despite other sources contributing to the development of individual character, there is nevertheless a certain unchanging human essence which would reach its fulfillment in the future, would have been anathema to Horkheimer's hesitancy about the idea of an enduring human nature, his rejection of the idea of a "meaning" of history, and his affinities with Schopenhauer's pessimism (Abromeit 148-9; Jay, *Dialectical Imagination* 55-6). Fromm's early work may have avoided a possible confrontation on this issue; Fromm's most overt arguments for humanism and messianism come later, beginning in the 1950s. He would later title his political program "socialist humanism," and nearly all of Fromm's work after leaving the Frankfurt School addressed questions of an enduring human nature and its future fulfillment. Another, related factor at work in Horkheimer's evolution from excitedly hiring Fromm to nervously distancing himself from him may have been Horkheimer's evolution of ideas with regard to the Enlightenment; as Abromeit's biography suggests, the early Horkheimer seems to have been a defender of the Enlightenment ideal of reason against proto-fascist and *lebensphilosophische* ideologies (Abromeit 171). This defense of the Enlightenment would have meshed well with Fromm's own concerns until Horkheimer's disappointment stemming from the Moscow Trials and the conformist character of U.S. culture led Horkheimer to a greater degree of hesitancy with regard to the Enlightenment promise of freedom through reason, education, and democratic equality. We will return to the events surrounding Fromm's break from the Institute later in this chapter.

In what follows I offer a chronological overview of Fromm's writings and their significance, from the time when Fromm first came into contact with the Institute in 1929 to the time of his parting with the Institute in 1939. This is necessary in order to show that Fromm's early writings made a significant contribution to the Frankfurt School and to present some of the ideas that Fromm would later develop in greater detail, which will be explored further in later chapters. Later in this book it will become evident that Fromm's post-Institute work emerged logically out of his earlier work and is usually in harmony with it, seriously engaging many of the same themes, contra the common charge that Fromm's post-Institute work flew off on an irrational and flaky tangent.

We can begin by exploring Fromm's early article "Psychoanalysis and Sociology." The article was written at the end of 1928 and published in 1929 in a psychoanalytic journal, before Horkheimer became director of the Institute in 1930 (Funk, "Major Points" 2). In that article Fromm laid out the basis of his synthesis of Freud and Marx, explaining psychoanalysis's need for sociology and vice versa. It pointed to Freud's recently published *Future of an Illusion* as an indication that Freud recognized the need for exploring the historical genesis of the psyche ("Psychoanalysis and Sociology" 2). Kevin Anderson suggests that the essay might better have been titled, "Psychoanalysis and Marxism" and that Fromm's commitment to a "revolutionary Marxist" position is already evident in it (Anderson [2000] 92). Marxism is the only sociological theory addressed in the article, and Fromm calls Marx "the greatest sociologist of all" (92). Fromm's essay concludes with a quote from *The German Ideology* that expresses an idea of Marx's that Fromm would frequently reference in his later work on messianism: "History does nothing, it possesses no immense wealth, it fights no battles. It is instead the human being, the real living person, who does everything, who owns everything, and who fights all battles" (92; "Psychoanalysis and Sociology" 3). As Anderson rightly notes, Marxist themes recur throughout Fromm's work, including his early essays, which frequently offer a radical critique of the reformism of Social Democrats Kautsky and Bernstein (95).

In 1930-1, Fromm published three studies on criminology in psychoanalytic journals and a lengthy class analysis and psychoanalysis of early Christianity, "The Dogma of Christ." Despite the surface appearance of a large divergence between the two topics, the criminology essays and the essay on early Christianity address relatively the same issue: the way in which authority is maintained through becoming internalized in the psyche of the individuals subject to it, who sado-masochistically seek punishment for their repressed desire to rebel.

The three essays on criminology explored the social function of punishment in maintaining the authority of the state. Fromm reflects that the threat of punishment does not deter crime, since most crimes either have economic causes or result from unconscious motives, not rational premeditation ("State as Educator" 124). Although punishment rarely deters crime, the purpose of punishment does not seem to be mere retribution either—the modern criminal justice system considers itself therapeutic or educational, not merely punitive, Fromm points out (124). Instead of being a means of deterrence or retribution, Fromm suggests—long before Michel Foucault's *Discipline and Punish* investigated this phenomenon—that punishment is employed by the state in order that the populace will psychologically internalize the state's authority. Once this internalization occurs, the masses' desire to revolt is turned inward masochistically towards self-punishment. By wielding the power to punish, the state becomes a father-figure (125-6). The criminal can derive satisfaction through submitting to the father-figure's punishment; some people will even commit crimes with an unconscious wish to be punished ("State as Educator" 126; "Psychology of the Criminal" 146). The rest of the populace, the non-criminals, find in punishment an outlet for their aggressive impulses, finding sadistic satisfaction in learning of the punishment of others ("State as Educator" 126). War, Fromm notes, also serves as an outlet for the sadism of the masses (126). The state's power of force is thus "Janus-faced," with one face turned towards the criminal or the enemy, the other towards the obedient masses ("Psychology of the Criminal" 147).

Fromm's other important work of 1931, "The Dogma of Christ," was framed as an application of the synthesis of Freudian and Marxian theory to an analysis of early Christianity. In fact, the book-length essay operates on a variety of levels, and in it Fromm's Marxist radicalism and his originality are again evident. According to Fromm, early Christianity was a movement of the impoverished masses, and early Christian communities were communistic in organization. The message of early Christianity was messianic and revolutionary; it was not a "social-reform program" (reformism) but rather "the blessed promise of a not-distant future in which the poor would be rich, the hungry would be satisfied, and the oppressed would gain authority" (DC 77). The early Christians fully expected this messianic future to come soon, within history and in their lifetimes, not in an other-worldly afterlife (93).

In contrast with the view of the Church later that Jesus was divine and *became human*—the Homoousian doctrine—Fromm contends that the early Christians were Adoptionists, believing that Jesus began as an ordinary human being and *became divine*. Adoptionism inspired a radical belief that all human beings had the potential to become gods, and this belief was linked to a spirit of revolt against authorities, both God the "Father" and earthly rulers. A major shift in the doctrine occurred as the Roman Empire became Christianized and the ruling classes converted, Fromm contends. "*The decisive element was the change from the idea of man becoming God to that of God becoming man*" (90, Fromm's italics). The emphasis shifted from immanent, historical empowerment of the masses and feverish messianic expectation, to the acceptance of fate and of the unchanging providence of a transcendent deity. After that shift, revolution no longer seemed like a possibility, so the only solution was to submit to the authority of the father-figure and to love him (DC 91). The masses were still enraged about the injustices they were suffering, but their rage was turned inward against the self. Through accepting earthly misfortunes as just punishments, the Christian masses now hoped only for bliss in the afterlife and turned to the Church and to the cult around Mary as images of the forgiveness and love that could be obtained through obedience and passive acceptance of authority (93-5).

"The Dogma of Christ" was hailed by a review in the Institute's *Zeitschrift* as (Michael Löwy's paraphrase) "the first concrete example of a synthesis between Freud and Marx"—no small achievement (Löwy, *Redemption and Utopia* 155). "The Dogma of Christ" was also a political statement: as Michael Löwy points out, Fromm intended his analysis of early Christianity as a criticism of the Soviet Union (155). The decline of the early Christian communes with their revolutionary enthusiasm and the rise of a hierarchical Church structure, obediently submissive to the Roman ruling class, was an allegory for the collapse of the early, enthusiastic workers' councils (soviets) and the submission of the Russian working class to the Stalinist state after the death of Lenin (155).[13]

Importantly, the essay also contained a political critique of "Gnosticism." Fromm was writing at a time when a sizeable subculture, including some proto-fascists as well as some sincere leftists, were claiming to be returning to the worldview of ancient "Gnosticism," especially its despairing belief in the world's fallen-ness and its vision of goodness and the messianic future as wholly other. Fromm described the ancient Gnostics as "the well-to-do Hellenistic middle class...[who] wanted to accomplish too quickly and too suddenly what [they] wished...before the consciousness of the masses could accept it" (DC 75). They were—one might paraphrase—the ancient world's Romantic nihilists. In "The Dogma of Christ," Fromm stressed that there *was* an alternative to the failed options of compliant obedience (Stalinism), "revisionism" (Bernstein and Kautsky's reformism), and Gnosticism (romantic or reactionary yearning for destruction or return to the past) (75). In early Christianity, Montanism emerged as an alternative to these failed options. The Montanist movement was a revolt "against the conforming tendencies of Christianity" and "sought to restore the early Christian enthusiasm" (75). It is not clear where Fromm located the contemporary equivalent of the ancient Montanist rebirth of messianic enthusiasm, such as whether he would have equated it with Trotskyism or some other emerging movement, or whether he would have described it as something that he wished for and did not yet see happening. Wherever Fromm may have seen hope for change in his context, however, his essay was plainly radical and was plainly critical of Stalinism, reformism, and nihilist "Gnosticism." One may justifiably assume that it was more than Fromm's Jewish background that caused the Nazis later to add the "The Dogma of Christ" to their list of prohibited reading materials (Roazen, "Exclusion" 2).

Some would argue that "The Dogma of Christ" presents an inaccurate account of the history of Christianity, but the point is somewhat irrelevant to the aims of Fromm's essay. "The Dogma of Christ" was not primarily about Christianity. In addition to critiquing the situation of the left of the time, the essay addressed the same important question that Fromm's work on criminology had addressed: the way in which external political authority becomes internalized in the psyche of individuals, with politically conservative consequences: either compliant submission or destructive nihilism. This concern has far-reaching political implications, beyond specific questions about early Christian history. It may indicate something at the core of the Nazis' rise to power and may even provide a useful critique of political events today.[14] At any rate, "The Dogma of Christ" may be read as Fromm's first major work on messianism. Like his later work on messianism, the essay presented messianic hope as an alternative to conformism and nihilism.

By comparison with "The Dogma of Christ," Fromm's next two major publications may have been a bit reductionist and less dialectical, but they are both rather famous, and they demonstrate the strengths and weakness of Fromm's brief period of relatively orthodox Freudianism. These two 1932 essays for the Institute's *Zeitschrift*, "Psychoanalytic Characterology and Its Relevance for Social Psychology" and "The Method and Function of an Analytic Social Psychology" continued Fromm's project of melding Marx and Freud, exploring applications of various psychoanalytic categories. The first article, focusing on object relations, concluded with an account of the bourgeois character structure as anal-erotic (CP 137-8). The continuation of anal impulses associated with toilet-training into adult life becomes sublimated into tendencies to "orderliness, punctuality, cleanliness, and stinginess" and an obsession with "duty" (142-3). This stage of development is also characterized by "pride" and a feeling of being utterly unique and special in comparison to everything and everyone else (143). People who are fixated at this stage "are inclined to regard everything in life as property and to protect everything that is 'private' from outside invasions. This attitude does not apply to money and possessions only; it also applies to human beings, feelings, memories, and experiences" (144). In this article, one can already see Fromm's later thesis in *The Sane Society* that it is possible for an entire society to be psychologically ill without knowing it—that is, neurosis is not necessarily limited to a minority of deviant individuals who stand out as abnormal. Particular socio-economic structures may foster the development of particular neuroses.

The second 1932 article, "The Method and Function of an Analytic Social Psychology" (hereafter, "Method and Function"), is Fromm's best-known early work, in part because it is one of the few works by Fromm that Marcuse praises in *Eros and Civilization*, though I will not address Marcuse's interpretation of the article here (*Eros and Civilization* 241-2). The article is noteworthy since it offers one of Fromm's first critiques of Freudian orthodoxy, though the article is still very close to the orthodox Freudian "line." In the essay, Fromm explores the family as a mediating link between the individual psyche and social and economic structures (*Eros and Civilization* 241; CP 117). The example of the family demonstrates for Fromm that psychoanalysis and Marxism need one another and must meet through an analytic social psychology that "*seeks to understand the instinctual apparatus of a group, its libidinous and largely unconscious behavior, in terms of its socio-economic structure*" (CP 116, italics Fromm's). The socio-economic structure delimits the ways in which the sexual instincts can be expressed or sublimated. Although Freud did not abstract the individual from social relationships, he mistakenly absolutized his contemporary bourgeois society, underestimating the degree to which social relationships are shaped by differing socio-economic conditions (115, 117). In a spunky challenge to one of Freud's most prized theories, Fromm also suggests that the Oedipus complex is not universal but is only a feature of patriarchal societies, not matriarchal ones (119).

"Method and Function" had a certain political subtext. It was a response to Wilhelm Reich's 1929 manifesto, "Dialectical Materialism and Psychoanalysis" (Erös 1). Reich's pamphlet had been an attempt to convince Stalinists of the merits of psychoanalysis. In order to give the method of historical materialism a wide berth and prevent psychoanalysis from colliding too much with it, Reich had limited the function of psychoanalysis to a merely *negative* critique of society, such as exploring the "irrational motives which have led a certain type of leader to join the socialist or national-socialist movement" or "[tracing] the effect of social ideologies on the psychological development of the individual" (1). Fromm responded to Reich in "Method and Function" by arguing that psychoanalysis also made a *positive* contribution to Marxism and that psychoanalysis could have *any* object, "only and wholly insofar as psychic factors play a role in the phenomenon" (Erös 1, CP 114). Psychoanalysis's usefulness to Marxism was not limited to uncovering neuroses in individuals or doing ideology critique. Fromm's ongoing commitment to coupling a negative critique of society with a positive account of the goals for which it could strive can already be seen here.

Despite its renown and despite its significance as a response to Wilhelm Reich, "Method and Function" is not Fromm at his most nuanced. This early attempted synthesis of Freud and Marx was less reductionist than either orthodox Freudianism or orthodox Marxism, but one could argue that here, as in his other early works on this topic, Fromm is somewhat reductionist in his emphasis upon a materialist explanation of human phenomena as outgrowths of biological drives and the economic base (CP 129). The article opens with the assertion, "Psychoanalysis is a materialistic psychology, which should be classed among the natural sciences" (110). As noted previously, Fromm later developed a more nuanced account of the interaction between base and superstructure in Marxist thought than that demonstrated in this article. He also later placed less emphasis upon the libido than he did in "Method and Function," accepted something more like the "social drive" he rejects in this early essay, and shifted from his early presentation of psychoanalysis as a "natural science" to classifying it as a "human science" (CP 110, PR 6).

Fromm's work on J. J. Bachofen (1815-1887) marked a further development by Fromm away from the limitations of Freudian orthodoxy, having already challenged Freud's ahistorical approach to psychoanalysis and his theory of the Oedipus complex. In 1933-4, Fromm published two pieces on Bachofen's theory of matriarchy in the Institute's *Zeitschrift*. Writing on Bachofen had only recently become acceptable, and any serious consideration of him, only shortly before this time, would have jeopardized one's academic credibility, partly because Bachofen had influenced both Engels and Nietzsche, neither of whom were accepted subject matter in academia

(Noll 164). In the ideological battleground of the 1920s, however, Bachofen had made a comeback. Among proto-fascists, his work was taken as a mythical, Teutonic alternative to Freud's more rationalistic approach to psychoanalysis. Fromm warned of this right-wing enthusiasm surrounding Bachofen, and he also pointed out that Bachofen's work had been used by Engels and other radicals, not just the right-wing, and thus might be salvageable.

Fromm responded to and defended the radical interpretation of Bachofen, arguing that the differing political interpretations were made possible by the contradictions in Bachofen himself, an aristocrat discontented with capitalism and fascinated by the past, though not a Romantic (CP 92). Fromm writes of Bachofen:

> There is obviously a sharp contradiction between the Bachofen who admires gynocratic democracy and the aristocratic Bachofen of Basel who opposed the political emancipation of women...It is a contradiction that crops up on several different planes. On the philosophical plane, it is the believing Protestant and Idealist over against the Romantic and the dialectic philosopher over against the naturalistic metaphysician. On the social and political plane, it is the anti-Democrat over against the admirer of a Communist-democratic social structure. On the moral plane, it is the proponent of Protestant bourgeois morality over against the advocate of a society where sexual freedom reigned instead of monogamous marriage. (93)

These contradictions in Bachofen made possible the varying interpretations of his work, but it is Marxism, according to Fromm, that can best account for the dialectical contradictions in Bachofen's work. Though it is not a return to the past, Marxism is the heir of the pre-historic matriarchal system, of its values of equality and fraternity (108-9).

The Bachofen articles represented a further development of the dialectical approach of Fromm's "Dogma of Christ" and demonstrated greater nuance than Fromm's "Method and Function." In the more substantive of the two Bachofen articles, one can see Fromm's emerging commitment to a highly *future-oriented messianism*, away from any "restorationist" desires for a mere return to Paradise. The proto-fascists Ludwig Klages, Alfred Bäumler, and Alfred Schuler praised Bachofen's theory because they "looked back to the past as a lost paradise," while the radicals (Marx, Engels, Bebel, and others) praised Bachofen's theory from an opposite standpoint, since they "looked forward hopefully to the future" (CP 85). Everyone at that time would have known that Klages and Bäumler had turned to Bachofen in search of a psychology that would provide an alternative to Freudian psychoanalysis and in search of a *lebensphilosophische* alternative to Neo-Kantianism, which was now perceived as stale and bourgeois (Lebovic, "Beauty and Terror" 2, 10). (For further discussion of Klages and *Lebensphilosophie* in relation to the Frankfurt School, see Section 2.4 in Chapter 2.) Unlike his proto-fascist contemporaries Klages and Bäumler, Fromm was not abandoning Freud's rationalism in favor of Bachofen's irrationalism. Rather, he was drawing upon Bachofen in an attempt to transcend the limitations of both Freud and Bachofen through a dialectical synthesis of the pre-historic "matriarchy" envisioned by Bachofen with the modern, Enlightenment insights of psychoanalysis.

In the same essay on political responses to Bachofen, one can see Fromm's emerging psychoanalytic critique of Nazism, which he would revisit and rework throughout his career, even exploring the question at great length in his very late work *The Anatomy of Human Destructiveness* (1973). In the early essay, Fromm analyzed the desire among the masses for regression to a state of helpless infancy and dependence upon an all-giving, all-nurturing mother. This mother figure was to be honored symbolically through passive submissiveness towards nature (manifested by belief in history as "fated" or cyclic), a strong preference for those to whom one is related by blood, a predilection to honoring the dead through rigid repetition of rituals, and an attachment to land and soil, symbolically associated with motherhood and feminine fertility. The conservatives looked to Bachofen's theory of matriarchy for these traits, which were already being exalted by the Nazi Party. Although the fascist movement oppressed women, Fromm points out that the reactionaries' sympathies for Bachofen did not conflict with their opposition to women's liberation. Rather, the reactionaries liked Bachofen's theory of matriarchy because they liked the idea that there were natural, essential differences between the sexes (which, while not Bachofen's main point, was a point on which Bachofen agreed), and because they were attracted to the submissive acceptance of fate that had supposedly characterized the matriarchal world (CP 90).

In 1933, the Institute collided with Nazi power and sought refuge in Geneva, and in 1934 it moved to New York. Although the Nazis had closed the Institute, it may have been possible to remain a while longer. But considering Fromm's psychoanalysis of Nazism, the members of the early Institute were not surprised by the Nazis' rise to power, and they knew that they needed to escape Germany quickly (Löwenthal 27). The pathologies of Nazism and the trend towards compliant obedience among the German working class were ever on Fromm's mind. Furthermore, Fromm's theory and personal experiences had given him cause to fear nationalism. Nationalism had long been a major intellectual concern for Fromm. One of the formative experiences of his adolescence was his startled discovery of the irrationality of the patriotic fervor in support of World War I (BC 7). Moreover, his early participation in and rejection of the Zionist movement added to his concerns about nationalism.

In addition to his worries about nationalism, Fromm's research project on the German working class convinced him that the danger of Nazism was far greater than most of his contemporaries yet realized. His study of the German working class was based upon the premise that, although most German workers were ideologically opposed to Nazism, this was not sufficient indication that they would resist the Nazis (DC 151).[15] It was unclear whether the German working class' opposition to Nazism was merely superficial or "rooted in [their] character structure" (151). The study concluded that the majority of the German citizens would be neither enthusiastic Nazis nor dissidents but would quietly acquiesce to the rise of National

Socialism, since their professed support for freedom was only superficial. Even more worryingly, the study found that some workers affiliated with the left would be drawn into the Nazi movement by their love of authoritarianism. For example, asked to list their heroes, some left-wing participants responded with a list like, "Marx, Lenin, Nero, and Alexander the Great," while others responded to the effect of, "Marx, Lenin, Socrates, and Pasteur" (OD 35). While both respondents professed support for socialism, for the former respondent socialism was a mere "ideology" or "rationalization" covering over a love of power, while the latter respondent truly admired "benefactors of mankind" (35). While the latter respondent would likely support the resistance, the former might support the Nazis. Not surprisingly, considering the results of this study, the Institute moved almost as far away from Germany as geographically possible, leaving Europe entirely, long before many others fled.

By 1935, as the Institute settled into its new home in New York, the seeds of Fromm's expulsion from the Institute had been planted. Fromm was popular in the U.S. and probably felt at home more quickly than others in the Institute, since he already had many contacts in the U.S. through psychoanalytic circles. (However, Wiggershaus's claim that Fromm's popularity implied that Fromm had friends who were less radical and that this caused his break from the Frankfurt School is dubious.) Frequently traveling, Fromm was not in New York as steadily as the other members of the early Institute were. In addition to his ability to settle comfortably into the U.S. more rapidly, perhaps his work on Bachofen had created some tension between him and others in the Frankfurt School. Some in the Institute's broad social circles may have disagreed with Fromm's attack on Ludwig Klages in that work, and Fromm's critique would not have gone unnoticed by Adorno or by Adorno's friend Walter Benjamin, both of whom had crossed paths with Stefan George's and Ludwig Klages's Cosmic Circle and had formed their own opinions on the Bachofen debate—I will return to this briefly in Chapter 2.

Despite these factors that may have brought into question Fromm's role in the Institute, it was the response to Fromm's 1935 essay for the *Zeitschrift*, "The Social Determinants of Psychoanalytic Theory" that most explicitly demonstrated the rift that was growing between Horkheimer's close circle of followers and Fromm.[16] Adorno at this time was trying to get closer to Horkheimer but was still an outsider and knew little about the Institute's earlier work. He responded to Fromm's article with a polemical rant in a letter to Horkheimer, accusing Fromm of being a reformist who needed to read more Lenin:

> [Fromm's article] is sentimental and wrong to begin with, being a mixture of social democracy and anarchism, and above all shows a severe lack of the concept of dialectics. He takes the easy way out with the concept of authority, without which, after all, neither Lenin's avant-garde nor dictatorship can be conceived of. I would strongly advise him to read Lenin. And what do the anti-popes opposed to Freud say? No, precisely when Freud is criticized from the

left, as he is by us, things like the silly argument about a "lack of kindness" cannot be permitted. This is exactly the trick used by bourgeois individualists against Marx. I must tell you that I see a real threat in this article to the line which the journal takes... (McLaughlin, "Origin Myths" 118-9)

It is a perplexing rant indeed, especially the admonition to "read Lenin." If Adorno were genuinely concerned that Fromm's approach were reformist or anarchist, then he might have turned to Marx for a critique, not Lenin. Perhaps Adorno believed that Horkheimer was an orthodox Marxist and would be concerned about deviation from orthodox Marxism, but Adorno seems to miss the fact that that debate would have been about *Stalin*, not Lenin. Nor does Adorno seem to realize that one of the Institute's main theoretical projects to that point had been a study of authority commissioned by Horkheimer. There is a certain absurdity in Adorno's claim that Fromm's study "took the easy way out with the concept of authority."

Although Adorno ends up looking confused, the letter is significant because it suggests the flawed equation that would later be used in an attempt to marginalize Fromm from the left: Freudian "revisionism" = Marxist revisionism = reformism. It should be pointed out that although critical of *Freud*, Fromm's article was not at all critical of Marx or of revolutionary sentiments; the article's Freudian revisionism was in no way connected to Marxist revisionism. In fact, the article condemned the weaknesses in Freud's theory and Freud's personal character as essentially the results of a *bourgeois, class bias* on the part of Freud, and the article harshly criticized the merely reformist, liberal attitude of mainstream psychoanalysis, which was condescending and authoritarian despite its appearance of objectivity and "tolerance." According to Fromm, the orthodox Freudian psychoanalyst subtly sends the following message to the patient:

> "Here you come, patient, with all your sins. You have been bad, and that is why you suffer. But one can excuse you. The most important reasons for your misdeeds lie in the events of your childhood for which you cannot be made responsible. Furthermore, you want to reform, and you show this in coming to analysis and in giving yourself up to my directions. If, however, you do not comply...then you cannot be helped." (Social Determinants 158-9)

In contrast to this patriarchal and authoritarian attitude towards the patient, Fromm urged an attitude of unconditional (matriarchal) love for the patient. But far from suggesting that such love was absent in Marx or Marxism, Fromm presented his article as a critique of bourgeois attitudes and also rejected any Romantic or unscientific return to feudal values (for which he critiqued Groddeck) (159). The article plainly suggests that psychoanalysis must struggle to transcend both feudalism and capitalism, though the article is focused primarily on a critique of Freudian psychoanalysis and does not proceed to discuss socialism directly.

By 1935 Fromm had already challenged Freudian orthodoxy on a variety of points, but his critique had not previously been so vehement. Almost from the very beginning of his work on psychoanalysis, Fromm had questioned the ahistorical character of psychoanalytic categories as posited by Freud. He had argued that character and neuroses are shaped differently in different socio-economic contexts. He had even argued quite early on that the Oedipus complex, one of Freud's most prized theories, was not an enduring feature of human experience but a result of patriarchal social arrangements. His writings on Bachofen, a thinker whom many considered an alternative to Freud, would also have raised eyebrows among Freud's most loyal disciples. However, the 1935 article marked Fromm's public, dramatic break from orthodox Freudianism, perhaps analogous to his earlier published break from Orthodox Judaism, the 1927 Sabbath article. Flouting psychoanalysis's father-figure, the 1935 article was a joyful act of iconoclasm, condemning Freud repeatedly as bourgeois, conservative, patriarchal, repressed, and incapable of love.

Considering the radical tone and content of Fromm's article, it is indeed puzzling that Adorno condemned it as reformist. If the article could reasonably be expected to trigger an offended outburst in defense of orthodox Marxism, it was not due to any opposition to Marx in the article but only due to the article's rejection of biological reductionism. (As Fromm later pointed out, however, the article was attacking Freud's materialism, which was quite different from Marx's materialism [McLaughlin, "Origin Myths" 119n21].) The article marked the most decisive rejection of biological reductionism to be found in Fromm's work up to that point. It is more likely, however, that Adorno had more pragmatic reasons for his response. Fromm was a more established member of Horkheimer's circle at this time and was popular and well-known in various circles in the U.S. Adorno was not yet even a formal member of the Institute—he was not hired by the Institute until 1938—but he was already angling for a position in it. He may have judged it beneficial for his career to present himself to Horkheimer as a defender of Marxist orthodoxy against Fromm, although one may dispute how orthodox a Marxist Horkheimer would actually have been in 1935.

Fromm remained a central member of the Institute for several more years despite the controversy over the 1935 article. He engaged in a number of empirical studies on U.S. workers and students in the late thirties, while reviewing the findings of the study of the German working class and preparing the manuscript of *Escape from Freedom*. The *Studies on Authority and the Family*, on which Fromm and Horkheimer had collaborated, was published in 1936 in Paris, and Fromm was listed as one of the authors, along with Horkheimer and Löwenthal. It was clear to those in the know that Fromm had contributed a substantial portion of this important work. Richard Wolin writes that, "In retrospect it is quite clear that it was the concept of 'analytical social psychology' advanced by Fromm that served as the inspiration and model for the project as a whole," through Fromm's emphasis upon the family as a mediating link between the individual and socio-economic structures (*Terms of Cultural Criticism* 53). The *Studies*, as well as some essays of Horkheimer's from the late 1930s, explored themes upon which Fromm had been at work since the late

1920s: the role of the state in socialization as it took over a role once consigned to the family (the rise of "the state as educator," as Fromm had put it), increased sadomasochism among the masses, and a "loneliness that craved authority" (Bronner 82). Horkheimer's earlier work had focused more upon philosophical questions concerning social totality, ontology, the relation between theory and practice, and the Institute's research program in relation to various other philosophical and theoretical approaches in vogue at the time (positivism, orthodox Marxism, phenomenology, Neo-Kantianism). The *Studies'* development of the theory of the authoritarian personality and its relation to the family was almost entirely a product of Fromm's theoretical work.

It was not until 1939 that Fromm formally broke from the Institute. It should be clear by now that the break was not due to a lack of substantive contributions on his part. In fact, it was quite the opposite. It is difficult to determine, however, whether Fromm's break from the Institute was mainly caused by Horkheimer, Adorno, or both equally. In *The Frankfurt School in Exile* (2009), Thomas Wheatland lays the blame squarely on Horkheimer. By contrast, Neil McLaughlin stresses Adorno's role in Fromm's break from the Institute; some evidence for this view is already suggested by Adorno's angry response to Fromm's 1935 article.

According to Wheatland's interpretation, as the Institute adjusted to exile in New York in the late 1930s, Horkheimer was solidifying his relationship with new allies—Adorno, Otto Kirchheimer, Franz Neumann, and Walter Benjamin—and distancing himself from some old ones, especially Fromm (Wheatland 61). Fromm's centrality to the Institute and his public persona were making Horkheimer nervous. Wheatland writes,

> Of all the Horkheimer Circle's members, Fromm became the most visible and popular at Columbia during his first years in the United States. He was less guarded than his colleagues, and he was in a position, as the group's functional director of social research projects, to develop strong contacts with U.S. social scientists. (76)

Horkheimer was frequently concerned about maintaining the loyalty of members of the Institute, and his often authoritarian grip made the Institute resemble the authoritarian family structures it was researching (80). This view of Horkheimer's authoritarian grip upon the Institute corresponds to Jürgen Habermas' later assessment of Horkheimer's character in the 1950s. According to Habermas, "Horkheimer was an 'authoritarian' and 'bullied' all the young assistants" (Specter 32). In a 1934 letter to Pollock, Horkheimer wrote,

> [Fromm] does not particularly appeal to me. He has productive ideas, but he wants to be on good terms with too many people at once, and doesn't want to miss anything. It is quite pleasant to talk to him, but my impression is that it is quite pleasant for very many people. (83)

According to Wheatland, Horkheimer wanted to find a small group of loyal supporters, perhaps Adorno and Marcuse, and even break with them from the Institute if necessary, in order to focus on research for a book (what eventually became *The Dialectic of Enlightenment*) (81). Meanwhile, Horkheimer was worried that the Institute would be targeted by the rising Red Scare, and he strictly forbade members of the Institute from any political involvement (72). Though Horkheimer's fears about the Red Scare were not unfounded—the Institute's office had been visited by detectives and was frequently under FBI surveillance—this prohibition may have seemed stifling to Fromm, who became politically active soon after leaving the Institute (73). Fromm later complained that the results of his study on the German working class remained unpublished because Horkheimer was worried the study would be too Marxist for the U.S. political climate (McLaughlin, "Origin Myths" 116).

Faced by a financial crisis in the Institute, Horkheimer decided to cut Fromm's salary first (Wheatland 83). In 1939, Horkheimer and Friedrich Pollock informed Fromm that they would stop his pay after October, asking him to agree "based on his ability to survive solely on his psychoanalytic practice" (83). Fromm objected and demanded a twenty thousand dollar severance package, to which Horkheimer conceded (83-4).

Stephen Eric Bronner provides further evidence for the case that Horkheimer was largely to blame for Fromm's firing. It was also in 1939, according to Bronner, that Horkheimer began a conservative turn (Bronner 83). Although Horkheimer was fairly supportive of the Communist Party throughout the 1930s, the Hitler-Stalin Pact may have been the breaking point, and after that time his focus turned away from practice-oriented theory towards a focus on the individual (80). There were earlier indications, however, that Horkheimer was shifting from his earlier theoretical commitments to praxis and totality, towards a new emphasis upon the individual; his 1936 essay defending pleasure and egoism, which prefigured some of his later work in *Dialectic of Enlightenment*, was one signal of the shift (Jay, *Dialectical Imagination* 58). Further, Horkheimer had stated as early as 1930 that Marxism was not to be identified with "the grasping of a 'totality' or of a total and absolute truth," perhaps implying a criticism of Lukács's method (Tar 23). It is possible that Horkheimer was never fully at home with Fromm's holist, roughly Lukácsian synthesis of the individual and the social.

While Wheatland stresses Horkheimer's role in Fromm's firing, Neil McLaughlin stresses Adorno's role. Enmity between Fromm and Adorno was fairly evident. According to Wiggershaus, Adorno tended to refer derisively to Fromm as a "professional Jew" (McLaughlin, "Origin Myths" 117). And as noted above, Adorno responded to Fromm's 1935 article with the peculiar polemic in which he accused Fromm of being a reformist or an anarchist. In a letter to Martin Jay explaining the causes of his firing, Fromm himself seemed to lay the blame more upon Adorno. Since this is one of the few places where Fromm speculated openly upon the causes for his break from the Institute, it is worth quoting at length:

In the first years of the Institute, while it was in Frankfurt and Geneva, Horkheimer has [sic] no objection to my critique of Freud, which began very slowly before I left the Institute. It was only in the years after the Institute had been for some time in New York, and maybe since I began to write *Escape from Freedom*, that Horkheimer changed his opinion, became a defender of orthodox Freudianism, and considered Freud's attitude as a true revolutionary because of his materialistic attitude towards sex. A strange thing for Horkheimer to do incidentally, because it is pretty obvious that Freud's attitude toward sex corresponded to the bourgeois materialism of the 19th century which was so sharply criticized by Marx. I remember that Horkheimer was also on very friendly terms with [Karen] Horney in the first years of [Horkheimer's] stay in New York, and did not then defend orthodox Freudianism. It was only later that he made this change and it is too personal a problem to speculate why he did so. *I assume partly this had to do with the influence of Adorno, whom from the very beginning of his appearance in New York I criticized very sharply.* Considering the whole situation of the Institute it is not surprising that when Horkheimer made this change, Lowenthal and Pollack [sic] did the same. *Adorno was in this respect probably not influenced by Horkheimer, but rather the other way around.* (McLaughlin, "Origin Myths" 119n21, italics mine)

This passage strongly suggests that Adorno's mid-1930s letter to Horkheimer, with its polemical admonition that Fromm should "read Lenin" (as though Fromm hadn't read Lenin!) was indeed an indication that Adorno was seeking to push Fromm out of the Institute in order to work more closely with Horkheimer. However, in spite of this conclusion, one must also bear in mind Horkheimer's powerful position in the Institute and Fromm's remark elsewhere that "the unwillingness of Horkheimer to publish [the study on the German working class] was one of the many conflicts which led to [Fromm's] departure" (116).

Whatever the causes, Fromm's firing resulted in a major set-back for the Institute both financially and for its public image. Not only did the Institute have to pay Fromm a sizeable severance package—$20,000 was no paltry sum in the Great Depression—but Fromm's firing resulted in the Institute losing funding from Columbia University. Fromm had played a crucial leadership role in the studies of the German working class and on authority and the family, and in the late 1930s he had directed empirical research studies of unemployed men in Newark and female students at Sarah Lawrence College (Wheatland 66, 70). Prominent Columbia sociologist Robert Lynd, a friend of Fromm's, was angered by the Institute's treatment of Fromm and denounced the Institute with the claim that Fromm had been fired for being too Marxist, an assessment with which Fromm himself concurred (85). And since Fromm had been considered the leader of the Institute's empirical research, and since Columbia's Sociology department emphasized empirical research, which was the trend in academic sociology in the U.S. in 1939, it appeared to Columbia that the Institute no longer had much to contribute. At Lynd's recommendation, another research group (Paul Lazarsfeld's) replaced the Institute's former position at Columbia (86). The Institute then turned to research on anti-Semitism, partly in a desperate search for grant funding (88).

We are not concerned here with the Institute's further work after the break with Fromm, so we leave off this historical account at the point of Fromm's break from the Institute. In Chapter 2, some Frankfurt School figures appear again in relation to the messianic milieu of fin de siècle Germany and the apocalyptic *Zeitgeist* of the 1920s. We also return in Chapters 3 and 4 to the work of some members of the Frankfurt School, especially Herbert Marcuse, along with some examination of Walter Benjamin and others, in relation to Fromm's work on messianic hope.

As has been demonstrated, although he has long been marginalized by canonical historical accounts of the Institute for Social Research, Fromm's contributions to Critical Theory were vast. Before joining the Institute, he had already explored the theme of alienated labor through his dissertation under Alfred Weber and had begun a theoretical synthesis of psychoanalysis and Marxism, applying psychoanalysis to societal questions in his article on the Sabbath. After being invited into the Institute by Horkheimer, Fromm's explorations of the possibility of a theoretical synthesis of Marx and Freud helped to shape the Institute's inter-disciplinary research program. Fromm applied his synthesis of Marx and Freud to studies on criminology, early Christianity, the Russian revolution (the underlying theme of "The Dogma of Christ"), Bachofen's theory of matriarchy, the family, and the authoritarian personality, all while working with the Institute. As we have seen, Fromm's thought evolved over the course of his membership in the Institute, as he rejected biological and economic reductionism, explored Bachofen while criticizing his reactionary acolytes, and finally concluded that orthodox Freudianism (though not psychoanalysis itself) had to be rejected. Fromm's daring critique of Freud, his popularity, and perhaps his desire to become involved in radical political activism may all have played a role in his eventual exclusion from the Institute. Personal conflicts among members of the Institute and the emerging intellectual partnership between Horkheimer and Adorno probably contributed as well.

Whatever the reasons for Fromm's break with the Institute, it should now be evident that Fromm's work during his approximately ten years of involvement with the Institute was substantial and central to the Institute's program. Further, it should be evident that Fromm was not merely a peripheral member of the Institute, was not conservative or a liberal reformist, and was not an unserious or merely derivative thinker. Instead, he was central and radical, forging a bold theoretical synthesis between psychoanalysis and Marxism, applying this method to concrete problems, and developing important critiques of the psychoanalytic establishment, orthodox Marxism, and fascism. Although one must reject the claim of some that all the essential ideas of Fromm's later thought are contained in his 1930s writings—in particular, his later writings were transformed by his encounter with the writings of the early Marx—the explorations of human nature, history, and political power in these early works were central to Fromm's later work (Knapp 23). More importantly, he had launched the first major attempt to combine psychoanalysis and Marxism, and to apply this theory to society through concepts like that of the authoritarian personality; this was a profound contribution to the Frankfurt School's early research program and, more broadly, to sociology and social psychology. His later work on messianism, prefigured in his early work, will be the focus of later chapters. There we will see that his critique of Freud, his dialectical account of Bachofen and of early Christianity, and his early attempts to meld the Marxist and psychoanalytic methods laid the basis for a radical philosophy of history and of Marxist messianic hope.

INTERLUDE: FROMM FROM MEXICO TO SWITZERLAND

Almost immediately after his exodus from the Frankfurt School, Fromm became publicly engaged in left-wing activism. He also continued to challenge Freudian orthodoxy, and he did so publicly and for a wider audience, including through a controversial book-length case study of the master himself, *Sigmund Freud's Mission*. I have examined Fromm's early life, demolishing some common misconceptions about Fromm's place in Critical Theory. The later events in Fromm's life do not need to be covered at equal length here, but I will elucidate Fromm's later life and work briefly with respect to two themes: psychoanalysis and the left.

Erich Fromm and the High Priests of Psychoanalysis

To explore Fromm's later life and work with regard to psychoanalysis, I begin by tracing Fromm's professional migration from Freud's psychoanalytic organization, the International Psychoanalytic Association, to his role in founding a new international psychoanalytic movement, the International Federation of Psychoanalytic Societies, which is still large and active today. Finally, I address Fromm's psychoanalytic legacy and his critique of orthodox Freudianism.

Fromm and Professional Psychoanalytic Organizations

Due in large part to his public rejection of orthodox Freudianism and his scathing critique of Freud and his circle, Fromm had rocky interactions with the International Psychoanalytic Association (IPA).[17] The IPA was the professional psychoanalytic organization founded by Freud and representing Freudian orthodoxy. Although some facts regarding the history of Fromm's interaction with the IPA are unclear—in part because his last wife destroyed large amounts of Fromm's correspondence after his death—the following facts are known. In 1935, Fromm was contacted by Carl Müller-Braunschweig, then head of the Berlin branch of the IPA, known as the DGP, which was still operating in Berlin under Nazi rule. Müller-Braunschweig rather pointedly demanded that Fromm pay the dues he owed to the DGP. Fromm offered to pay by installments, but in the spring of 1936, he withheld his last payment, writing a sharp letter to Müller-Braunschweig, asking whether it was true that the DGP had "excluded its Jewish members" and objecting that he had not even been informed of this (Roazen, "Exclusion" 10). Müller-Braunschweig and Ernest Jones (more on Jones momentarily) wrote back assuring Fromm that the Jewish members of the DGP had resigned voluntarily (in late 1935) and apologizing for not having informed him earlier (10, 12). Following this response, Fromm submitted the remainder of his dues (12-3). (In that same year, the reader may recall, Fromm wrote his feisty article attacking orthodox Freudianism, "The Social Determinants of Psychoanalytic Theory," which was scorned by Adorno and later praised by Marcuse in *Eros and Civilization*.)

Fromm could not have known the full extent of the concessions that the DGP was making in order to stay in operation under the Nazi regime. The situation gradually worsened until November 1938, when the Nazis at last moved to close down the DGP (Roazen, "Exclusion" 13). By that time, the DGP was a subsection of the "Göring Institute," directed by "enthusiastic Nazi" M.H. Göring, a distant cousin of Hermann Göring (Goggin and Goggin 24). A photograph of Freud had been replaced by one of Hitler, and all members were required to read *Mein Kampf* and were forbidden to treat Jews, homosexuals, and soldiers suffering "battle fatigue" (what we now term PTSD) ("Exclusion" 12-3). The DGP had held a celebration of Freud's eightieth birthday two years before, but Jews were not welcome. Müller-Braunschweig was heavily involved in the transition of the DGP into a branch of the Göring Institute. He also turned over the names of Jewish psychoanalysts in Italy to the Nazis, and the other major leader of the DGP, Karl Boehm, publicly endorsed the genocide of homosexuals and turned over for execution the soldiers determined to be "malingerers" (14, Goggin and Goggin 203).

Fromm also probably did not know that the removal of Jewish members of the psychoanalytic institute had been dubiously "voluntary," considering that they had been presented with the catch-22 of resigning or closing the entire German branch of the IPA. Since it was not until almost three years later that the Nazis forbade Jews from practicing medicine or law, it may have been possible to keep the Center running with its Jewish members for a while longer, but the Jewish psychoanalysts in Berlin were not given the opportunity to evaluate this possibility by the IPA (13). Later, in *Sigmund Freud's Mission*, Fromm subtly references Freud's non-confrontational stance towards the Nazis, pointing to Freud's fear of anti-Semitism and his early wish that Jung would be the "Aryan" successor and that psychoanalysis would expand beyond Jewish circles in Vienna in order to survive (SFM 48-9).

In questioning the IPA's policies, Fromm was jeopardizing his one source of professional accreditation as a psychoanalyst. In the United States, psychoanalysis was the province of physicians, so as a non-physician Fromm was at a significant disadvantage and was not eligible to join the New York branch of the IPA. In the late 1930s or early 1940s, Fromm discovered Harry Stack Sullivan's Zodiac Club in New York, a center for psychoanalytic and related intellectual discussion where he was welcome. The Zodiac Club was an informal circle including such prominent humanistic psychoanalysts as Karen Horney (with whom Fromm was romantically involved) and Clara Thompson, along with noteworthy anthropologists Ruth Benedict and Margaret Mead. In 1950, Fromm moved to Mexico, partly for the health of his new wife Henny Gurland. He continued to travel back and forth from the United States and Europe, generally remaining in Mexico for five month intervals at a time (Funk, *Life and Ideas* 127; Millán 208).

Fromm did not interact with the IPA again until 1953, when he noticed that he was no longer listed as a member and contacted the organization to find out why (Roazen, "Exclusion" 16). This time, he was coldly and bureaucratically dismissed. The claim was that Fromm had been dropped from the membership rolls because the IPA had decided to get rid of the special "direct" memberships that had existed during World War II and to require instead that everyone belong to a specific branch of the IPA. In fact, only one exception seems to have been made; a direct membership had been granted to Werner Kemper, who had been involved in genocide in Nazi Germany and had fled to Brazil with the help of Ernest Jones (16). (Kemper was later accused of involvement in torture in Brazil (16).) As a non-physician, Fromm did not qualify for admission into the New York branch of the IPA (13). It was conceded that Fromm could re-apply for acceptance if he wished to be a direct member of the IPA again, but in his view this requirement was spurious, since he had never left the organization, and at any rate, the letter from an IPA representative subtly implied that if he did apply again, he would not be accepted (17-8). In the early 1960s, after his exclusion from the IPA, Fromm helped to found the International Federation of Psychoanalytic Societies (IFPS), an alternative to the IPA. The IFPS still exists today and is active; the important William Alanson White Institute in New York is one of its member organizations, and the IFPS also has branches in Finland, Italy, Brazil, Chile, Switzerland, Mexico, Austria, Lithuania, Norway, Greece, Canada, and Spain, according to the IFPS website.

Fromm always insisted that he was loyal to the core insights of psychoanalysis, especially the importance of the unconscious. "I never gave up psychoanalysis," Fromm wrote in a letter to Martin Jay, sounding irked at the suggestion:[18]

I have never wanted to form a school of my own. I was removed by the International Psychoanalytic Association…, and I am still [1971] a member of the Washington Psychoanalytic Association, which is Freudian. I have always criticized the Freudian orthodoxy and the bureaucratic methods of the Freudian international organization, but my whole theoretical outlook is based on what I consider Freud's most important findings… (Jay, *Dialectical Imagination* 89-90)

It was the dispute over what those "most important findings" were that undergirded Fromm's exclusion from the IPA. He had been told that he could apply for re-admittance and that it was unlikely that anyone who agreed with the basic tenets of psychoanalysis would be excluded, but Fromm realized that what was at stake was exactly the identity of those basic tenets.

Fromm's Psychoanalytic Legacy

As Neil McLaughlin explains, the basic theses of the "humanistic psychoanalysis" in which Fromm was engaged (although he resisted being classed strictly as a member of the humanistic school) are now more widely accepted than the views of Fromm's orthodox opponents:

> Today one can find few serious defenders of the death instinct, the primal horde or orthodox libido theory. Most of the interesting work in psychoanalysis rejects instinct theory and deals with, as Fromm suggested it must, relatedness and identity. Fromm's neo-Freudian former collaborator Karen Horney is now being rediscovered as an early proponent of feminist object relations. Sullivan's work has given rise to the emergence of interpersonal psychoanalysis, an important school of thought within contemporary Freudian theory. In addition, Fromm's position on Freudian theory has gained new influence in recent years. (McLaughlin, "Origin Myths" 8)

Few of Fromm's ideas have been credited to him in the canon of psychoanalytic theory today. These ideas are generally viewed in disjunction from Fromm's contribution to Critical Theory. It is telling, for example, that an Oxford *Dictionary of Psychology* lists Horkheimer, Adorno, and Marcuse under its definition of "Frankfurt School" and does not mention Fromm, although it does have a separate entry on "Fromm's [character] typology" (Colman 287, 290).

Although Fromm is still too often overlooked, the ideas he and others advanced are now more widely accepted, which has paved the way for an ongoing revival of Fromm's contributions to psychoanalysis. In Europe, his insights are enriching certain psychoanalytic circles, such as the circle around the recently deceased Italian psychoanalyst Romano Biancoli. In Mexico, the International Federation of Psychoanalytic Societies (IFPS) holds conferences that seek to draw from Fromm's psychoanalytic insights. The editorial of a 2000 issue of the journal of the IFPS was headlined, "Erich Fromm: A Rediscovered Legacy." In 2009 a new introductory book to Fromm's psychological thought was published, Annette Thomson's *Erich Fromm: Explorer of the Human Condition*. While encumbered by a sometimes overly simplistic style of argumentation,[19] the book discusses ways in which Fromm's insights underlie developments in psychology that are now widely accepted. Fromm's work is also currently contributing to the development of "psychologies of liberation" (cf. Shulman and Watkins, Bruce Levine).

Much remains to be done towards recuperating Fromm's psychoanalytic legacy. As Paul Roazen writes, "A central silence in the official story of the history and development of psychoanalytic thought has to do with Erich Fromm's contributions" (Roazen, "Escape" 239). The time is ripe for a revival of interest in Fromm's humanistic psychoanalysis. The reputation of psychoanalysis itself has suffered since the 1950s and 60s, especially as the Reagan-era drug war and neoliberal laudations for individual responsibility found the behaviorism of B. F. Skinner more useful for its ideological aims. Although Skinner rejected the use of punishment ("aversives") as a means of behavior modification, others were less humane. That was a time in which James Dobson of Focus on the Family, with his manuals on corporal punishment of children, was at an all-time height of popularity, as the progressive, humanistic approach to childrearing of Benjamin Spock (who worked with Fromm on peace activism through anti-nuclear weapons organization SANE) was losing popularity. In that era, behaviorism supplanted psychoanalysis. Although the tide of professional opinion has turned against the more aggressive versions of behaviorism of the past (electric skin shock and other "aversive" therapies, for example), it remains the case that behaviorist and pharmaceutical methods are privileged over talk therapy.[20]

Fromm's Critique of Freud and His Circle

Fromm's critiques of orthodox psychoanalysis include critiques of Freud himself as well as of Freud's disciples. Three of Fromm's major criticisms of orthodox psychoanalysis are based upon his assessment of Freud's personality and its influence on the movement: (1) Freud was overly pessimistic, (2) Freud's thinking was limited by his Victorian context, and (3) Freud had an authoritarian personality, reflected in his manner of leading the IPA.

According to Fromm, while Marx's vision was imbued with messianic hope for the future, Freud's view was "tragic" (BC 39). Freud's pessimism was increased by the bloodbath of the First World War, which Freud enthusiastically endorsed at the outset. ("All my libido is given to Austro-Hungary" (SFM 101).) According to Fromm, Freud's theory of the death drive, developed in the wake of the war, was the chief indication of Freud's increased pessimism. In addition to Freud's pessimism, a keynote of Fromm's critique was that Freud was limited by his Victorian context, in that he had a patriarchal worldview and was obsessed with sex. The charge of Freud's patriarchy was not unique to Fromm but was advanced by Karen Horney among others, and other humanistic psychoanalysts challenged what they considered Freud's over-emphasis upon sexual desire in the development of the psyche.

Finally, Fromm charged that Freud had an "authoritarian personality" and was unable to love. Fromm continued to maintain this charge after he advanced it in his controversial 1935 article, to which Adorno responded with such hostility, and in which Fromm portrayed Freud as a tyrannical leader who sought to crush all dissent within the early psychoanalytic organization. Fromm's *Sigmund Freud's Mission* (1959), in another act of unabashed and celebratory iconoclasm, turns Freud's psychoanalytic method upon Freud himself, casting him as unloving and repressed, "a typical Puritan" who "had little love for people in general, when no erotic component was involved," and claiming that Freud "made love an object of science, but in his life it remained dry and sterile" (SFM 33, 28, 31). More to the point, the book turns on a lengthy analysis of Freud's dependence upon authority figures and his tremendous need for followers to serve as objects of his authoritarian impulses.

Fromm's critique of Freud's loyal followers builds upon the critique of Freud's authoritarian personality. From Freud's own *modus operandi* arose an organization that nearly killed the radical, non-conformist, revolutionary faith of early psychoanalysis, replacing it with a conservative bureaucracy and staid ideology. (There are parallels here, of course, to the Soviet Union. As with Fromm's critique of early Christianity in the "The Dogma of Christ," Fromm's critique of orthodox psychoanalysis serves also as an implicit critique of orthodox Marxism.)

Aside from his critiques of Freud's personality, Fromm's remaining critiques of orthodox psychoanalysis may be summarized in two points: (1) orthodox psychoanalysis was "fanatical," and (2) orthodox psychoanalysis as a professional discipline was bureaucratic, dehumanizing, and gate-keeping.

Firstly, Fromm asks of psychoanalysis as he asked also of the Frankfurt School and Marxism: "*How could psychoanalysis...be transformed into this kind of fanatical movement?*" (DC 143; italics Fromm's). He traces the problem to Freud himself, whose youthful desire to participate in political struggle was channeled into the formation of an apolitical psychoanalytic "International." According to Fromm, the "fanatic" is a narcissist who deals with her removal from the world and withdrawal into herself by means of a "cause" that becomes her source of strength and connection (156). Fromm characterizes the fanatic as "burning ice," motivated by "cold passion" (156). When it was not fanatical, psychoanalysis was conformist, Fromm asserted—not only internally, but in its relationship to society, orthodox psychoanalysis was a bulwark of the status quo.

Secondly, Fromm issues a prophetic call for psychoanalysis to abandon its "sterile bureaucracy" and recommit itself to the quest for truth (DC 148). According to Fromm's theory of religion, all human societies are religious in some way, but the religion they actually believe and practice is not necessarily the one they profess to follow. When a religion deteriorates from a living system into a dead ideology, bureaucracies arise. These bureaucracies are then administered by priests—not prophets—who keep tradition alive through rituals, after the beliefs that animated the religion have become stagnant (have become "idols") (MPP 124). Fromm states that members of each psychoanalytic "school" had to be "properly 'ordained,'" implying that their members were priests, not prophets (AB 65).

Fromm was unique in unabashedly criticizing Ernest Jones's three-volume, hagiographic "court biography" of Freud. He responded to Jones repeatedly, including in *Sigmund Freud's Mission*, in his essay "Psychoanalysis—Science or Party Line?", and in *The Crisis of Psychoanalysis* (SFM *passim*; DC 135-138; CP 9-12). For example, he objected to Jones's branding of Sándor Ferenczi and Otto Rank as mentally unstable at the time of their break from orthodox Freudianism (CP 19; DC 136). Fromm probably knew that Jones's book also involved a degree of cover-up of the situation of psychoanalysis in Nazi Germany. Jones claimed in the biography, "This year [1934] saw the flight of the remaining analysts from Germany and the 'liquidation' of psychoanalysis in Germany," a claim that Jones probably knew was false or at least grossly oversimplified, since Jones had written to Ana Freud in 1933, approving of Karl Boehm's efforts to "save" psychoanalysis in Germany by continuing to keep the IPA running in Berlin with the agreed resignation of the Jewish members (Roazen, "Exclusion" 6, 10).

By the 1950s, in *The Sane Society* (1955), Fromm had worked out most of his criticisms. In the foreword to that work, Fromm noted some shifts in his thought with regard to Freud since Fromm's earlier books *Escape from Freedom* (1941) and *Man for Himself* (1947). According to Fromm, the "basic thesis" of the "humanistic psychoanalysis"[21] to which he now subscribed was "that the basic passions of man are not rooted in his instinctive needs, but in the specific conditions of human existence, in the need to find a new relatedness to man and nature after having lost the primary relatedness of the pre-human stage" (SS viii). Here it is clear that Fromm's humanistic psychoanalysis had the same aim as his messianism: to grapple with the loss of the primeval paradise and to seek a better future without resorting to psychological regression. Despite his disagreements with Freud and orthodox psychoanalysis, Fromm notes in *The Sane Society* that there are aspects of Freud's theory that he still found valuable and was retaining, including "[Freud's] scientific method, his evolutionary concept, [and] his concept of the unconscious as a truly irrational force" (SS viii). Yet Fromm concluded his observations about psychoanalysis in *The Sane Society* with the warning that "there is a danger that psychoanalysis loses another fundamental trait of Freudian thinking, the courage to defy common sense and public opinion" (SS viii).

Erich Fromm as Left-wing Activist

Fromm was an activist. As we have seen, Fromm was certainly an organizer even before arriving at the Institute for Social Research (and his radicalization long preceded his contact with the Institute). We turn now to Fromm's activism after his exodus from the Institute, at which point, freed from Horkheimer's restrictions on political involvement, Fromm was more able to engage in activism and soon joined the Socialist Party of America (SP-SDF). Among Fromm's first major political endeavors in the United States was his involvement in the founding of the leading anti-nuclear weapons organization in the U.S., "SANE" (named after his book *The Sane Society*), for which he went on an important national speaking tour. Later he assisted with anti-war protest candidate Eugene McCarthy's Presidential bid (even writing suggested speeches for McCarthy), continued his extensive activist speaking tour, collaborated with Trappist monk and peace advocate Thomas Merton in the attempt to coordinate an international conference on peace to be sponsored by the pope (which never came to fruition but had many endorsers), fought to get his leftist cousin Heinz Brandt freed from political imprisonment in East Germany, and—probably his crowning organizing achievement—organized and published an international "symposium" of "socialist humanists" seeking a socialist alternative to capitalism and Soviet Communism (*Socialist Humanism: An International Symposium*). He corresponded and collaborated with a range of leading activists and public intellectuals, including Raya Dunayevskaya (who also carried on a correspondence with Marcuse) (Anderson and Rockwell *passim*). Dunayevskaya was the founder of a "Marxist Humanist" tendency on the U.S. left and the only prominent Marxist organizer in the U.S. who took the influence of Hegel upon Marx very seriously. In addition to his many books, articles, and speeches, Fromm wrote at least three important radical pamphlets that were widely circulated, two for the Socialist Party of America (SP-SDF) (*Let Man Prevail* and *We Have a Vision*) and one for the American Friends Service Committee (*War Within Man*). Fromm's influence on the U.S. left became widespread in the 1950s, with his bestsellers *The Sane Society* (1955) and *The Art of Loving* (1956) challenging the sterility of 1950s life. Martin Luther King later cited *The Art of Loving* as one of the philosophical influences in his development of a "love ethic" (hooks [2010] 1).

Given this background, it should be no surprise that the FBI had a file on Fromm over 600 pages long (Funk, *Life and Ideas* 145). Nor should it be surprising how vocal were his conservative opponents, nor that a polemical advocate of laissez-faire capitalism like Ayn Rand would include a polemic by Nathaniel Branden against Fromm's concept of alienation in her *Capitalism: The Unknown Ideal* and would later say that Fromm's ideas about love were reflected in her villain character James Taggart in *Atlas Shrugged* (Rand 259-285; Binswanger 3). Nor should it startle the reader to learn that Isaiah Berlin attacked Fromm's idea of "positive freedom" in his *Four Essays on Liberty*, nor that even in the late 1980s, Fromm was still a favorite whipping boy for conservative critics like Allan Bloom, in his *Closing of the American Mind* (Berlin xlii; McLaughlin, "Critical Theory" 6).

It is more interesting, perhaps, that Fromm was driven from the circles around the New York Intellectuals—he was cut off from Irving Howe, for example, who resented *The Art of Loving* and the manifesto that Fromm wrote for the Socialist Party of America (SP-SDF) (McLaughlin, "Forgotten Intellectual" 226). Howe's rejection was especially damaging to Fromm since Howe was editor of *Dissent* magazine, "the natural home for [Fromm's] moderate democratic socialist politics" (according to Neil McLaughlin) (226). Fromm's work was famously harshly criticized by Sidney Hook as well, and Fromm faced similarly intense public criticism from Daniel Bell in the 1970s (by which time Bell was a Cultural Cold Warrior), against whom Fromm had contended that there was deep continuity between the early and late Marx (225-6, cf. Frances Stonor Saunders on Bell in *The Cultural Cold War*).

Despite Fromm's long life of activism, not only has the history of his contributions to Critical Theory and psychoanalysis been revised in a way that downplays and misrepresents his role, but so has the history of Fromm's contribution to the left. Due to the lack of scholarship on Fromm and due to various "origin myths" of the Frankfurt School and the left, it often appears as though Fromm did not contribute much to the left. Fromm is often simply omitted in discussions of the movements in which he played an important role. Some confusion stems from the myth that the Frankfurt Institute or "Critical Theory" was the architect of the New Left or one of its chief theoretical influences. The related myth that Herbert Marcuse was "the guru of the New Left" obscures Fromm's contribution and misconstrues Marcuse's. (Consider as an example of this obscuring of Fromm's contribution to the left, the recent book *Scriptures for a Generation: What We Were Reading in the '60s*; the book contains approximately fifty entries on authors who influenced the 1960s, and there is no entry on Fromm, though there is one on Marcuse [Beidler 140, 179].)

To turn to the problem of the myth of Marcuse as "guru of the new left," one must consider the way in which Marcuse's role has tended to displace Fromm's in histories of the New Left. For example, Jamison and Eyerman's *Seeds of the Sixties* explores Fromm along with Marcuse, C. Wright Mills, Hannah Arendt, and a few others. Although Jamison and Eyerman consider Fromm's contribution, they malign Fromm peculiarly (though characteristically, for the genre), while presenting Marcuse as a radical upstart:

> When his old [i.e., former] colleague Erich Fromm grew too successful in his popular psychoanalysis and turned radicalism largely into a personal quest for mental health, Marcuse took him on and questioned whether Marxism was really a humanism at all, as Fromm claimed. Unlike Fromm, Marcuse never ceased being—or at least trying to be—a revolutionary. Marcuse sought to keep the radicalism of Marx from being watered down, from being transformed into a toothless liberalism; but he also resisted the attempts to freeze Marxism in its own past, to reify the writings of Marx as dogmatic truths that were in no need of amendment. (Jamison and Eyerman 120)

Jamison and Eyerman never present an argument for what they take to be obvious truths: Fromm's alleged conformism, "liberalism," dogmatism, and lack of radicalism. These criticisms echo the typical presentation of Fromm according to the "origin myth" of the Frankfurt School addressed earlier.

It is an oft-repeated adage, first proclaimed by *Time* magazine and later reinforced by Douglas Kellner, that Herbert Marcuse was "the guru of the New Left," a claim that seems to displace Fromm's contribution and a claim that Marcuse himself desperately tried to put to rest (cf., for example, video footage of Marcuse contesting this claim in *Herbert's Hippopotamus,* and Wheatland 269) (Kellner, Introduction xi, xxxvi; N. Braune 5). Although the New Left had no single "guru," Fromm was significantly more influential on the New Left in its early stages. The myth that Marcuse was the guru of the New Left is only now being debunked (cf., Bronner 2002, Wheatland 2009). Although Marcuse's writings show that he was attentive to changes on the New Left, it seems that, as Wheatland puts it, "the New Left meant more to him than he meant to the New Left" (Wheatland 334). Marcuse was more of a student of the New Left than its mentor (334).

> [Marcuse] neither set the waves of student protest in motion nor shaped U.S. student opinion on a large scale once the New Left was on the rise. Instead, he recognized the significance of the Movement and the events that he was witnessing, and he sought to counsel the New Left as it grew and tried to articulate a new agenda for the late 1960s. (334)

It was only in the late 1960s that Marcuse began to gain the attention of parts of the left in Europe and in the U.S., especially the Weather Underground (N. Braune 5). There were some left activists in the U.S. who were seriously influenced by Marcuse—Angela Davis, Ron Aronson, Mike Davis, Stanley Aronowitz—but Marcuse was almost never discussed in the leading publications of the New Left: *New Left Notes*, *Studies on the Left*, and *Ramparts* (317).

It has been suggested that Marcuse did not initially catch on with the New Left because they found his writing inaccessible, presupposing philosophical knowledge and drawing upon such thinkers as Plato, Rousseau, Schiller, Kant, Hegel, Marx, and Freud (Wheatland 298). Anti-intellectualism on the left and Marcuse's opposition to this anti-intellectualism further increased the distance between Marcuse and the New Left (298). There is a great deal of truth in both these claims. The sheer difficulty of reading Marcuse, enhanced by his struggles with writing in English, and the anti-intellectual mood of the left would not have worked to his advantage. Although Fromm also drew heavily upon the history of philosophy, his style of writing was more publicly readable.

However, perhaps another reason that Marcuse was inaccessible was that he was not trying to be accessible. Fromm had consciously decided to write for a wide audience and had written books for the general public since 1941. Marcuse, on the other hand, may have believed it impossible to reach the masses with his message in the 1960s (as is suggested by the pessimism of *One-Dimensional Man*) and consequently did not attempt it. One can observe a significant change in Marcuse's style in the late 1960s.[22] Along with others in the Frankfurt School of the 1950s, it is possible that Marcuse had accepted the *Flaschenpost* method, sending out "messages in a bottle" for a future time at which the culture of the masses would be capable of seeing their value (Wheatland 88, 203, 267-8).

David Wellman, though not a key player on the left at the time, is worth quoting at length, since his comments typify the opinion of the 1960s left towards Marcuse:

> I'm not surprised that you haven't found much mention of Marcuse in the archival materials on the American New Left. I don't remember him being an important figure to us during the Radical Education Project. Our idea of education during that period didn't pertain to theoretical, philosophical issues but much more basic understandings of American society and how to change it. That said, I remember people reading *One-Dimensional Man* later on...I can't estimate how many other people were reading it. I guess there was some interest since I recall discussing it with people in informal settings. I personally was turned-off by the book. It struck me as incredibly pessimistic and unhelpful to people trying to make change. I read him to be saying that change was impossible given the one-dimensionality of modern society and since that was what I was trying to do, the book was less than useful to me. It was an argument for why my activism was doomed to failure. I did, however,

find his notion of repressive tolerance incredibly important. It gave voice to my experience in the student and civil rights movement. It gave a name to the way we were treated by people in power. (Wheatland 317)

Wellman's remarks appear prototypical in their skepticism concerning *One-Dimensional Man*, considering its message of pessimism and a totally administered society, along with their gratitude for Marcuse's "Repressive Tolerance," which was more widely read by the New Left than *Eros and Civilization* or *One-Dimensional Man*.

As for the other members of the Frankfurt School, their influence on the New Left was negligible. [23] Nor were Fromm and Marcuse viewed by the public as members of the "Frankfurt School" or of "Critical Theory." Stephen Eric Bronner writes, offering some chronological perspective on the titles generally identified with the tradition of "Critical Theory" and their availability to the U.S. public in English translation:

> *History and Class Consciousness* by Georg Lukács appeared only in 1971, Korsch's *Marxism and Philosophy* was first published in 1970, and a severely edited version of Benjamin's *Illuminations* only in 1969. Horkheimer's collection titled *Critical Theory* and his and Adorno's *Dialectic of Enlightenment* were published in 1972, and Adorno's *Negative Dialectics* in 1973, while Ernst Bloch's *Principle of Hope* appeared in 1986. None of these works were known when the movement was on the rise, or even when the future of Martin Luther King's Poor People's Movement was on the agenda, but rather only when the original flame had begun to flicker (Bronner 166).

By contrast, as Bronner points out, Fromm's *Escape from Freedom* (1941), *The Sane Society* (1955), and *The Art of Loving* (1956) had all been bestsellers in the U.S., before Fromm's *The Revolution of Hope* was published in 1968. Fromm's *Marx's Concept of Man*, published in 1961, "introduced the young Marx to America and provided the dominant interpretation of this thinker" (Bronner 166).

Fromm significantly influenced the development of the New Left. For example, in addition to Fromm's influence on Martin Luther King's love ethic, it was sometimes claimed that Fromm's *Sane Society* was one of four or five books that influenced Tom Hayden's Port Huron Statement (Bronner 165). Annette Thomson writes of Fromm's fame on the left:

> At the height of Erich Fromm's popularity in the United States and Mexico in the 1960s, he received around 30 invitations per month to give lectures and talks. These events attracted huge audiences—for example 2000 students at Chicago University and over 3000 in Mexico City. Some of Fromm's books became international bestsellers and were translated into most major languages. (Thomson 1)

By the 1970s, after his campaign for Eugene McCarthy, Fromm's influence upon the New Left in the United States began to fade. Fromm moved back to Europe in the early 1970s, where he remained a prominent public figure to his death, and his influence in Europe grew as it waned in the U.S.

Fromm's impact over the course of his career was global. Paulo Freire, the founder of contemporary critical pedagogy, was considerably influenced by Fromm (Freire 11). (Fromm also points to the importance of Freire's work [ROH 116].) Freire and Fromm met at Fromm's home in Cuernavaca, Mexico, through the introduction of Ivan Illich, who was a friend of Fromm in Mexico (Freire 44, 90). (Fromm also wrote a nice introduction for Illich's book *Celebration of Awareness*.) Fromm also influenced socialist humanists in Eastern Europe (especially the Yugoslav Praxis Group), with the help of his important book/organizing project, *Socialist Humanism: An International Symposium*.

Various reasons have been offered for Fromm's decline in popularity in the New Left towards the end of the 1960s. I hold that Fromm seemed too hopeful or optimistic in the climate of growing despair, as some on the left began to feel helpless, in the wake of Cointelpro and protracted struggle, and as some turned to drugs, violence, and spiritual escapism. As will become apparent in Chapter 3, such escapist responses were the very kinds of things Fromm was warning against and to which he was presenting messianic hope as an alternative. Stephen Eric Bronner explains Fromm's fall from popularity thus: "With the fragmentation of the New Left and the rise of postmodernism, [Fromm's] work appears almost quaint. The old concern with inner development and the emancipatory content of new social relations is no longer what it once was" (Bronner 171). Fromm was unlikely to be the hero of desperate or retreating activists, which was the majority by that point. I argue in the Epilogue that current political developments make Fromm more relevant today than ever, in a present resurgence of resistance.

As has been shown, Fromm had considerable influence upon the early development of the New Left. His radical critique of society, combined with his popularity, won him both enemies and friends. Now that we have surveyed Fromm's work up through the end of his life with regard to his early theoretical synthesis of Marx and Freud, his break from the Frankfurt School, and his interactions with and critiques of psychoanalysis and the left, it is necessary to discuss the context of the debates concerning messianism in which Fromm was engaged, the tumultuous situation of German intellectual life from shortly before the First World War to the late 1920s.

NOTES

[1] Although I sometimes follow the convention of using the terms "Frankfurt School" and "Institute" interchangeably—Fromm was certainly a member of both—it should be remembered that the Frankfurt School is sometimes interpreted as a broader category that can include scholars like Karl Korsch and Ernst Bloch, who were not members of the Institute for Social Research.

[2] Fromm's absence in the book is particularly unfortunate considering that Tar's thesis—i.e., the Institute became pessimistic (partly through the influence of Schopenhauer on Horkheimer) and abandoned Marxism—jibes with Fromm's own concerns about the Institute.

3   Fromm distinguishes between the bureaucratic "priest" and the revolutionary "prophet." I return to these concepts later in this chapter.

4   Jay is a bit vague about who should be given the most credit for the study of the German working class, noting that the study was mentioned in Horkheimer's inaugural lecture as director of the Institute but, unlike some other scholars' accounts, Jay's does not give Horkheimer all of the credit for the idea or the research (*Dialectical Imagination* 93).

5   Although Leo Löwenthal is known to have engaged seriously with Jewish thought, his parents were not religious. He accompanied Fromm at the *Lehrhaus* and at Fromm and Reichmann's experimental religious commune/psychoanalytic treatment center, the Therapeuticum, but like most members of those circles, he was rebelling against his parents' secularism and rediscovering Judaism for himself. Max Horkheimer was raised in a Conservative Jewish family but had less exposure to Jewish tradition and broke from the practice of Judaism more quickly than did Fromm.

6   Fromm cites Alfred Weber in *The Sane Society*, where he mentions his "scheme of historical development which has some similarities to the one in my [Fromm's] text. He assumes a 'chthonic period' from 4000 to 1200 B.C. which was characterized by the fixation to earth in agricultural peoples" (SS 51). Alfred Weber seems to have been an influence on Fromm's concern about reactionary attachments to land and soil.

7   Of course, I am referring here to Conservative Judaism (as opposed to the Orthodox, Reform, or other branches) and not to Nobel's politics, which were left.

8   Although Franz Rosenzweig is often credited as founder, Fromm's involvement in the *Lehrhaus* predates Rosenzweig's, who later became the director (cf., Funk, "Jewish Roots" 2).

9   Fromm and Reichmann are also said to have met through Frieda's "childhood friend" Golde Ginsburg, whom Fromm was dating and who later married Fromm's friend Leo Löwenthal (Hornstein, Funk).

10   Scholem's book is peppered with similarly biting remarks about others in these circles who rejected Scholem's interpretation of Judaism and messianism, so one need not assume that Fromm's demeanor towards Scholem was offensive or condescending.

11   Fromm's later work on the Sabbath also highlighted the Sabbath's radical implications as a foretaste of the messianic time, in which labor would be ended, harmony restored, time and death conquered, and enjoyment instituted (FL 247–9; TB 42).

12   Zilbersheid's article "The Idea of Abolition of Labor in Socialist Utopian Thought" and his book *Jenseits der Arbeit. Der vergessene sozialistiche Traum von Marx, Fromm und Marcuse* suggested that Fromm and Marcuse both followed upon Marx's conception of an *Aufhebung* of labor, with Fromm interpreting this *Aufhebung* with an emphasis upon the *transformation* of labor (into a free, creative process) and Marcuse stressing the aspect of an *Aufhebung* as *abolition* of labor (freedom from the misery of toil).

13   This use of allegory is not especially surprising. Fromm often employs historical narratives (such as that of Robespierre or of seventeenth century false messiah Sabbatai Zevi) and myths (Antigone, Adam and Eve, etc.) to present subtle critiques of contemporary problems. Even when he is explicitly critiquing a contemporary social movement (for example, psychoanalysis), it often seems that his criticism is directed elsewhere (for example, towards the current direction of the socialist movement). For example, Fromm's book *Sigmund Freud's Mission*, which mocks Freud's attempt to form a psychoanalytic "International," should probably be read as a not-too-subtle critique of orthodox Marxism, not just orthodox Freudianism. Fromm's use of historical narratives and myths is in some sense of a typical Freudian trope; psychoanalysis frequently draws from mythology, literature, and history to discuss basic human neuroses. However, Fromm's application of this method to a critique of contemporary social problems is unique.

14   For an example of an interesting contemporary application of Fromm's theories of the authoritarian personality and "escapes from freedom," see Max Blumenthal's use of Fromm for building a compelling critique of the U.S. religious right in *Republican Gomorrah: Inside the Movement that Shattered the Party* (New York: Nation Books, 2009).

15   Incidentally, Rolf Wiggershaus also misunderstands the premise for the study of the German working class. He condemns it as pessimistic about revolution, and he objects that one cannot determine whether an individual will support a socialist revolution through exploring their authoritarian

sentiments (for example, as manifested in their attitude towards the role of women in society, or their support for or opposition to corporal punishment of children). What Wiggershaus misses is that the study never was trying to determine whether the workers in Germany professed support for a socialist revolution—in fact, the study was begun with the knowledge that many of the German workers were self-professed socialists. Rather, Fromm's study was evaluating the contradictions in the thinking of the German workers and examining what results could be expected from political engagement on the part of the workers. Even if an upheaval of some sort could be expected, the question was not whether it would choose to label itself a "socialist revolution" but whether its consequences would be more like Stalinism or more like the society envisioned by Marx in which human freedom would be its own end. Wiggershaus asks rhetorically whether most workers in Russia before the revolution, if surveyed, would have supported equality for women and humane treatment of children; the answer of course is "no," but that is not the point; authoritarian attitudes are relevant to the long-term success of a revolution, and Fromm did not view the Soviet Union as fully socialist. Wiggershaus conveniently ignores that the so-called "gloomy," "pessimistic" study was proven correct in its prediction that the German working class was not ready to lead a socialist revolution or an effective anti-fascist resistance.

[16] Marcuse, interestingly, loved this essay by Fromm, lauding it later in *Eros and Civilization* even in the midst of pillorying much of Fromm's other work (*Eros and Civilization* 243). Although it is ironic that Marcuse praises the most manifestly anti-Freudian of Fromm's early essays—Marcuse at the time was condemning Fromm's Freudian "revisionism"—it is not surprising that Marcuse would like the essay. The essay challenged the Freudian illusion of the analyst's political and philosophical "neutrality" and rejected the bourgeois value of "tolerance" (the subject of a later, important essay by Marcuse), and it condemned contemporary society as overly sexually repressive.

[17] In this section on Fromm's interaction with the IPA, I am chiefly indebted to Paul Roazen's essay, "The Exclusion of Erich Fromm from the IPA."

[18] Incidentally, Fromm sounds irked in every quotation from correspondence with Martin Jay that is quoted in Jay's *Dialectical Imagination*. This is probably because, judging from the criticisms that Fromm is quoted responding to, Jay's letters to Fromm accused him of being an optimistic Pollyanna and of abandoning psychoanalysis.

[19] For example, Thomson suggests that Fromm's discussion of the similarities between world religions is encumbered by his failure to discuss the B'hai Faith--a point which she does not explain further. More problematic is her odd dismissal of Fromm's socialist humanism on the grounds that "his suggestions gnaw away at the very essence of our Western and arguably global system of capitalism" (as though Fromm did not know this!) (Thomson 139).

[20] "Aversive therapy" is not wholly a thing of the past. Some more aggressive programs of behavioral reward and punishment still exist, including (as this goes to press), the controversial Judge Rotenberg Educational Center in Canton, Massachusetts, which employs painful electric skin shocks to patients as an "aversive." The Center's practice has been condemned by the United Nations as torture.

[21] In *The Sane Society*, Fromm still labels himself as a member of humanistic psychoanalysis, though he becomes hesitant about this label later and does not want to be classified as a member of the humanistic "school."

[22] For example, consider the difference in tone between *Eros and Civilization* (1955) and *Essay on Liberation* (1969). Here is *Eros and Civilization*: "The Orphic and the Narcissistic Eros engulfs the reality in libidinal relations which transform the individual and his environment; but this transformation is the isolated deed of individuals, and, as such, it generates death" (209). And here is *Essay on Liberation*: "The majority of the black population does not occupy a decisive position in the process of production, and the white organizations of labor have not exactly gone out of their way to change this situation" (*Essay on Liberation* 58).

[23] This claim applies only to Horkheimer's generation; in the next major generation of Critical Theory, the young Jürgen Habermas did have some influence on the New Left in Germany.

WEIMAR GERMANY, PROPHETIC TO APOCALYPTIC

A sea change began in German thought during the First World War. The new rebels (Peter Gay's "outsiders as insiders") of fin de siècle Germany rejected the old Enlightenment ideals of culture and cultivation (*Kultur*), popular education towards morality and autonomy (*Bildung*),[1] immanent historical progress, reason, and humanism. Such ideals were now scorned as overly safe, under-confrontational, "liberal." The new view reveled in the apocalyptic, the "Gnostic," and the occult, and it glorified the aesthetic over the rational and the ethical. It wanted to confront social structures head on and *in toto*, and it demanded immediate change. The new, more apocalyptic messianism was not a marginal trend but was nearly ubiquitous in German culture, including in Jewish intellectual circles. Nearly everyone in German intellectual circles of the time advocated some sort of messianism and defined his or her projects in relation to it.

This chapter cannot provide an overview of the philosophical perspective of each of the thinkers it touches upon; rather, it focuses on certain elements, especially their attitude towards the future and their interpretations of messianism. The groundwork laid in this chapter makes it possible to contextualize Fromm's work in later chapters. Of course, the period was massively complex. For example, some of the new apocalyptists rejected the concept of "totality" and were critical of universals, preferring a return to the individual. Others, however, viewed society as an organic whole and were caught up in what Peter Gay has called "the hunger for wholeness" (Gay 70).[2] Further, one finds that a common vocabulary does not always indicate a common political outlook. As Anson Rabinbach writes,

> In Germany protagonists of the earthly kingdom and prophets of the divine, enthusiasts of the war and its more pacifistic opponents, left-wing revolutionaries and fascists *avant la lettre*, all shared a similar vocabulary of decline and destitution, and many competed to portray themselves as avatars of the "new man." (*Shadow of Catastrophe* 6)

The new messianism was spread across the political spectrum, although the new, apocalyptic version of messianism appears to have been more heavily concentrated among the revolutionary left and the proto-fascist right than among moderates. Given complexities such as these, and given the moral gravity of the questions surrounding the time due to the atrocities that followed, there is far from being a scholarly consensus upon any interpretation of Weimar culture. This chapter does not attempt to explicate all or even most of these complexities but to clarify some themes that are necessary for making sense of Fromm's messianism.

After the bloody defeat of the 1918–1919 socialist and anarchist revolts in Berlin and München, the Social Democratic compromise pleased almost no one. The way forward was unclear, however, and revolt did not seem viable. The *avant garde* of Weimar Germany sought liberation neither through revolution by the proletariat (as had Karl Marx and Rosa Luxemburg) nor reformist social programs; rather they envisioned a return to a primordial state and a nihilistic break with the given. In a *Kulturpessimismus* crisscrossing political divides, they sought to escape from declining European "culture" and return to "cult." The attitude of the time was encapsulated in the motto *"origin is the goal,"* by Vienna journalist Karl Kraus, quoted by Walter Benjamin in his "Theses on the Philosophy of History" (Rabinbach, "Between Enlightenment" 84; Benjamin, *Illuminations* 253). Only a rejection and refusal of the fallen world and a return to pre-civilizational innocence—in allegorical terms, to the Garden of Eden—could liberate humanity from the toilsome cycle of history and the burden of *Zivilisation*. Apocalyptic or catastrophic messianism proclaimed a new age that would arise from that destructive (nihilistic) break from history. That break could occur through the intervention of seemingly transcendent powers, such as charismatic leaders, artistic novelties, "magic," or calculated violation of social norms, either in a controlled and ritualized or abrupt and total fashion.

Most thinkers straddled the divide between the earlier and the later messianism, caught between progress and apocalypse, reason and Gnosis, humanistic culture and chthonic myth, the anticipatory vision and the backwards glance, and a myriad of other dichotomies characterizing the age. Thus, the messianic thinkers of the time range along a spectrum, from the more "prophetic" to the more "apocalyptic." After outlining some characteristics that make it possible to locate thinkers along this spectrum, this chapter discusses the shift from the prophetic to the apocalyptic, beginning with some of the more "prophetic" thinkers, like Hermann Cohen and Rosa Luxemburg. Martin Buber, addressed after Cohen, is an intermediary figure, while Gershom Scholem and Franz Rosenzweig appear to fall into the apocalyptic camp, each in a different way. I then show how two young friends in Heidelberg—Ernst Bloch and Georg Lukács—made a different shift, from the apocalyptic back to the prophetic. Finally, the chapter explores one of the triumphs of the apocalyptic *Zeitgeist*—Stefan George's circle—and its influence upon some members of the Frankfurt School *avant la lettre*.

In order to demonstrate the shift from prophetic to apocalyptic/catastrophic messianism, some related shifts in the intellectual climate need to be addressed. The issues include (1) the shift in emphasis from *Geist* to *Seele*, (2) discourse of "life" and the popularity of *Lebensphilosophie*, (3) "neo-Gnosticism," and (4) nihilism and antinomianism. After an overview of these themes, I offer an overview of political options available to left-wing Jews in fin de siècle Germany, including Marxism, anarchism, and Zionism.

(1) The Death of Geist

"One can say that Hegel died."
Carl Schmitt

The first issue to be addressed is the peculiar cultural reaction that occurred against the idea of *Geist* (spirit/mind) and the embrace of *Seele* (soul) in its stead. The intellectual move from *Geist* to *Seele* was in large part a conservative reaction against Hegel, Marx, and Enlightenment rationalism. Even before *Geist* became Hegel's watchword for the French revolution (the masses in motion), *Geist* had a radical history. Jacob Taubes (an interesting figure in his own right in terms of this evolution from *Geist* to *Seele*), adroitly summarizes:

> *Spirit* [*Geist*] is the watchword for all the Joachimites,[3] from the Spirituals Müntzer and Sebastian Frank, to Böhme, Lessing, and German Idealism. Armed with the "spirit," they join in battle with the sacrament of the Catholic Church, the word of the Lutheran Church, the dogma of the Orthodox Church, the dogmatism of philosophy and the systems of bourgeois society (Taubes [2009] 139).

The subsequent rejection of *Geist* in the name of *Seele* was an exultation of the emotional over the rational. *Geist*, after all, is not just "spirit" but also "mind" or "intellect." To a lesser extent, the shift rejected the radical power of the masses in favor of a focus on the individual.

The proto-fascists of the Cosmic Circle, examined in the final section of this chapter, certainly embraced *Seele* and shunned *Geist*. The Cosmics produced titles such as Stefan George's *Das Jahr der Seele* (1897) (*The Year of the Soul*) and—one of the central texts of the debate over *Seele* and *Geist*—Ludwig Klages's three-volume *Der Geist als Widersacher der Seele* (1929) (*Spirit/Mind as the Adversary of the Soul*) (Gay 80). Carl Jung, likewise, analyzed the "soul," which in his thought had racial connotations, as the concept did for many of the Nazis.[4] However, the exultation of *Seele* over *Geist* was a complex phenomenon, not confined to those who actively identified with the political right. There were also those on the avant-garde left, including the early Georg Lukács, who sided with *Seele*. Before his turn to Marxism, Lukács's early, Romantic book on aesthetics was significantly entitled *Soul and Form* (*Seele und Formen*).[5] The book finds the expression of soul in a yearning that is conveyed within the finitude of artistic form. (Lukács did not remain a partisan of *Seele*—later in this chapter, I trace Lukács's return to the prewar radicalism of *Geist*.)

(2) The Discourse of Life

Sometimes the war against *Geist* was promulgated not in the name of soul but in the name of "life" or "inwardness," as one also finds in Lukács's *Soul and Form*.

The language of "life" invokes the tradition of *Lebensphilosophie* or life philosophy, which arose in the eighteenth century and garnered support in the nineteenth from German Romanticism in its struggle against the Enlightenment ideal of gradual progress in *Bildung* (Lebovic, "Beauty and Terror" 26). For the anarchist Bakunin, "life" was a non-intellectual alternative latent in the masses, sidestepping ivory tower rationalism: life was not objective "science," and it had priority (as action) over "ideas" (Kolakowski, *Main Currents* 204-5). By the Weimar period, life was still contrasted with science—sometimes, more specifically, to scientism and positivism—but the enthusiasm for life did not turn into the revolt of the uneducated underclass that Bakunin had envisioned. Rather, the enthusiasm for "life" had become a movement for an intellectual elite. And "life" was no longer the watchword only of outsiders, of anarchists like Landauer and Bakunin, of marginalized homosexuals and Bohemian artists reveling in Walt Whitman's poetry, but also of established academics like Wilhelm Dilthey, Martin Heidegger, and Henri Bergson. Eventually, "life" became a kind of slogan of the Third Reich. In retrospect, the migration of "life" (or any similar concept) from the left to the right is hard to grasp, but one must remember that fascism too, at its nascent stages, was not clearly confined to the political right.

By the time of Ludwig Klages and Alfred Bäumler, "*Lebensphilosophie*" was, metaphorically speaking, a banner waved in "protests against the elitist Prussian bureaucracy launched by both the green movement[6] and the youth movement, [and] it inspired the *Lebensreformbewegung* (life reform movement)"[7] (Lebovic, "Beauty and Terror" 26). The *Lebensreformbewegung* "advocated nudism and natural therapy as a means of liberating the soul and casting away all formal conventions and false pretensions" (26). Oswald Spengler wrote, "*life* is the alpha and omega, and life has no system, no programme, no rationality; it exists for itself and through itself, and the profound order in which it realizes itself can only be intuited and felt—and then perhaps described" (Lukács, *Destruction of Reason* 464-5). The Nazi extermination campaign later employed in its propaganda a demand for "life-room" (*Lebensraum*) (Neumann 1).

Naturally, to be a defender of "life" in Weimar Germany could have meant any number of things and did not automatically make one a proto-fascist. As the later Lukács pointed out, *Lebensphilosophie* was not a school of thought in the sense that neo-Kantianism or phenomenology were; rather, *Lebensphilosophie* was a "general trend pervading all schools or at least influencing them" (Lukács, *Destruction of Reason* 403). *Lebensphilosophie* was not exclusively the property of the right. Defense of "life" was often a critical response to the rightward tide of politics—it was a way of celebrating newness and countering the yearning for return.[8] Nor should Husserl's theorizing of the lifeworld (*Lebenswelt*) be considered a nod to obscurantism. For some, life signified change, and for some, even revolution. And probably no one offered such a profound psychoanalysis of the Nazis' obsession with death (their "necrophilia") and such a stirring defense of the love of life (biophilia) as did Erich Fromm himself. Fromm's eminently political critique of fascist necrophilia can only be understood as a response to an era that exalted death for the forces of reaction, an era in which Wagner had characteristically written, "I have... found a sedative which has finally helped me to sleep at night; it is the sincere and heartfelt longing for death: total unconsciousness, complete annihilation, the end of all dreams—the only ultimate redemption" (Janaway 121). Although the enthusiasm for "death" was also at its core reactionary, Weimar's enthusiasms for "life" and for death were often oddly not at odds; *Lebensphilosophie* was not concerned chiefly with the *preservation* of life, and if there is anything life is (at least in the biological sense), it is finite, ending in death. Fromm's messianism, by contrast, resists this finitude by its paradoxical faith in a future fulfillment of human hopes.

(3) The New "Gnosticism"

The rise of a neo-Gnosticism, like the rise of *Seele*, was a sign of the increasingly apocalyptic mood. Anson Rabinbach draws the connection between the new apocalyptic messianism and an attraction to secret knowledge: "Whereas the prophetic tradition involved public testimony, the messianic[9] tradition involves an esoteric or even secret form of knowledge" (*Shadow of Catastrophe* 32). Neo-Gnosticism and apocalyptic messianism went hand in hand. The apocalyptic/Gnostic mood was ever watchful for omens of the approaching cataclysm. It was perhaps in this spirit that Walter Benjamin uttered the famous line attributed to him by Gershom Scholem, "A philosophy that does not include the possibility of soothsaying from coffee grounds and cannot explicate it cannot be a true philosophy" (Buck-Morss, *Dialectics of Seeing* 13).

A prominent source in discussions of the neo-Gnosticism of Germany is Hans Jonas's important book *The Gnostic Religion: The Message of the Alien God and the Beginnings of Christianity*. Though published in 1957 and focused upon the history of Gnosticism as an early Christian heresy, the book concludes with a discussion of Heidegger and other contemporary "Gnostics"; the book may be used to describe an aspect of the tenor of fin de siècle Germany (Jonas 335-8). This chapter takes some cues from Jonas. However, one can also find references to Gnosticism directly in the texts of the time, including frequent praise of Marcion of Sinope, partly under the influence of Ernst Bloch's *Spirit of Utopia* (1918) and of Adolf von Harnack's important text in 1921 defending Marcionism as useful for Protestantism due to Marcionism's opposition between grace and the world (Taubes, *Cult to Culture* 140). One also notices in the literature of the time the presence of the Gnostic tropes of secret knowledge, the message of a God that is "wholly other," the myth of a fall and return, and the rebellious retelling of classic myths in which the roles of villain and hero are reversed. Benjamin Lazier's recent book *God Interrupted: Heresy and the European Imagination between the World Wars* (2008) is also a useful resource; Lazier masterfully distinguishes "pantheist" and "gnostic" mysticism in Weimar Germany.[10]

Recall from the previous chapter that Erich Fromm challenged the rising Gnostic movement in his "Dogma of Christ" and in his critique of Bachofen's right-wing interpreters. The "well-to-do Hellenistic middle class" sought to force the creation of the society they wanted "before the consciousness of the masses could accept it" (DC 75). Although generally "Gnosticism" refers to an early Christian heresy combated by neo-Platonists like Plotinus and Church fathers like Irenaeus and Tertullian, in 1920s Germany it described a cultural phenomenon ranging in influence from Theosophist educator Rudolf Steiner (Steiner's "Lucifer-Gnosis") and Stefan George to Walter Benjamin and (to a more limited extent) Ernst Bloch (Lazier 28, 29, 32). According to Lazier, this cultural phenomenon spanned the intellectual environment from "Gershom Scholem, Walter Benjamin, Franz Rosenzweig, Leo Strauss, and Ernst Bloch" to "crisis theologians" including Karl Barth and Adolf von Harnack in his *Marcion: Das Evangelium vom fremden Gott* (1921) (29, 32). All were attracted to "the gospel of the alien God," the message of a spiritual reality that was wholly other, antithetical to worldly creation (31).

Although it negates the world in its entirety and therefore might at first blush seem very radical, Gnosticism's "negativity" should not be equated with that of Marxist or Hegelian dialectics, as has sometimes been done.[11] Gnosticism's "negativity" conceives the world as evil, the product of an inferior god (literally or metaphorically). Gnosticism wages war not against the *present* state of the world but against history and the world *as such*. There is a revolutionary, potentially dialectical alternative to Gnosticism, sometimes associated with neo-Platonism or pantheism, though it may be independent of both. There is no universally acknowledged name for this alternative, but one finds in many thinkers the view that there are good forces immanently at work, moving the world towards redemption, and that humanity may participate in this work of redemption. This revolutionary alternative refuses to deify or reify any part of the whole (perhaps, like Fromm, condemning such a practice as "idolatry"). Instead, it values the whole as a self-conscious, unfolding process. (Fromm would likely have identified this view with some of his predecessors: Spinoza, Hegel, Marx.)

Gnosticism, as a Christian heresy, was generally hostile to Judaism. Second century Gnostic Marcion of Sinope's plainly anti-Semitic views make him an odd hero for 1920s Jewish leftists. Lazier writes,

> Marcion had undertaken to emancipate early Christian teaching from its Jewish corruptions. If Christianity evolved out of Judaism, it nonetheless ought to be understood as its strictest opposition. The God of the Old Testament he described as an evil demiurge and all creation his malicious work. The God of the new dispensation, incarnated by Christ and best described by Paul, was in turn the God of salvation, love, and mercy. (Lazier 29)

There was thus an irony and indeed rebelliousness in Jews like Gershom Scholem and Walter Benjamin flirting with Gnosticism. Scholem is often referred to as a Gnostic, and conservative Jewish intellectual Harold Bloom actually embraced the title of Gnostic (Spirer 4).

Scholem's friend, the rabbi Jacob Taubes, agreed that Gnosticism had an anti-Semitic past, but nevertheless he found Gnosticism salvageable for his apocalyptic messianism:

> It is certain that the protest of late ancient Gnosticism is deeply connected with the rebellion against antimythic Jewish monotheism. But this counterattack comes not only from outside, from the pagan surroundings but also is carried out from within, from the environment of early Judaism. (*Cult to Culture* 72)

What attracted twentieth century Jewish radicals to Gnosticism was in large part its doctrine of an absolute divide between God and creation, such that creation was totally fallen and God wholly other, like the dramatically "other" messianic age that they longed to see dawn. Although a vision of a totally fallen world may not be universal in Judaism, it certainly appealed to many Jewish radicals who wanted to see a dramatic transformation of society.

Although the new Gnosticism had radical dimensions, I will show that it was not the property only of the left, and in fact, some of its political implications are quite reactionary. Finally, in addition to this neo-Gnosticism of Weimar Germany and the shift away from the social radicalism of *Geist* to the individualized inwardness and spiritual resoluteness of *Seele* and *Leben*, a final theme of the times, that of nihilism and antinomianism, remains to be examined before we can unfold the narrative to which Fromm's writings on messianism were a response.

(4) Nihilism and Antinomianism

Fourthly and finally, we turn to the theme of nihilism, and what can be categorized as a species of it, antinomianism. At the time there was a renewed fascination with the Jewish Sabbatean heresy and its doctrine of "redemption through sin," discussed below in section 2.2 (under "The Anarchic Break-in of Transcendence"). The term "nihilism" can be used in many different ways, though it originates in a description of a movement of Russian anarchist revolutionaries in the 1860s. Here I use the term to point to the fulfilled yearning for annihilation as a political project. It is this sense of nihilism that concerned Fromm.

One might say that there are basically two types of antinomianism. Isaac Deutscher, Leon Trotsky's biographer, offers two poignant stories that I suggest can be taken as examples of these two antinomianisms. The first story involves a knave who sought to corrupt Deutscher in his youth, encouraging him to sneak away from his family on Yom Kippur to violate the fast by eating in secret in a graveyard. Deutscher felt pressured to participate and later that day felt ashamed and burdened by the secret of his participation in this ritual. The second was a tale that influenced him in his youth, a tale of an honored rabbi's scholarly and heretical mentor, who respected the rabbi's obedience to the Law but himself found it too constraining and disobeyed it. I suggest that the former, the knave, symbolizes an antinomianism that "forces the Messiah" through seductive, "magical" means. This antinomianism is obscurantist and proto-fascist. It represents brokenness, fallenness, failure. Since the world is hopelessly corrupt, according to this view, it concludes that the only "hope" for change lies in a nihilistic rejection of all that is. Carl Schmitt's *Ausnahmezustand* (state of exception) may be seen as antinomian in this sense. Although Schmitt's legal philosophy sought to legitimize the Nazi state, it celebrated not so much the state as raw, lawless power. (There is also a resemblance to Georges Sorel, who influenced both the left [Antonio Gramsci, Walter Benjamin] and the right [Mussolini].)

However, there is a second kind of antinomianism, symbolized by the rabbi's mentor, the heretic. The humanistic heretic's antinomianism does not seek to force the time. It violates the law only in passionate celebration of the lawbreaker's own, human, immanent power and does not try to seduce or overwhelm the will of others. This humanistic antinomianism celebrates universality and tries to spark revolutionary transformation of the whole, refusing to settle for the partial. Its passion for universality includes the excluded and re-communicates the excommunicated (i.e., accepts radical "heretics" like Spinoza or Joachim of Fiore). When it tramples the sacred and smashes idols, it does so not defiantly, semi-magically ushering in the break-in of transcendence (e.g. God's intervention), but rather with the understanding that human beings themselves are called to inaugurate the new order, in which the law will be different (if not abolished in its entirety). Prometheus, Marx's hero, who bravely defied the gods in the name of humanity, and Antigone, who likewise defied irrational authority in the name of higher ideals, might be taken as archetypes of this spirit. Like Prometheus or Antigone, this second form of antinomianism disobeys not in order to abolish law as such, but out of fidelity to a higher law.

2.1 THE GERMAN JEWISH LEFT AND THE MILIEU OF WEIMAR GERMANY

Now that some underlying controversies have been outlined, we can offer a preliminary overview of the left-wing political options available to German Jews in the 1910s and 1920s. Before and during the First World War, many European Jews saw an international socialist or anarchist revolution as a viable expression of Judaism. Many in this group rejected the Zionist movement because they viewed it as nationalist.[12] Others, especially in Fromm's parents' generation, opposed Zionism because it seemed too radical and fringe, a rebellious youth movement. Yet many leftists and internationalists opposed it because they believed that Jews had a politically radical, religious mission to spread throughout the world and proclaim the coming of the revolution and the messianic age. For example, Erich Unger speaks this way: "The Jews owe the psychic force they may now possess to their tradition and to their exceptional non-territorial position," as does Walter Benjamin's friend Rudolf Kayser, who argued for replacing the Zionist movement with a radical Jewish alliance (*Bund*) "to make the earth a homeland of men" (Löwy, *Redemption and Utopia* 173; Lowy, "Jewish Messianism" 113). The focus on settling a particular land seemed to endanger that mobile, international mission.

Although for various reasons a religious Jewish mission of mobile socialist or anarchist evangelism might sound heterodox today, it was a relatively mainstream option even in religious Judaism at the time. Leading Jewish intellectuals like Hermann Cohen and Fromm's highly respected Talmud teacher Rabinkow, discussed in the first chapter, were on board. Even in the 1920s, after the socialist revolts in Germany had been crushed, the great Jewish scholar Franz Rosenzweig (1886-1929), though not a revolutionist, still held that the Jews had a diasporic, mobile vocation and rejected Zionism partly on those grounds (Bouretz 152). Non-Zionist Jews were not only contesting the idea of a Jewish *state*—in fact, many Zionists were roughly anarchists, including Martin Buber and Gershom Scholem[13] —but also the idea of Jewish *stability*. To be a faithful Jew meant to be on the move (as Fromm constantly was, throughout his life), spreading the radical idea that all people were created equally by the one God and were meant to live in justice and peace as brothers and sisters.

Although Hermann Cohen's combination of Enlightenment-style messianism and ethical socialism was rejected by broad swaths of the radical youth during and following the First World War, prior to the war Cohen's messianism was not considered conservative—far from it. Cohen was not a Marxist, but Marxism in its early stages was also largely driven by a rationalist, universalist, Enlightenment worldview akin to Cohen's, albeit with less emphasis on ethics and greater distance from religious tradition. As Anson Rabinbach writes,

> The unproblematic understanding of Judaism as "the religion of Reason," as Hermann Cohen called it, was equally characteristic of secular nineteenth-century Jewish Socialist intellectuals like Rosa Luxemburg, whose universalism permitted no special pleading for Jewish suffering, and Eduard Bernstein, who took Marx and Kant as the gospel of a self-assured Socialist future. (*Shadow of Catastrophe* 27-8)

In general, the understanding of Judaism as the religion of reason was a mainstream, left-leaning worldview in the German Jewish community shortly before World War I. There should be little surprise that such revolutionary optimism reigned; Germany had undergone fifty years of rapid industrialization and urbanization. As Richard Wolin points out, "in 1870 some 70 percent of Prussian Jews lived in small villages," and by 1927, this statistic had shrunk to 15 percent (*Labyrinths* 47). Meanwhile, the socialist movement had continued to grow internationally since the death of Marx. However, the shocking reemergence of nationalism and collapse of the Second International that occurred in tandem with the First World War dramatically threatened hopes for a socialist revolution in Germany.

After the horrifying, irrational bloodbath of the world war (workers killing workers, not uniting for socialism), the Jewish leftist internationalist movements in Germany were dealt a near-deadly blow by the defeat of the 1919 revolts in Berlin and München and the subsequent assassinations of revolutionary leaders Rosa Luxemburg and Gustav Landauer. Luxemburg in Berlin and Landauer in München— the leading Marxist revolutionary and the leading anarchist revolutionary of the time, respectively—were both of Jewish origins, and perhaps both (definitely Landauer) were victims of anti-Semitic violence. The Weimar Republic that emerged in the wake of the revolts was a compromise that pleased few, not least because Germany's first attempt at a capitalist democracy coincided with a devastating economic depression in the wake of the Treaty of Versailles. After the revolts of 1919 were crushed and the crisis deepened, the ideology of Jewish political movements began to shift dramatically towards apocalyptic messianism, though apocalyptic tendencies had already existed before the war. After 1919, migration to Palestine became a more common choice, as many left-wing Jews were attracted to the Zionist movement and the anarchism or utopian socialism that often accompanied it. Others looked further east, to the Soviet Union, believing that Eastern Europe would be the site of the coming revolution, as the Russian Revolution of 1917 rippled outwards.[14] Some preceded them in the move to the east, however, including some Jews with Zionist inspiration, seeking a vehicle for their socialist utopianism in Russian communes and the burgeoning Russian revolutionary movement.

Since the first Russian revolution of 1905, hope had already aimed eastward (Landauer, *Revolution* 176). And during the First World War, solidarity with Russia and rejection of the imperialist spread of German *Kultur* to that supposed backwater took on a plainly radical tone (Gay 91). The pull to the east was not a purely left-wing phenomenon. Oswald Spengler, for example, predicted the rise of Russia in *The Decline of the West* ("Interview with Ernst Bloch" 44). From both the left and the right, Russia became identified in German popular culture with religious passion, over against the coldness of reason—Russia was Dostoyevsky and Tolstoy (43-4; Rabinbach, *Shadow of Catastrophe* 61-2). Others, such as novelist Hermann Hesse, held that a turn to obscure mystical traditions and Asian religions might be a way forward. Overall, the shift to the East reflected growing skepticism and suspicion towards the Enlightenment.

Some Jewish radicals, religious and not, chose neither the Communist Party nor Zionism, but rather a socialism or anarchism independent of these options. Trotskyism was an alternative before long, of course, but it was not the only one. Erich Fromm was one of those who clung to socialist internationalism while rejecting the more established options. He was in the minority who kept talking about this history publicly, into the 1960s, criticizing Zionism and arguing that the heart of Judaism was an internationalist, socialist, messianic revolution. The movement around Nikolai Bukharin, for another example, was also a socialist alternative to Stalinism. Fromm's socialist cousin Heinz Brandt, a union organizer who was imprisoned first by the Nazis and then by East Germany, was part of Bukharin's movement in the 1930s and wrote an insightful book about it called *My Search for a Third Way*, to which Fromm wrote a stirring introduction about the need to revive the hopes and dreams of the pre-World War I Jewish socialist movement. (Fromm was not in a party until the 1950s, when he joined the Socialist Party of America (SP-SDF).) Fromm's allegiance in the 1920s and 30s was probably not strictly to Trotskyism and certainly not to Stalinism, but to a different sort of socialism.

Those who stayed in the socialist movement after its 1919 collapse in Germany, for various reasons tended to feel obliged to choose between religiously observant Judaism and an ethically, Jewishly-motivated commitment to the revolution, and many chose the latter. In a sense, they *converted* to Marxism. In his wonderful little book *The Non-Jewish Jew*, Isaac Deutscher explained why he still identified as Jewish despite joining the Communist movement, opposing Zionism, and abandoning Jewish religious practice and belief. Deutscher's "non-Jewish Jew" transcends Judaism from within, turning to atheism and communism as the solution to, one might say, the antinomies of Judaism. As a demonstration of this attitude, Deutscher recounts a *midrashic* tale that influenced him in his childhood, of the saintly Rabbi Meir and his intellectual mentor, a heretic named Akher ("The Stranger"). This story was mentioned briefly above, as an example of a humanistic antinomianism. As Deutscher tells the tale:

> Once on a Sabbath Rabbi Meier was with his teacher, and as usual they became engaged in a deep argument. The heretic was riding a donkey, and Rabbi Meir, as he could not ride on a Sabbath, walked by his side and listened so intently to the words of wisdom falling from his heretical lips that he failed to notice that he and his teacher had reached the ritual boundary which Jews were not allowed to cross on a Sabbath. The great heretic turned to his orthodox pupil and said: "Look, we have reached the boundary—we must part now; you must not accompany me any farther—go back!" Rabbi Meir went back to the Jewish community, while the heretic rode on—beyond the boundaries of Jewry. (Deutscher 25)

The young Deutscher, raised in an Orthodox Jewish home, was puzzled and enthralled by the tale. This tale from his youth became a metaphor for Deutscher's solidarity with the "heretics" of Marxist internationalism. He writes:

> My heart, it seems, was with the heretic. Who was he? He appeared to be in Jewry and yet out of it. He showed a curious respect for his pupil's orthodoxy, when he sent him back to the Jews on the Holy Sabbath; but he himself, disregarding canon and ritual, rode beyond the boundaries. (26)

Deutscher explains,

> The Jewish heretic who transcends Jewry belongs to a Jewish tradition. You may, if you like, see Akher as a prototype of those great revolutionaries of modern thought: Spinoza, Heine, Marx, Rosa Luxemburg, Trotsky, and Freud. You may, if you wish to, place them within a Jewish tradition. They all went beyond the boundaries of Jewry. They all found Jewry too narrow, too archaic, and too constricting. They all looked for ideals and fulfillment beyond it, and they represent the sum and substance of much that is greatest in modern thought. …(26)

Deutscher eventually concluded that the truth of Judaism lay in its sublation. Judaism was not a race, a nation, or a religion but "unconditional solidarity with the persecuted and exterminated" (51).

One such "non-Jewish Jew," Gustav Landauer, was particularly influential on radical Jewish thought in early twentieth century Germany. In the following section, we are not concerned primarily with his connection with Jewish religious belief and practice, of which he had little, but rather with Landauer's expression of a commitment to mobile, international revolution. Although Landauer saw something worth preserving in individual cultures and languages, and although shades of Romanticism color his thought, he was most of all an heir of the German philosophical and Enlightenment tradition.

Landauer: Anarchism and Romanticism

In his 1955 *Sane Society*, Fromm offers this stunning line: "When [Rosa Luxemburg] and Gustav Landauer were murdered by the soldiers of the German counter-revolution, the humanistic tradition of faith in man was meant to be killed with them" (SS 239). Today—or even in the 1950s, when Fromm wrote this line—one would likely be taken aback to find Fromm saying that the 1919 assassinations of Gustav Landauer and Rosa Luxemburg were meant to deal a deathblow to prophetic messianism. Today one would expect Fromm to speak of Luxemburg and (Karl) *Liebknecht*, not Luxemburg and *Landauer*. The great anarchist revolutionary Gustav Landauer has been all but forgotten—for that matter, so has the threat of "prophetic messianism" (at least as known by that name) to the established order. But both thinkers—Luxemburg and Landauer—could have represented many things to a thinker like Fromm: international revolution and the Jewish contribution to revolution, the dream of a very different future, the possibility of universal human emancipation, and martyrdom at the hands of reactionaries and anti-Semites. Beyond that, Luxemburg and Landauer together represented an era at the turn of the century when optimism for international revolt was high and pessimism and obsession with decline were yet to take hold.

Luxemburg stood closer to the Enlightenment than did Landauer. Landauer thought socialism could be constructed from communal land ownership, "national spirit" (*Volksgeist*), and in some part, it seems, a return to the Middle Ages (*Aufruf* 3; *For Socialism* 34). Of course, as an anarchist, Landauer's enthusiasm for the Middle Ages was no nostalgia for monarchy—he was trying to recover a time when the bonds of community were stronger and based upon less flimsy ground. Despite his use of some language (like *Volksgeist*) that sounds worrying in retrospect, Landauer's watchword was spirit, not *soul*—he was not a proto-fascist partisan of *Seele* over *Geist*. Nevertheless, Landauer's use of *Volksgeist* (national spirit) sets him apart from Hermann Cohen's assertion in *Religion of Reason* that *Volksgeist* is outdated and has been superseded by Hegel's *Weltgeist* (world spirit) (*Religion of Reason* 360).

Rosa Luxemburg and Gustav Landauer—both "prophets" in their own way—denounced the injustices and idolatries of their time.[15] Both held that socialism could not come about by a single event, like a lightning bolt of transcendence intervening into reality. Rosa Luxemburg made that clear in her critiques of Blanquism and of Karl Kautsky.[16] Although Luxemburg realized that revolutions can spring up unpredictably, she did not believe that the revolution was a single, apocalyptic event but rather viewed revolution as a long, unsteady and messy development. Luxemburg's and Landauer's shared rejection of determinism, mechanism, and nihilism made them prime candidates to lead in a humanistic, socialist/anarchist movement.

Probably Landauer's most important and influential book was his 1911 *Aufruf zum Sozialismus* (*Call to Socialism*, translated in the English edition as *For Socialism*). There Landauer defines "socialism" as:

1. "A tendency of the human will and an insight into conditions and ways that lead to its accomplishment" (*For Socialism* 29).
2. "A striving, with the help of an ideal, to create a new reality," although the ideal itself will never be brought into reality (29-30).
3. "The tendency of the will of united persons to create something new for the sake of an ideal" (31).

One notices a few things about these definitions. First, Landauer's socialism is an ethics and an object of the will; it is the result of a moral decision. Further, socialism is guided by an ideal, an ideal which remains unattainable but which human societies approach through continual "striving" (a probable allusion to Fichte). Finally, socialism is achieved through the effort not of isolated individuals but of a community.

Although he obviously wrote a book calling for "socialism" (*Aufruf zum Sozialismus*), Landauer was more properly an anarchist in today's terminology—according to Fromm, Landauer was "one of the last great representatives of anarchist thought" (SS 252). Landauer sometimes called his philosophy "anarchism," sometimes "socialism." He never identified as Marxist, opposing the positivism and determinism with which the term had become equated. In opposition to those who would wait patiently for the revolution to come of its own accord, he writes, "Socialism need not come…But socialism can come and should come, when we wish it" (Berman 3).

Landauer's socialism or anarchism was agrarian, eschewing technology (*For Socialism* 40-1). Scorning the notion of "constant progress," he offered a somewhat pessimistic, cyclical view of history: "nations have their golden ages, the high points of their culture, and they descend again from these pinnacles" (32). Marx would have considered Landauer's thought a return to primitive socialism, and there is a worrying anti-intellectualism in Landauer's polemics against bourgeois scholars ("Philistines") deceiving the people and in his over-emphasis on attempting to write in a manner accessible to the masses (39).

Some further themes of Landauer's messianism need to be addressed: (1) his puzzling blend of internationalism and apparent particularism, (2) his openness to "the New," and (3) his view of the totality of society, rather than atomistic individuals. Finally, I draw some parallels between Landauer's and Fromm's approach to the future: both sought seeds of potential latent in the present, warned of fanaticism, stressed the need for hope while simultaneously cautioning against determinism, and steered clear of the neo-Gnostic and apocalyptic cultural tendencies of their times.

First, to begin with the topic of nationalism and internationalism in Landauer, it must be affirmed at the outset that Landauer was most definitely an internationalist in that he supported an international revolution and global workers' solidarity. For his journal *Der Sozialist*, he covered topics as diverse as the Mexican revolution, the trial of the McNamara brothers for the 1910 bombing of the *Los Angeles Times* office, the execution of twelve anarchists in Japan, and Spanish anarchist Francisco Ferrer. He even spoke respectfully of tribal ("rested") peoples, stressing what Europeans needed to learn from them (*Revolution* 117-8). But Landauer's internationalism differed from Fromm's. Landauer wrote that "blood is thicker than water" and that communities could be built based upon common blood and ties to ancestors (104). Of course, Landauer, the great leftist Jewish revolutionary, was not some strange proto-fascist; although that should be no surprise, it bears saying considering his talk of "blood" and "nation." In retrospect, one cringes at such language, at Landauer's assertion that individuals do not exist, and at his troubling pairing of such statements as "there are no autonomous individuals" and "the great hereditary communities are real; the work of the ancestors can be felt today" (102, 103). But Landauer was not in favor of conflict between communities, of annihilation of some communities by others, or of cultural isolationism. He wanted to preserve cultural uniqueness. The idea of a universal language like Esperanto horrified him. However, he believed in a human unity made possible by what he considered to be ineradicable cultural and ethnic differences:

> The German, French, English, and Italian understood one another incredibly well at the conference. They embraced one another with open and curious eyes. No stammering could get in the way of understanding. Shall we give up such moments of deep unity for Esperanto? Never! (278)

Landauer had a profound appreciation for cultural difference, but he also saw it as a source of unity-in-difference, without which unity would be stale and meaningless. His insistence on heterogeneity did not mean freezing cultures in a state of stasis, however. Deeply Spinozist, he viewed reality as in constant transformation: "Turn this world into a world of becoming, of transition, infiniteness, diversity, unpredictability, and inextricableness!" he exclaimed (135).

The embrace of newness, in addition to enabling him to steer clear of reactionary or nostalgic nationalisms, should be considered a second important aspect of Landauer's messianism. Landauer's involvement in the (now nearly forgotten) intellectual fight in Germany over Walt Whitman, offers further insight into his vision of the world as a constantly evolving process, moving towards redemption, not a world of essentialist nationalist categories. By translating Whitman into German, he staked a claim in the fight, adopting Whitman's enthusiasm for America as a representation of the "New" (*Anarchism in Germany* 22–3, 26). His embrace of Whitman was further evidence of his rejection of certain romanticisms of regression and return, despite Landauer's enthusiasm for certain aspects of Medieval culture. (Under the influence perhaps of Landauer or perhaps of humanistic psychotherapist and socialist Richard Maurice Bucke, Erich Fromm too was an admirer of Whitman, holding him up as an example of the biophilic character orientation [HOM 60–1, Bucke 215–237].)

Thirdly, Landauer's messianism (like Georg Lukács's later) placed the social totality at the center and critiqued bourgeois society's fixation on atomistic individuals. Landauer's Spinozist totality sometimes seemed to go too far, obscuring the role of the individual (*Revolution* 99). One might say that this near-erasure of the individual was an over-compensation for Landauer's sympathies for Max Stirner's anarchism. Landauer saw his own work as a correction of Stirner. Stirner was a great enemy of reification, Landauer argues, but Stirner was inconsistent, replacing the abstraction of God with the abstraction of the individual (101). In a sense, Landauer is also inconsistent, replacing the abstraction of the individual with the abstraction of hereditary community. Nevertheless, one at least finds that Landauer's messianism was played out more in the key of *Geist* than that of *Seele*.

With these three themes of Landauer's messianism in mind (internationalism, "the New," and social totality), we can now explore some significant parallels between Landauer and Erich Fromm. Like Fromm, Landauer offered an ethical interpretation of socialism and stressed "constructive" action, allowing the future to "grow" organically from the seeds of the present—in this respect, he remains in the prophetic-messianic camp. In a famous passage, Landauer argues that his socialist anarchism would not be a consequence of "smashing the state" but of a new social contract, possible on the basis of the potentialities of the present:

> One can throw away a chair and destroy a pane of glass; but those are idle talkers and credulous idolators [of] words who regard the state as such a thing or as a fetish that one can smash in order to destroy it. The State is a condition, a certain relationship between human beings, a mode of behavior; we destroy it by contracting other relationships, by behaving differently toward one another—One day it will be realized that socialism is not the invention of anything new but the discovery of something actually present, of something that has grown. ...We are the state, and we shall continue to be the state until we have created the institutions that form a real community and society of men. (*Anarchism in Germany* 4)

In this commitment to the latent presence of socialist possibility within contemporary society, Landauer is aligned closely with Fromm. Landauer also issued this Fromm-like warning about the danger of fanaticism and the need for hope:

There are prophets with poetic visions who anticipate and create the future; and there are fanatical speakers appealing to our consciousness with clarity and insight. It is the latter who bury the past by understanding and pronouncing the horror of the present. When the common qualities of the individuals who form societies turn into words and battle cries, when inwardness and confidence turn into opposition and demagogy, then an intensity and combativeness is created that might appear youthful and new—yet in reality it only proves that the old is disappearing without hope. (*Revolution* 138)

To an extent, Landauer's thought was grounded in a worldview preceding the three matters of dispute outlined at the beginning of this chapter (*Geist* and *Seele*, neo-Gnosticism, and the interconnected themes of nihilism and antinomianism). He was not impacted by these divisions in the same way as later thinkers, who lived under the Weimar Republic.

Further, Landauer's writings demonstrate a plenitude of psychological and spiritual insights that are echoed (whether under Landauer's direct influence or not) in Erich Fromm's work. For example, in Landauer, self-transformation and class consciousness are key to revolution. He even mentions the *unconscious*, buried knowledge of the workers and their inability to face themselves and "think their own thoughts" (*Revolution* 226).

Like Fromm, Landauer abandoned Jewish religious practice in his twenties, was influenced by Buddhism and German mysticism (e.g., Meister Eckhart), and considered himself an atheist in spite of profound interest in religious topics. Landauer was also drawn to Hasidism under Buber's influence, as was Fromm. Further, Landauer and Fromm shared a devotion to the value of human life that excluded all war and terroristic action (for example, see Landauer's response to the incident of the McNamara brothers (*Revolution* 258-9) and Fromm's pamphlet for the American Friends Service Committee, *War Within Man*). Fromm did not condemn violence without qualification—in that sense, he was not strictly a pacifist—but he was deeply troubled by the impact of violence upon the human psyche, as his multiple references to Simone Weil's profound essay on violence attest (e.g., DC 188; WW 9; October 1955 letter to Thomas Merton).[17]

Landauer's statement in a newspaper interview on the difference between hope and certainty closely resembles Fromm's own understanding of hope and faith:

Certain? No, I definitely cannot be certain! It signifies the decay of our times that people always want external certainties. In reality, this only increases the external uncertainty of their situation, and the unstableness of their mind and their conviction. When it comes to our ultimate means to preventing atrocity, we can neither rely on God nor on Marx to provide us with any certainty. We need certainty in ourselves. This is the certainty that has always led the way to victory; it is called *courage*. We need to have the will to be victorious, and we have to try. (*Revolution* 224)

Like Fromm, Landauer held that radicalism—that is, in the sense of "going to the root"—must be differentiated from frenzied activism and fanaticism. "Even wild agitation and excessive hate can be very superficial. On the other hand, quietness, contemplation, and caution can be very radical. I see Tolstoy as an eminently radical figure, much more so than many who have risked their lives..." (258). There is a parallel here to Fromm's assertion that the true revolutionary is a person of strong conviction who still shuns fanaticism (DC 151). Fighting in a revolution is not a sufficient condition for being a true revolutionary, as Fromm explains in his essay on the "revolutionary character" (154). Rather, the true revolutionary loves life and does not desire power, while the mere rebel is envious of those in authority and secretly wants their appreciation and acceptance (163, 165, 154). Further, notice that Landauer, like Fromm, rejects determinism (certainty).

Finally, Landauer warned of the rising Gnosticism and apocalypticism that he saw lurking in German culture:

> The minds of the workers—and nowhere is this truer than in Germany—are twisted and wrecked. They are not sober people, and it is difficult to rely on their ideas; they put all their hopes in spontaneity, in the unknown, in miracles. They have no understanding of hope to realize ideas step by step and stone by stone, and this is why all they do is feverishly dream of a sudden transformation in which night turns to day and mud to gold...Their entire idea of socialism is a fairy-tale...Yet, we must not despair. Rome was not built in a day either. (*Revolution* 226)

Despite Landauer's warnings, the German "fairy tale" would turn into the Nazi nightmare—but only later. The rise of the nightmare was precipitated by the loss of a worldview yet to be described, i.e., of the messianic optimism of neo-Kantian philosopher Hermann Cohen and the various responses to it. Landauer's ardent revolutionism has a surprising amount in common with the sober Kantian socialism of Cohen.

The Religion of Reason

Hermann Cohen is often taken as archetypical of pre-World War I, Enlightenment-style prophetic messianism (Rabinbach, "Between Enlightenment" 79; Wolin, *Seduction of Unreason* 95; Lilla 244). Cohen's messianism is essential for understanding Fromm's context. Cohen's messianism can stand in for the attitudes of a generation of Jews who saw a harmony between the Enlightenment, German culture, socialism, and religious messianism.

One need not rely upon Cohen as an example of Enlightenment-style Jewish prophetic messianism. For example, Rabbi Leo Baeck (1873-1956) also represented a mainstay of Enlightenment optimism and Kantian rationalism that many of the young radicals of the 1920s repudiated as outmoded. Baeck also saw messianism as the central component of Judaism. In defining the "essence of Judaism" (as his most widely known book is entitled), Baeck "envisioned the kingdom of God on Earth as a distinctive trait of Jewish messianism, while ascribing an escapist attitude to Christianity," which attitude he saw evidenced in St. Augustine's *civitas dei* (Idel 29). Baeck also wrote of Judaism's ability to handle paradox and considered it a synthesis between transcendence and immanence (Baeck 174). Like others of his time, he stressed that Judaism's role was to be active in transforming history and society and, like Cohen, he was not a Zionist. Nevertheless, since Cohen ended up being of particularly great significance in the messianism fight, with his philosophy held up as an exemplar of the old messianism that was to be rejected, we will focus upon Cohen here as opposed to others, like Baeck, whose approach to messianism was very similar.

According to Hermann Cohen, messianism was the core of Judaism, and the Messiah was *humanity as a whole,* making world history together—an idea that was first advanced by the Hebrew prophets (Poma 236). The possibility of world history and the idea of a universal humanity were products of the prophets and of the idea of monotheism (235). Monotheism was most significant not quantitatively (in terms of the number of gods) but *qualitatively*—what was most significant about monotheism was the idea of a God who was universally the creator of all people; Jewish monotheism was the source of the idea of a universal humanity (*Religion of Reason* 35, 238-9; Poma 236). The Jewish people, as the first recipients of the message of monotheism, were chosen to proclaim it and to live as a *symbol* of it, through their willingness to suffer religious persecution for the monotheist idea and for their rejection of idolatry (Poma 236, 245). However, individuals' awareness of belonging to a universal humanity is still only partial; until the messianic age arrives and this consciousness becomes universalized, humanity does not yet fully exist, and nor in fact does any individual have full selfhood (237; Cohen, *Religion of Reason* 235 and *passim*). The messianic age both fulfills human nature and completes the process of individuation.

Cohen's messianism contrasts sharply with the later, cataclysmic, semi-Romantic messianism of some German-Jewish intellectuals. Explicitly rejecting talk of the end times, Cohen contrasted his messianism with the "myth of eschatology" (Fiorato 135). Cohen writes:

> Messianism, however, in opposition to eschatology remains in the climate of human existence. And if it makes the future of mankind its problem, then it is the task of the historical future, the future of the infinite history of the human race, which becomes the task of the holy spirit of man. (*Religion of Reason* 307)

Cohen's messianism is teleological but deeply anti-eschatological. He foresees a future in which human beings will be more capable of pursuing virtue, continually approaching the ideal of perfection; the messianic future concludes the struggle of humanity in history but not the struggle of the individual to be ethical. Although history's goal will be reached, time will not end. For Cohen, messianism must be radically future-oriented, but the messianic event does not result from a complete rupture with the present (Poma 237). A "bridge" must be maintained between the vision of the ideal and the concrete, material world. If the messianic age is conceived as existing beyond the end of time, humans are incapable of conceiving how to bring it about and are unable to fulfill their ethical obligation to do so.

Cohen rejected Zionism, criticizing the idea of a Jewish "nation" as well as any proposals for Jewish isolation from culture (*Kultur*), an isolation that he held was connected with Zionism. In Cohen's view, the idea of a nation as a "naturally given fact" was outdated, long superseded by the state. The state was now being superseded by the (Kantian) idea of a "confederation of states," establishing world peace and fulfilling the messianic promise (Cohen, *Religion of Reason* 361). Thus, according to Cohen, the "backwardness of Zionism with regard to the concept of the nation" should be overcome through a rejection of the cultural isolation that he identified with it (362). In the sense that Jews were to remain isolated, it was only in the realm of religious practice. Jewish religious isolation was to sublate itself and be seminal, spreading virtue and enhancing the culture of society (69). Notice that Cohen's critique of Zionism is not chiefly directed against the idea of a Jewish "state," as per the discussion of anarchist Jewish anti-Zionism above. Although Cohen holds that Judaism was an advance over Greek culture precisely because Judaism had no need of a state either in theory or in practice, he wants to get beyond the state dialectically, not return to a past historical situation (251).

According to *The Religion of Reason*, the arrival of the (universal, non-nationalistic) messianic age depends upon humanity becoming the object of its own *knowledge* and *love*. Cohen seems to agree with Marx that human nature (species-being) is yet to be fulfilled. Until world history becomes possible through knowledge and love, *humanity does not fully exist* (Poma 237). Because he holds that humanity evolves through knowledge and love, Cohen rejects any equation of Jewish messianism with a pagan mythology of a pre-historic Golden Age (*Religion of Reason* 248). The messianic age is not a Rousseauian state of nature; it is "a new heaven and a new earth" (248, 250). Intervening between prehistoric Eden and the present is the irreversible birth of human knowledge and culture, and the messianic future does not relinquish these achievements (130-1, 248). Knowledge of God's law made possible the first "sin," Adam and Eve's disobedience, which was "the origin of culture insofar as its consequence is the establishment of labor" (130-1). The first serious sin, for Cohen, is represented not by Adam and Eve's disobedience, which God rewards through encouraging human culture (agriculture), but rather the fratricide by Cain, that is, the crime against the brotherhood of humanity. Cain's fratricide symbolizes war, which the peace of the messianic age brings to an end (130-1).[18] The messianic age redeems humanity's lost innocence through the universalization of knowledge. The redemption occurs through a more equitable distribution of intellectual life, not through a return to the state of nature. Cohen thus categorically rejects the idea of a past "Golden Age," as he rejects "idolatry" and "magic" as pagan (i.e., pre-monotheist) (248, 232).

Although the classical world longed to return to a primeval Paradise, "Messianism is directed to the *future*" and opposes both the past and present (Cohen *Religion of Reason* 248, 249). In accordance with Moses Maimonides' vision, according to Cohen, the messianic future is one of "ethical *socialism*" (Cohen's italics), a project to be pursued at all times: "The material and economic conditions should never become a hindrance to the realization of the moral and spiritual culture of *all* men without any distinction" (311, Cohen's italics). For Cohen, the future is not an ever-unreachable "not yet," but rather "must fill every moment of existence, without 'waiting for the future'" (Fiorato 149, Fiorato's words).[19]

According to Cohen, the achievement of the messianic age is intimately tied to suffering and to the possibility of martyrdom, freely chosen out of compassion and fidelity to ethical principles (Poma 242). (On this view, Gustav Landauer's martyrdom could be considered an especially significant event in the messianic struggle.) Through compassion, one perceives the suffering of the other (especially the poor) and recognizes the other as a fellow human, or *Mitmensch* (Poma 242; Cohen, *Religion of Reason* 143). Cohen distinguishes the *Mitmensch* from the mere *Nebenmensch*, who is perceived as just another individual in a series (*Religion of Reason* 114). The *Mitmensch* stands out from the series and becomes real to me once I feel pity for her suffering (141). The *Mitmensch* is discovered only through recognizing the universality of humanity, which is clarified through the command to welcome the "stranger," precisely the one who is outside of one's own clan and nation (116; HOM 89).

For Cohen, the paradigmatic example of the suffering *Mitmensch* is the person in poverty. Judaism was an advance over pagan myth because it viewed suffering—not power and heroism, whether human or divine—as the engine of historical victories of good over evil (Poma 242). From the Jewish standpoint, the poor and the suffering are those who most please God (242). The poor become the leaders of messianic transformation; the suffering of the poor in the course of their struggle is characterized by "humility," or anti-authoritarianism, demonstrated in "opposition to the acceptance of superficial human reality as displayed in power, in splendor, in success, in dominion, in autocracy, in imperialism; as an opposition to all these signs of human arrogance" and as transcending mere individual piety (244). This humility is a humanism: "The humble man bears the whole of mankind in his heart," Cohen writes (244).

Cohen's virulent rejection of myth, paganism, and magic, his argumentation against return to a past Golden Age, and his messianic goal of universal knowledge separate him from the Gnostic camp. Additionally, with regard to the second concern outlined above, Cohen was also more a partisan of *Geist* than *Seele*. For example, he writes, "Monotheism…sets for man another origin: god has created man, and he has created man not only as soul but also as spirit" (*Religion of Reason* 304). The future of humanity depends upon spirit's action in history, in its future-orientedness. Humanity's fundamental immortality differed from the mythical view, which emphasized the soul's cyclical journey through death and rebirth (304).

Martin Buber, Franz Rosenzweig, and others in the *Lehrhaus* circle who were influenced by Cohen eventually broke from identification with his thought. One of the leading reasons was Cohen's jarringly inconsistent endorsement of the German entry into World War I. The war itself, however, and the defeat of the Berlin and Münich uprisings in its aftermath, also trampled the optimistic messianism that had been associated with Cohen and Baeck. Symbolically, after Cohen died in 1918 and Marburg neo-Kantianism disintegrated, Martin Heidegger was the new rising star at Marburg (Norton 628). Heidegger was a figure of the new gnosis, as his student Hans Jonas later pointed out, and Fromm identified Heidegger as one of the figures of despair in the wake of the world wars and Stalinism (Jonas 334-7; HOM 15). Erich Fromm stands out as one of the few intellectuals of this context who remained devoted to Cohen's Enlightenment-style humanism and optimism.

2.2   THREE FROM THE FREIES JÜDISCHES LEHRHAUS

The Frankfurt *Freies Jüdisches Lehrhaus* was a bustling hub of Jewish intellectual life in 1920s Germany. In chapter 1, we saw that Fromm helped to found the *Lehrhaus*, which emerged out of the circle around the charismatic Rabbi Nehemiah Nobel. Hermann Cohen died before the founding of the *Lehrhaus* but was also central to its conceptualization. The list of the participants was a who's who of German-Jewish intellectual life in the 1920s: Martin Buber, Gershom Scholem, Franz Rosenzweig, Ernst Simon (a close friend of Fromm), Abraham Heschel, Eduard Strauss, Richard Koch, Rudolf Hallo, Siegfried Kracauer, S. Y. Agnon (Frieda Reichmann's cousin), Bertha Pappenheim, Leo Strauss, Leo Löwenthal, and Nachum Glatzer (Funk, *Life and Ideas* 39; Pollock 25; Hornstein 63; Knapp 14).

In this chapter, I explore three figures—Martin Buber, Gershom Scholem, and Franz Rosenzweig—who were part of the *Lehrhaus* circle and developed three prominent and very different strands of contemporary messianic thought. All three remained faithful to religious Judaism, and all three emigrated to Palestine. Michael Löwy groups them with Leo Löwenthal as representatives of "religious Jews tending to anarchism" (Löwy, *Redemption and Utopia* 47). Theirs was a quiet anarchism that sometimes spoke of mighty cataclysms but was lived out peacefully amid utopian communities or religious ritual. Nevertheless, I suspect that their messianism is not as demure in its implications as one might infer from their lives. Scholem, the strongest in his defense of catastrophic or apocalyptic messianism, also issued some of the strongest warnings against it, and by the end of his life, he defended it only with tremendous caution.

Paths in Messianism

In Martin Buber (1878–1965), Landauer's anarchism encounters a mix of Jewish religious inwardness and Zionist socialism or anarchism. However, in the early

1900s, Martin Buber's "renewal" movement represented another option for German Jews, one not of outward revolutionary struggle but of inward (yet social) spiritual transformation.

The similarities between Buber and Fromm are frequently noted (Jay, *Dialectical Imagination* 89; Hausdorff 50; Bronner 168). Both were committed to ethical socialism. Like Fromm, Buber held that utopian thinking encourages people to strive for a better future, as opposed to disempowering them by leading them to seek the impossible (Buber 58; MFH 30[20]). Buber was a leader in propagating revolutionary messianism in Germany in the early 1900s, with the publication of his *Three Speeches on Judaism* (1909, 1911) (Wolin, *Labyrinths* 49). He was probably a major influence on Fromm's distinction between prophetic and apocalyptic messianism and Fromm's concept of "alternativism." Buber distinguished between prophetic and apocalyptic messianism and defended the former against the latter in his *Paths in Utopia* (which Fromm cites in his *Sane Society*), and in his essay "*Prophetie und Apocalyptik*," Buber argued that apocalypticism was not essential to Judaism and was, in fact, foreign to Judaism (Iranian in origin) (Buber 8; SS 258; Biale, "Gershom Scholem" 526). In *Paths in Utopia*, Buber prioritizes the prophetic over the apocalyptic and contrasts rupture with "revolutionary continuity" (Buber 13). However, unlike Fromm, Buber did not consider Marx messianic, although Buber did consider the "utopian" socialists messianic (10).

Like Fromm, Buber asserts that the prophet poses alternatives, while apocalypticism rejects alternatives (Taubes, *Cult to Culture* 13-4). Judaism was alternativist, emphasizing the possibility of changing the future through either human repentance or God's turning towards humanity (both meanings captured by the Hebrew word *teshuva*) (xxvi). *Paths in Utopia* concludes with a reflection on "crisis," in a chapter that includes the offering of an alternative for "contemporary man": "Can he or can he not decide in favour of, and educate himself up to, a common socialistic economy?" (Buber 133). And, like Fromm, Buber rejected the cultural "Gnosticism" of the time. At a time when many were praising Marcion, Buber charged that Marcion had made "an intellectual contribution to the destruction of Israel" (Taubes, *Cult to Culture* 141).

It is not surprising that Buber would have influenced Fromm, since in fact Buber was profoundly influential on an entire generation of young Jewish radicals. Fromm was personally acquainted with Buber through the *Lehrhaus*, and he employed three of Buber's texts in his dissertation on the Jewish law (*Die Geschichten des Rabbi Nachman, Vom Geist des Judentums, Der große Maggid und seine Nachfolge*) (JG 191). However, Buber had stronger affinities with anarchism than did Fromm. Svante Lundgren writes that "[Buber's] socialism was not as Marxist as Fromm's" and that Buber "was closer to the anarchist tradition through his friend Gustav Landauer" (Lundgren 103). Buber also saw potential in the Kibbutzim and chose Zionism, seeing it as a utopian socialist movement, which as we have seen, Fromm rejected as a political option. Buber emigrated to Palestine in 1938 (Löwy, *Redemption and Utopia* 57).

* * *

Now that some similarities and differences between Buber and Fromm have been addressed, we can offer a brief overview of Buber's life before delving more deeply into his messianism. In 1899-1901, Buber studied in Berlin with two scholars who were influential for *Lebensphilosophie*: Georg Simmel and Wilhelm Dilthey (Swedberg and Reich 30-1; Morgan 98). In 1900, he joined the Berlin *Neue Gemeinshaft* (New Community) group, where he first met Gustav Landauer, who became his friend and profoundly influenced Buber (Löwy, *Redemption and Utopia* 49; Schaeder 24). Buber later participated in the Bar-Kochba Club (around 1909-11), "the German Jewish organization of Prague" (Löwy, *Redemption and Utopia* 49; Lebovic, "The Jerusalem School" 108). In an important lecture to *Neue Gemeinschaft*, Buber argued for a new community based not upon national origin but "elective affinities" (*Wahlverwandtschaft*), i.e. the free choice of its members (Löwy, *Redemption and Utopia* 49).[21] According to Buber, the new community would be a new social arrangement differing from the modern city, feudalism, and primitive life (49-50). From 1909-1913, he was extremely influential in the revival of Judaism (Rabinbach, "Between Enlightenment" 88). His "renewal" movement emphasized personal, inward religious experience and *Lebensphilosophie* (88-9). In the early 1920s, he became involved with the Frankfurt *Lehrhaus*, along with Fromm, Scholem, Rosenzweig, and others (Löwy, *Redemption and Utopia* 151).

After Buber eventually migrated to Israel, he stayed in contact with Fromm periodically, working with him on a couple of causes. In 1948, he agreed at Fromm's request to sign a statement for *The New York Times* for the rights of Palestinians[22] (Funk, *Life and Ideas* 146). The letter was also signed by Leo Baeck, Albert Einstein, and others (146). Buber was also among the international sponsors of anti-nuclear weapons group SANE, which Fromm helped to found (Katz 71). There was, however, some tension over Buber's Zionism; in a 1957 letter to Norman Thomas, Fromm expressed frustration with Buber's refusal to sign a petition supporting a Palestinian right of return (Lundgren 104, 109).

* * *

Buber's future-oriented prophetic messianism linked him to the messianism of Hermann Cohen, and so did Buber's assertion that messianism was "Judaism's most profoundly original idea" and that the messianic age would harmonize human creativity with social order (Löwy, *Redemption and Utopia* 51, 53-4). But in some ways Buber was closer to the apocalyptic camp. For example, Buber asserted that messianism sought "an absolute future that transcends all reality of past and present as the true and perfect life" (51). This manner of speaking—"absolute future," "all reality," etc.—suggests that Buber's messianism was aimed more at rupture than continuity. According to Buber, the messianic age could arrive only through

69

a profound rupture with history; the messianic age would be a "renewal." "For by 'renewal,'" he explained, "I do not in any way mean something gradual, a sum total of minor changes. I mean something sudden and immense (*Ungeheures*) by no means a continuation or an improvement, but a return and transformation"—one should desire "the impossible" (52).[23] While phrases like "sudden and immense" and "by no means a continuation" may sound far placed from Buber's commitment to "revolutionary continuity" mentioned earlier, one notices that crucial extra piece: both a *return* and a *transformation*. For all his hostility to Hegel, Buber was a deeply dialectical thinker.

According to Buber, Zionism was a *Lebensphilosophie*, and he offered a "romantic recasting" of Hasidism, but he himself remained distant from the Hasidic Eastern European Jews (Rabinbach 1985, 89). (In this, he differed from some young radicals, such as Leo Löwenthal, who were volunteering their time to help Eastern European refugees in Germany.) In terms of the distinction drawn at the opening of this chapter between *Seele* and *Geist*, one might say that Buber was on the side of *Seele*, not *Geist*; his concern centered upon the individual in relationship to other individuals, not the moving force of the collectivity. This is the wider context of Buber's hesitancy about Hegel. Buber was not, however, one of the neo-Gnostics of Weimar Germany who stressed the absolute fallenness of the world and the impotence of all immanent forces.

Like Fromm, Buber believed that human beings could play a role in bringing about the messianic age. According to Michael Löwy, Buber "more than any other modern religious Jewish thinker, placed the active participation of men in redemption—as God's partners—at the heart of his messianism" (Löwy, *Redemption and Utopia* 52). This was not a rejection of divine omnipotence; rather, according to Buber, God "does not *will* redemption without the participation of man" (52). Buber saw the messianic event as both a result of human effort (moving "forward," horizontally) and divine intervention (vertically, from above), holding that the messianic age required both human effort and divine intervention. Although Buber also drew a distinction between between messianic eschatology and utopia (the former requiring divine intervention, the latter being capable of resulting from human will alone), in both cases, human action was required (57). Buber's commitment to the participation of a universal humanity in messianic transformation, along with his simultaneous Zionist commitments, led to confrontation between Buber and Hermann Cohen around issues of humanism and national identity.

Initially caught up in enthusiasm for World War I, Buber was persuaded by his friend Gustav Landauer to repudiate the war (Löwy, *Redemption and Utopia* 53). Buber commenced a debate with Hermann Cohen, in which he critiqued Cohen's capitulation to German nationalism by chastising him with Cohen's own philosophy: "Humanity—and to say that, Professor Cohen, is now more than ever the duty of every man living in God—is greater than the state" (53). Buber's and Cohen's positions on the emerging Zionist movement were also a major cause of the rift between the two thinkers, even more so than their positions on World War I. Buber wrote an "open letter" to Cohen on Zionism, to which Cohen responded with his own "open letter." Cohen's response was a peculiar mix of particularism and universalism. On the one hand, he argued that Jews were "patriots" of the European countries to which they belonged. On the other hand, he opposed Zionism on the grounds that true Judaism was a message for all people, not a single nation. The connecting thread between Cohen's German particularism and his humanist, Jewish universalism was his commitment to *Aufklärung*. Cohen posited an "innermost accord between the German spirit and our Messianic religiosity"; "the German spirit is the spirit of classical humanism and true universalism," he wrote (*Reason and Hope* 168-9). Cohen's messianism does not seek the restoration of a lost Golden Age: "The classical concept of our religion points towards the future of mankind, and not towards the past of an ethnic community whose holiness, rather than being tied down to a geographical location, is bound up with its historical idea" (170).

In summary, perhaps one could accurately say that Buber moved from Gustav Landauer's optimistic, humanistic messianism to the dark apocalypticism of the post-war era—after all, Buber tempered his messianism with a mystical turn towards individuality and inwardness. And according to Jacob Taubes, "In the later writings of Buber (after the First World War) the mystic-immanent interpretation of messianism gives way to a more religious transcendent view" (*Cult to Culture* 18). However, the assessment that Buber moved from a prophetic to an apocalyptic messianism would be true only in a very limited sense. Buber stands with a complex network of affinities, many of them shared by Fromm. To an extent, Buber belongs to an earlier era. Although Buber does not belong to Cohen's messianism, his socialism and Zionism were forged before Weimar and cannot be neatly categorized in terms of that era. A much clearer case of the catastrophic or apocalyptic messianism that Fromm opposed can be found in the work of Gershom Scholem, whose messianism is addressed in the next section.

The Anarchic Break-in of Transcendence

Gershom Scholem (1897–1982) is a chief representative of the catastrophic/apocalyptic messianism that Fromm opposed (OBH 142; YSB 148).[24] Obsession with catastrophe was widespread in German thought following World War I and held sway over many of the Frankfurt School thinkers, including Walter Benjamin, but this obsession was perhaps most prominent in Benjamin's friend Scholem. Scholem writes:

> Jewish messianism in its origins and by its nature—this cannot be sufficiently emphasized—is a theory of catastrophe. This theory stresses the revolutionary, cataclysmic element in the transition from every historical present to the Messianic future…The elements of the catastrophic and the vision of the doom are present in peculiar fashion in the Messianic vision. (Idel 31)

Moshe Idel writes, "[Scholem] was more attracted by the dramatic, revolutionary, and public manifestations of messianism than by its private, inner, or spiritual aspects…Scholem had 'an obsession with the imagery of catastrophe'" (31).

In an iconic passage, Scholem characterizes messianism as catastrophic and anti-Enlightenment:

> The Bible and the apocalyptic writers know of no progress in history leading to the redemption. The redemption is not a product of immanent development such as we find it in modern Western interpretations of messianism since the Enlightenment where, secularized as the belief in progress, messianism still displayed unbroken and immense vigor. *It is rather transcendence breaking in on history, an intrusion in which history itself perishes, transformed in its ruin because it is struck by a beam of light shining into it from an outside source.* (The Messianic Idea 10, italics Scholem's)

According to Scholem, "there can be no preparation for the Messiah. He comes suddenly, unannounced, and precisely when he is least expected or when hope has long been abandoned" (11). The Messiah will arrive at the time of humanity's greatest corruption (11-2). Not only is human action incapable of creating the messianic utopia, but all human action is futile. Messianism is a "*life lived in deferment*, in which nothing can be done definitively, nothing can be irrevocably accomplished. One may say, perhaps, the Messianic idea is the real anti-existentialist idea" (35; italics Scholem's).

In contrast to Hermann Cohen, Scholem insisted that redemption could not be the result of historical evolution or human ethical action, only of a "break-in of transcendence...in which history itself perishes" (Moltmann 37). As Hegelian Protestant theologian Jürgen Moltmann suggests, Scholem's messianism seems to make any form of "anticipation" (read: hope) illegitimate (38). Consider again this excerpt from Scholem's important essay, "Toward an Understanding of the Messianic Idea in Judaism" (1959):

> The redemption which is born here is in no causal sense a result of previous history. It is precisely the lack of transition between history and the redemption which is always stressed by the prophets and apocalyptists...there can be no preparation for the Messiah. He comes suddenly, unannounced, and precisely when he is least expected or when hope is abandoned. (Morgan 103; *The Messianic Idea* 10-1)

If there is "no preparation" for the Messiah, who comes in a time of despair, then it seems that short of actually worsening the situation and increasing despair in society, one could do nothing to assist in the coming of the messianic age.

Scholem was a representative of the return to a strand of Medieval Jewish apocalypticism, a return which rejected the Enlightenment Jewish tradition in which Cohen stood. Of traumatic irruptions in Jewish history, Scholem writes with enthusiasm at some times and with warnings and trepidation at others, but always with a zest for the "imagery of catastrophe" (Bloom, "Scholem" 217). As he later wrote of Cohen and his ilk, "I think one can say without disrespect that hardly ever had there been a Jewish theology of such vacuity and insignificance as existed in the decades before World War I" (*The Messianic Idea* 321). Scholem argued that an apocalyptic and pessimistic messianism was at the core of the true Jewish tradition, and Enlightenment-style messianism was a recent invention in contradiction to Judaism:

> We have been taught that the Messianic idea is part and parcel of the idea of the progress of the human race in the universe, that redemption is achieved by man's unassisted and continuous progress, leading to the ultimate liberation of all the goodness and nobility hidden within him. This, in essence, is the content which the Messianic ideal acquired under the combined dominance of religious and political liberalism--the result of an attempt to adapt the Messianic conceptions of the prophets and of Jewish religious tradition to the ideals of the French Revolution. (*The Messianic Idea* 37)

The idea of messianism that Scholem's generation "had been taught" was essentially that of Hermann Cohen. In Chapter 4, I show how Fromm revived this idea of messianism, embracing a cautious critique of the Enlightenment but still situating his messianism within the Enlightenment tradition.

* * *

Reviving the study of Jewish mysticism is Scholem's claim to fame. Unquestionably, his scholarship filled a serious gap in the literature, but its rapid rise to canonical status is troubling. Treating Scholem as a disinterested accumulator of facts obscures the eccentricity of his project and does not do justice to Scholem's own understanding of his work. He was making a controversial argument for a particular understanding of Judaism, by exploring subterranean, borderline-heretical traditions that had long lingered on the margins of Judaism. Two of the most noted commentators on Scholem, Harold Bloom and David Biale, both refer to his objective, historical, scholarly style of presentation as a "mask" concealing his passionate devotion to his subject matter and to a very esoteric and radical interpretation of it (Biale [1987] 58; Bloom, "Scholem" 214). Scholem is not concerned only with memory; he speaks also from a position of the mysterious erasure or loss of certain parts of the tradition and the cautious embrace of other, long marginalized and heretical currents. As early as 1918, he was intensely critical of canonical thinkers like Moses Maimonides and Saadia Gaon, along with Hermann Cohen, and in his later work as well, he classified Cohen with Maimonides and Saadia as non-messianic (Lazier 182-3; Scholem, *Major Trends* 38).

As noted above, in the summer of 1923, Scholem taught a class at the *Lehrhaus* on the apocalyptic Book of Daniel, evidencing his early commitment to an apocalyptic messianism (Funk 42). In that same year, he moved to Jerusalem, as Fromm exited the Zionist movement (Magid 3; Funk, *Life and Ideas* 40). (With Martin Buber, Scholem later spoke out against violence towards the Palestinians and joined the peace organization *Brit Shalom* [Löwy, *Redemption and Utopia* 25, 65].)

The influences upon Scholem's youth resembled those of contemporary German Jewish youth. Like many of his generation, he opposed World War One. He even attended some antiwar meetings of a radical faction of the Social Democratic Party with his older brother Werner and distributed the Marxist journal *Die Internationale,* which was tied to the radical faction of the Social Democratic Party that would eventually become that of Luxemburg and Liebknecht (Scholem, *From Berlin* 52). However, Scholem reported later that he had been more interested in the non-Marxist "socialism" of Proudhon, Kropotkin, and Landauer than the "supposedly scientific kind" of socialism, and he was particularly impressed by Landauer and devoured his *Aufruf zum Sozialismus* (52-3).[25] Scholem states in his autobiography that he later began to have doubts about anarchism as a political program after his initial enthusiasm (53). Scholem was also initially impressed by Buber, meeting him while Scholem was a youth, and was influenced by Franz Rosenzweig, though he rejected the options Buber and Rosenzweig represented (55). Scholem critiqued Rosenzweig's *Star of Redemption* for its "profound tendency to extract the apocalyptic sting from the organism of Judaism" and for being insufficiently catastrophic (Moltmann 36).[26]

Scholem's apocalyptic messianism played well into the philosophical and cultural phenomenon of life philosophy and the prevailing antinomianism. The sudden catastrophe and apocalyptic transformation would occur almost by law of nature, the result of an anarchic life force that refuses to be controlled or repressed—the "anarchic promiscuity of all living things" (Lazier 187). For Scholem (as Benjamin Lazier explains), "Life is anarchic. It is wild and ungovernable. It defies in the end every effort to bring it to order, to subdue it to the dictates of law, any law. It is the wellspring of lawlessness, a primary earthly force" (Lazier 187).

Types of Messianism in Scholem

In "The Messianic Idea in Judaism," Scholem locates Jewish messianism at an intersection of three tendencies:

1. *Conservative*, aiming at the preservation of Jewish practice and law, i.e. *Halakhah.*
2. *Restorative*, "directed to the return and recreation of a past condition which comes to be felt as ideal."
3. *Utopian*, seeking "a state of things which has never yet existed," of which he sees Ernst Bloch's *Spirit of Utopia* and *The Principle of Hope* as examples. According to Scholem, Medieval apocalypticism was "utopian" in this sense, viewing history as a Manichaean battleground between good and evil and the future as the product of a "catastrophic and destructive" situation (the "birth pangs of the Messiah," "the terrors of the Last Judgment") (*The Messianic Idea* 3, 6, 7-8, 341).

As it will be argued in Chapter 4, this three-part characterization excludes Erich Fromm's messianism, which does not seek the preservation of the present, a return to the past, or a future that is totally other. According to Scholem, the Hebrew prophets (to whom Fromm looks for his radical messianism) addressed humanity universally, claimed no secret knowledge, and visualized the coming of the messianic age as an *historical* event (*The Messianic Idea* 5). The prophets' view is not conservative, restorative, or utopian, Scholem asserts, and ergo not messianic (4-5). Scholem's account of the worldview of the prophets matches Fromm's prophetic messianism: universal, non-hierarchical, historical, utopian. Fromm's messianism is thus *de facto* excluded.

Jewish messianism is not "rationalistic," Scholem claims (*The Messianic Idea* 32). In Scholem's view, the rationalistic interpretation was a defensive move to make Judaism palatable to Christians by severing ties to true messianism (i.e., apocalyptic or catastrophic messianism). This concession to Christianity exiled true (apocalyptic) messianism to the margins of society, away from centers of confrontation with Christian power (33). The implication is clear: according to Scholem, Cohen's messianism was not faithful to the spirit of Judaism and was a subservient concession to Christianity.

Although Benjamin Lazier rightly points out that Scholem did not single-handedly revive interest in the Sabbatean movement as is often claimed, Scholem unquestionably contributed massively to the study of Sabbateanism (Lazier 144). Scholem's biography of its founder, enigmatic seventeenth century Messiah-figure Sabbatai Zevi (1626-1676), was an especially important contribution. The Sabbatean movement sought to "force the Messiah," endorsing various antinomianisms. In 1648, Zevi declared himself the Messiah and announced that the messianic age would begin in 1666 (YSB 146). Perhaps due to this being a time of crisis and rampant persecution, many devout Jews throughout Europe believed his message and sold their homes, preparing to move to Jerusalem; their hopes were dashed when Zevi, after being threatened, converted to Islam (147). Yet the Sabbatean movement endured as one of Zevi's followers, Nathan of Gaza, became its leading apologist. In order to save humanity, Nathan argued, Zevi was required to sink to its lowest level through infidelity to the faith. This doctrine became known as "redemption through sin." The Sabbateans were divided in their interpretation of the doctrine, some holding that Zevi was the only one called to sin for the sake of the redemption, while others honored the doctrine through ritualistic violation of social and religious norms. Scholem would have been aware of the parallels between Sabbateanism and the later antinomian practices of the 1920s neo-Gnostics.

Scholem was a student of "Jewish Gnosticism," even writing a book on early Jewish Gnosticism (*Jewish Gnosticism, Merkabah Mysticism, and Talmudic Tradition*). Although he is often labeled as a scholar of "Jewish mysticism," Scholem's "gnosticism" makes him more a partisan of *myth* than of pantheism (of which he was harshly critical) or of mysticism (especially when mysticism could be taken to include a rationalistic humanism, of Meister Eckhart's type, for example). In fact, Scholem saw mysticism and messianism as opposed (Lazier 155-6, Idel 2). According to Harold Bloom, who wrote extensively on Scholem, "Scholem's work helped inaugurate [an age of] Jewish gnosticism" (Lazier 147).[27] Scholem did link Kabbalism and messianism, but Kabbalism may be difficult to classify according to the categories employed here (Idel 28). Benjamin Lazier suggests that both pantheist and gnostic currents exist within the tradition of Kabbalah and that both are therefore present in Scholem's work, but Lazier notes that the gnostic current predominates in Scholem's approach (Lazier 147).

According to Scholem, the doctrine of redemption through sin (or "the holiness of sin") led to a belief that the material world and one's external actions upon it are irrelevant and essentially unreal (*Major Trends* 319). Obviously, there is a resonance here with Gnosticism's eschewal of created and material reality, but Scholem insists that Sabbateanism was a rejection of the abstracted, rational, philosophical God of the Gnostics and an affirmation of the God of Israel, whom the Gnostics rejected (323). The unreality of the world followed from both of the major Sabbatean interpretations of the doctrine of redemption through sin. One interpretation suggested that the messianic age had already come for the elect who had accepted Zevi's message and that the law had hence been abrogated. The elect could not sin, as even what was adjudged to be sin on their part was really holiness in disguise. The alternate interpretation was that although the messianic age had not yet arrived, it was holy to sin if necessary to combat evil. Whichever interpretation one adopted (that the world was already secretly already redeemed or that it would be redeemed through sin that was secretly good), the existing world was illusory. In consequence, two possible approaches could be taken, each with political implications: quietism (withdrawal into inwardness) or nihilism (319).

Although Zevi was by no means the first Jew to announce himself as the Messiah and achieve a popular following, Sabbateanism had surprisingly far-reaching philosophical and political influence. Later, the Sabbateans—and the Jews broadly, by proxy—were accused of fomenting the French Revolution when a new Messiah-figure, Jacob Frank, claimed to be the incarnation of Zevi. (While Zevi converted to Islam, Frank eventually converted to Catholicism.) Sabbateanism undoubtedly played an explosive role in Judaism, but it is a matter of debate whether it contributed meaningfully to substantive revolutionary change. (Predictably, considering Scholem's anti-Enlightenment proclivities, Scholem despised the Frankists, although he expressed qualified admiration for them in his essay "Redemption through Sin" [Lazier 143, 144].)

According to Scholem, the doctrine of redemption through sin arose from the Lurianic Kabbalah, which conceived creation as a three-part process: *zimzum* (God's "contraction"/withdrawal), *shevirah hal-kelim* ("breaking of the vessels"), and *tikkun* (restitution/redemption) (Bloom, *Kabbalah* 39). According to this narrative, since God is infinite and the existence of two infinities is logically impossible, God could not create a perfect, infinite creation. God had to withhold some of God's goodness in order to create something other. The concept of *zimzum* was Isaac Luria's unique contribution to Kabbalah (Scholem, *Major Trends* 260). *Zimzum* differentiated Lurianic Kabbalah from pantheism, Scholem points out, because the doctrine of *zimzum* affirmed unequivocally that there had to be at least *something* that was not God. Notice, then, that this places Lurianic Kabbalah, and Scholem's enthusiasm for it, away from the "pantheism" option, in the possible alternative of pantheism and Gnosticism (262).

God created "vessels" of goodness, the Lurianic account goes, which burst and shattered their containers; the resultant "sparks" of goodness were lost and scattered, and now remain concealed throughout creation (Bloom [1975] 40-1). The task of human life is to assist in the redemption by freeing these sparks through good deeds. Drawing on Scholem, Harold Bloom argues that according to Lurianic Kabbalah, God could create only through destruction (shattering of the vessels), and this was surely a standpoint that appealed to many activists of the time (and earlier, to Bakunin under Nietzsche's influence[28]) (41). Scholem eventually interpreted Zevi's story as a cautionary tale about the dangers of "religious nihilism" (Habermas 144; Magid 7). Messianism was potentially explosive, but it only became truly dangerous when united with secular movements. As Scholem stated in a 1975 interview:

> I've defined what I thought was the price the Jewish people have paid for messianism. A very high price. Some people have wrongly taken this to mean that I am an antimessianist. I have a strong inclination toward it. I have not given up on it. But it may be that my writings have spurred people to say that I am a Jew who rejects the messianic idea because the price was too high. (Wolin, *Labyrinths* 53)

Rather than simply rejecting messianism, Scholem warned that "the failure to distinguish between messianism and secular movements is apt to trip up movements" and that "such a mix-up becomes a destructive element" (53). Since he was convinced that all true messianism posited a total rupture from preceding history, one can see why he would fear that it would lead to violence if mixed with politics. Such an absolute break requires the destruction of many existing structures. Without a political impetus, however, it would seem that messianism is reduced to quietist waiting, with its grand vision of cosmic transformation bracketed away and kept safe from the realm of the political.

Scholem's ambivalent discourse on technology resembles his ambivalent attitude towards messianism, expressing both a fear and a celebration of destructive power. His 1965 use of the Jewish folk tale of the Golem seemed to condemn technology's destructive power and simultaneously revel in it (Lazier 191). According to Scholem, humanity will eventually be defeated by nature, which will rise up against it. Lazier writes, "Like the pit of promiscuity out of which all that lives comes to be, this tellurian power both gives rise to creation and undoes it" (192). Scholem's vision of the threat of humanity's creations rising up to destroy humanity resembles that of others in the romantic tradition, including Mary Shelley's *Frankenstein* (192-3).

Scholem appears to have shifted his position on messianism over time. In his youth he had even toyed with the idea that he personally was the messiah, but by the late 1970s, the rise of extreme conservative political factions in Israeli politics (Menachem Begin, Likud Party, Gush Emunim) appears to have led him to issue warnings about the dangers of messianism (Lazier 195-6). At that time he made an effort to differentiate Zionism from messianism, defining Zionism's aims as merely temporal (Lazier 196). Even as early as the 1930s, however, Scholem was wary of mixing messianism with politics, since he was opposed to Communism and considered it a manifestation of messianism (Dubnov 144).

Scholem's rejection of the Enlightenment and ideals of progress, his stress on rupture and the intervention of transcendence, his determinist interpretation of messianism, and his view that the messianic age arrives in a time of human failure and collapse are all main features of the catastrophic or apocalyptic messianism with which Fromm was contending. The manner in which Scholem has been taken as canonical is highly problematic and has aided in the neglect of Fromm's sort of messianism or a "defining it out of existence," through which messianism is restricted by definition to the catastrophic or apocalyptic form, or to the three-part typology offered by Scholem (restorative, utopian, conservative).

The Star of Inwardness

The conclusion that Scholem eventually reached while in Israel—that the dangers of apocalyptic messianism must be rejected in favor of quietism and inwardness—had been reached far earlier in post-WWI Germany by the young scholar of Judaism, Franz Rosenzweig (1998-1929).

In 1913, Rosenzweig was on the brink of converting to Lutheranism when he recommitted to Judaism (MacIntyre 150-1). One month after his reversion, Rosenzweig attended a lecture by Hermann Cohen, and he was influenced by Cohen's reading of Kant for some time thereafter—so much so, in fact, that he reports in a letter to his parents that he gushed with praise of Cohen to a Russian child who merely asked what Rosenzweig did for a living (MacIntyre 152; Bouretz 101). Rosenzweig was especially influenced by Cohen's later work (the period of Cohen's *The Religion of Reason*), which he saw as a move away from idealism towards "existentialist, dialogic thought," focusing not on universal humanity but on "man as a concrete individual and God as his interlocutor" (Poma 303).

Although Rosenzweig was not the sole founder of the *Lehrhaus* as is sometimes claimed, he was its leader and heavily involved in organizing the group. Rosenzweig later broke from Cohen, accusing him of having "betrayed the messianic idea" through his emphasis upon gradual progress (Löwy, *Redemption and Utopia* 59). After the catastrophe of World War I, Rosenzweig published *The Star of Redemption* in 1921. He had already published an important two-volume work on Hegel's political philosophy, but *Star* was unquestionably one of the most important twentieth century works of Jewish thought, urging European Jews to stop assimilating and seek "redemption from history" as opposed to redemption *through* history (Moltmann 33). Like Scholem later, Rosenzweig held that the messianic age would be "a complete change, the complete change...that would put an end to the hell of world history" (Löwy, *Redemption and Utopia* 59).

Change was in the air. Along with Rosenzweig's *Star*, Karl Barth's *Epistle to the Romans* appeared in the early 1920s. *Romans* marked a shift in Christian theology that paralleled the shift occurring within Jewish theology, from immanence to transcendence, and from the prophetic to the apocalyptic. The pendulum had swung away from the Hegelian God-in-history. The coming God was a God who would *end* history, who would triumph over it rather than complete it, who would through transcendent intervention reveal the contingency of all temporal and human affairs (Lilla 264, 267-8).

Just as Scholem is often taken as canonical despite the fact that he was presenting a new interpretation, Rosenzweig is often taken as a mere defender of traditional Judaism in the midst of upheaval when, in fact, he was doing something new and contesting tradition in certain respects. Rosenzweig's return to Orthodoxy, as well as his adherence to a messianic hope based on ritual practices and distanced from revolutionary upsurge, might seem to represent the Judaism of an earlier time. And, in fact, a good many Jews of the time, having not really read it, presumed that *Star* was a mere apology for Judaism. "Everybody thinks [the book] is an admonition to eat kosher," Rosenzweig complained (Galli 4). Yet Rosenzweig was a child of his time, enraptured by the rich possibilities of the present into which the Messiah could enter. Although Barth and Rosenzweig are classed as exemplars of "neo-orthodoxy," in both cases one should lean heavily upon the "neo" and lightly upon the "orthodoxy" (Lilla 267). Just as Jewish and leftist messianism were shifting from prophetic to catastrophic in the wake of World War I, so too was Christian eschatology, and Barth was an exemplar of this shift in Christian theology; Barth's *Romans* was imbued with "esoteric gnosticism" (262). Likewise, comparisons are drawn between Gnosticism and some of Rosenzweig's thought (Lilla 277; Pollock 6).

Enraptured by the spirit of the times, Margarete Susman wrote (in a review of Rosenzweig's "The New Thinking") a passage worth quoting at length, if for no other reason than that it so neatly encapsulates the apocalyptic mood discussed at the opening of this chapter. (Note the themes of inwardness, otherness, transcendence, destiny, and fate.)

> A peculiar life is commencing today in our country. At the moment when all the stars above it seem extinguished, and when its reality stares at us greyer and more wasted than ever, an odd lightning and flashing is beginning above it in the sky of its spirit, as if from new, unknown stars. Strange cloud formations and configurations of light gather above its head: Forms of pure inwardness arose, appearances foreign to everything that pertains to the life of the day, and yet finally determined and winged, again to transcend it. One asks oneself, in view of these manifold and yet essentially profoundly interrelated formations, whether it will not nevertheless at all times be Germany's fate and destiny to be thrown back again and again into its inwardness, whether its ultimate destiny cannot, despite all threats and dangers of annihilation—indeed because of them, be determined only in its inwardness. (Susman 106)

The apocalyptic tone of this passage, a tone so widespread throughout contemporary literature, is impossible to miss. These "strange cloud formations and configurations of light" are omens of the end, the "annihilation."

While Moses Hess, Hermann Cohen, and other progressive philosophers of Judaism had challenged Hegel's exclusion of the Jews from future world history,[29]

Rosenzweig apparently accepted Hegel's claim and saw it as a peculiar advantage of Judaism (Avineri 52-3). According to Rosenzweig, messianic hope had protected the Jews from muddying themselves in the atrocities of history, creating a safe distance from the temporal. The Jews avoided politics and found meaning instead in the cyclically recurring events of their religious calendar, which prefigured the messianic time (Pollock 13). Needless to say, this anti-teleological messianism was a significant shift from Rosenzweig's earlier discipleship to Cohen.

According to Rosenzweig, political enthusiasm for the making of history was a Christian phenomenon, an undesirable effect of their theology for which Christians should be forgiven. As pilgrims pining after another world, living in constant tension between the immanent and the transcendent, Christians continually had to seek consolation in history through the political (Lilla 266). As Mark Lilla puts it, the Christians were thus the *Shabbas goyim* (gentiles who help Jews by working on the Jewish Sabbath) of politics (267). The Jews, for their part, found meaning not in the vagaries of history but in being the "eternal people." They were nevertheless to participate in inaugurating the messianic age, but not by force—Rosenzweig opposed forcing the Messiah, condemning the "fanatic" who tries to make the kingdom come before its time (Rosenzweig 274-5). And certainly not through politics, either—it was simply a spiritual task. To the extent that *Star of Redemption* had a political message, it could be read as a boringly benign anarchism, in the absence of there being Christians around to do politics. According to Lilla, this anarchism (as one might call it) was more hesitant than the utopianism of the early Zionists, which Rosenzweig rejected (Lilla 274).

In contrast to Mark Lilla's interpretation, there are differing interpretations of *Star of Redemption*, including one that stresses the ambiguous passage entitled "Revolution" and finds in *Star* an enthusiasm for the Russian revolution, albeit not directly expressed (Löwy, *Redemption and Utopia* 60). One must also bear in mind that hostility to "politics" in German culture did not always entail quietism. Nevertheless, neither the book nor Rosenzweig's own life demonstrates a manifest call to political action.

Star opens with a discursus on mortality (human finitude), and the book as a whole is a meditation upon the interaction between finitude and infinity. Specifically, it is a reflection on the way in which the eternal and infinite enters the realm of the temporal and finite, through a religious community relating itself to God in tradition and ritual. This emphasis upon the relationship between the finite person and the infinite God shows the continuing influence of Hermann Cohen on Rosenzweig despite his break from Cohen, especially with regard to Cohen's concept of the priority of relation ("correlation") over relata (Large 62). Rosenzweig, however, had shifted from Cohen's prophetic messianism to the rising apocalyptic or catastrophic messianism. Although Rosenzweig, after his break with Cohen, emphasized the *caesura* between present and future and rejected the view that the messianic future would be the outcome of historical progress, Rosenzweig still believed that human action was essential to the coming of the messianic age, but this action was religious ritual, not politics (Leaman 802).

Like Landauer, Rosenzweig saw the messianic age as the product of an organic, natural human development and creativity. "…God in his love freed the soul for the freedom of the act of love, just as he gave creation the power to grow vitally within itself" (Rosenzweig 267). In a section titled "Hope," Rosenzweig emphasizes that life is incomplete and growing (284). Hope was the last of a Joachimite progression of three ages: "As Augustine loves, and Luther believes, so Goethe hopes. And thus the whole world enters under this new sign" (284).

* * *

Erich Fromm would probably consider Rosenzweig's political quietism and Scholem's flirtation with nihilism two sides of the same coin. In Chapter 3, exploring Fromm's notion of hope, it will become apparent that Fromm sees lack of hope producing both quietism and nihilism. Martin Buber's prophetic hope, at its best, stands opposed to both quietism and nihilism; under the influence of his friend Landauer, Buber's messianism posits the ability of human beings to construct a utopian future through small communities. Scholem and Buber sensed the dangers of apocalyptic messianism, their suspicions enforced by their encounter with the sway of politicized apocalyptic messianism over the right-wing in Israel. However, they may have failed to see a way out of this dilemma due to their unwillingness to abandon their convictions about the sterility of Hermann Cohen's messianism. We turn now to two thinkers—Ernst Bloch and Georg Lukács—who were influenced by apocalyptic messianism but nevertheless found a way out and a way forward, embracing prophetic elements and a revolutionary, Marxist messianism.

2.3 TWO "THEOLOGIANS OF THE REVOLUTION"[30]

Ernst Bloch and the young Georg Lukács were both of Jewish origins, although they were not members of the *Lehrhaus*. Both were socialists whose spirit, like Fromm's, may be described as "atheistic religiosity." Like many of their time, Bloch and Lukács longed to fill the chasm of meaninglessness that followed in the wake of the First World War, and they entered Marxism through an experience akin to religious conversion. Unlike many of the *Lehrhaus* thinkers, however, Bloch (to an extent) and especially Lukács found fidelity to a pre-war messianic vision as the solution to their intellectual difficulties. For Bloch and Lukács, the initial path to that vision may have been an existential, absurd choice, not a mere rational argument along Kantian lines, as would have been expected by Hermann Cohen's tradition. Both also had early flirtations with Romantic, pessimistic, or "gnostic" tendencies, yet both Bloch and Lukács, in different ways, eventually ended up affirming reason, hope, prophetic messianism, and the unfinished project of the Enlightenment. Their move to Marxism was not a flight from reality but a way of accessing the *this-sidedness* (*Diesseitigkeit*), to use Marx's term,[31] of truth. Both realized that hope depended upon a unity of theory and practice, and only from the standpoint of this unity could one advance the revolution.

The World is Not Yet True

Ernst Bloch (1885-1977) and Georg Lukács (1885-1971) were both members of Max Weber's circle in Heidelberg from 1912-1914 (Lowy, "Capitalism as Religion" 71). In the first decades of the twentieth century, Max Weber and Stefan George were Heidelberg's intellectual celebrities (Bouretz 426). Both derived their influence from their lack of affiliation with the University of Heidelberg, marking them as outsiders, which at that time translated into a peculiar kind of cultural capital. Weber's group met on Sunday afternoons at his house. According to Bloch, "half of the Stefan George Circle" also attended the Weber gatherings ("Interview with Ernst Bloch" 35). In recalling those years later, in the 1970s, Ernst Bloch resisted Michael Lowy's suggestion that the Weber circle was radical and anti-capitalist and indicated that a separate grouping of radical thinkers existed in Heidelberg, including Bloch, Lukács, and Karl Jaspers, among others (35).

Bloch and Lukács were close friends and intellectual collaborators. They were developing a method unlike anything Weber had seen before, but which he found promising. Ernst Bloch said later that as he got to know Lukács, "[they] quickly discovered that [they] had *the same opinion on everything*, so much so that [they] founded a 'wildlife preserve' (*Naturschutzpark*) for [their] differences of opinion, so that [they] wouldn't always say the same things" ("Interview with Ernst Bloch" 36, italics Lowy's). Weber felt forced to choose allegiances between the two students, who were bright and seemed to be in total agreement. Weber chose Lukács, whom he saw as the more theoretical of the two; Bloch, by contrast, seemed not to have his feet on the ground (Bouretz 427). Weber described Lukács as "one of the types of German 'eschatologism,' at the opposite pole from Stefan George" (Löwy, *Redemption and Utopia* 147). (George will be discussed further in the following section.) However, "[Bloch] is possessed by God," Weber concluded, "and I am a scientist" (Bouretz 427). Max Scheler apparently agreed, describing Bloch's early writings as "a running amok to God" (427).

Although he was an atheist, Ernst Bloch employed Christian and Jewish concepts, history, and symbols throughout his scholarly career. Bloch has been a formidable intellectual influence upon Christian theologians including Gustavo Gutierrez, Jürgen Moltmann, and Wolfhart Pannenberg (Gutierrez 124). Although Bloch did not consider himself a theologian, it is constantly tempting to read him as one; what Gershom Scholem said of Walter Benjamin might be equally true of Ernst Bloch: he was *a theologian marooned in the realm of the profane*—or, to play upon the title of Bloch's book on the German peasant revolt, a "theologian of the revolution." (As we will see, one might say that there are also theological moments in Lukács, although he would have rejected the title of theologian with even greater vehemence.)

Contrary to some Marxists who consider religion mere "ideology" and demand that theological language be jettisoned, Bloch was convinced that Marxists needed to employ the language of religion and myth. This was partly for tactical purposes, to prevent such tools of persuasion from becoming the exclusive property of Marxism's political enemies. In fact, the basic thesis of Bloch's 1935 book *Heritage of Our Times* is that the left permitted the rise of fascism and was partly culpable, since the left had failed to engage with the myths that were captured and repurposed by fascist ideology and propaganda. But Bloch also saw an intrinsic value in some aspects of religion, as did Fromm. Humanity's highest hopes throughout history had been expressed in religious language, Bloch reasoned, and thus a theory of the socialist future would have to draw from this intellectual resource. The realization of human hopes could only occur through a critical yet empathetic engagement with religious thought. Socialism was not a mere negation of religion—Marx himself had pointed that out in his critique of Feuerbach—but was the heir of the yearnings of the past and was in Bloch's view a new religious movement—the "red faith" (Bloch, *Man on his Own* 146). (*Aufhebung*, after all, the German word for dialectical synthesis, means both cancelation and preservation; socialism's defeat of religion is also religion's realization.)

Many thinkers affected by this time—Walter Benjamin, Theodor Adorno, and the vastly underrated Simone Weil, among others—turned to the desolate theological realm, now abandoned by its God, in search of an antithesis to the sunny Enlightenment and an account of the darkness of human suffering (Waggoner 5). What the mature Ernst Bloch sought from theology, however, was different. He sought not an understanding of the depths of suffering so much as that light of reason and liberation for which the Enlightenment had come (somewhat inaccurately) to be the reigning symbol. Some have commented that Simone Weil understood the cross (suffering) but not the resurrection (hope, promise).[32] In these terms, one might say that Bloch understood both the cross and the resurrection.

Bloch's messianism is eschatological and more focused on rupture than continuity. To some extent, Bloch supports an unpredictable, transcendent intervention into history, although in his later work he warned against the desire for transcendence. An opening epigraph of his *Atheism in Christianity* states, "What is decisive: to transcend without transcendence" (viii). In contrast to Buber and Fromm, Bloch was sympathetic to Gnosticism, and he defended the Gnostic Marcion throughout his career (as Jacob Taubes points out), from the time of Bloch's early book, *The Spirit of Utopia*, to *The Principle of Hope* in the 1950s and *Atheism in Christianity* in 1968 (Taubes, *Cult to Culture* 142). (Bloch's discussion of Marcion in *Spirit of Utopia* in 1918 preceded Harnack's book on Marcion in 1921 and thus helped to shape the debate that followed.) Bloch never completely broke from the neo-Gnostic apocalypticism that influenced his first edition of *The Spirit of Utopia* (1918), but he underwent a significant shift away from it.

The first edition of *The Spirit of Utopia* may be understood as Marxist, and it distinguished Marxism from "state socialism" (Löwy, *Redemption and Utopia* 140). It was skeptical of Zionism and included a section entitled "*Symbol: die Juden,*" which argued along the lines of Hermann Cohen that the Jews, along with the Germans and the Russians according to Bloch, were to play a crucial role in bringing the Messiah, but definitely not through Zionism (141-2). Bloch was giving a nod to the cultural eastward tide, not to Palestine in this case but to Russia; still, he continued to see Germany as integral to the revolution. The section "*Symbol: die Juden*" was later absent from the 1923 edition, which removed about a hundred pages from the original text, including laudations for Stefan George and for other "esoteric teachers" (*Geheimlehrer*), along with a lengthy philosophical discussion of Kant, Hegel, Nietzsche, Bergson, and Husserl (*Geist der Utopie* 237–342). In 1923, Bloch was distancing himself from some of his earlier ideas. However, the strangely apocalyptic, mysterious final chapter, aptly entitled "Karl Marx, Death, and the Apocalypse," remained in the second edition, suggesting that Bloch was conflicted on this issue.

After the first edition of *Spirit of Utopia* in 1918, Bloch's next major undertaking was a text on the leader of the sixteenth-century German peasant revolt: *Thomas Müntzer als Theologe der Revolution* (1921). The book posited the persistence of utopian longing throughout history but did not link it well to changing historical developments. It proved to be a breaking point between Bloch and Lukács, who harshly criticized it in 1923 (Toscano 80). Perhaps Lukács underestimated the importance of religious motivations in sparking the German peasant revolt, but his critique of Bloch's utopianism as endorsing quietism is interesting—Bloch's Gnostic and apocalyptic leanings are compatible with quietism, he argued—and he claimed that Bloch's views represented an inaccurate account of human nature (82).

When Bloch and Lukács were reunited following the First World War, they found that they had developed significant disagreements. According to Bloch in a late interview, one of the major disagreements was over Schopenhauer ("Interview with Ernst Bloch" 37-8). Bloch saw Schopenhauer as radical due to his complete negation of the world and was attracted to Schopenhauer's view that, "The world as it exists *is not true*" (37, Lowy's italics). Lukács's subsequent rejection of Kierkegaard and Dostoyevsky, which Bloch chocked up to Lukács's conversion to "the Party," marked a further division, about which more will be said later (38-9).

Ernst Bloch's Messianism

Bloch envisioned the messianic age as a synthesis of the achievements of history—including heretical movements of the Middle Ages, radical aspects of the Reformation, and the Enlightenment—with the perfections of a pre-historic paradise (Löwy, *Redemption and Utopia* 143). Like Fromm's messianism, Bloch's messianism was future-oriented and sought to synthesize history and pre-history. However, Bloch seems to undercut any real understanding of historical syntheses and specificity when he begins to emphasize the total newness and *absolute otherness* of the messianic future, though in his later work he tempers this insistence upon absolute otherness. This insistence upon absolute otherness seems to place Bloch within the "Gnostic" camp that conceived the future messianic age as analogous to the coming of the "alien God."

In the second volume of his *Tübinger Einleitung in die Philosophie*, Bloch distinguishes "renewal" and "new life," explaining that he seeks "new life," not "renewal" (*Man on his Own* 80). According to Bloch, Martin Buber's Renewal movement sought return to a primordial state through a process akin to Platonic anamnesis. For the Renewal movement, "the New" is never fully new, Bloch objects, but only new to the person who rediscovers it (82). "Renewal" thus lacked hope and proved "untenable" once material production increased and new philosophies of "generation and process" arose (82).

Like Fromm, Bloch sees "mysticism" (under which he includes Joachim of Fiore, Meister Eckhart, and Thomas Müntzer) and "humanism" as allies, not adversaries (cf. "Marx and Meister Eckhart on Having and Being" in *On Being Human*; *Atheism in Christianity* 51-2). Yet Bloch also embraced Gnosticism to a limited extent. Melding the pantheist notion of human dignity with the Gnostic view of an absolute divide between God and world, Bloch writes:

> It is of course true that when the mystics place God within men they equally presuppose an Other-world (and indeed one that is even over-transcended within itself) which, with lofty paradox is, in its turn, one that wipes away the whole business of Other-worldery, and does so for the sake of man, and in man. (52)

Furthermore, Bloch adds, the paradox of messianism is that the Messiah both has and has not arrived (a Spinozist claim).

In *Atheism in Christianity*, as before, Bloch's messianism is highly future-oriented. Eschatology has its origins in the Jewish scriptures, not in Greek thought, he insists (echoing Cohen's differentiation of Judaism from Greek thought, but unlike Cohen embracing eschatology) (44). In contradistinction to the "mere anamnesis" found from Plato to Hegel, eschatology is "something still open within itself, open with Not-yet-being" (45).

Bloch expresses admiration for Albert Schweitzer (as does Fromm) but celebrates the apocalyptic, eschatological side of Schweitzer's thought, "the highly explosive coming of God's Kingdom...the not only war-like but also cosmic catastrophe" (*Atheism in Christianity* 41). Schweitzer's "notes read rather like jottings from around the year 1000, or even from around 1525, when the end of the world was really thought close at hand" (42). Bloch contrasts Schweitzer with Hermann Cohen, the latter's messianism having a rationalistic "anti-mythical feeling" from which the "Total-*Futurum*" was absent (45). This is a crucial point in relation to Fromm, who rejects this "total" future theory.

Atheism in Christianity follows the Gnostic trope of inverting stories, making villains into heroes (Jonas 92). The serpent and Lucifer (like Prometheus, a rebellious bearer of light) are a few of the heroes celebrated in Bloch's *Atheism* (40, 72). (Lucifer is likewise celebrated in *Spirit of Utopia* [*Spirit of Utopia* 217].) Nevertheless, Bloch concedes that the Gnosticism of Marcion and the parallel insistence by the Jacobins upon a future that is totally other, while radical in certain respects, should not be wholly translated into the realm of contemporary revolutionary politics (*Atheism in Christianity* 178).

To untangle the reactionary from the revolutionary threads among many apocalyptic messianic thinkers of the early twentieth century is a difficult task. That Bloch was a self-professed Marxist—first as a critic of the Soviet Union, then a supporter, and then a critic again in his later years—raises more questions than it answers. The political implications of Bloch's work are ambiguous. As Wayne Hudson writes,

> The issue is not straightforward. Bloch was influenced by the widespread revolt against Zivilisation and capitalism among German youth before 1918. He shared the general hostility to positivism, abstract rationalism, and egoistic materialism; the enthusiasm for Eckhart, Boehme, Dostoevsky and Nietzsche. …(Hudson 12)

As we have seen, Bloch praises Gnosticism and sees the revolution as at least partly a product of transcendence. He wrote in a style that some believed obscurantist. Had he been older, he might himself have been one of the mysterious Messiah figures of the 1920s, like Stefan George; instead, he was a member of Max Weber's group, which was fortunately less cult-like than George's group. Stephen Eric Bronner emphasizes Bloch's fidelity to the earlier time, even if not exactly to Cohen's style of messianism:

> [Bloch's] philosophy harked back to intellectual tendencies existing prior to World War I when cultural radicalism was defined by a commitment to the "new dawn" foreshadowed by Nietzsche, the visionary communitarian socialism associated with figures like Gustav Landauer, the concern with reification and alienation exhibited by neo-Kantians like Emil Lask and Georg Simmel, the rebirth of interest in Jewish mysticism and Christian chiliasm, and the manifold experiments of the modernist avant-gardes. (Bronner 69)

Ultimately, Bloch does not fit neatly into either the Gnostic or anti-Gnostic camp, and one should not be too hasty to classify him. His gradual evolution from his early to later work is reflected in a more dramatic way in the work of his friend Lukács.

Conversion to Totality

The following section explores the second "theologian of the revolution," Georg Lukács. Together with Karl Korsch's *Marxism and Philosophy*, Lukács's *History and Class Consciousness* revived the study of Hegel for Marxism and returned the focus of Marxist thought to human nature and history, while opposing economism and determinism. Lukács's Marxist philosophy was made possible by a shift in focus more complete than any undergone by Bloch, a dramatic "conversion" that moved Lukács and his philosophy from the standpoint of the spectator to that of the revolutionary subject. Bloch's continued reliance on notions of transcendence and a future that is totally other are positions that Lukács was able to overcome through this conversion.

I must briefly explicate the central themes of two Lukács essays in *History and Class Consciousness* —"What is Orthodox Marxism?" and "The Marxism of Rosa Luxemburg"—before exploring the following problem: Lukács's presentation of the dialectical method (i.e., the standpoint of totality), suggests that one must obtain this methodological perspective through a simultaneous shift in one's theory and practice. To stand *outside* totality—either *theoretically* outside (as a non-class conscious worker) or *practically* outside (as a non-involved spectator)—leaves one incapable of comprehending totality. This raises the question of what initially leads the individual to encounter totality both theoretically and practically. Once what I call the "leap" to totality is made, Lukács's conception of totality provides a meaningful worldview, but it is difficult—if not impossible—to justify the leap to totality from any standpoint outside totality. But by what means does one attain the standpoint of totality? I pursue this question both in terms of Lukács's philosophical assessment of the issue and in terms of a biographical reflection upon Lukács's own "conversion" to Marxism.

Notes on "What is Orthodox Marxism?" (March 1919)

What Lukács calls "orthodox Marxism" is a far cry from what mainline Soviet Marxists call orthodox Marxism (which is what usually goes by the name). Lukács issues a daring challenge to reigning orthodoxies. The true essence of Marxism, he argues, lies not in any particular statements made by Marx but only in Marx's dialectical method. Genuine orthodox Marxism "is the scientific conviction that dialectical materialism is the road to truth" (*History and Class Consciousness* 1). It is a method or standpoint, the method of dialectical materialism or, what is the same thing, the standpoint of totality. This method is revolutionary and provides the crucial link between theory and practice (2).

The dialectical method conceives of reality as a unity, a social "totality" that is continually becoming. All of existence is a product of human activity, and thus the totality is a human creation, which includes humanity itself (19). One might say the totality is the process of humanity's self-creation. All of the parts of the process of production (distribution, exchange, consumption, etc.), which appear as so many distinct, static entities in bourgeois economics, are really only interconnected parts of this single, total process, which is reality itself (13). The goal of this total, social process—the emancipation of the proletariat—is immanent, and Marxism is the "prophet" of this emancipation (23–4).

However, the standpoint of totality has not been attained by the "blinkered empiricist," who focuses only upon individual "facts," wrenched from their social-historical context, and who fails to see the total process (5). Numerous problems result from the attempt to treat facts in isolation from the totality; the blinkered empiricist cannot recognize the following truths:

- Any presentation of the facts already implies an interpretation (5).
- Any change in any part of the economic/social/historical totality affects the whole (13).
- The facts are meaningful only in context.
- Apparent "contradictions" in the facts have two sources: some are only illusory and are resolved by the standpoint of totality, while others reveal the inherently contradictory nature of capitalism itself (10-11).

Only the proletariat, through becoming class-conscious, can comprehend totality. And in comprehending the totality, it comprehends itself. The knowledge of the object (totality) is also the knowledge of the subject (the proletariat); the subject becomes the object, and the object becomes the subject.

Lukács's critique of Hegel is illuminating. Lukács does not think that Hegel's lack of "materialism" is the most important difference between the Marxist and Hegelian dialectics (a surprising claim for an "orthodox Marxist"!) (34). He praises Hegel for understanding the importance of totality but reproaches him for believing that knowledge of the totality can only occur after the fact (i.e., "The Owl of Minerva only flies at dusk."). Contra Hegel, Lukács believes that the class-conscious proletariat is able to perceive and comprehend totality simultaneously with its present unfolding; the proletariat can grasp totality in the present, in a "single, undivided act of cognition," seeing its past, present, and even—to some extent—its future (14).

Notes on "The Marxism of Rosa Luxemburg" (January 1921)

Lukács believed that Rosa Luxemburg, like himself, understood the significance of the standpoint of totality. Unlike reformists like Bernstein, Luxemburg was a revolutionary who knew that revolution is the product of a perspective on totality and cannot be an "isolated act" (*History and Class Consciousness* 29). (Her account of capitalist accumulation places accumulation into the context of totality [36].)

In order to choose Marxism, one must declare one's theoretical commitment to the standpoint of totality (30). This involves rejecting the specialization of knowledge, refusing to "[confine] oneself to the analysis of isolated aspects in one or other of the special disciplines" (30). And since Marx realized "economic reality" is not "governed by…eternal laws of nature," to reduce Marxism to a series of formulae (Aristotle's M-C-M, C-M-C discussed in *Capital*, etc.) is erroneous; the Marxist must realize that these formulae are only a part of the total picture (31).

In contrast with the simplistic, formulaic approach of Marx's vulgar interpreters, Hegel, Marx, and Luxemburg realized that attempting to understand even one thing historically leads to an historical explanation that is broader in scope (34). Historical investigation of phenomena through Hegel's method reveals the identity of the philosophy of history and the history of philosophy and the fundamental unity of thought and existence (33-4). This historical method goes far beyond the bourgeois tradition of "taking the achievements of their forerunners into account" (35).

Luxemburg rightly distinguishes, according to Lukács, "the total and the partial, the dialectical and the mechanical view of history" (39-40). The partial/mechanical perspective leads to the attempt to force the revolution through small-group conspiracies and coups (Blanquism, which in Fromm's terms would be a form of "forcing the Messiah") (40). By contrast, the total/dialectical perspective finds the unity of theory and practice in the whole proletariat (not a small group who force the revolution upon others). *The proletarians come to know themselves and transform society through the same act.* "By recognizing its situation [the proletariat] acts. By combating capitalism it discovers its own place in society" (40).

As neat and clean as such summaries sound—know by acting, act by knowing—in reality the proletariat's merger of theory and practice is spontaneous, unpredictable, not mechanical; in short, it is *messy* (40-1). As anyone who has participated in social activism knows, the success of events is inscrutable; an excellently organized event sometimes draws a turn-out of two people, while a poorly planned, last-minute endeavor suddenly wins over hundreds, who enthusiastically crowd into the back rows and aisles. Luxemburg wrote of the mass strike, wherein the working class suddenly, world over, begins to reach the same realizations. 1968, to use a more recent example, was a "mass strike" year; for reasons that will never be entirely clear, there were revolts all over the world.

According to Lukács, the (messy) class consciousness of the proletariat takes the form of the Party. Hence, he rejects bureaucratic or mechanical understandings of the Party. The Party is not simply "a form of organization" (41). The Party is the effect, not the cause, of revolution. It gives expression to the "free, conscious action" of the proletariat and is the "incarnation of the ethics" and consciousness of the proletariat (41-2).

Lukács concludes the essay with what one might call a profession of faith (i.e., "faith" in Fromm's non-religious sense of the term: a paradoxical certainty that something uncertain will occur [ROH 14]). Responding to those who sneer that Marxism is "religious faith," Lukács does not reply, as one might expect, by insisting that Marxism is not a faith but a science. In fact, he responds by criticizing science and stating that there is "no 'material' guarantee" of the proletariat's success (*History and Class Consciousness* 43)! He then professes his "certitude that regardless of all temporary defeats and setbacks, the historical process will come to fruition in our deeds and through our deeds" (43). Here Lukács expresses a faith in the coming of socialism, not a scientific conclusion that the coming of socialism is "determined" (43).

Granted, Lukács goes on to say that the fall of capitalism will result from "method," which sounds a bit more scientific (and safer!) than "faith." But what Lukács means by method is something that cannot be proven on mere theoretical grounds but can only be proven through a transformation of the life of the proletariat, in their commitment to "living and dying for the revolution" (43). He finishes by stating that it is just as impossible to understand Marxism for a mere a scholar of Marxism, unengaged in this revolutionary struggle of living and dying, as it is for the economic determinist (43). Marxism can only be understood *from the inside*. This presents a problem: It seems that one must adopt Marxism before one can understand it. Surely this is paradoxical?

A Possible Answer, Through a Biographical Reflection on Lukács

We can consider the process of attaining the standpoint of totality as a "conversion." I will take "conversion" here to mean a simultaneous shift in both one's practice and one's theory, through which one identifies oneself with a particular group of people or a particular historical tradition and through which one obtains a new understanding of oneself in relation to a larger whole. (In this sense, one could probably "convert" to anything from Freudianism to the Republican Party to Surrealism; it would not have to be a religion.) The comparison between conversions and the process of attaining the standpoint of totality is helpful, because in this process one does not necessarily first assent to beliefs and then adopt new practices, or vice versa, but it is often through a simultaneous shift in practice and belief that one undergoes a conversion.

In his puzzling little book on phenomenologist Edith Stein (*Edith Stein: A Philosophical Prologue: 1913-1922* [2006]), Alasdair MacIntyre reflects upon the way in which the personal lives of philosophers, especially their "conversions," impact their philosophies. In a chapter entitled "Three Conversions," he discusses Franz Rosenzweig's conversion to Judaism, Georg Lukács's conversion to Marxism, and Adolf Reinach's conversion to Christianity. Lukács's case is illuminating.

In 1910, Lukács was an aspiring drama critic with left-wing politics but little interest in fomenting revolution (MacIntyre 154). Lukács's first major work, *Soul and Form*, was published in that year; his perspective at this time was what he would later classify as "Romantic anti-capitalism" (Butler 1). It embraced a tragic view of life and alluded to Novalis's blue flower, the symbol of Romanticism. Around the same time, he also wrote a dialogue about suicide and unrequited love resembling Goethe's *Sorrows of Young Werther*, a favorite text of the Romantics. Yet Lukács moved away from the Romanticism and Schopenhauerian pessimism of his early work quickly, transitioning from *Seele* to *Geist* (a move Bloch had also made— notice that Bloch's book was *The* Spirit *of Utopia*, not *The* Soul *of Utopia*, and the second edition of his book and later work, including *Heritage of Our Times*, distanced him further from the partisans of *Seele*).

Around 1911, living in Germany, Lukács initiated what became a ten-year correspondence with Martin Buber, whom he greatly admired, and began a serious study of Judaism lasting several years (Löwy, *Redemption and Utopia* 145-6). Lukács became swept up in the spirit of messianism, and somewhat indiscriminatingly (148). He was attracted to Hasidic mysticism, and his notebooks around that time discuss a distinction between an authoritarian "Jehovaic" strand in the Old Testament and a radical messianism, which excited him, and which he linked to Sabbatai Zevi and Jacob Frank (145, 147). In 1914, Bela Balazs wrote of Lukács: "Gyuri's great new philosophy...*Messianism*. Gyuri has discovered in himself the Jew! The search for ancestors. The Chassidic Baal Shem. Now he too has found his ancestors and his race. Only I am alone and forlorn" (Rabinbach, "Between Enlightenment" 80; Löwy, *Redemption and Utopia* 146, italics in original). Shortly before his conversion to Marxism, he had begun to speak of a revolution that would be "Christ's advent" (Löwy, *Redemption and Utopia* 148). The faith of the atheist revolutionaries, according to Lukács, was a faith in "a new, silent God, who needs our help" (148). At this time, Lukács was also drawn towards the thought of Kierkegaard and Dostoevsky, and in 1913 he began work on a book that would synthesize Kierkegaard and Hegel, which he never completed (Jay, *Marxism and Totality* 87).

In 1915, after a break from Max Weber around German nationalism and World War I, Lukács returned to his native Hungary (MacIntyre 157). Lukács soon after published his *The Theory of the Novel*, in which he contemplated whether Dostoevsky might be the herald of a new age that would synthesize art and political life. Lukács was still pessimistic, considering his time an age of absolute sinfulness, in Fichte's expression (*Theory of the Novel* 152-3; Löwy, *Redemption and Utopia* 147; MacIntyre 158). But he also envisioned a new unity, an end to all dualisms: a world of "pure soul-reality in which man exists as man, neither as a social being nor as an isolated, unique, pure and therefore abstract interiority…a new complete totality could be built out of all its substances and relationships. It would be a world in which our divided reality would be a mere backdrop" (*History and Class Consciousness* 152). His full conversion to Marxism came in 1918, when he declared the proletariat to be the "Messiah-class of world history" and formally joined the Hungarian Communist Party (Löwy, *Redemption and Utopia* 149; MacIntyre 154).

MacIntyre calls Lukács's conversion to Marxism a "deliberate act of faith" and states that "as Lukacs had approached the question of Bolshevism he had confronted himself with a recognizably Kierkegaardian 'Either-Or,' a choice so fundamental that it cannot be supported by reasons" (MacIntyre 159-60). Only after his "conversion" did Lukács develop a philosophically-grounded defense of Marxism as the resolution to the "antinomies" of German idealism (also in *History and Class Consciousness*) (160). MacIntyre explains,

> To become a Marxist is through participation in such practice to move beyond the limitations of pre-Marxist philosophy and so to become able to identify those limitations. And Lukács understands himself as someone who has achieved this new standpoint. Where in 1918 and 1919 he had still spoken in Kierkegaardian terms, so that his choice of Marxism was represented as an act of arbitrary, nonrational faith, now he presents his Marxism as the rational solution of his earlier philosophical difficulties. His new standpoint excluded what he was in the future going to characterize as Kierkegaardian irrationalism. (160)

The fact that Lukács had moved from bourgeois philosophy to Marxism through an existential leap of faith would not have been well-received by all of his new comrades, and this was a fact that he never openly discussed (MacIntyre 157).

The influence of "irrationalist" thought on the young Lukács served as a continual source of embarrassment to him in his later years. Yet in the two essays addressed above, Lukács suggests that Marxism is only comprehensible for one who has already attained the standpoint of totality. It would appear that this standpoint is initially achieved—despite however vigorously Lukács would deny it—through a kind of leap of faith. If this is so, many Marxists would consider Lukács's totality a dangerous obscurantism. Martin Jay leans that way, stating that the role that the concept of totality has played in the history of Western Marxism has tended to be one of obscuring the truth, not revealing it (Jay, *Marxism and Totality* 297). However, Lukács's core insight, that theoretical and practical transformation depend upon a vision of one's unity with an active, self-creating whole, runs throughout much of Western philosophy (Heraclitus's *Logos*, Spinoza's *Natura Naturans*, Hegel's *Geist*), and this strand of thought influences Fromm's own work on hope.

Lukács lived at a time when Marxism was plainly a viable object of conversion. He was far from alone in his leap of faith, even if his philosophy provides a uniquely useful basis for theorizing it. In addition to many in Germany, one finds a rash of similar conversions to Marxism in France throughout the twentieth century. Martin Jay describes Merleau-Ponty's move to Marxism as a conversion experience or Pascalian wager (*Marxism and Totality* 363-4, 370). Sartre in turn claimed that Merleau-Ponty had "converted" him to Marxism (361). Simone Weil, of course, drew her inspiration for social transformation from a conversion experience, in her case a perhaps more conventionally religious one. Henri Lefebrve arrived at Marxism from his early Joachimist fantasy of spreading a "cult of the Holy Spirit," for which he envisioned that he would be willing to be a martyr (Lefebvre 223).

Lukács's productive "totality" could be summarized as a political reconstrual of Spinoza's *natura naturans*. Totality, this almost-divine substance, the beatific vision of which is granted to the class conscious proletariat, offered the individual worker the opportunity for self-consciousness as a subject. Lukács would have been offended, most likely, by Merleau-Ponty's charge in the 1950s that Lukács's philosophy could be classified as a "Marxist Gnosticism" (Merleau-Ponty 51). Although his thought showed echoes of the Romantic anti-capitalism of his early work, especially in his vision of the achievement of the standpoint of totality as a kind of conversion, he firmly rejected the Gnosticism that may have attracted him at the time of his early *The Theory of the Novel*. While Lukács never wholly abandoned his early philosophical influences—and his Marxism was richer for it—Merleau-Ponty was wrong: Lukács had left Gnosticism behind. He had successfully moved from Gnosticism to something bordering on pantheism, and from inwardness and *Seele* (as in his *Seele und Formen*) back to Hegel's *Geist*. By the 1950s, he had become a leading defender of reason against its opponents from Schopenhauer and Nietzsche to Ludwig Klages, whom we will explore further in the following section.

Ernst Bloch, for his part, never underwent the dramatic conversion experience of Lukács. In an interview done late in his life with Michael Lowy, Ernst Bloch reflects upon his friendship and break with Lukács. Part of the problem underlying Bloch's misunderstanding of Lukács in the interview is that Lukács finally made the decision, the leap or conversion, that both of them were seeking, while Bloch chose not to and to remain somewhat an outsider. Perhaps Bloch resented Lukács's fame, considering that Bloch probably saw himself as having more integrity for remaining independent in spite of how much he could have gained by committing himself to the West, to the East, or to Christianity or Judaism. But Bloch was wrong if he believed that Lukács's rejection of Kierkegaard, Dostoyevsky, and Schopenhauer was a cheap capitulation, i.e., that Lukács was deceiving himself and accepting the Soviet Union as the coming of the Messiah. Lukács's conversion experience simply opened up new truths to him that were not available to Bloch, partially because of Bloch's lingering tendency to see historical change as an interruption from outside. Although Lukács was wrong in his assessment of the Soviet Union (and Bloch was also, for at least a time), Lukács's standpoint as an epistemologically privileged revolutionary subject granted him a hope and optimism denied to Bloch. Seeing totality as a process that is moving towards redemption, and consequently rejecting the pessimism of Schopenhauer, was not a sunny daydream or a self-deception; it was simply how the world looked to Lukács as a subject in the midst of a revolutionary moment.

2.4   AIR FROM OTHER PLANETS: STEFAN GEORGE'S REACTIONARY ANTINOMIANISM

The ideology of the Stefan George circle was far removed from the emancipatory intent of Ernst Bloch and George Lukács. The George circle represents another kind of response to the widening abyss perceived between the corrupt present and the messianic, fulfilled future. For Stefan George and his conservative admirers, the abyss between present and future was so wide it that could only be bridged by irrational, "magical," or aesthetic means. Styling themselves the protectors of a subterranean "secret Germany" that would one day ascend to reign, George's elite group was not engaged in debates in left-wing Jewish intellectual circles over the meaning of messianism—in fact, it was a rather anti-Semitic grouping, despite having some Jewish members—but it nevertheless possessed a peculiar type of messianic tendency. Their messianism was in large part a deference to a leader, a Messiah-figure—Stefan George. Their ideology was conceptually linked to some previously discussed figures and movements by its gnostic orientation and by its sense of doom, decline, and apocalyptic expectation.

Stefan George (1868-1933) was a mysterious figure, a poet and the leader of a kind of cult. His circle emerged out of the Cosmic Circle, founded at the turn of the century by Ludwig Klages in the Bohemian borough of Schwabing in Münich (Lebovic, "Beauty and Terror" 27). Stefan George, Ludwig Klages, and Alfred Schuler "used to walk the streets of Munich disguised in Dionysian masks and robes, sometimes carrying knives" (Lebovic, "Dionysian Politics" 5). The Cosmic Circle lasted until 1905, when the more virulently anti-Semitic faction represented by Klages and Schuler (who later became infamous as the popularizer of the swastika) split from George (Lebovic, "Beauty and Terror" 27; Norton 153, 585-6). After the disintegration of the Cosmic Circle, George created his own circle in Heidelberg. Heidelberg became "the secret capital of the Secret Germany," where one could catch a glimpse of that celebrity, Stefan George: "I certainly saw him," Walter Benjamin said later, "even heard him. It was not too much for me to wait for hours on a bench reading in the castle park in Heidelberg in expectation of the moment when he was supposed to walk by" (Norton 475).

George's circle was ostensibly a literary circle, but everyone knew it was far more than a writers' workshop. It preached the message of a secret- and sacred Germany that could be recuperated through a return to Germany's primordial Teutonic and heroic past. Like radical Vienna journalist Karl Kraus, George viewed the *origin as the goal*; it was through rupture with the ordinary that one could return to the past, and it was from the past that the new order (or *Reich*, as in the title of George's 1928 chapbook *Das Neue Reich*) would emerge (Norton 679).

Although George was anti-Semitic, anti-Semitism does not seem to have been the primary source of his reactionary politics (Norton 155-6). Several in George's circle were Jews, including most notably Friedrich Gundolf and Karl Wolfskehl. The Circle's ritual practices and its hierarchical, secretive nature do more to suggest its political affinities. In *Secret Germany: Stefan George and His Circle*, Robert Norton writes:

> Elitist, hierarchical, antidemocratic, and deeply suspicious of all forms of rationalism, George held many of the beliefs and values that were shared by antimodern intellectuals in early-twentieth-century Germany. For George and his followers, who typically expressed nothing but contempt for the democratic experiment of the Weimar years, their own "Secret Germany" provided a surrogate ideology that looked back to a heroic European past for cultural and political models to provide the patterns to inform some future—German— state. Stefan George and his circle, then, offered kind of miniature model of the way that state might look: enthusiastic followers who submitted themselves without question to the example and will of their charismatic leader, who they believed possessed mysterious, even quasi-divine powers. (xi)

The George circle organized secret costume parties at which members dressed as mythological deities, conducted orgies to "Wagnerian" drumbeats, and formed a cult of veneration around select teenage boys (Norton 311ff, 329-330; Lebovic, "Dionysian Politics" 5). Although they consciously and deliberately violated the norms of their society, their movement was not recruiting widely. Theirs was a conservative revolution not intended for the masses.

Although the George circle should be considered proto-fascist, it does not appear to have collaborated directly with the Nazi regime. When Hitler came to power, George moved to Switzerland. At the time, his disciples claimed this did not indicate opposition to Hitler, though they later explained that it was a strategic retreat from Nazism (Cartwright 3). After George's death in 1933, two of his followers, the von Stauffenberg brothers—among the young men celebrated by the circle for their beauty—attempted to assassinate Hitler. The assassination was motivated by aristocratic, not democratic aspirations. Claus von Stauffenberg is said to have faced the firing squad proclaiming, "Long live sacred [or secret] Germany!" (Norton 745).

The George circle was fascinated by J. J. Bachofen's theory of a pre-historic matriarchal society, and Bachofen's book *Matriarchy* has been called "the bible of the Cosmic Circle" (Norton 361). Recall from Chapter 1 that Fromm's essay on the radical and reactionary adherents of Bachofen had targeted Ludwig Klages, Alfred Bäumler, and Alfred Schuler—all were members of the Cosmic Circle. The revival of Bachofen was tied to "post-Nietzscheanism" and *Lebensphilosophie*, and like so many of the Cosmic Circle's concerns, the Bachofen controversy centered upon the political implications of the yearning for return to a prehistoric past (Lebovic, "Beauty and Terror" 26).

Cosmic Circle member Ludwig Klages's book *Vom Cosmogonischen Eros*, which opened with a note of gratitude to Bachofen's work on matriarchy, was hugely popular in Germany and was considered a contribution to *Lebensphilosophie*. It also had a profound effect on some left-wing Jewish thinkers, including Walter Benjamin. In *The Destruction of Reason*, Georg Lukács later identified Klages as the founder of a fascist *Lebensphilosophie* (Lukács, *Destruction of Reason* 526-7). Klages's magnum opus was a three-volume work positing a conflict between soul (*Seele*) and mind (*Geist*), *Der Geist als Widersacher der Seele* (Gay 80). Mind (*Geist*) he identified with "the killing of life," and he foresaw a resurgence of soul, when "an extra-mundane power [would] burst into the sphere of life" (Lukács, *Destruction of Reason* 524). At this apocalyptic moment, the old forces of myth would rise up to take vengeance on the forces of intellect and to save the soul; the struggle for soul was a return of the past, a rescuing of myth, and in turn, its enemy was the future (which was "not a property of real time") (525).

George's influence was certainly in the air in post-World War I Germany, and his admirers were not confined to the political right. As noted above, in 1918 Ernst Bloch's first edition of *Spirit of Utopia* praised Stefan George, though Bloch removed the remarks for the second edition in 1923. Bloch later attacked Ludwig Klages in *Heritage of Our Times* (1935).[33] Walter Benjamin carried on a correspondence with Klages, an interesting matter that will be explored later. T. W. Adorno and the early, pre-Marxist Georg Lukács both wrote admiringly of Stefan George (Fleming 98-9 and *passim*; Lukács [2010] 98-110). Although George is now almost forgotten, "in 1929, a newspaper published a photograph of [George] alongside the likenesses of Woodrow Wilson, George Clemenceau, Hindenburg, Gandhi, and Lenin" proclaiming them "contemporary figures who have become legends" (Norton ix).

George's circle is a particularly important example of the many cultish circles of the time and was one of the more influential ones, but it was far from being the only circle of this type. Along with Stefan George's circle, some similar figures such as Oskar Goldberg, Carl Jung, and Rudolf Steiner had circles of followers that shared at least some of the characteristics of having a charismatic leader, an intentionally esoteric writing style, a close-knit group of disciples, and a belief that a new age would be ushered in by a "magic" return to the primordial past.

Herbert Marcuse and Apocalyptic Messianism

Considering the peculiar history of the Cosmic Circle it is interesting to consider its wide influence. In particular, it would be worth exploring the following question, which I propose to treat at some length: Why does Herbert Marcuse quote Stefan George in *One-Dimensional Man* and conservative nineteenth-century writer Heinrich von Kleist in *Eros and Civilization*? This question also opens up an exploration of an apocalyptic/catastrophic tendency within Marcuse's work. This enquiry naturally divides into two parts, the first concerning Stefan George and *One-Dimensional Man* and the second concerning Heinrich von Kleist and *Eros and Civilization*. The latter enquiry will take us away for a moment from the George circle, but the themes of Marcuse's encounter with Kleist's work are related, as we shall see.

First, a disclaimer: This is neither an exercise in guilt-by-association nor an attempt to ascribe to Marcuse a reactionary conservatism which Marcuse himself would disavow. Even in his early years, Marcuse joined the Spartacist uprising of in Berlin, later recalling his admiration for Rosa Luxemburg as a great orator. Of course, he was politically active on the left again later as well, in the 1960s in San Diego and into the 70s. Fromm offered high praise for Marcuse's *Reason and Revolution: Hegel and the Rise of Social Theory* (1941) (MCM 60-1). Marcuse's moments of hope and optimism are to be found most prominently in *Reason and Revolution* and again in *Essay on Liberation*, at the height of the New Left. Nonetheless, I argue, with Fromm, that Marcuse had a crisis of despair that is manifested itself in *Eros and Civilization* and *One-Dimensional Man*. To point out Marcuse's affinities with conservative or even reactionary thinkers during the pessimistic period of his *Eros and Civilization*[34] and *One-Dimensional Man* merely highlights questions concerning the history of Critical Theory and the continuing influence of Weimar culture upon it, questions that have often been fearfully avoided in the literature on the Frankfurt School. Richard Wolin has begun to break through this wall and has suggested that the key to understanding Walter Benjamin is not, as many have suggested, Benjamin's alleged 1924 conversion to Marxism (the date of which should probably be set later). Instead, Wolin suggests that the key to Benjamin's philosophy may in fact be 1922, when he was in discussion with Ludwig Klages ("Benjamin Meets the Cosmics" 4). Benjamin has plenty to offer to left theory, and he was not a reactionary—those were complicated times, and not even hindsight is 20/20. But it may mean that Benjamin's work needs to be read differently in light of that history. Similarly, facing the inconsistencies in Marcuse's oeuvre does not force one to reject Marcuse, but rather opens up space for new readings that are cognizant of the complex history out of which his work emerged.

Two Quotations from Stefan George

Marcuse quotes Stefan George twice in *One-Dimensional Man*, both times without translation. The first quotation is simply a phrase: "*Luft von anderen Planeten*"—air from other planets (*One-Dimensional Man* 65). The line is from George's poem "Rapture" ("*Entrückung*"), which was set to score in Arnold Schönberg's String Quartet No. 2. (In its atonal rejection of the *status quo* and its meditation upon the experience of exile, Schönberg's quartet was almost as significant as George's poetry to the spirit of the times [Taubes, *Cult to Culture* 344n1]). Marcuse's second quotation from George refers to worries about "over-population": "*Schon eure Zahl ist Frevel!*"—even your number is an outrage (*One-Dimensional Man* 244). After some brief historical context, I explore these quotations within the context of *One-Dimensional Man*.

I suggest that Stefan George's circle and Herbert Marcuse expressed aspects of an "apocalyptic messianism," if one is willing to treat messianism as a broader cultural phenomenon that is no longer limited to religious Judaism but expressed the revolutionary sentiments of Europe at the turn of the century. With Gershom Scholem, Walter Benjamin and others, Herbert Marcuse was caught up in an enthusiasm for a sudden and total transformation of society. This messianism differed from the prophetic messianism of Hermann Cohen, Rosa Luxemburg, and Erich Fromm, among others—prophetic messianism is more open to Enlightenment ideals and to reason. While it may take either a revolutionary or reformist form, prophetic messianism warns strongly against trying to *force* the messianic age to arrive without the involvement of the masses. Apocalyptic messianism, by contrast, posits a future that emerges from a dramatic rupture with the present, ushering in something that is *totally other*. Therefore, for apocalyptic messianism the future is necessarily *unthinkable* from the standpoint of the present. From the prediction of a total break between present and future emerges a kind of nihilism or antinomianism. The attempt to bridge the abyss between the present and the future may occur through irrational, "magical" or aesthetic means; as we have seen, many thinkers of the time rejected both gradual reformism and organizing for mass revolt, preferring to compel the intervention of mysterious, transcendent forces into history.

Marcuse may not have met Stefan George or other members of the George Circle, but he certainly knew Walter Benjamin, who had been influenced by Ludwig Klages. The director of Marcuse's Ph.D. thesis on the German artist-novel (*Der Deutsche Künstlerroman*), Philip Witkop, was also influenced by Stefan George (Kellner, *Herbert Marcuse* 18). Further, according to Douglas Kellner, Marcuse's dissertation drew heavily from the pre-Marxist Georg Lukács, including Lukács's *Soul and Form*, which contains a chapter praising Stefan George and which serves as a prime example of the "Romantic anti-capitalism" of the pre-Marxist Lukács that the later Lukács decried. Any direct contact between George and Marcuse is unlikely to have occurred and it is unclear to what extent even George's published writings influenced

Marcuse. Nevertheless, Marcuse quotes Stefan George not once, but *twice* in *One-Dimensional Man*, and this with very little clarification of the mysterious quotations or of his reasons for employing George.

Let us now examine the two George quotes in the context of *One-Dimensional Man*. The first quotation, about "air from other planets," occurs in the course of a discussion about aesthetics. According to Marcuse, all works of art participate in the Great Refusal, regardless of any particular artwork's explicit political content and regardless of the artist's intent. Art creates a "rupture" with social reality through either "magic or rational transgression" and by "refuting, breaking, and recreating" (63). Art thus renders the familiar *strange*, and in virtue of this, ushers in the *air of other planets*. Rather than operating immanently within the established order, art is a disruption of the here and the now, which makes Marcuse's Great Refusal possible. Art is a means of confrontation with established norms, which art violates in order to open up space for further refusal, beyond the limits of art. "Air from other planets" is an apt image for the yearning for a messianic age that would be *totally other*, something *not of this world*.

Art's "transgression" may be "rational," according to Marcuse, or irrational, "magic" (*One-Dimensional Man* 63). "Magic" has a host of connotations, of course, from the Romantic "magical idealism" of Novalis to aspects of Kabbalah. To speak of magic and transgression is to invoke the fascination of Weimar Germany with *Rausch*—ecstatic, trance-like intoxication (Lebovic, "Dionysian Politics" *passim*). For Nietzsche, the Dionysian spirit was one of *Rausch*: "the result of all great enthusiasms...all the extreme movements; the *Rausch* of destruction, the *Rausch* of cruelty; the *Rausch* of meteorological influence, for example, the *Rausch* of spring; or the influence of narcotics" (3). For Nietzsche, according to Nitzan Lebovic, transgression was not a free choice but was written into the nature of reality; existence itself was returning to its prehuman state, was itself transgressing social norms (3). Georges Bataille is another figure in the background of Marcuse's reference to magic and transgression. For Bataille's vitalism, transgression for transgression's sake, like war and violence broadly, could liberate the life forces of humanity and create an organic community (Wolin, *Seduction of Unreason* 159, 163). By placing a reference to George beside this call for "magic or rational transgression," Marcuse is doing more than making an idle literary reference; he is recalling an era and bringing George back into the discussion—performing a metaphorical séance.[35]

Why would Marcuse want to bring Stefan George back into the conversation? This is somewhat different from the question of Heidegger's possibly problematic influence on Marcuse, considering that unlike Heidegger, George could not be described as an academic philosopher. (In fact, George's cult influence relied on his distance from academia and his lack of affiliation with the University of Heidelberg.) Whatever his poems offer, it does not seem to be propositional, so much as a sometimes peaceful and melodic, sometimes thundering succession of images. They seem to capture the mood of intoxication and trance that swept through Germany, perhaps the sort of "trance" in which Löwenthal describes writing his early essay on the "the Demonic" (Löwenthal 49).

Marcuse's second quotation from George occurs in a discussion about privacy, capitalist over-production, and worries about world population. According to Marcuse, civilization is on a continual quest to conquer nature and to obtain new space to dominate, such that even the individual's rational autonomy is constantly infringed:

> The crime is that of a society in which the growing population aggravates the struggle for existence in the face of its possible alleviation. The drive for more "living space" operates not only in international aggressiveness but also within the nation. Here, expansion has, in all forms of teamwork, community life, and fun, invaded the inner space of privacy and practically eliminated the possibility of that isolation in which the individual, thrown back on himself alone, can think and question and find. (*One-Dimensional Man* 244)

To break free from this tyrannical, totalitarian intrusion upon privacy, the individual must fight for private space in which she can think through her thoughts independently. Since this is next to impossible in a completely administered society, Marcuse's discussion concludes with a fantasy of sabotaging the mainstream media. The absence of television media and entertainment would plunge the individual into a "traumatic void," forcing her to re-educate herself and acquire new modes of living (*One-Dimensional Man* 245-6). This proposal is characteristic of a problematic aspect of apocalyptic messianism, i.e., that it sees the only hope of social change in mere destruction of the present order, rather than the creation of alternative structures or dual power (e.g., through the alternative news media and local organizing, alternative systems of governance like the "general assemblies" of the Occupy movement, etc.).

It is also puzzling that Marcuse links theories of over-population and the need for privacy and intellectual autonomy with the issue of capitalist over-production. Marxists have traditionally rejected theories of over-population as Malthusian apologetics for capitalism (i.e., competition is needed to kill off the weak), and they have interpreted capitalist "over-production" not as evidence of the dangers of technological reason but as evidence that capitalism produces resources that transcend its limits, pointing the way to a system where resources could be better allocated. Of course, if we are to agree with Lukács, accepting all of Marx's economic theories is certainly no prerequisite for being Marxist. Although Marcuse is free to deviate from standard Marxist tropes, it is nevertheless somewhat troubling to find his worries about over-population coupled with a Stefan George quote, especially considering the history it evokes of the Nazis' campaign for "living space" (*Lebensraum*) for the Aryan race. Marcuse knows that he quickly has to follow his George quotation with a clarification, which he rightly does. Marcuse is calling for "life-room" not for the state or for an ethnic group, but simply for individuals. Although Marcuse is presumably correct that people need more privacy and autonomy, why quote Stefan George in this context? And why couple a discussion of the need for increased personal space with a discussion of global population and over-production? The answer is not evident, but it raises interesting questions concerning which aspects of the cultural milieu of Weimar Germany, a milieu which remains under-explored by the contemporary literature on the history of the Frankfurt School, Marcuse is seeking to re-examine or revive.

On a broader scale, Marcuse's presentation of the topic of "living space" seems to miss the significance of inter-subjectivity and historicity. Although there is much to be said about the loss of privacy in modern society, and while he is surely right to mock the shallowness of contemporary capitalist society's confidence in "teamwork, community life, and fun," he still seems to be missing something about the importance of inter-subjectivity (a charge Fromm also makes against Marcuse in *The Art of Loving* [AL 131]). Rather than seeing community, solidarity, or love as tools for dismantling totalitarian technical control of the mind, Marcuse seems to propose increased isolation, unlike, for example, Axel Honneth, who has recently emphasized the role of inter-subjectivity in relation to structures of reification. No doubt many in contemporary society, especially the poor, suffer from a lack of time and space for quiet reflection, as Marcuse rightly notes, yet one finds it doubtful that placing them in situations of increased isolation would spark revolutionary transformation. In addition to neglecting the significance of inter-subjectivity in his discussion of living-space, Marcuse's account at this point in the text also does not appear to give proper weight to *historicity*; it presumes, in remarkably un-dialectical fashion, that the individual can "break free" of the limits of capitalism and think in other categories entirely of her own making. This is either remarkably naïve or a hypothetical example intended to demonstrate the futility of trying to liberate society due to the impossibility of this exercise. This is Marcuse at a moment of despairing pessimism—it is later, as a student of the New Left, that his hope is rekindled and that he is able to contribute to revolutionary change.

To his credit, in *One-Dimensional Man* Marcuse rejects the idea of a return to a mythological "Golden Age." This rejection of return occurs in the context of an argument that modern progress makes it impossible to discuss certain concepts in ways that do not seem mythical (188-9). He distances himself from reactionary destructiveness like that of Ludwig Klages, following his critique of a mythological Golden Age with a critique of *Lebensphilosophie* and "irrational pseudo-philosophies" (189). He also states that critical theory only needs to engage mythological concepts because of the irrational nature of capitalism itself—in this, he is like Ernst Bloch. In *One-Dimensional Man*, Marcuse is clearly trying to avoid flying off on any strange mythological tangent, because he is aware of the complexities of the history he is engaging. He is somewhat less cautious in his earlier work *Eros and Civilization*, which bears further affinities to the George Circle and the Weimar era yearning for return to the past.

Eating from the Tree of Knowledge

Now that the two quotes from Stefan George in *One-Dimensional Man* have been addressed, we may turn to the other mysterious quote mentioned in the introduction to this section, the Heinrich von Kleist line about "eating from the tree of knowledge" quoted in Marcuse's *Eros and Civilization*. Marcuse writes: "If the guilt accumulated in the civilized domination of man by man can ever be redeemed by freedom, then the 'original sin' must be committed again: 'We must eat from the tree of knowledge in order to fall back into the state of innocence'" (198). The line about eating again from the tree of knowledge is a quotation from Kleist, whom he cites (198n1). Marcuse's use of this puzzling image, like the "air of other planets" image, reveals something about his context and the uniquely "apocalyptic" nature of his messianic yearning.

Simply referring to Heinrich von Kleist is not all that odd, but it is awkward, because Kleist was held up as a hero by the Nazis. It seems more awkward from the standpoint of an American audience than referring to Nietzsche, who, although he was also held up by the Nazis, was more widely known in 1950s America and had a wider berth of adherents. Kleist lived well before the Nazi era, from 1777 to 1811, and was a prominent German playwright and short story writer, and there is no consensus on the political implications of Kleist's work. Kleist was being rediscovered in Weimar Germany. As Peter Gay points out, the Weimar revival of Kleist meant different things to different people: for some, Kleist was "the tormented Christian," for others "the aristocrat out of his time," for others "a rebel," for the Nazis, "the pure strong German," for Stefan George's circle, "the poet of the lonely elite," for the Communists, "an early revolutionary," for others, simply a German patriot (Gay 62). Not long before this revival, however, Kleist had been considered a hero of the conservative anti-Enlightenment. "Nietzsche coupled Kleist with Hölderlin as a victim of pretentious cultivation—that cursed German *Bildung*" and painted Kleist as an opponent of Enlightenment ideals of progress (60). Friedrich Gundolf, a member of the *Georgekreis*, wrote a book on Kleist (Norton 615). According to Peter Gay, the ultimate result of the Kleist hoopla in Weimar Germany was that "the so-called better interpreters of Kleist only gave new respectability to the love affair with death that loomed so large over the German mind" (Gay 62). Kleist's plays about war seemed to celebrate German nationalism, while his eerie story of a post-earthquake, quasi-sacrificial slaughter is disturbing ("The Earthquake in Chile"); his political writings against Napoleon are also notorious for their hypernationalistic sentiments.

Marcuse was surely aware of the debate about Kleist; it would have been impossible to ignore it in Freiburg (where Marcuse studied under Martin Heidegger) and Frankfurt in the 1920s. Marcuse's later writings, like Fromm's, hark back to that time. Even the title of Marcuse's *Eros and Civilization* invokes a troubled past, a time in German culture when Eros was celebrated and the Enlightenment ideal of *Zivilisation*, condemned. Ludwig Klages's 1922 work *Vom Cosmogonischen Eros* almost certainly crossed Marcuse's mind. Marcuse was dredging up the past. It is not clear, however, to what purpose.

The quote about eating from the tree of knowledge is from Kleist's short text "The Puppet Theater" (or "On the Marionette Theater"), a kind of anti-humanist parable. The narrator recounts a discussion with a friend whom he takes to be very wise. The friend suggests that an unconscious puppet is a better dancer than a human, and a trained bear, a better sword fighter. Turning to a mythological account of human nature, the character describes a fallen humanity, wandering in search of lost innocence. He states, "The gates of Eden are barred against us and the angel drives us on. We must make a journey round the world and see whether we can perhaps find another place to creep in at" (Kleist 85). The story concludes:

> 'You mean,' I said rather tentatively, 'that we must eat again from the tree of knowledge in order to relapse into the state of Innocence?'

> 'Certainly,' he replied. 'That is the last chapter of the history of the world.' (88)

The suggestion quoted by Marcuse that humanity must eat again from the tree of knowledge resembles his remark in *One-Dimensional Man* that art is radical because of its ability to contribute to "transgression."[36] Kleist's parable exemplifies a mysticism of return: according to Kleist, humanity's *telos* is the return to innocence— God and non-conscious matter are alike in their innocence, while the fallen human soul is on a journey of return: origin is the goal, as Vienna journalist Karl Kraus had quipped. This quasi-Romantic yearning for return was a thread running through Weimar culture and is a prime example of the theme of neo-Gnosticism addressed at the opening of this chapter.

The difficulty is that one cannot encounter the world from a standpoint abstracted from human history, as Marx masterfully argued in the 1844 Paris Manuscripts. ("Man is no abstract being squatting outside the world" [*Early Writings* 43]). We have no concept of life before myth, theology, or other attempts at the world's explanation. Thus, a return to primordial innocence lies beyond our powers of conceptualization, outside of all of our categories. We are being asked by Marcuse to create a future that is, in effect, impossible to describe. There can be no blueprints or utopian models. Marcuse's messianic event is unlikely to be a product of strategizing and movement-building (at least for Marcuse in the period of *Eros and Civilization* and *One-Dimensional Man*). One wonders if Marcuse's eventual embrace of third world revolutionism—in a 1968 Paris interview, he stated that a revolution in the United States would be impossible—is related to a desire for the intervention of what lies outside (*The New Left* 106). One can yearn for a return to innocence, but the gates to Paradise are barred behind us.

Eros and Civilization lacks some of the careful qualifications Marcuse offers later in *One-Dimensional Man*. In *Eros*, Marcuse's affinities with Klages, George, et. al., appear in high relief. The Kleist quote is situated in a discussion of the need to return to a state prior to civilization, in order to jettison surplus repression. According to Marcuse, liberation from surplus repression will necessarily appear to be a regression to a pre-civilizational state (*Eros and Civilization* 199). The return to innocence would be possible only through a transgression of the present order that could only appear as "barbarism" from the standpoint of that order (198).

We can now return to the question asked at the outset of this section on Marcuse and apocalyptic messianism: Why does Marcuse quote Stefan George and Heinrich von Kleist in *One-Dimensional Man* and *Eros and Civilization*? This question will not be answered here, as the reader was warned at the outset. However, one may suggest an avenue for further exploration. In the mid-1950s to early 1960s, Marcuse was re-evaluating the optimistic Hegelian Marxism of his early *Reason and Revolution*, which he only recovered in *An Essay on Liberation*, albeit in a modified form, with greater emphasis upon the role of "catalyst groups" as an alternative to the proletariat. *Essay on Liberation* recaptures the enthusiasm of his earlier Marxist work of the 1940s, and this did so under the influence of the 1960s protest movements. It concludes not with the ambiguity of *One-Dimensional Man*, which ends with a statement about loss of hope and an absence of concepts bridging the gap between the present and the future, but instead with the clarity he received from a young Black militant saying, "For the first time in our life, we shall be free to think about what we are going to do" (*One-Dimensional Man* 257; *Essay on Liberation* 91). But it is not this recovery of hope that concerns us here, but the period of *Eros and Civilization* (1955) and *One-Dimensional Man* (1964). We turn now to the final thinker to be addressed by this chapter: Walter Benjamin.

Soothsaying from Coffee Grounds

In 1914, Walter Benjamin (1892-1940) met Ludwig Klages in München and invited him to speak to the Berlin Free Students Association, and he corresponded again with him in 1920 (Lebovic, "Beauty and Terror" 28; Wolin, "Benjamin Meets the Cosmics" 11). Benjamin also published contributions to the Bachofen fight, and according to Lebovic, "Benjamin's texts, after this debate, are filled with hidden and explicit references to this debate, a fact largely unrecognized in the fertile Benjaminian scene" ("Beauty and Terror" 24). In the early thirties, as Fromm was writing on Bachofen for the Institute's *Zeitschrift* and rejecting the idea of the "collective unconscious," Benjamin "considered writing a book about the theory of the collective unconscious, relying on the insights of Klages and Carl Jung," focusing on Klages's theory of Eros and its relevance for politics (Funk, Introduction 7; Lebovic, "Beauty and Terror" 30).

In 1929, Benjamin's essay "Surrealism: The Last Snapshot of the European Intelligentsia" sought out sources of "profane illumination," like "esoteric love" (175). He wrote of the need for a "history of esoteric poetry" (presumably including Stefan George and Dada) presenting it less as an "historical evolution" than as "a constantly renewed, primal upsurge" (177). Apparently George circle member Max Kommerell's *The Poet as Leader in German Classicism* (*Der Dichter als Führer in der deutschen Klassik*) (1929) did not fit the bill, however (Norton 670). According to Benjamin (as Norton summarizes Benjamin's review of the book), "Kommerell's talk of sacrifice and death, his worship of sharp blades and flashing lances, and his glorification of the inexorable German conquest, were no mere figures of speech but rather the solemn tenets of a shared and lived faith," a faith which Benjamin rejected (674).

Despite the influence of the George circle on Benjamin, he also poked fun in 1930 at the "habitués of the chthonic forces of terror, who carry their volumes of Klages in their packs" (Lebovic, "Beauty and Terror" 24). He harshly criticized two publications by members of the George circle. And Benjamin was critical of Friedrich Gundolf's polemical book on Goethe, which was a thinly disguised encomium to Stefan George ("Goethe's *Elective Affinities*" *passim*; Norton 585). According to Martin Jay, the essay critiquing Gundolf on Goethe's *Elective Affinities* led to Benjamin being "ostracized from the scholarly world into which [the George circle's] influence extended" (*Dialectical Imagination* 204). "Ostracism" may be an exaggeration, however; it is possible that Benjamin was simply involved in an internal faction fight among people belonging to the broad social circle influenced by George and relatively sympathetic to him.

It is difficult to know how to assess the influence. Benjamin was a person of deep and profound contradictions. He was drawn to Romanticism but also to the Enlightenment, to anarchism but also to socialism, influenced by conservatives like Carl Schmitt and leftists like Lukács (Löwy, *Redemption and Utopia* 102-3). He was excited by surrealism and advances in technology but feared the loss of the sacred aura that surrounded the things of the past. As we noted above, Richard Wolin has suggested that Benjamin's connections to the political right may be the Rosetta stone to his esoteric philosophy. Although Benjamin's messianism was unquestionably catastrophic/apocalyptic, like his friend Scholem's, Benjamin shared messianism and atheistic religiosity ("negative theology," in Richard Wolin's terms) with Fromm, Lukács, and Bloch (Buck-Morss, "*Walter Benjamin*" 744).

Benjamin's Restorative Messianism

It is likely that Benjamin's messianism was "restorative" in Scholem's sense of the term mentioned above, in the sense of seeking an absolute past. As Michael Löwy and Richard Wolin point out, Benjamin's ideal in the past was a prehistorical or ahistorical Golden Age (Löwy, *Redemption and Utopia* 117-8, 232n85; Wolin, *Walter Benjamin* 180). It was not a reactionary yearning for the Middle Ages or lost fatherlands, and whether Benjamin would actually consider it possible to return to or meaningfully restore a prehistoric ideal is open to dispute (Löwy, *Redemption and Utopia* 117). But unlike Fromm's, Lukács's, and Bloch's messianisms, Benjamin's messianism was oriented more towards the past than the future, more towards remembering and recovering a lost pre-historic harmony (117). Under the influence of Charles Fourier, Friedrich Engels, and J. J. Bachofen, Benjamin held that such a prehistoric state existed (116-8). Michael Löwy presents Benjamin's method as a dialectical synthesis of the pre-historic state of Paradise and the historical achievement of the Enlightenment, as in Lukács or Bloch (or Fromm). Yet Löwy also links Benjamin to "revolutionary romanticism" (117). Benjamin himself, in the "Theo-Political Fragment," called his messianism *restitutio in integrum*, a legal term for remedying a wrong by returning a situation to its condition before the wrong was committed (*Reflections* 312ff.; Löwy, *Redemption and Utopia* 102).

For Benjamin, the messianic age could only be the outcome of an explosive rupture with the present. Ever skeptical of the Enlightenment ideal of progress, he wrote, "The Messiah breaks history; the Messiah does not come at the end of an evolution" (Löwy, *Redemption and Utopia* 124). His early writings refer to his political thought as "nihilism" (100, 102). According to "Fragment," the messianic event is destructive "eternal and total passing away," which is "the task of world politics, whose method must be called nihilism" (313). Further, Benjamin's "studies of Sorel and his defense of anarchist spontaneity…against any Marxist 'programming' of action" underlie his nihilism (xli). This rejection of political "programming" or planning is itself political, and this same rejection of programming can be found in Marcuse's work during the period of *Eros and Civilization* and *One-Dimensional Man*, and it differentiates Fromm from Benjamin and Marcuse.

In his "Theologico-Political Fragment," Benjamin rejects the possibility of employing prophetic messianism as a political program (*Reflections* 312). According to Benjamin, the political quest for utopia and the spiritual quest for the Messiah proceed in different directions; the "order of the profane" seeks happiness, not the Messiah. Although the establishment of earthly happiness may assist in the coming of the Messiah, it is not possible to consciously and effectively direct one's political action to the coming of the messianic age (312). Like Marx's contemporary Moses Hess, who following in the footsteps of Spinoza held that Judaism had a unique ability to overcome dichotomies (Father/Son, Judaism/Christianity, etc.), Walter Benjamin saw in his philosophy the potential to integrate the messianic and profane trajectories (xxiv; Avineri 25). Despite this promising synthesis, however, it would seem that Benjamin's messianism cannot ground political planning, since the aim of utopian activity differs from that of messianism, at least according to the Theologico-Political Fragment.

According to the standard narrative about Benjamin's intellectual evolution, he converted to Marxism in 1923 or 1924, which was around the time that his wealthy family went bankrupt, that he read Lukács's *History and Class Consciousness* and met Ernst Bloch, and that he was exposed to Communist ideas by agitprop theater director Asja Lacis (Löwy, *Redemption and Utopia* 103; Wolin, *Walter Benjamin* 109). By 1923, "Benjamin had already made his mark as a leader of the radical Jewish student movement during the 1910s, where he developed a distaste for the communitarian *Lebensphilosophie* of Martin Buber" (Jay, *Marxism and Totality* 246-7). He did not immediately become a Communist, however. In a 1926 letter to Scholem, Benjamin mentioned that he was considering joining the Communist Party but still considered himself an anarchist (Löwy, *Redemption and Utopia* 103). As late as 1929, as we have seen, Benjamin hailed the Surrealists and still spoke often of anarchism and "nihilism" in a favorable light; after 1930, he no longer seemed to discuss anarchism (105-6). He became more typically Communist in his political views, and in the wake of the 1936 Moscow Trials, he moved towards Trotskyism (109).

The complexity of Benjamin's affinities is further revealed by his aesthetics. For example, although Benjamin seems to celebrate technology's potential to make art accessible to the masses, another interpretation is that Benjamin's work on art is *reactionary*, opposed to the revolt of the masses and anti-technology (Löwy, *Redemption and Utopia* 109). According to Michael Löwy, however, Benjamin was not demanding an end to technology but rather "mastery not of nature but 'of the relation between nature and man'" (105). Benjamin's worries about technology and progress were partly humanistic, linked to a critique of Soviet mechanistic materialism (which he depicted as a humanoid robot) (115). "In '*Erfahrung und Armut*' [1933], Benjamin hailed the end of culture as a healthy *tabula rasa*, but the words he uses to refer to the new civilization—'sombre and cold', like glass and steel—are hardly joyful: 'a new barbarism'" (109).

Although Benjamin may sometimes be difficult to locate on the political spectrum, he is certainly an example of a broader movement that explores the idea of a complete break between the present and the future, with a vast annihilation of the present order, and the revolutionary power of art and disruption. This phenomenon in Marcuse and Benjamin finds expression in Adorno as well, who headed off to Vienna to join a movement in music that sought to disrupt the status quo (cf. Wiggershaus 72; Jay, *Dialectical Imagination* 23; on the eccentric cultural milieu of Vienna, Janik and Toulmin 67, 74 and *passim*).

We have now briefly surveyed the influence of the Stefan George circle upon both Herbert Marcuse and Walter Benjamin within the specific context of their work on certain concepts, such as art and technology. For Marcuse, the quotations from George serve to indicate both that Marcuse was not a mainline Marxist at the time of *Eros and Civilization* and *One-Dimensional Man* and also that Marcuse was not immune to the yearning for the past and for advocating a dramatic break, in the tradition of Heinrich von Kleist. The George circle's system of tight control and manipulation of its adherents, its secrecy and mysticism, its yearning for return and its apocalyptic expectation—all of these combine to place it in a camp of worrying gnosticism, obscurantism, and elitism. One looks back at its first edition publications, many adorned on their covers by a swastika (before it became the symbol of the Third Reich), and cringes. Walter Benjamin did not know what horrors were soon to follow in Germany, but he was sometimes prescient and warned of the proto-fascist ideology of the George circle.

The themes of this time were later addressed in different ways in the work of Herbert Marcuse and Erich Fromm. Marcuse sought to salvage an apocalyptic messianism for a project of future liberation. Fromm was far more critical of attempting to re-appropriate the apocalyptic messianism of Weimar Germany. The themes and internal tensions of the thought of this time continue to haunt the present.

* * *

The options represented by Hermann Cohen and Gustav Landauer had virtually vanished by the time of Fromm's best-selling *Sane Society* in 1955, in which he affirmed the tradition of prophetic messianism that had been nearly crushed by the assassinations of Landauer and Luxemburg (SS 239). In the movement for socialist humanism, Fromm sought a renewal of the prophetic-messianic spirit, after the *Freies Jüdisches Lehrhaus* had long since been divided by questions pertaining to Zionism, Marxism, and religion, and after a Gnostic proto-fascism had crept over the political and cultural landscape. Perhaps Bloch and Lukács, after going their separate ways, come closest of the figures in this chapter to representing the messianic hope that Fromm defended.

It would be difficult to over-estimate the degree to which the trauma of World War I, worsened by the brutal defeat of the leftist uprisings of 1918–1919, the rise of Nazism, the Holocaust, and subsequent historical developments, have threatened prophetic messianism. The result of the series of catastrophes marking the twentieth century has been a socio-political "shattering of hope" (in Fromm's terms, discussed in Chapter 3) on a grand scale. Writing in honor of his cousin Heinz Brandt, who spent many years as a political prisoner both of Hitler and of East Germany, Fromm calls him a member of a "generation of authentic revolutionaries,"[37] of "socialists and Communists born before the First World War" who stood against both the Social Democrats and Stalin (Foreword to Brandt xii). "This generation of authentic revolutionaries has almost been forgotten," writes Fromm, and this was not only because many were killed by Stalin and Hitler and others were fooled by Stalin's claim of fidelity to Marxism (xii). This generation's revolutionary legacy was nearly forgotten and lost due to the *despair* that arose at the time of the First World War:

> Events since the First World War have increasingly shaken and shattered illusions about ideas and principles. A cynical attitude of disbelief, which is presented as realism, has become dominant, and persons who uncompromisingly adhere to their beliefs and their principles are frequently viewed as neurotics, madmen, or worse. (xii)

In few places does Fromm so poignantly display his devotion to the dreams of the earlier, Enlightenment-inspired generation to which he remained loyal, as his own generation abandoned its hopes in favor of a newfound pessimism, cynicism, or despair. Heinz Brandt's story, writes Fromm, "is not only a ...human document of faith, courage, and independence," but also "an important historical document, above all because only a few eyewitnesses of this epoch have survived whose vision has not been blurred by helplessness, cynicism, or disenchantment" (xvi).

In the following chapter, I outline Fromm's definition and defense of hope. Responding to the crisis of the First World War, Fromm argued for the need for hope. His concept of hope is closely related to his concept of messianism: hope must be actively engaged in trying to transform the world. Nevertheless, hope does not attempt to "force the time" but recognizes the need for a combination of patience and impatience. The fourth and final chapter of this book outlines the main characteristics of Fromm's messianism and how it differs from the prevailing account of the messianism of the Frankfurt School.

NOTES

[1] The German ideal of *Bildung* had blossomed from an intellectual movement which had been designed to fly beneath the radar of government censors—Friedrich Schiller's *Gedankenfreiheit* (Gay 72). This is partly why it was later seen as overly conformist by some in Weimar. The term has a complicated history, popping up in the work of mystics like Meister Eckhart and later employed by Pietists speaking of education in virtue and by progressive reformers seeking to give aesthetic experience a more central role in education. In the 1800s, however, it became identified with the training of bourgeois youth for their future economic success, so it is not surprising for this reason too that the term came to be rejected (Cocalis *passim*). Unfortunately, however, the idea of popular education that *Bildung* once represented seems to have been rejected by apocalyptic messianism along with related baggage accruing to the term.

[2] They tended to be united, however, by a rejection of traditional humanism; under the influence of late Romanticism, the desire for wholeness was manifested in a yearning for union with the non-human "cosmic," not with the totality of humanity or of human history (Lebovic, "Dionysian Politics" 3).

[3] Followers of Joachim of Fiore (1135-1202), the medieval Franciscan who predicted a coming "Age of the Holy Spirit" that would end oppression and inter-religious strife.

[4] Jung writes: "The 'Aryan' unconscious has a higher potential than the Jewish; that is both the advantage and the disadvantage of a youthfulness not yet fully weaned from barbarism. In my opinion, it has been a grave error in medical psychology up to now to apply Jewish categories— which are not even binding on all Jews—indiscriminately to German and Slavic Christendom. Because of this the most precious secret of the Germanic peoples—their creative and intuitive depth of soul...—has been explained as a mass of banal infantilism, while my own warning voice has for decades been suspected of anti-Semitism" (Goggin and Goggin 75).

[5] "Form" was an ambiguous term as well, sometimes used to describe the "conservative revolution" (Gay 84). Much later, in *The Destruction of Reason*, Lukács himself classified "form" as "one of the central categories" of a proto-fascist vitalism and linked it to Oswald Spengler's "morphology" and Ernst Jünger's esotericism (Lukács, *Destruction of Reason* 528, 530, 532).

[6] The environmental movement in Weimar Germany is well known to have included significant ties to the right, and considerable research has been done on the continuation of environmental concerns under the Nazi regime.

[7] Incidentally, the rhetoric about political "movements" (*Bewegungen*) was as odd as that about life (*Leben*). The Nazis spoke of themselves as a "movement," rather than a static "Party," as a way of expressing a commitment to conceiving society as an organic whole (Gay 77).

[8] Thomas Mann linked aristocracy to death and democracy to life (Gay 126).

[9] Like many of those involved in recent scholarship on messianism, Rabinbach uses the term "messianism" only to describe the apocalyptic/catastrophic variant. This is of course one of the problems in the scholarship that this book is trying to correct.

[10] Lazier concludes that pantheism was a "catchall" for many tendencies of the time (Lazier 73). Since pantheism does not seem to offer an adequate contrast for Gnosticism for our present endeavor, I focus here on Gnosticism, though there are similarities between the fight over Gnosticism in Weimar Germany and the *Pantheismusstreit* over Spinoza approximately a century earlier.

[11] Cf., e.g., Jacob Taubes, Ernst Topitsch, J. J. Altizer. (At the end of Chapter 4, I critique Rainer Funk's use of Topitsch and Funk's classification of Fromm as a Gnostic.)

[12] Walter Benjamin and Ernst Bloch, for example, both came to this conclusion around 1912 (Rabinbach, *Shadow of Catastrophe* 43). Erich Unger, of the Oskar Goldberg circle of Kabbalistic Nietzscheans, likewise rejected the Zionist program in favor a mobile Jewish revolutionary mission (Löwy, *Redemption and Utopia* 173; Rabinbach, *Shadow of Catastrophe* 58).

[13] Here is the young Gershom Scholem writing in his diary about Theodor Herzl and defending an anarchist Zionism against Herzl: "We reject Herzl. He is to blame for the Zionism of today [...] which is an organization of grocers, who grovel before everyone powerful!" (Lowy, "Messianism in the Early Work" 180). And, "[Herzl's] only thought was the Jewish *State*. And that we reject. For we preach anarchism...We do not go to Palestine to found a state—oh, you little Philistines!—and to ensnare ourselves in new chains [forged] out of the old, we go to Palestine out of thirst for freedom and yearning for the future, for the future belongs to the Orient" (Lazier 150; italics Scholem's). (In addition to anarchism, one notices here a kind of determinism that is evident in Scholem's work—the direction of the future is pre-decided--a theme we will return to later. Also, notice the turn towards the East—"the future belongs to the Orient.")

[14] This eastward tide did have earlier influences. For example, according to Jacob Taubes, "Kireyevski, Bakunin, Belinsky, Dostoevsky, and Count Czieskowski interpreted the role of the Slavic nations in messianic terms" (*Cult to Culture* 15). One also finds this attitude in Moses Hess, following in the footsteps of Czieskowski.

[15] For example, in her 1905 essay, "Socialism and the Churches," Luxemburg argues that Christianity is at its basis socialistic and charges the clergy, especially the Russian clergy, with abandoning their principles and perpetuating exploitation. Here she proclaimed, "The bishops and the priests are not the propagators of Christian teaching, but the worshippers of the Golden Calf and of the Knout which whips the poor and defenceless" (3). In her stirring conclusion, she again references the "Golden Calf" and issues a prophetic condemnation of the clergy, in a tone that sounds like something straight of out of Amos:

Also: These servants and worshippers of the Golden Calf support and applaud the crimes of the Czarist Government and defend the throne of this latest despot who oppresses the people like Nero.

But it is in vain that you put yourselves about, you degenerate servants of Christianity who have become the servants of Nero. It is in vain that you help our murderers and our killers, in vain that you protect the exploiters of the proletariat under the sign of the cross. Your cruelties and your calumnies in former times could not prevent the victory of the Christian idea, the idea which you have sacrificed to the Golden Calf; today your efforts will raise no obstacle to the coming of Socialism. Today it is you, in your lies and your teachings, who are pagans, and it is we who bring to the poor, to the exploited the tidings of fraternity and equality. It is we who are marching to the conquest of the world as he did formerly who proclaimed that it is easier for a camel to pass through the eye of a needle than for a rich man to enter the kingdom of heaven (19–20).

[16] Regarding Kautsky's critique of the "mass strike," she charges Kautsky with advocating "one, 'final,' pure political mass strike, disengaged from economic strikes: which once only, but with absolute conclusiveness, smashes down like thunder out of the clear blue sky" (*Theory & Practice*, 1).

[17] For further on the connection of Simone Weil to Erich Fromm and Thomas Merton, see my "Erich Fromm and Thomas Merton: Biophilia, Necrophilia, and Messianism" in *Fromm Forum* and reprinted in *Reclaiming the Sane Society: The Life and Scholarship of Erich Fromm in Critical Theory for the 21st Century* (Sense Publishers, 2014). On Merton's encounter with Weil in particular, see Merton's essay "The Answer of Minerva: Pacifism and Resistance in Simone Weil" and his book *A Vow of Conversation* (citation information below under References).

[18] Fromm notes that he was inspired by Cohen in *You Shall Be as Gods* (YSB 13). The book includes an account of the disobedience in the garden as the libratory first act of human history. I explore this allegory further in Chapter 4.

[19] Cohen's radically future-oriented messianism is also reflected in his *Ethics* (*Ethik des reinen Willens*). There Cohen stresses that history, not nature, is the realm of human freedom (Deuber-

Mankowsky 175). The will is temporal and oriented towards the future, and because it is concerned with the will, ethics must also be future-oriented (175-6).

[20] "Utopias are visions of ends before the realization of means, yet they are not meaningless; on the contrary, some have contributed greatly to the progress of thought, not to speak of what they have meant to uphold faith in the future of man" (MFH 30n17).

[21] The theme of "elective affinities" was drawn from Goethe's novel by that name and Max Weber's use of the concept in *The Protestant Ethic and the Spirit of Capitalism*. It acquired further significance later with Walter Benjamin's important critical review of a book on Goethe by Friedrich Gundolf, a member of the Stefan George circle.

[22] Svante Lundgren suggests that Buber may have initiated this (Lundgren 108).

[23] According to Ernst Bloch, this "rupture" was illusory and was only a return to past, as I will discuss in Section 2.3.

[24] This classification of Scholem is discussed further in Chapter 4.

[25] "Scholem met with Landauer between 1915 and 1916, when the anarchist philosopher was lecturing to Zionist circles in Berlin; the subject of their conversations was their common opposition to the war and their criticism of Martin Buber's positions on it" (Löwy, *Redemption and Utopia* 65).

[26] In a 1922 letter to Rudolf Hallo, Rosenzweig expresses contempt and suspicion of Scholem, labeling him a "nihilist" and an "ascetic" with *Ressentiment* and rejecting Scholem's Zionism (Lazier 189-90).

[27] Harold Bloom also considered himself a "Jewish Gnostic" (Spirer 4). Scholem's reading "seems to me to account much better [for] the whole nightmare of Jewish history than the normative Jewish religion can possibly do," Bloom states (5). For Bloom, Scholem represented an alternative to the "normative tradition" in Judaism, Cohen's sort of Judaism (Spirir 4; Bloom, "Scholem" 220).

[28] "The joy of destruction is a creative joy," Landauer writes, quoting Bakunin (*Revolution* 160).

[29] According to Hegel, the Jews were part of the Oriental world and thus stagnant and incapable of producing world-historical subjects (Avineri 52). Hegel held that the Jews had "initiated the break between East and West," and that their involvement in world history had ended with this act (Kouvelakis 122). Naturally, this was a contention to which the Young Hegelians were forced to respond. Moses Hess responded by arguing that through going into exile, the Hebrews had in fact become capable of being "intermediaries" between the East and West (Avineri 53). Their mobility—their exile—was evidence that the Jews could be makers of history and were not part of the apparently unchanging, non-historical "Oriental" world (53). In his early work *The European Triarchy* (1841), Hess argued that messianism was the Jews' chief contribution to world history (25, 69–70). Jewish messianism—characterized by restlessness, lack of rootedness and stability, and dissatisfaction with the world in its present state—was actually the engine of world history (70). This conception of messianism seems to contrast sharply with Hess' later advocacy for the establishment of a Jewish state in Palestine.

[30] This classification of Ernst Bloch and Georg Lukács is a satisfying one for a number of reasons, although it runs the risk of confusing the reader into thinking either that the two thinkers were theologians by professional discipline or that they were simply obscurantists, neither of which is the case. I am adopting this terminology of "theologians of the revolution" from Richard Wolin and will return to this terminology again shortly (Wolin, *Labyrinths* 45).

[31] "The question whether objective truth can be attributed to human thinking is not a question of theory but is a practical question. Man must prove the truth, i.e., the reality and power, the this-sidedness [*Diesseitigkeit*] of his thinking, in practice" ("Theses on Feuerbach" 1).

[32] This is partly on the basis of her famous statement that "if the Gospel omitted all mention of Christ's Resurrection, faith would be easier for me. The Cross by itself suffices me" (Johnston 4).

[33] In a section on Klages in *Heritage of Our Times*, Bloch argues, contra the proto-fascist yearning for return to the primordial, that it would be impossible to return to the beginning of time, because one cannot find an "original" human being to tell us what that state was like. (Marx makes a very similar argument in the 1844 Paris *Manuscripts*—imagining a world prior to human beings involves one in a contradiction, Marx argued [*Early Writings* 166].) Continuing, Bloch asks: "But did this 'original' human being, this untreated new wine ever exist? And even if he should have existed, is there a

living witness to the fact anywhere to be found, is there a way back to this unknown Adam anywhere to be found?" (*Heritage of Our Times* 304).

[34] *Eros and Civilization* is sometimes contrasted with *One-Dimensional Man* as the optimistic book to which *One-Dimensional Man* can be counter-posed as pessimistic (Farr 77). There is some truth in the claim that *Eros and Civilization* is a more optimistic work than *One-Dimensional Man*, certainly in the sense that *Eros and Civilization* very clearly expresses the possibility of revolution and of sloughing off excess repression through liberation of the drives and instincts. Fromm thought the book possessed a sort of childlike naiveté, a claim that may be compatible with my assessment. However, as this section will make clear, *Eros and Civilization* has affinities with the pessimistic ideology of decline that could be found in Weimar Germany. Marcuse's turn to Eros as a source of liberation from *Zivilisation* should be revisited in the context of Ludwig Klages and the George Circle.

[35] Another reference to this prior time in *One-Dimensional Man* is Marcuse's allusion to the controversies of Vienna journalism "during and after the First World War," a reference to Karl Kraus (196).

[36] There may also be a connection here to the fascination in some despairing German Jewish left circles, after the crushed socialist uprisings of 1919, with the history of the seventeenth century heretical Sabbatean sect and its doctrine of "redemption through sin," mentioned above, according to which the messianic age would be brought about through violation of social norms or of certain elements of religious law.

[37] Fromm's use of "authentic revolutionaries" here harks back to his distinction between the true revolutionary and the illusory revolutionary, the mere "rebel," mentioned above in the section on Gustav Landauer.

PART II

ERICH FROMM'S CONCEPTS OF HOPE
AND MESSIANISM

The next two chapters explore Erich Fromm's interconnected concepts of hope and messianism, terms that Fromm appropriates from disputes among German-Jewish intellectuals of his time. He frequently couples his discussion of hope with the theme of messianism. The opening of *The Revolution of Hope* provides Fromm's most thorough discussion of hope, including a three-part negative definition and a more restricted positive definition. *You Shall Be as Gods* follows a discussion of false Messiahs throughout Jewish history with a section of the book entitled "The Paradox of Hope."

Fromm distinguishes two conflicting types of "messianism": "prophetic" messianism and "catastrophic" messianism, both of which are viewpoints on political struggle. He sees prophetic messianism as hopeful and progressive, motivating the Old Testament prophets' denunciations of injustice and the radicalism of the Enlightenment and Marxism, and catastrophic messianism as despairing and regressive. Catastrophic messianism awaits a messianic event that will follow a catastrophic situation, into which some force or individual from outside of history will intervene to save a corrupted humanity from itself. Prophetic messianism views the messianic event as the outcome of historical progress and united human effort.

Fromm's support for prophetic messianism and opposition to catastrophic messianism served as a challenge to certain predominant political perspectives on the left, including within the Frankfurt School. Within Critical Theory, Walter Benjamin and Herbert Marcuse advocated a messianism more rooted in the "catastrophic" than the "prophetic." Although the following chapters focus on Fromm's conceptions of hope and messianism, they also indicate how Fromm's messianism challenged other prevailing conceptions of messianism, including those of other members of the Frankfurt School. The differing implications and consequences of the prophetic and catastrophic outlooks, I argue, demonstrate that Fromm's prophetic messianism is more useful to political praxis than catastrophic messianism.

WHAT HOPE ISN'T AND IS

Hope is central to Erich Fromm's prophetic messianism. Far beyond simply inspiring people to work for the messianic age, hope, properly defined, offers an account of the relationship between the present and the future and of the implications of that relationship for social change. Furthermore, hope is the chief "proof" that Fromm offers for the attainability of the messianic age: it is only from the standpoint of hope that the possibility of the messianic age becomes visible. Hope stems not from a scientific conclusion but from an act of faith. Holding in tension a confident faith in the future with the urgent need for action, hope is paradoxical. Although hope is not based upon empirical calculations of probability, according to Fromm, it is ultimately the most "realistic" approach to political problems, because it expresses something central to human life itself and reveals the potential latent in the present.

This chapter focuses upon Fromm's *definition* of hope and his philosophical *justification* for hope. The chapter begins by addressing Fromm's negative definition of hope—the three things "hope is not"—followed by his intentionally terse positive definition of hope. A careful explication of Fromm's *The Revolution of Hope: Towards a Humanized Technology* (1968) forms the substance of the definitional work. Following this definitional work, I discuss the philosophical basis for hope in Fromm's thought, beginning with his more moderate, early account of hope grounded on a distinction between "existential dichotomies" and "historical contradictions," and then addressing the more radical account of hope he developed later, in the 1960s. Throughout Fromm's career, his defense of hope is grounded upon humanism. Hope springs from faith in human nature and in the future; it is not a conclusion inferred from empirical data. Drawing on Gabriel Marcel, who may have influenced Fromm's work on hope, I then distinguish between the philosophical *justification* for hope and the phenomenological *experience* of hope. Hope is not experienced as an object of the will but rather as the only possible response to human suffering, or sometimes as a gift from something beyond the self. The standpoint of hope provides access to truths not accessible without first adopting the position of hope.

3.1 WHAT HOPE IS NOT

At first approach to the topic, one might propose to define hope simply as a desire or wish for something combined with the expectation of obtaining it. This definition seems to accord with the way that hope is often spoken of in ordinary discourse (e.g., "I hope I remembered to roll up the car windows before it started to rain.").

But this definition also appears to be inadequate as a philosophical definition of hope. Although a broad historical overview is not possible here, one notes that philosophers as diverse as Saint Thomas Aquinas, Immanuel Kant, and John Dewey would have been dissatisfied with this definition. For Aquinas, for example, an optimistic desire would not qualify as hope unless it were also grounded upon confident faith (not mere optimism) in the future attainment of its object and unless the object of desire were truly worthy of being desired. The object of hope would have to be essentially directed to the proper *telos* of human life, the state of blessedness that can only be bestowed by God (Mittelman 51). For Aquinas, the object of hope must *actually* be attainable, not merely believed to be so; there is no hoping for the impossible. (One recalls Dante's depiction of hell: "Abandon hope, all ye who enter here.")

Immanuel Kant and John Dewey also rejected the ordinary, everyday definition of hope (desire plus expectation of obtaining its object). In Kant's essay "On the Common Saying, 'This May be True in Theory, but it Does Not Apply in Practice,'" Kant argues that one has a duty to seek to improve the world for future generations and to ensure that this duty itself is passed on to future generations (Kant 306). Hope is a prerequisite for fulfilling these obligations; therefore, hope for Kant is not merely an expectant or optimistic wish, but an engine of socio-political action. John Dewey, in turn, stressed that hope includes the "belief in the realizability of good," a good which "can never be demonstrated to the [senses], nor proved by calculations of personal profit" (Fishman and McCarthy 19). This definition of hope therefore restricts hope's possible objects—for Dewey, one cannot hope for just anything that one might expect to receive, but only for that which is good and only without being driven solely by self-interest (19). Gabriel Marcel, as we shall see shortly, also offers a definition hope that challenges the colloquial definition of hope as desire plus expectation. Like Aquinas, Kant, Dewey, and Marcel, Fromm sees hope as more than desire plus expectation. Although he begins by explaining that a mere desire is not hope, which might lead one to believe that the only other needed element is expectation, it becomes clear that hope for Fromm is a much more complicated affair.

Fromm's discussion of hope rests primarily on a negative definition, an account of "what hope is not." He holds that the question of "what hope is not" is easier to answer than the more difficult question of "what hope is," which he suggests can be more adequately addressed through the arts than philosophical treatises (ROH 6, 11). Fromm describes three kinds of non-hope, which tend to give the false appearance of hope. According to Fromm, hope is not (1) mere desiring or wishing, (2) passive and inactive waiting (for future salvation, fulfillment, revolution, etc.), nor (3) "forcing...what cannot be forced," or "forcing the Messiah." The first two can be explained fairly briefly, while the third requires a longer exegesis, since Fromm draws from a specific debate about "forcing the Messiah," the context of which must be explained.

1. Hope is Not Desire or Wish

There are three reasons that hope cannot be mere desiring or wishing (although Fromm does not list them but discusses them together): (A.) hope requires expectation, which is closely linked to Fromm's idea of "faith" ("paradoxical certainty"), (B.) hope is active, and (C.) only some objects of desire can serve as objects of hope.

(A.) Fromm uses the term "faith" to describe the expectation of the achievement of hope's object. "Faith" for Fromm is not propositional, and it is not a scientific hypothesis concerning future events. Rather, it is a "paradoxical certainty" regarding the future achievement of the desired object. Desire can exist without such faith. Fromm employs the term "faith" to describe much more than what is usually associated with specifically "religious" faith. Not surprisingly considering his warnings against idolatry,[1] Fromm's definition of faith is mainly negative and avoids linking faith to any slogan or formula that could become an idol. (Even his account of religious experience he denotes with a mere "X," too cautious to assign it a name [YSB 58].) Fromm consciously limits his discussion of faith, writing, "Can one say more about the practice of faith? Someone else might; if I were a poet or a preacher, I might try. But since I am not either of these, I cannot even try to say more…" (AL 128). However, Fromm does offer us the following rather limited definition of faith:

> [Hope] is closely linked with another element of the structure of life: faith. Faith is not a weak form of belief or knowledge; it is not faith in this or that; faith is the conviction about the not yet proven, the knowledge of the real possibility, the awareness of pregnancy. Faith is rational when it refers to the knowledge of the real yet unborn; it is based on the faculty of knowledge and comprehension, which penetrates the surface and sees the kernel. Faith, like hope, is not prediction of the future; it is the vision of the present in a state of pregnancy. (ROH 13, italics Fromm's)

While not propositional, faith is both "knowledge" and "vision"; it beholds the seeds of potential planted in the present.

That hope requires faith suggests that the object of hope must be attainable and that the person who hopes must know that it is attainable. One may certainly desire the unattainable, or daydream about various odd things that would be nice—the ability to fly like an eagle or swim like an octopus—but desire or dreaming are not a sufficient condition for the attainment of what one desires. Yet even when one desires something that is both attainable and worthwhile—for example, if one desires to end global starvation—one is not hopeful if one does not believe that the object of one's desire is attainable. If one simply gives up—"Well, the problem of global starvation can never be solved, because too much power rests in the hands of global corporations and banks"—then one lacks hope, even if one simultaneously agrees that, for example, "It would be desirable to end global starvation. I wish that we could."

117

(B.) A second reason that hope cannot be mere desiring or wishing is that hope requires "activeness" aimed at bringing about its object. In fact, the activeness of hope is the reason why Fromm is wary of associating hope with "waiting," as we shall see in the following section ("Hope is not passivity or inactivity"). For now it suffices to note that the person who desires or wishes may in fact be completely inactive, and whether a person takes action on behalf of her desires has much more to do with whether she is hopeful than with the strength of her desires. One only has to consider the example of unrequited love for it to be quite evident that strong desire can coexist with inactivity and the absence of hope.

(C.) A final reason that hope cannot be reduced to mere desiring or wishing concerns the content of hope. Unlike mere desiring or wishing, which can have any object, hope is not indifferent to content. One reason has already been offered: if hope requires expectation (paradoxical certainty, faith), then it follows that the object of hope must be seen as attainable. (For example, one must believe that it is possible to end global starvation in order to be "hopeful" about doing so.) Nor is it sufficient for hope if a person erroneously believes, with great strength of conviction but ignoring all the evidence to the contrary, that an unattainable object is attainable. There must be at least some possibility (even if the probability is low) of actually achieving the object of hope. The grieving mother who witnessed her child's death yet retreats into denial, insisting that the child has not died and can still be saved, is not thereby "hopeful" when she arms herself and sets out fearlessly to rescue her already-dead child from its attackers. As will become apparent in later sections of this chapter (on "forcing the Messiah" and "grounds for hope"), although hope is not based upon a scientific calculation of probable outcomes, hope must maintain a degree of contact with present reality. Far from being a naïve, dreamy optimism that turns its eyes away from the harsh reality of human failure, hope looks reality in the face and beholds it with greater accuracy than the cynical despair that claims to be wise to the ways of the world. Hope, not cynicism, is the true "realism" for Fromm. Objects of hope are humanly achievable.

The content of hope must be specified further: even achievable objects of desire are not necessarily objects of hope. Some achievable objects of desire contradict the nature of hope (e.g., a desire for the destruction of the human race) or are simply too trivial to be objects of hope (e.g., a desire for an iPhone). In the former case, the desire for the destruction of humanity is not hopeful because hope is always connected with love of life. In fact, as we shall see, Fromm holds that all living things are at least unconsciously hopeful, while he identifies hope's opposite, despair, with hatred of life. The reasons why Fromm connects hope with life will be explored subsequently, in the section on Fromm's positive definition of hope. In the latter case (the desire for an iPhone), Fromm rejects consumerist desires as contrary to hope because, despite the fact that it involves being "busy," consumerism is passive, while hope is fundamentally active. The enthusiastic consumer of commodities wants to "drink in" the world rather than transform it. She misconceives supreme happiness or "heaven" as a world in which one may consume anything that one wants, rather than the experience of creativity and of being in relationship with others (Mike Wallace Interview).

Although hope can be expressed in ordinary, everyday activities, according to Fromm, hope is directed towards a goal that is central to human life, not to just any particular, everyday goal. A particularly useful example of this can be drawn from existentialist philosopher Gabriel Marcel, who offers a similar account of the proper content of hope in his essay "Sketch of a Phenomenology and a Metaphysic of Hope" in *Homo Viator*. According to Marcel as well as Fromm, hope is not indifferent to content (Marcel 29). For example, Marcel suggests that only a "diluted" kind of hope is expressed in the statement, "I hope that James will arrive in time for lunch to-morrow and not just in the afternoon." Even if "I should like to have James with me for as long as possible," and "I have reason to think that what I want will come about: I know that he does not intend to return to his office and could therefore catch an early train, etc.," this is not hope in the highest sense of the term. Hope is more than just "a wish and a certain belief" (the conventional definition of hope, which both Fromm and Marcel contest) (29). Hope can have as its object only that which must be, by its very nature, the object of hope. Such necessity does not adhere to the desire for James's arrival. Whether or not one desires James's punctual arrival is contingent on various factors. If one needed some extra time to clean up the kitchen, for example, or if one knew that James is just the sort of person who is always late, then one would not "hope" for him to arrive on time. The case of James arriving early or late differs, however, from the hope for salvation or the hope for liberation from a state of fundamental "captivity." While it makes equal sense to "hope" that James arrive late or on time, it does not make sense to hope that one will not be saved or that one will not be liberated. Marcel writes:

> The "I hope" in all its strength is directed towards salvation. It really is a matter of my coming out of a darkness in which I am at present plunged, and which may be the darkness of illness, of separation, exile or slavery. It is obviously impossible in such cases to separate the "I hope" from a certain type of situation of which it is really a part. Hope is situated within the framework of the trial, not only corresponding to it, but constituting our being's veritable *response*. (30)

Hope comes into the darkness of human suffering to offer the light of another possibility.

Although Fromm might disagree that hope must always be a response to acute suffering—in fact, Marcel qualifies this claim later in the essay, linking hope to the fundamental human desires to create and to love, a connection Fromm also draws—Fromm would agree with Marcel that hope's object must be central to the human condition, not a contingent desire, such as a desire for James to arrive early or late (Marcel 57-8, 66). (If one wishes to push the example, of course, one can imagine a situation in which James arriving on time to lunch would be at the very center of one's hope—if, for example, James will arrive bearing with him a letter of pardon from the governor, sparing my sister from her imminent execution for a crime of which she is innocent and I am guilty. However, Marcel means to point to a boring, everyday wish: "lunch" is usually a pretty mundane affair.) Later, we will see that Fromm links hope to life (as does Marcel, incidentally) and even goes so far as to equate hopelessness with death; hope is so fundamental a component of human experience that despair (hope's opposite) stands in opposition to human life itself (67).

A large portion of Fromm's definition of hope has now been articulated in the process of explaining why hope cannot be mere desire or wish. We have established that, according to Fromm, hope must be coupled with faith, the object of hope must be attainable, and the object of hope can neither be trivial nor contradictory to life itself. However, even the confident expectation of the future attainment of some lofty object of desire ("fuller life," "liberation," "salvation," "revolution") is insufficient for hope, according to Fromm, if this confident expectation does not lead to *action*. The claim that hope is active (or, more precisely, the claim that hope is *not inactive*) is one of the three central components of Fromm's negative definition of hope, and as such, it requires a lengthier explication.

2.   Hope is not Passivity or Inactivity

The second part of Fromm's three-part negative definition of hope is that hope is not passive, inactive waiting (ROH 6). *True hope actively seeks to bring its goals into reality* (6). Although hope's "activeness" need not be frantically busy—in fact, it might not even look active to those who imagine "activity" as frantic consumption or paid labor—hope's orientation towards the world is one of involvement and transformation. Through its alliance with activity, hope expresses something fundamental to human nature. Fromm's socialist humanism seeks to liberate humanity for a fuller, freer expression of activeness. In contrast to Herbert Marcuse's charge that Fromm was advancing the "performance principle" of capitalist society, I argue that Fromm's understanding of hope's activeness is a radical challenge to capitalist profit-making "efficiency."

Passive waiting, by contrast with true, active hope, can become a "cover for resignation," "mere ideology," or even idolatry of history or progress, in which history and progress become gods to which humans submit rather than realities that they actively shape (ROH 6). (Here Fromm references Marx's adage, "History is nothing and does nothing. It is man who is and does" [8].) As mentioned in Chapter 1, according to Fromm's account, ideology and idolatry render living things dead and easily administrable, but in the process, ideology and idolatry become purely cerebral and renounce affective ties to the ends they seek. The cold, "scientific" prediction of a coming international revolution in Soviet ideology was detached from any actual hope of building an international socialist movement. If one accepts historical determinism, one need only wait passively for history to do its work. This passive waiting is antithetical to hope, according to Fromm.

Passive "hope" is dangerous. Even when the hoped-for event presents itself as a very real possibility—when, one might say, the revolution is imminent—the person who has cultivated a false, passive form of hope may, like the man in Kafka's parable of the gatekeeper in *The Trial*, be unable to seize the opportunity and take action (ROH 6-7). In Kafka's parable, the main character seeks entrance into "the Law," the object of his hope, but instead of entering the gate by simply shoving aside the gatekeeper, he spends his life submitting to his bureaucratic commands and waiting to be allowed in, until at last he is too old and tired to disobey the gatekeeper's orders, to fight him if necessary, and to obtain entrance. Similarly, Fromm offers this tale:

> [A] man, trapped in a fire, stands at the window of his room and shouts for help, forgetting entirely that no one can hear him and that he could still escape by the staircase which will also be aflame in a few minutes. He shouts because he wants to be saved—and yet it will end in complete catastrophe. (EF 175)

This example is from Fromm's first published book, on the psychological allure of fascism to those seeking to submit to leaders (*Escape from Freedom*). The person who has the ability to rescue herself may not do so if her attention is fixed upon the expectation of a salvation that will come from outside, from external forces or authorities.

Although Fromm states that hope requires "activeness," he is quick to clarify that not all activities qualify as the "activeness" he advocates. The contemporary consumerist trend-follower, for example, as she busily fills her shopping cart, is not "hopeful." While people in our society often appear to be "busy," that does not mean that they practice "activeness." He writes,

> Our whole culture is geared to activity—activity in the sense of being busy, and being busy in the sense of busyness (the busyness necessary for business). In fact, most people are so "active" that they cannot stand doing nothing; they even transform their leisure time into another form of activity. (ROH 12)[2]

Thus, although hope cannot be passive and inactive, hope need not look frantically busy either, like the harried shopper.

Nor must activeness be miserable toil. Here is where Fromm is able to respond to Marcuse's "performance principle" critique. Indeed, the truly "active" person, in Fromm's sense of the term, despises exploitation and would be useless to many employers. In *Man for Himself* (1947), he explains that true productivity or activeness, which is central to human nature, can run up against a society's established division of labor:

> The statement that productiveness is an intrinsic human faculty contradicts the idea that man is lazy by nature and that he has to be forced to be active. This assumption is an old one. When Moses asked Pharaoh to let the Jewish people go so that they might "serve God in the desert," his answer was: "You are lazy,

nothing but lazy." To Pharaoh, slave labor means doing things; worshipping God means laziness. The same idea was adopted by all those who wanted to profit from the activity of others and had no use for productiveness, which they could not exploit. (MFH 106)

Here Fromm suggests that his concept of activity or productiveness is one that inherently makes exploitation impossible. One imagines how "useless," from the point of view of the employer, a factory worker becomes, if a new-found love of contemplation leads her to become less focused upon her work. Similarly, Fromm's thought on the radicalism of the Jewish Sabbath ritual emphasizes that the Jewish Sabbath is a time of "activity" despite its appearance of calm. Giving people a day off from work every week hardly seems advantageous for a capitalist who wishes to exploit workers to the fullest possible extent, and as long as there is a "reserve army of the unemployed," one can easily find new workers when the old ones wear out through overwork. (The modern first-world weekend was a product of workers' agitation, not of the capitalist quest for efficiency.) Yet even if the Sabbath appears as laziness or inefficiency to the employer, it is not experienced by the practitioner as a time of passivity.

Fromm's point is that activeness flourishes in a state of human freedom. This is in contradistinction with Herbert Marcuse's later claim, in the epilogue to *Eros and Civilization*, that Fromm's concept of productivity contributed to the "performance principle" of capitalist society (*Eros and Civilization* 242, 259). According to Marcuse, Fromm's conception of human nature was not "explosive" of the current order but rather encouraged "adjustment," by not challenging the values of capitalist society. A point that Marcuse glosses over in this discussion, however, is that pre-capitalist ideas can take on radical implications within a capitalist system. By employing pre-capitalist concepts, Fromm presents the inadequacies and contingency of capitalist arrangements.

In claiming that human beings are naturally productive, Fromm is not admonishing the working class to keep its nose to the grindstone. Rather, he emphasizes that leisure time (which socialist humanists like Fromm hope to increase) need not be a time of mere recuperation from the strain of labor, as it so often is. Under capitalism, Marx argues in his early writings, leisure becomes a time for satisfaction only of our most brutish, least human needs ("eating, drinking, and procreating"), while our uniquely human activities are stunted by alienation (MCM 82). Although Fromm's debate with Marcuse in *Dissent* magazine and in the pages of *Eros and Civilization* and *The Art of Loving* preceded Fromm's later study of Marx's 1844 *Manuscripts*, Fromm would at least have known Marx's famous remark in *The German Ideology*. There, envisioning a future in which human flourishing would be its own end (to paraphrase the *Grundrisse*) and in which abundant leisure time would be filled with a multitude of activities, Marx wrote of a coming society in which it would be "possible for me to do one thing today and another tomorrow, to hunt in the morning, fish in the afternoon, rear cattle in the evening, criticise after dinner, just as I have a mind" (MCM 34).

Fromm remained committed to the view that activeness is central to human nature. Activeness, like the hope upon which it depends, is central to life, and as such, it is open to growth and transformation. In his late work *To Have or To Be?* (1976), Fromm develops his distinction between two orientations towards the world: a "having" orientation, which (like ideology and idolatry) fears change and sees the world as a fixed thing that can be possessed, and a "being" orientation, which identifies being with becoming and with "*process, activity, and movement*" (TB 21; Fromm's italics). Arguing that humans are by nature active as opposed to lazy and passive, Fromm clarifies his concept of activity through the work of Aristotle, Aquinas, the author of *The Cloud of Unknowing*, Meister Eckhart, Spinoza, Marx, and Albert Schweitzer, demonstrating that "activity" for each included contemplation or rational thought (75-9, 81). Spinoza, especially, seems to have been significant to Fromm's concept of activeness and the priority that Fromm places on activity over passivity. In *The Art of Loving*, for example, Fromm draws upon Spinoza's *Ethics* to define activity as "inner freedom and independence" from control by the passions and to emphasize that activity can include thought and need not be limited to those events that change external reality (AL 21-2).

As we have seen, the second component of Fromm's negative definition of hope—hope is not passivity or inactivity—demonstrates that hope is not merely a combination of a noble desire and the expectation of success. Rather, hope is *actively engaged* in bringing to fruition the object of its hope. Although hope is active, it is not necessarily "busy." Fromm differentiates the activeness of hope from consumerism and immiserating toil. Rather, activeness is central to human nature; far from being an admonition to obedience, it expresses joy at the basic desire for free use of human power. A final dimension of Fromm's negative definition of hope remains to be addressed—the one that is the most overtly political in its implications and fills an important gap in our discussion of hope thus far, by addressing the relationship of hope to time. This final dimension is Fromm's assertion that hope does not attempt to "force the Messiah."

3. Hope Does not Attempt to Force the Messiah

The third and final component of Fromm's negative definition is that hope does not "force what cannot be forced," or "force the Messiah"—a complicated and historically situated concern that will require careful explication (ROH 8). As Fromm points out, the Jewish Talmudic tradition warns against "forcing the Messiah," which usually takes the form of attempting to calculate the date of the Messiah's arrival or announcing that the Messiah has come (YSB 153). The prohibition upon announcing the Messiah's arrival traditionally precludes proclaiming oneself or another individual to be the Messiah, and it precludes destructive action aimed at pressuring God to intervene into the world to save it.

Although the previous section, stressing hope's "activeness," might lead us to think that hope is fundamentally impatient, in a hurry to "get out there and make

123

it happen," this is only partly the case. Recall that hope retains contact with reality and does not desire the impossible. Hope is impatient in the sense that it does not postpone action out of the belief that human action is unnecessary. But hope is also patient, in the sense that it is always tempered by the limits presented by reality. To "force the Messiah" is essentially to fail to acknowledge reality and to try to institute the messianic age (the object of hope) before it is possible to do so.

According to Fromm, hope is a paradoxical combination of patience and impatience. The *impatience* of hope pushes the hopeful to act and presents the situation as urgent, yet hope's *patience* ensures that hope remains in harmony with reason and does not attempt to force the impossible. Following this same theme, Fromm refers to two conflicting trends within the socialist movement—a tendency to (impatiently) believe that "the new Socialist society, a new age for humankind, will be achieved now" (or has already been achieved) and a tendency towards "endless patience based on a scientific [prediction] of how things had to be" (PN 74-5). According to Fromm, both of these currents were mistaken. The proper standpoint (a dialectical synthesis of the two) could be found in the "Messianic paradox, by which I mean patient and impatient at the same time" (75).

In one of Fromm's essays on psychoanalytic practice, he compellingly describes the tension between hope's patience and impatience in a discussion of the psychoanalyst's hope for the cure of a client. There he calls hope a kind of "patience-impatience," a concept drawn from Talmudic literature (Fromm, "Being Centrally" 11). To be a human being, he argues, is to be constituted by paradox, which includes the paradox of being a fundamentally unique individual while also fundamentally lacking individuality and uniqueness, through being formed by and influenced by society (10-11). With regard to time, he then states, the proper human attitude is also one of paradox—that of "patience-impatience" (11). In the case of the psychoanalyst, this means that the recognition that the patient could "wake up" and become psychologically liberated at any moment must be held in tension with the knowledge that it will probably take many years for the patient to achieve this. This two-sided approach to the patient enables the psychoanalyst to avoid despair when the patient is not cured quickly but also keeps open the possibility of change in the patient, rather than blocking it through conveying to the patient a sense that the cure is impossible or will be long delayed (11). Fromm is acutely aware that the concept of "patience-impatience" in the Talmudic tradition concerned the proper attitude towards the coming of the Messiah. According to Jewish tradition, one must be "prepared every moment" for the coming of the Messiah, but one also knows that "it may happen now or in thousands of years" (11).

Although it is an exhortation to a certain kind of patience, the prohibition of "forcing the Messiah" is not, in Fromm's view, an admonition to be submissive to divine authority. Jewish tradition is in favor of forcefully confronting God, as Fromm points out. He even references a Hasidic tale that illustrates a narrow sense in which it is permissible to "force" the Messiah: A man informs a rabbi that he had bargained with God that if God would forgive him for his own, minor sins, he would in turn forgive God, whom, he charges, "[has] separated mothers from children and permitted people to starve" (YSB 152; PR 47). The rabbi responds that the man was foolish to demand so little and should instead have forced God to send the Messiah (PR 48). Fromm clearly likes this story; it illustrates the non-authoritarian religious attitude that he prefers to the authoritarian one. He sees the heart of the Jewish tradition as anti-authoritarian, which he frequently contrasts with the authoritarianism of Lutheranism and Calvinism. According to Fromm, the story of the Hasidic rabbi demonstrates that, "If God fails to put an end to the suffering of man as he has promised, man has the right to challenge him, in fact to force him to fulfill his promise" (48). Here "forcing" God to send the Messiah means something like "commanding" or "being pushy" with God, not issuing elliptical, gnostic or occult predictions, nor instigating catastrophes that would pressure the populace to change quickly—practices that are among the chief targets of Fromm's critique of "forcing the Messiah." Although God is generally considered sufficiently powerful to resist human commands, far from smiting pushy people, God does not seem to mind being commanded. The Old Testament is full of prophets who argue with God and speak to God in a demanding way, as Fromm was definitely well aware. It is not necessarily irreverent to "call" God out on God's failure to intervene in the world to stop injustice. A demanding prayer made to God is quite different from claiming gnosis about God's coming, claiming that the Messiah has already arrived, when in fact it has not—if one looks about, it should be evident that a world of justice and peace has yet to be attained—or attempting to force God to send the Messiah through nihilistic action.

The concept of "forcing the Messiah" plays a multitude of roles in Fromm's thought, as a critique of fascism, Zionism, Stalinism, the psychoanalytic movement, and some 1960s first-world revolutionists. Forcing the Messiah "was the attitude of the false Messiahs and the *Putsch* leaders, who had contempt for those who did not under all circumstances prefer death to defeat," Fromm writes (ROH 8). This is a political critique on Fromm's part, no doubt including a critique of fascism's attempt to make leaders and nations into Messiahs, as the reference to the Beer Hall *Putsch* clearly implies. More interestingly, the critique of "forcing the Messiah" applied also to left politics, including Soviet Communism's attempts to make leaders or the Party into Messiahs and its claim to have created "real, existing socialism" (a false/idolatrous image of the messianic age, in Fromm's sense of "idolatry"). (It is not surprising that the Soviet Union was referred to by Cold Warriors as "the God that failed.") It was also a critique of certain anarchist or Blanquist strategies of small-group sabotage, i.e., trying to force revolutionary change without building a movement and winning the support and involvement of the masses. Furthermore, Fromm employed the critique of forcing the Messiah as a critique of Zionism, as we shall see, and even of Freud's psychoanalytic movement in *Sigmund Freud's Mission*, which stresses Freud's peculiarly authoritarian pleasure in molding his students into loyal followers and discusses his creation of a quasi-political, secretive psychoanalytic "International" at the head of which he was to be a kind of Messiah-figure, a new "Moses."

Why would Fromm employ such an archaic concept as "forcing the Messiah" to critique contemporary political and social movements? The answer begins with Fromm's adamant opposition to Gershom Scholem's catastrophic messianism, along with Scholem's peculiar fascination with the enigmatic seventeenth century false Messiah Sabbatai Zevi. In Fromm's "radical interpretation of the Old Testament," *You Shall Be as Gods*, he offers a brief history of some messianic figures in Jewish history, from Bar Kochba in the second century to Jacob Frank in the eighteenth (YSB 143, 147). Among those he discusses is Zevi, the subject of Scholem's famous biography. Scholem and others celebrated the Sabbatean (Zevi's) movement's doctrine of "redemption through sin," i.e., that in order to save humanity, Zevi had to descend to the lowest level of human life through infidelity to his faith. The doctrine of redemption through sin was popularized in the 1910s and 1920s, as the German Jewish left gradually shifted its allegiance from the ideals of *Aufklärung* to the new, apocalyptic vision of a transcendent intervention into history. Since this change was perceived to be a product of extra-human, extra-mundane forces, redemption through sin held appeal as a metaphor for the coming revolutionary upheaval. The dream was that one could force the messianic age to arrive through antinomian practices, i.e., through dramatic disruption of established society—as seen in the thought of Gershom Scholem, Walter Benjamin, and Ernst Bloch in his more apocalyptic moments—or through the ritualistic violation of social norms as seen in Stefan George and Ludwig Klages's Cosmic Circle. In Chapter 2, we noted how such practices became characteristic of the new messianic radicalism that abandoned Cohen's messianic radicalism in favor of apocalypticism.

Fromm's *You Shall Be as Gods* is largely a response to Gershom Scholem, though not explicitly. As we saw in Chapter 1, Fromm saw both Scholem and Zevi as exemplars of a catastrophic messianism, so it would not be surprising if Fromm's critique of Zevi and "forcing the Messiah" were also a critique of Scholem. *You Shall Be as Gods* is in large part an argument for the legitimacy of prophetic messianism against the view of Scholem and others that Jewish messianism is fundamentally apocalyptic and catastrophic. Several pages are devoted merely to refuting Scholem's claim that Hasidism (which Fromm likes) was not messianic. And although Fromm does not say so in *You Shall Be as Gods*, he would certainly have known that Scholem had published his massive, definitive biography of Zevi several years earlier. In Fromm's mind, Scholem's insistence upon catastrophic messianism would have been seen as an endorsement of forcing the Messiah and of the doctrine of redemption through sin, since catastrophic messianism left only nihilistic antinomianism as a course of rebellious action.

Fromm's critique of "forcing the Messiah" was no doubt also an adamant denunciation of the Messiah-figures of the lost generation, from Stefan George to Oskar Goldberg, Rudolf Steiner to Martin Heidegger, and of their admiring, often uncritical followers. The catastrophic/apocalyptic exaltation of Messiah-figures penetrated political theory and eventually, at the hands of Nazi legal theorist Carl Schmitt, was employed as an endorsement of Hitler's rule. In the absence of the

Enlightenment ideals of reason, progress, and education of the masses, Schmitt's voluntarist "decisionism" seemed to be the only alternative to passive inactivity. Later, decisionist apocalypticism was employed within the Zionist movement, as it slowly abandoned its early, utopian anarchist vision and moved towards support for a powerful military state. Jacob Taubes, then in Jerusalem, emerged as an advocate of the turn to decisionist apocalypticism. As Nitzan Lebovic explains, describing Taubes in a compelling article on this topic (which includes a discussion of Buber's and Scholem's growing hesitancy about apocalyptic messianism in the face of its adoption by the far right of the Israeli settler movement):

> Against the passive hope of those confronting the end of the world, Taubes emphasized in 1947 the need for an immediate decision: the time for a Buberian "veiled choice" had passed. Taubes had in mind a Schmittian operation from within the destructive situation: it involved using and abusing destruction as a tool, acknowledging its inevitability. The apocalypse, he argued, entailed "a form-destroying and a forming power...If the demonic, destructive element is missing, the petrified order, the prevailing positivity of the world cannot be overcome." (Lebovic, "The Jerusalem School" 106-7)

The influence of apocalyptic messianism on Israeli politics would not have been lost on Fromm. Beginning in the late 1920s, Fromm considered Zionism an abandonment of Jewish principles and an attempt to force the Messiah, a nationalist movement with a false, idolatrous image of the messianic age. By 1966, when he was writing *You Shall Be as Gods*, the early, anarchist-utopian ideals of the Zionist movement played a minimal role in guiding Israeli politics. In a sympathetic, almost pleading tone, Fromm writes, "even one of the greatest humanists among the sages, [Rabbi] Akiba, could not withstand the seduction of the false hope" (YSB 153). He wrote this knowing that he was writing for close friends like Ernst Simon, then in Israel, trying to convince them to redirect their political efforts and change their allegiance (Funk, *Life and Ideas* 39; Lundgren).

Fromm's critique of "forcing the Messiah" was also a warning to the left in the United States and Europe, where he worried about the rise of a destructive left-wing "nihilism." Fromm suggests that, in the context of politics, the hopelessness that leads to forcing the Messiah is characterized by "phrase making and adventurism" and "disregard for reality" (ROH 8). He writes that such hopelessness is rapidly becoming characteristic of his time (8).

In a 1968 note for the Eugene McCarthy presidential campaign, possibly intended as a campaign speech, Fromm warned of what he called the "Maoist alternative" in the U.S. left:[3]

> This [Maoist] alternative proceeds from the premise that the system is moving towards catastrophe, and that no reform of any kind can change this course. The only chance for avoiding the catastrophe is a change of the system itself, and this change can occur only through revolution on an international scale,

meaning that when all the underdeveloped countries turn against the industrial countries, and particularly their leader—the United States—they will be able to overthrow the system, just as the Chinese peasants overthrew their rulers in the cities. (OBH 53)

What Fromm objects to is not the proposal for international revolution but the pathologically self-destructive and nihilistic desire of the young "Maoists," including their desire that their own country (implicitly, themselves) be destroyed by revolutionists from the outside. Their aim was not really to create a more just society but to see their own society obliterated in an act of gloriously destructive, aesthetic, cosmic justice. As we saw in Chapter 2, the exaltation of the aesthetics of violence, so frequently identified with fascism, appears also in thinkers identified with the left, including Walter Benjamin, Gershom Scholem, and Georges Sorel.

Not long after the publication of *The Revolution of Hope*, groups such as the Weather Underground in the United States and the RAF/Baader-Meinhof in Germany arose, attempting to "force" a revolution without building a mass movement. The Baader-Meinhof's explicit goal was to "reveal" the truly destructive, fascistic power of the state by forcing the state to employ violence against them. In 1976 Fromm turned down an invitation to testify for the defense in the trial against the Baader-Meinhof in Germany, and in *To Have or To Be?*, published that same year, he was critical of such terroristic impulses (TB 62, 85).

At the request of their lawyers, Jean-Paul Sartre had agreed to meet with the Baader-Meinhof in prison. He denounced the conditions of their imprisonment and portrayed them as martyrs, giving a quick boost to their public image. However, the lawyers still needed the support of a public figure like Fromm, whose German Jewish background and psychoanalytic training made him a prime candidate for a persuasive expert witness for the defense in the trial of the Baader-Meinhof (Fedderson). Knowing that his appearance as witness for the Baader-Meinhof could be taken as an endorsement of their tactics, Fromm brusquely declined (Fedderson). He wrote in reply to the lawyers:

> I very much appreciate your wish—that is, the wish of the accused—to meet with you and Frau X. But I must confess that I am rather astonished that the accused wish to have this meeting, since they must know my work. I would have thought that my political beliefs would be repellent to them, the same way theirs are to me. To put it bluntly, I am completely against your strategy and tactics, which I view as totally repulsive—both politically and humanly. (Vickrey 1)

Adding that he personally opposed solitary confinement, Fromm stated that he nevertheless could not denounce it as "torture" per the lawyers' request (Fedderson).

Fromm believed that the Baader-Meinhof's tactics were emblematic of a problematic despair that afflicted much of the left. Warning that despair can lead to both self-destructiveness and violence towards others, he had written of Ulrike Meinhof a year earlier:

WHAT HOPE ISN'T AND IS

It is often the case that people who have lost the capacity to love replace this inability with the thought of sacrificing their own life, and then take this self-sacrifice as some kind of proof that they can indeed love. In some cases terror is the only escape from a completely hopeless and desperate situation. (Vickrey 1-2)

Fromm's analysis appears to be borne out by Meinhof's suicide and the subsequent suicides of the other leaders of the organization (2).

In *The Revolution of Hope*, Fromm had written, foreshadowing his later concern with the RAF's desperation and destructiveness:

In these days, this pseudo-radical disguise of hopelessness and nihilism is not rare among some of the most dedicated members of the young generation. They are appealing in their boldness and dedication but they become unconvincing by their lack of realism, sense of strategy, and, in some, by lack of love for life. (ROH 8)

The desperate, nihilistic side of the left critiqued by Fromm failed to account for reality; they despaired in many cases because they expected the world to accord too quickly with their vision for it, without taking the necessary steps between the present and the future. According to Fromm in *The Revolution of Hope*, Herbert Marcuse had fallen prey to a similarly reality-disregarding, false-messianic hope, adding in a footnote after the above passage, "Such hopelessness shines through Herbert Marcuse's *Eros and Civilization* and *One-Dimensional Man*" (8). He then quotes from Marcuse's conclusion to *One-Dimensional Man*:

The critical theory of society possesses no concepts which could bridge the gap between the present and its future; holding no promise and showing no success, it remains negative. Thus it wants to remain loyal to those who, without hope, have given and give their life to the Great Refusal.

Fromm replies to this passage:

These quotations show how wrong those are who attack or admire Marcuse as a revolutionary leader; for revolution was never based on hopelessness, nor can it ever be. But Marcuse is not even concerned with politics; for if one is not concerned with steps between the present and the future, one does not deal with politics, radical or otherwise. Marcuse is essentially an example of an alienated intellectual, who presents his personal despair as a theory of radicalism... This is not the place to show in detail that it is a naïve, cerebral daydream, essentially irrational, unrealistic, and lacking love of life. (ROH 8-9)

Despite Fromm's uncharitable tone, these statements are more than a mere *ad hominem* jab. Fromm's *Revolution of Hope* is largely a reply to Marcuse's *One-Dimensional Man*, even though Marcuse is only discussed in a footnote. *Revolution of Hope* was initially to include a full chapter on Marcuse, but as Fromm explained

129

in a letter to Raya Dunayevskaya, he removed the chapter because he did not want to focus negative attention on Marcuse, because during the summer of 1968 Marcuse had been receiving death threats (Anderson and Rockwell 158, 165n.48).

As a psychoanalyst and social psychologist, Fromm attempted to diagnose pathologies that he observed in society at large, especially in certain sectors of the left. There is some important truth in the claim that the attempt to "force what cannot be forced" had become prevalent on the left at the time (the late 60s), and there certainly was a climate of despair and a lack of life-lovingness in the air, which was manifested not only in the behavior of organizations but in the psychological states of individuals. Moreover, Fromm held that Marcuse's Great Refusal was unrealistic as a revolutionary strategy, lacking hope due to its expectation of a revolution that would be fundamentally "explosive" and an apocalyptic end to time, coming from outside the mainstream social order, not a process of planning, emerging from a mass movement. More will follow about this in Chapter 4, however, where I distinguish Fromm's concept of messianism from the prevailing view of radical, messianic thinkers of his time, and I will contrast Marcuse's understanding of the relationship between the present and future with Fromm's.

It is a bit too simplistic to say that Marcuse rejects hope; he merely draws hope from different sources. However, the variation between his sources and Fromm's sources indicates a crucial difference between the two thinkers' conceptions of hope. These sources, in Marcuse at that time, were largely aesthetic and libidinal. (Memory also served as a source of hope for the messianic age in Marcuse's work [e.g., *One-Dimensional Man* 98; *Eros and Civilization* 232-3].) Fromm's concern about the "nihilism" of Marcuse[4] and some of the New Left is related to Fromm's other major criticism of Marcuse, that Marcuse's thought encourages psychological regression to the state of the "satiated baby." The lack of alternatives that Marcuse finds in the present leads him to seek return to a Golden Age of the past, not a Golden Age of early human history or pre-history but within each individual lifetime, an early childhood Golden Age from which surplus repression was absent. Fromm sees Marcuse's Great Refusal as a mere rebellion, not revolutionary, and as a vision of mere "freedom from" (from rules, restrictions, repression) as opposed to "freedom to" (TB 62).[5]

To grasp the implications of Fromm's citation of the conclusion from *One-Dimensional Man*, it must be further noted that Marcuse's book technically concludes not with Marcuse's own words, but with a quote from Walter Benjamin: "It is only for the sake of those without hope that hope is given to us" (257).[6] Although Fromm does not mention Benjamin or include the quote in his footnote about Marcuse, it is likely that Benjamin was also a chief target of the critique. There may have been personal reasons why Fromm never mentions Benjamin in any of his published writings, despite the fact that Benjamin's messianism stands in sharp contrast with his own: Fromm's second wife, Henny Gurland, was among the last people to see Benjamin alive on his final journey through Spain. However, Benjamin was also not widely read in the United States at that time, in comparison with Marcuse.

Fromm's criticism of "forcing the Messiah" thus serves a multitude of purposes: it rejects the claim that the messianic age has already arrived, whether in the form of Soviet Communism or U.S. capitalism, and it warns against empowering Messiah-figures, whether political leaders, intellectuals, artists, or others, to whom the populace submits unquestioningly. It also, however, presents a rather subtle and useful problem for left revolutionary strategy: though one must not simply wait around for some "scientifically" foreordained time and objective condition for the revolution, neither may one announce the revolution any time a small group's whims decide. And although a "consensus" should not be defined too rigidly ahead of time, still the readiness and willingness (subjective condition) of the workers must be assessed properly. Fromm's condemnation of "forcing the Messiah" warns against the desire found among some of the young first-world Maoists and the Baader-Meinhof, or the conclusion that Fromm believes Marcuse's apocalyptic orientation forces him to draw, to simply destroy the entire social system through widespread rebellion and disruption, rather than to strategically construct the future by drawing upon the potential of the present.

As we have seen, according to Fromm's *negative* account of hope, hope is neither mere desire, nor passive and inactive waiting, nor destructive or gnostic "forcing of the Messiah." The struggle to attain true hope and avoid falling for illusory versions is for Fromm a necessary part of achieving psychological maturity, even in the hypothetical absence of political situations that tempt us to despair. All adults struggle against the desire to succumb to false hope, because every adult experiences a "shattering of hope" (ROH 20) (or "shattering of faith" [HOM 28]). This shattering of hope often results from the child's discovery of the disingenuousness of those whom she had previously trusted, or it may occur with regard to God, when a child witnesses an injustice she deems incompatible with the existence of a benevolent God (ROH 20; HOM 29). The initial shattering of hope occurs at a young age—four, five, six, or even earlier—yet the final, more complete shattering usually occurs later in life (HOM 29).

As with many of Fromm's key concepts, the shattering of hope describes a phenomenon both in the individual and in society as a whole (e.g., patience-impatience both towards the psychoanalyst's client and towards societal change). He writes:

> In my clinical experience these deep-seated experiences of loss of faith are frequent, and often constitute the most significant *leitmotiv* in the life of a person. The same holds true in life, where leaders in whom one trusted prove to be evil or incompetent. If the reaction is not one of greater independence, it is often one of cynicism or destructiveness. (HOM 30)

Some respond to the shattering by becoming independent and relinquishing their previous dependencies (29). On the other hand, some respond by withdrawal:

> ...the person remains skeptical, hopes for a miracle that will restore his faith, tests people, and when disappointed in turn by them tests still others or throws

himself into the arms of a powerful authority (the Church, or a political party, or a leader) to regain his faith. Often he overcomes his despair at having lost faith in life by a frantic pursuit of worldly aims—money, power, or prestige. (HOM 29-30)

The shattering of hope can be so painful as to cause the individual to seek escape from the world and from consciousness. This occurrence is further elaborated in Fromm's account of the three "mechanisms of escape," which he describes in *Escape from Freedom*: sadomasochism, destructiveness (usually combined with narcissism), and conformity (AHD 233; EF). Sadomasochism enables "the individual to escape his unbearable feeling of aloneness and powerlessness" and to escape freedom through symbiosis with the other (EF 173). "Destructiveness" is also founded upon the desire to overcome separateness, yet it seeks to annihilate its object rather than maintain it as dominator or dominated (202). The individual defends herself through destructiveness when she feels "threatened" or her potentialities are "thwarted," for example by societal norms (204). Destructiveness in particular may result from the shattering of hope:

> Precisely because men cannot live without hope, the one whose hope has been utterly destroyed hates life. Since he cannot create life, he wants to destroy it, which is only a little less of a miracle—but much more easy to accomplish. He wants to avenge himself for his unlived life and he does it by throwing himself into total destructiveness so that it matters little whether he destroys others or is destroyed. (ROH 21)

The third escape, "automaton conformity," seeks to overcome isolation through "withdrawal from the world" or through "inflation of oneself psychologically to such an extent that the outside world becomes small by comparison" (EF 208).[7] In the struggle to get beyond these traps, one requires not only a negative understanding of what hope is not, but also a positive understanding of what hope is.

3.2 WHAT HOPE IS

Although Fromm warns that it is difficult to give a *positive* definition of hope, he offers a brief positive account. His aversion to making positive statements about hope may have stemmed from his concern with "idolatry"; he insists that the experience of hope transcends language and that words may "obscure," "dissect," and "kill" experience (ROH 11). Here he reflects implicit support of the *Bilderverbot*, the Jewish ban on idolatry that influenced Critical Theory. (I return to the *Bilderverbot* in Chapter 4 to show how Fromm differs from Horkheimer and Adorno's take on the imaginability of the messianic future in *The Dialectic of Enlightenment*.)

Fromm's positive definitions of hope may be listed concisely as follows: hope is "a psychic concomitant to life and growth," a "state of being," an "inner readiness" ("to be ready at every moment for that which is not yet born, and yet not to become desperate if there is no birth in our lifetime"), "activeness," and a "mood" accompanying the intellectual act of "faith" (ROH 11-12, 9). Readiness and activity have already been addressed above. I will focus here upon explicating the connections between hope and life, and between hope and faith. I will also discuss the metaphor of pregnancy and birth, which Fromm often employs in his discussion of hope and faith, and which he connects to hope's readiness.

According to Fromm, hope has an *unconscious* component, found in all "life and growth"; even the growth of plants, the dreaming human, or the newborn infant express this component of hope (ROH 13). "When hope has gone life has ended, actually or potentially," he writes (13). There are a number of possible interpretations of this understanding of hope, though the best would probably be via Lawrence Wilde's sober reading of Fromm as an Aristotelian from whose standpoint all living things have a *telos* for which they are striving—thus, to stop striving for this *telos* would be both to die and to abandon hope (*Quest for Solidarity* 39). This Aristotelianism correlates with Fromm's ongoing defense of socialist humanism, according to which socialism would be the full unfolding of human potentiality.

Aristotle, however, is not the sole or even main source of Fromm's assertion of the fundamental "hopefulness" in all living things. It is not surprising, considering Fromm's skepticism concerning the ability of words to accurately describe experience, that Fromm would be drawn towards a more mystical metaphysics that lies outside the bounds of Aristotle's teleology. Although the fundamental dynamism of Fromm's account of hope parallels Aristotle in interesting ways, hope being in touch with life and rejecting *stasis* and the *status quo*, another important influence on Fromm's account of hope and life, one that he directly references, is Spinoza. Spinoza's rationalist pantheism deeply inspired Fromm, who would have viewed it as the Enlightenment alternative to the rise of obscurantist gnosticism in the 1920s (as evidenced in the conflict between pantheism and gnosticism discussed in Benjamin Lazier's *God Interrupted* and noted in Chapter 2). In the fight between the Spinozists and the gnostics of Jacob Taubes's ilk, there is no question that Fromm's allegiance lay with the former.

Also in the background of Fromm's identification of hope with life are some thinkers who were influenced by Spinoza's vision and emphasized more specifically the "life" of reality, of totality-in-process through history and evolution: Henri Bergson (whom Fromm employs in *The Sane Society* and recommends an essay from in *Escape from Freedom*), Pierre Teilhard de Chardin (whom Fromm suggests points the way towards a synthesis of prophetic and apocalyptic/catastrophic messianism), and Richard Maurice Bucke (friend of Walt Whitman and author of *Cosmic Consciousness: A Study in the Evolution of the Human Mind*, which Fromm also cites approvingly) (SS 165; EF 38n9). For these radical thinkers who transcended the chains of scientism and positivism, the natural world was not the nemesis of hope but was imbued with the power to transform. Far from being static or mechanical, the natural world for these thinkers was the silent ally of human progress. Without being theists in the traditional sense (with the possible exception of Teilhard, a Jesuit who was censured by the Vatican), these thinkers believed that there was something at the heart of reality, beyond all data and beyond all calculations (to paraphrase Marcel), that coincided with the good will of humanity. For these thinkers, as for Lukács, Spinoza's *natura naturans* was simultaneously a human and a divine and/or natural process, and human beings had the power to consciously direct it.

For Aristotle, Bergson, and Teilhard, hope was embedded into the structure of human life and was constitutive of the human person. One could even argue that there is such an implicit hope in Spinoza, for whom Fromm writes so much in praise. Although Spinoza warned against the emotion of hope when this meant an emotional attachment to something beyond what reason could know with certainty, Fromm may have seen himself as the heir of a tradition that saw the universe in Spinozist terms as a process of becoming (or naturing, *naturans*), a process of which human beings can become conscious and which they can then direct to their own ends, and it is this *consciousness of reality-in-process* that is so central to Fromm's conception of hope. In German idealism, one finds a similar commitment to this unfolding, most notably in Hegel's conception of *Geist* but also in Fichte's emphasis upon striving and conscious activity (*Tätigkeit*). Thus the hope expressed in the natural world, as articulated above, is present also in the realm of social life.

Hope's connection to faith is tied to hope's connection with life. As discussed earlier, Fromm defines faith as a kind of knowledge and as a "paradoxical certainty" concerning the future attainment of the object of hope. Hope and faith go hand in hand, according to Fromm, and each is "an intrinsic element of the structure of life" (ROH 13). Faith, like hope, also has an unconscious component; this can be disastrous, as in the case of ideology, in which a person's malignant faith is concealed beneath an outward appearance of another faith that really has no meaning for the person but which is simply a set of slogans or platitudes. But true faith, for Fromm, is not mere ideology; rather, true faith reflects reality and does not allow itself to be overpowered by propaganda. True faith is not faith in what is "scientifically predictable" (e.g., the Stalinist's confidence in the coming revolution), nor in what is "impossible" (e.g., the melancholic's conviction that her lost loved one will return). Rather, building upon the distinction between activity and passivity in Spinoza, Fromm asserts that faith is active and creative; it does not passively absorb the beliefs of authority figures or mass society (14).

Fromm also links "fortitude" (courage), a Spinozist concept, to hope (ROH 14). Negatively defined, fortitude's fearlessness stems neither from a desire to die (only a disguised *fear of life*), nor from having a leader to obey (which is only a disguised *fear of disobedience*). Fromm would agree with Aristotle that blind acceptance of all risk without proper precaution is not true courage. Positively defined, fortitude is "the capacity to say 'no' when the world wants to hear 'yes'" (15). It is the "the courage of love" that arises in its fullest form from "enlightenment," from seeing the whole in process and one's place within it (AL 8; ROH 15).

Paradoxically, Fromm says more about hope by saying what it is not than by saying what it is. All the same, his discussion of the connection between hope and the "structure of life" should not be discounted as hippie goofiness or the "neopaganism" that Jürgen Habermas is worried about, despite how odd it may sound to speak of an intrinsic connection between hope and all of life. Standing in the tradition of Lukács and others who drew inspiration from Spinoza's rationalist pantheism, Fromm was taking sides against the "gnostic" trend in radical social thought in favor of a humanistic pantheism that exalts human beings and empowers them to take control of the dynamic process of reality.

3.3 GROUNDS FOR HOPE

In addition to Fromm's positive and negative definitions of hope, along with the individual and sociopolitical consequences of hope, the question remains: upon what *foundation* does hope rest? There are at least two senses in which one may speak of the "foundation" of hope; one might mean the *philosophical justification for hope*, or one might mean the *cause of the individual's hope*. Although there is some overlap between philosophical reasons and individual motivations for hope, the two must not be equated. In this section, I focus upon Fromm's *philosophical justification* for hope, chiefly his optimistic theory of human nature and his account of "faith" as a basis for hope. I trace the development of Fromm's philosophical justification for hope from his earlier work on human nature to his later emphasis on messianic hope, under the influence of Marx's early writings. After exploring Fromm's account of human nature and faith as bases for hope, I conclude the chapter by arguing that the philosophical rationale for hope is quite different from the cause of hope in an individual, i.e., from the basis of hope as experienced, phenomenologically, by the hopeful subject. (I draw heavily from Gabriel Marcel to articulate this distinction.) Although hope can be rationally justified, the subject who hopes does not do so for reasons, but just the reverse—she beholds the reasons for hope only because she already hopes.

Fromm called his philosophy "socialist humanism," and he was firmly committed to grounding his philosophical views upon a conception of human nature. According to Fromm, "the socialist movement...was radical and humanistic," radical in the sense of "going to the roots, and the roots being man; humanistic in the sense that it is man who is the measure of all things, and his full unfolding must be the criterion of all social efforts" (Funk, *Courage* 206). Unlike Soviet Marxism and other left paradigms that have grown popular since, such as Louis Althusser's structuralism and Michel Foucault's post-structuralism, Fromm's Marxism held that society should be grounded upon an understanding of human nature, human needs, and the good life. Lawrence Wilde, a leading scholarly defender of Fromm's socialist humanism, argues that "Fromm is unique among social scientists of the late twentieth century in offering a thoroughly worked-out and well-defended view of human essence as a philosophical grounding for an appeal to solidarity" (*Quest for Solidarity* 4).

One might say that Fromm's major contribution to psychoanalysis was his attempt to offer an account of *psychological health*, as opposed to merely *diagnosing pathologies*. This also points to what may be his chief contribution to Critical

Theory: his commitment to not merely critiquing bourgeois society but presenting alternatives, and not merely describing pathologies but to providing an account of psychological (social) health. While other members of the Frankfurt School tended to confine their work to critiques of existing social conditions, Fromm's messianism offered a positive goal for which to strive: the sane individual (the productive character) and the sane society.

As a Marxist and as a psychoanalyst, Fromm acknowledged that people are influenced by socio-economic structures, biological drives, and other environmental factors, including the accidental characteristics of childhood home life. These influences are beyond one's control yet profoundly shape one's personality, beliefs, and way of life. However, Fromm did not believe that individuals were wholly determined by socio-economic, biological, and environmental forces. The individual stands in a complex matrix composed of her individual "character structure," on the one hand (for example, her personal tendency to hoard possessions, or her tendency to make many acquaintances but few close friends) and the universal human condition on the other.[8] The individual's character structure and the universal human condition constantly influence one another, yet they are nevertheless differentiable. The human condition is further subdivided into an unchanging and unalterable human nature and aspects of human life that can be changed in the course of history. Fromm agreed with Marx's statement in *Capital* that there are two elements to human nature, "*human nature in general*" and "*human nature as modified in each historical epoch*" (MCM 23).

In addition to the individual character structure, human nature, and the influence of socio-economic structures, biological drives, and other environmental influences, Fromm acknowledged a limited possibility for human free will. According to Fromm, some people have free will and others do not; free will is "a function of a person's character structure" (HOM 131). While average people have the ability to choose, in individual situations, for good or for evil, or for progress or for regression, some people have character structures that are so exemplary (insert favorite saint-like person here) or so pathological (insert favorite crazed serial killer here) as to make this impossible.

Two philosophical foundations for hope   In his relatively early book *Man for Himself: An Inquiry into the Psychology of Ethics* (1947), Fromm gives his most thorough account of his theory of human nature. There are some slight modifications to this theory of human nature in Fromm's later work, chiefly a greater degree of hope for resolving certain fundamental tensions within human experience, which I will address. I will begin by offering a summary of his account of human nature in *Man for Himself*, before addressing his move towards messianic hope and faith. Although references to messianism can be found in earlier works, Fromm's more serious thought on messianism seems to have come after *Man for Himself*, in the 1950s through 1970s, beginning with *The Sane Society* (1955). In order to determine whether the messianic age is achievable or whether one should hope for it, one must understand the foundation upon which hope for its attainment rests: Fromm's conception of human nature. One should bear in mind, however, that one does not first determine whether the messianic age is achievable before beginning to hope for it. Whether one is philosophically justified in hoping has very little to do with one's actual reasons for hoping, as I explain in the final section of this chapter.

In *Man for Himself*, Fromm states that human beings are differentiated from non-human animals by a host of factors: humans' comparatively diminished instincts in relation to animals, humans' ability to transform their environments rather than merely adapting to them, their capacity to "remember the past, to visualize the future, and to denote objects and acts by symbols," their use of reason in seeking to understand the world, and their "imagination" through which they "[reach] far beyond the range of [their] senses" (MFH 39). It is human nature to seek to know and to be "interested" in the world (ROH 81). Here he also states that human reason is not just a blessing but also a curse: it burdens the individual with boredom, discontentment, and a feeling of having been "evicted from paradise" due to the alienation she feels from nature (MFH 40-1).

Also central to human nature, for Fromm, is the desire to be "productive" or "active." Productiveness resolves the paradox of the human being's struggles for unity and independence. Further, productiveness is the root of love (MFH 96-7). According to Fromm, love is not a passion but an activity, and love is not a feeling but a state of being, brought about through effort, through "laboring" for what one loves (99-100). To explain what he means by productiveness or activity, Fromm draws upon Aristotle and Spinoza, both of whom he takes to be saying that "activity" is the actualization of human potentialities towards the fulfillment of human beings' unique function (25-6, 92). (He does not yet employ Marx in *Man for Himself* to make the case that human beings are by nature productive. In his later work, especially after reading Marx's 1844 *Manuscripts* and studying his idea of species-being (*Gattungswesen*), Fromm draws more heavily upon Marx's conception of human nature.)

According to Fromm in *Man for Himself*, every human being stands in relation to humanity and to nature in a complex relation of being both part and whole, both immanent and transcendent. Although an individual, each is simultaneously a representative of the whole and bears the whole of humanity within him or herself (MFH 38). (Fromm seems to see this as a possible foundation for solidarity or love, since one can see the possibilities for all human behavior within oneself.) In addition to being caught in a strange relation of being both part and whole in relation to humanity, the human being is caught in a relation of unity and difference with regard to nature, since she sees herself as being a part of nature and, simultaneously, transcending it (40).

Much of the problem of human existence depends, for Fromm, upon the tension between autonomy and relatedness in the human being's relation to other humans and to nature. In *Man for Himself*, this contradiction of autonomy and relatedness is presented as irresolvable, yet his later works suggest hope for a resolution of this contradiction. As we know, Fromm's later work construed the messianic age as a dialectical synthesis of humans' prehistoric unity with each other and with nature, on the one hand, and humans' later achievement of individuation and freedom through history, on the other. In *Man for Himself*, however, Fromm had not yet developed this messianic synthesis. Instead, he distinguishes between two kinds of contradictions: "existential dichotomies" and "historical contradictions" (MFH 41, 3). The former, under which he includes the human situation of being caught between autonomy and relatedness, immanence and transcendence, and the problem of human mortality, he states can never be wholly resolved but must simply be accepted as basic to the human condition. But the latter, "historical contradictions," *are* resolvable; among these he includes "the contemporary contradiction between an abundance of technical means for material satisfaction and incapacity to use them exclusively for peace and the welfare of the people" (43).

The distinction between existential dichotomies and historical contradictions is important, because people are too often convinced that alterable historical conditions are inalterable existential dichotomies (MFH 43). Consequently people submit to the advice of authorities who tell them to simply accept their "tragic fate" (43). Yet "all human progress" depends upon the ability of people to confront resolvable contradictions, the ignoring of which leads to the development of ideologies or rationalizations through which people attempt unsuccessfully to cover over their unconscious dissatisfaction (44). Since the mind cannot be passive in the face of contradictions, the person who attempts to avoid all contradictions will be left in anxiety and restlessness (44).

The best path, according to Fromm in 1947, is to boldly face and accept all existential dichotomies, while pledging oneself to the eradication of historical contradictions. With regard to existential dichotomies, the solution is "to face the truth, to acknowledge his fundamental aloneness and solitude in a universe indifferent to his fate, to recognize that there is no power transcending him which can solve his problem for him" (MFH 44-5). Upon accepting the truth, one is then able to change what really can be changed, by making one's own meaning:

> If he faces the truth without panic he will recognize that there is no meaning in life except the meaning man gives his life by the unfolding of his powers, by living productively; and that only constant vigilance, activity, and effort can keep us from failing in the one task that matters—the full development of our powers within the limitations set by the laws of our existence. (45)

Man for Himself is Fromm at his most prototypically existentialist (i.e., emphasis upon making one's meaning in life, accepting the prospect of death, etc.). We will soon see a shift in his thought from the acceptance of existential dichotomies and the need to make one's own meaning to an increased *messianic hope* for the resolution of contradictions, including even some existential dichotomies. Despite this evolution, however, Fromm never abandoned the basic features of the picture of human nature he articulated in *Man for Himself*.

Fromm does not seem to have done anything more with the distinction between "existential dichotomies" and "historical contradictions" in his later works.[9] It is not clear why. It is possible that he realized that the distinction was murkier than he initially thought. However, his intervening work on Marx's early writings probably helped him to move away from this distinction and towards a greater emphasis upon messianic hope. Marx himself expressed hopes that existential dichotomies could be overcome through this-worldly action, writing in his 1844 *Manuscripts* that communism would be "the solution to the riddle of history," the "resolution of the antagonism between man and nature, and between man and man...the true solution of the conflict between existence and essence, between objectification and self-affirmation, between freedom and necessity, between individual and species," "a *total redemption of humanity*," and the "resurrection of nature" (*Early Writings* 155, 58, 157; Marx's italics). At least in these early writings, Marx expresses (in rather messianic language) hope that even existential dichotomies can be resolved.

Along with the growing importance of messianic hope in Fromm's thought after *Man for Himself*, there is a related shift in Fromm's concept of "faith." In *Man for Himself*, Fromm had drawn a distinction between rational and irrational faith, a distinction he preserves throughout his later work. "Irrational faith" is "the belief in a person, idea, or symbol which does not result from one's own experience of thought or feeling, but which is based on one's emotional submission to irrational authority," while rational faith, by contrast, is "a firm conviction based on productive intellectual and emotional activity" (MFH 201, 204). Fromm maintained this basic distinction, never conflating the person of true faith with the authoritarian personality. Yet while in Fromm's 1947 work true, rational faith coincided with the acceptance of existential dichotomies and the rejection of any belief in the absurd, Fromm's conception of faith takes a *paradoxical* turn in his later work (203). In his later work *The Revolution of Hope*, Fromm sees "faith" as a paradoxical *certainty* that something *uncertain* will occur (ROH 14). It is a confidence that human beings will create a better future, despite the knowledge that progress is not inevitable. Faith still maintains the connection to rationality and activity that Fromm stresses in *Man for Himself*, yet the basis of faith for Fromm now seems to be something more than strong belief in a logical conclusion of an argument, which seems to have qualified as faith for Fromm in 1947.

Fromm's new articulation of faith as paradoxical and his new commitment to messianic hope marked an opening from the narrower hope of *Man for Himself*. Whereas his earlier work on human nature had urged people to confront historical contradictions while accepting existential dichotomies, his new approach suggested that both could be overcome, through radical hope and faith in human potential. A particular dimension of this radical, messianic hope and faith must be addressed. An account of human nature alone is insufficient to ground messianic hope for the resolution of both existential dichotomies and historical contradictions.

Hope for the messianic age in the absence of probability of success   Even if humans by their nature are capable of great good and of rising above the chains of necessity, are there grounds to hope that they will ever actually bring a messianic age to fruition? This question must be asked, because Fromm does not see the messianic age as a mere regulative ideal but as a pragmatically achievable goal. At first blush, the question certainly seems hard to answer in the affirmative, considering that time and again throughout history, human beings have failed to live up to their potential and have mired themselves in war and injustice of every kind.

In his social context, Fromm could find few empirical grounds for hope in the achievement of his ("awake," not dreaming) utopian aims (Wilde, *Quest for Solidarity* 4). He witnessed in his lifetime the failure of the Soviet experiment and its devolution into mechanized, bureaucratic "state capitalism," two catastrophic world wars, the Holocaust, nuclear annihilation in Japan, the arms race, and the rapid growth of U.S. economic and political dominance, coupled with an ever-widening gap worldwide between rich and poor, powerful and powerless. In the time of his youth before World War One, many expected to see a successful Marxist revolution in Germany, yet due to the events that followed, Fromm lived most of his life unsure if the human race would even consent to its own survival.

Fromm nevertheless sought to find seeds of hope within the present and to hold out hope for the resurrection of the prophetic-messianic movement after the near-deadly blows dealt it by the collapse of the Second International. He had no illusions about the probability for success; in fact, he estimated (more to drive home his point than as any kind of scientific calculation) that the odds of humanity surviving and progressing towards greater solidarity were about 2% (TB 160). What mattered to Fromm, however, was not the probability, but the existence of even a remote *possibility* for the messianic age. He wrote,

> Indeed, "it is part of the probability that the improbable happens," as Aristotle put it. The question is, to use a Hegelian term, of a "real possibility." "Possible" here means not an abstract possibility, a logical possibility, a possibility based on premises which do not exist. A real possibility means that there are psychological, economic, social, and cultural factors that can be demonstrated—if not their quantity, at least their existence—as the basis for the possibility of change. (ROH 142)

He believed that such possibility could be found through an honest assessment of human nature, which he saw as neither wholly good nor wholly evil.[10] Clinging to the hope that human potential could be realized was the only solution to the problems of his time.

Fromm was an activist, and as such he valued programs for action. He suggested a number of programs for political action himself, including his pamphlet *Let Man Prevail: A Socialist Manifesto and Program*, written for the Socialist Party of America (SP-SDF). His *The Sane Society* concluded with a call for worker cooperatives. His *The Revolution of Hope* concluded with a call for people to form "clubs" to discuss creating a more hopeful society and included a mail-in clip-out page for those who wanted to sign up to join the "clubs." His *May Man Prevail?* included recommendations for ending the nuclear arms race. His *To Have or To Be?* concluded with a call for leftists to unite with others in a campaign against the spread of consumerism and overly seductive techniques in advertising.

As an activist, Fromm was a defender of "humanistic planning"; he firmly believed that the future achievement of the messianic age would depend upon prior planning and "productive" action by many people, not upon mere destructiveness or the coup-like actions of small groups of leaders playing Messiah (ROH 95). Fromm's own proposed programs for action include some insightful recommendations but may sometimes also seem impractical, despite his great effort to make practical recommendations. But Fromm's prophetic messianism is not grounded on any particular program for action. It is grounded on a commitment to the *development* of programs for action: through reason, dialogue, planning, solidarity or love, and productive creativity. Prophetic messianism asserts hope in the face of hopelessness, clinging to even the smallest indication of possibilities for societal change. Clinging to a paradoxical, active, and rational hope is the only ethical and psychologically healthy course of action in a world that stands on the brink of catastrophe.

Towards a phenomenology of hope   Now that we have examined the *philosophical* foundation for hope, another sense of the foundation of hope remains: What is the foundation of hope for the individual who hopes? That is, what does the individual experience as the source of her hope? This question is an entirely different matter from the philosophical justifications that may be provided for hope. One does not become hopeful by becoming convinced by an argument for hope and subsequently deciding to be hopeful. In fact, one does not consciously "choose" to hope at all (though hope may be an indirect result of other choices). Rather than choosing to hope, the subject experiences hope as something that *happens to her* or in which she is *caught up.* Hoping is not an action so much as a state of being; the one who hopes is "in hope." Despite the fact that hope is not experienced as a choice, hope is active and not passive. To be hopeful is to be engaged in an activity of which one is not wholly the cause and which is not maintained solely by means of reasons or evidence. Although Fromm himself does not make all the points that follow in this section, one can supplement Fromm's work in this way, by drawing on Gabriel Marcel. The results are consistent with Fromm's general project and assist in better understanding how a Frommian hope can be grounded in individual experience.

In order to understand the difference between the philosophical justification for hope and the individual's motivation for hope, it is particularly important to understand the following: one does not hope *because* one decides that empirical evidence to the contrary is irrelevant; rather, such evidence is irrelevant *because* one hopes. Marcel convincingly explicates the irrelevance of evidence to hope. He calls the person who asks whether or not there are sufficient reasons for hope "the observer," and he calls the hopeful person who must respond to that question "the subject." This choice of terms is not accidental. Like Georg Lukács, Marcel believes that the position of subjectivity reveals truths denied to the detached observer. The subject understands the whole (including the observer), in a way that the detached observer cannot. (Fromm certainly agrees with Marcel and Lukács that access to the truth requires not an unbiased and uninvolved viewpoint but active and committed engagement with the world.[11]) The committed, hopeful subject, according to Marcel, has reached a state of understanding in which the question, "Are there sufficient reasons to hope?" is no longer relevant or even coherent. Marcel explains:

> [I]f the subject hopes, it would surely seem that the reasons for hoping are sufficient for him, whatever the observer may think about them.
>
> But in reality the question which the subject is supposed to ask himself ["Are the grounds for my hope sufficient?"]...does not arise for him unless he detaches himself in some degree from his hope. Actually, it comes from a different register and springs from a calculating factor of reason which, with the very approximate means at its disposal, proceeds to carry out a regular balancing up of chances. Without any doubt it may happen that, upon consideration, hope gives in for a variable space of time to those calculations of the reason; above all if the subject is engaged in a discussion with someone whom he wants to convince: It is none the less true, however, that hope and the calculating faculty of reason are essentially distinct and that everything will be lost if we combine them. (64-5)

The point of this richly insightful passage can be clarified through focusing on the case of a hopeful political activist who is engaged in a Frommian project of trying to build the messianic age. Let us examine whether such an activist would be able to explain the reasons and justifications for her hope to a disengaged observer and what would happen when she attempts to offer such an explanation.

Let us assume that the activist (the subject) is being asked by a non-activist (the observer), "Does activism work? Is there reason to hope that society can be changed to accord with your vision of it?" If the observer merely means to ask about the effectiveness of some particular course of action, such as mass demonstrations, and is not objecting to activism *in toto*, then the subject will find the question unobjectionable. (Activists themselves constantly discuss questions of strategy and tactics, seeking effective means to their desired ends.) But when the question at hand is really, "Why try to change society? What if you can't succeed?" the question seems very odd to the subject.

Upon discovering that the world is deeply mired in systemic injustice, many people immediately feel obligated to act. Shocked by the world's problems and by the hypocritical discrepancy between the cheerful picture of the world painted by ideology and the harsh reality of the exploitation and oppression that ideology defends and covers over, many people suddenly *find themselves* asking (rather than *choosing* to ask), "What should I do?" They do not first ask, "*Should* I do something?"

They immediately ask, "*What* should I do?" They do not so much *choose* to ask the question as experience the question *happening to* them. I remember, for example, a discussion with a fellow student at my alma mater as an undergraduate. She was planning to go to medical school and was taking a philosophy course focusing on the atomic bomb during her last year of undergraduate coursework. Suddenly horrified by the reality of nuclear weapons, she questioned whether she could pursue a career as a wealthy and satisfied physician or whether her life might have to take some other course. The question was experienced by her almost as an external attack. "I wish I didn't know this," she explained to the professor, "but now that I do, I feel like I have to do something." Hope often springs from such an experience, from the knowledge that there simply *must* be some solution to the horrors of the present, since I am compelled to act in opposition to these horrors. It is therefore unsurprising that hope has traditionally been considered one of the three "theological virtues" (along with faith and love), a product not of ordinary, freely willed human action, but of divine grace. Hope is not experienced as the result of one's own choice but as something that shakes up the placidity of experience, while helping the subject to cope with the burden of a new-found responsibility. If predisposed to do so, the subject may interpret this gift in theistic terms, as a special divine grace.[12]

Because hope is something that *happens to* the subject, the subject does not know how to reply when the observer asks, "Why do you hope?" If one believes that the world is broken and that one has an obligation to assist in its repair if possible—a belief that the observer often claims to have—then not acting due to doubt about one's effectiveness seems irrational. All the same, the subject may be caught off guard by the observer's question and may begin to offer empirical examples that demonstrate that well-intentioned people who stand up for what they believe in can make a difference in society and that history has not been wholly a history of failures. She makes a brief foray into "calculative reason," as Marcel would put it, bracketing her hope in order to defend it: "Gandhi's salt march..." she begins to say. "The Montgomery bus boycott..." But deep down, she is puzzled by her own reply, since the observer's question strikes her as somehow incoherent. She would rather ask the interlocutor simply, "Why do you ask?" She herself did not choose to act on the basis of stories about the effectiveness of other people's action but simply because it seemed imperative upon her to involve herself—at least to *try* to succeed in the struggle, even if she were to fail.

The disconnect between the observer and subject is made more acute by the fact that, in a certain sense, the subject is already in the messianic age. The messianic age has always been "already but not yet." In the objective sense, of course, the subject is plainly not in the messianic age; she looks around and sees all the same horrors as the observer. Yet she has faith, a vision of the pregnancy of the present. Because she has decided to work for the coming of the messianic age, she looks around for tools to use for that purpose, and the only material available to her is found in the present. She is forced to look for potential within the present if she does not wish to relinquish her hope. The subject thus has had a glimpse of the messianic age, which now presents itself to her as a goal towards which she can move, that is, towards which she can orient all her activity. It becomes real to her through her practical interaction with it. The observer's question—"Why are you doing this? How do you know whether it will *get you there*?"—strikes the subject as odd, because in a way the subject is *already "there,"* and she knows it, at least unconsciously. What is present to her as a goal remains a mere abstract idea to the observer. The subject will continue forward until she reaches the goal or gets as close to it as she can, while the observer has not yet brought herself into relationship with that goal.

The subject can also understand the observer's true situation in a way that the observer cannot. To the subject, it looks as though the observer is simply standing around, wanting to get there, *waiting* and *wishing* and *desiring*, but not moving. ("And they look at me like *I'm* unrealistic and a naïve dreamer!" the subject exclaims in exasperation.) To the subject, the observer is like the man Fromm describes in *Escape from Freedom* who waits at the window of a burning building, shouting for help and wanting to be rescued, desiring to be saved, when all he has to do is turn around and take the stairs out of the building in order to escape the fire (EF 175).

NOTES

[1] Fromm links idolatry and ideology. Ideology involves the profession of a religious belief that is not one's true religious belief (TB 138). Ideology arises through an individual's or a society's attempt to deceive both itself and others about the real motivations for its actions and beliefs (MMP 122). Nevertheless, one is not fully conscious of holding an ideology. For example, Fromm points out, although by 1961 the Soviet Union had become relatively isolationist, millions of Americans believed that a Soviet attack was imminent and could be prevented only through the threat of mutually assured destruction.

According to Fromm, the belief in such an exaggerated Soviet threat could not be explained on the mere basis of media disinformation or government propaganda; that is, the problem was not just that U.S. citizens did not know certain empirical facts. Their pathological fear could only be adequately accounted for through reference to the concept of ideology, through the widespread attempt of the society to deceive itself. Further, Fromm states that although the majority of Americans professed support for democracy, this did not entail that they would take action to defend it if it were threatened; their professed support for democracy was a mere ideology (PR 61-2). Ideology coincides with the deadening of beliefs that had once startled people out of indifference and which now produce "purely cerebral, alienated thought, instead of authentic experiences," and Fromm warns that this alienated, unemotional, robotic thought is beginning to replace all authentic experience (MMP 122).

[2] In a study of female college students at Sarah Lawrence College, Fromm found that most of the students were terrified at the thought of spending several days sitting around reading classic literature.

[3] Fromm adds the disclaimer that he is referring to a trend in the United States, not to Mao or other Chinese thinkers. It is not exactly clear which people or what group he is referring to here.

[4] Fromm likens Marcuse's philosophy to nihilism as early as their 1950s debate in *Dissent* magazine (McLaughlin, "Origin Myths" 9). There Fromm charged that Marcuse's "nihilism" left only the options of martyrdom or insanity, suggested by Marcuse's claims in *Eros and Civilization* that "curing" the psychoanalytic patient "would mean 'curing' the patient to become a rebel or (which is saying the same thing) a martyr" and by Marcuse's assertion of the "tension between health and knowledge" (Ibid.; *Eros and Civilization* 258, 261). Fromm repeats the charge of Marcuse's "nihilism" in *The Art of Loving* and *The Revolution of Hope* (AL 131; ROH 8).

⁵ Fromm develops the distinction between the revolutionary and the rebel in his essay "What is a Revolutionary?" in *The Dogma of Christ: And Other Essays on Religion, Psychology, and Culture*.

⁶ The original source of this quote is the conclusion of Walter Benjamin's essay "Goethe's *Elective Affinities*" (Benjamin 356). The quote also concluded a 1946 talk by Adorno critiquing Fromm's psychoanalysis, and the quote recurs in Adorno's *Negative Dialectics* in a section arguing that reason must defend the tradition of nihilism from attack (Jay, *Dialectical Imagination* 103, 105; Adorno 378).

⁷ In a sense, sadomasochism and destructiveness are less worrying than conformism. In the case of sadomasochism or destructiveness, one is at least trying to relate to the other, either through a power relationship or by annihilating the other, yet in the case of conformity one is not seeking to relate to the other, even violently or submissively, but simply to *avoid the reality* of the other. In Fichtean terms, conformism does not distinguish the *I* from the *not-I*; it beholds a single, undifferentiated reality. The conformist does not even reach the beginning of Hegel's account of the struggle for recognition, i.e., of the dialectic of lordship and bondage. The individual seeking pure destructiveness lies at the very beginning of that dialectic, where two self-consciousnesses become aware of one another as self-conscious and enter into the struggle to the death to annihilate the other and return to being the sole self-consciousness. Relationships of masochism and sadism are only able to exist after that point, once the slave submits to the rule of the lord, establishing a relationship of power and domination. But the conformist does not actively confront the problem of living in a world of other self-conscious beings. Instead, the conformist sacrifices her own self-consciousness in a sort of intellectual death, rather than attempting to preserve self-consciousness in a perverted or incomplete form. If one could place the conformist at a level of Hegel's *Phenomenology of Spirit*, that level would probably occur in one of the sections preceding that of "Self Consciousness," such as that of "Sense-Certainty" or "Perception."

⁸ Chapter 1 of *Man for Himself* is structured by this distinction and divided into two sections, "The Human Situation" and "Personality."

⁹ Of course, Fromm continues to speak dialectically in terms of historical contradictions. There is also a reference to "existential dichotomies" in Fromm's 1966 book *You Shall Be as Gods*, although the switch in emphasis is apparent, since there Fromm presents the messianic age as the *resolution* of existential dichotomies, although he does not explain how this is to occur beyond offering the allegory of the fall that will be discussed in Chapter 4 (YSB 123).

¹⁰ This is the theme of the first chapter of *The Heart of Man* and the first section of *War Within Man*. He argues that human nature is neither that of a vicious "wolf" nor a compliant "sheep," but that humans have the capacity to be either, or something better.

¹¹ Truth for both Fromm and Marcel is experienced affectively, not purely cerebrally, and it is found through an encounter with the whole, totality, or reality, not in fragments but in a viewpoint that includes both the other and the self (Treanor 8, 11; SFM 7; MMP 122; TB 16; AL 29). For Marcel, a higher level knowledge is gained through an encounter with mystery (as opposed to mere problems), and a mystery poses a "question" that necessarily includes the subject who asks it (Treanor 8). Similarly, for Fromm, the courage of love brings one into contact with a reality that is in process, not fixed and dead. For both Marcel and Fromm, the attitude of love for the other leads one to reject an understanding that seeks to dissect an object in order to understand it; Fromm is particularly worried by the attempt to manipulate or force human beings to "reveal the secret" of the human mystery (the attitude of the torturer) rather than to understand by love and relationship (AL 29).

¹² Thomas Merton challenged Fromm on whether the absence of a divine, transcendent being in Fromm's thought is problematic for his notion of hope. In an addendum to Fromm's antiwar pamphlet *War Within Man*, Merton associates hope with grace:

> Still I would like to conclude on a note of hope. It is precisely because I believe, with Abraham Heschel and a cloud of witnesses before him, that 'man is not alone,' that I find hope even in this most desperate situation. Man does not have to transcend himself in the sense of pulling himself up by his own bootstraps. He has, rather, to respond to the mysterious grace of a Spirit which is at once infinitely greater than his own and yet which, at the same time, offers itself as the total plenitude of all Gift, to be in all reality his "own spirit" (WW 50).

Merton suggests Fromm's messianic hope points beyond itself, indicating the need for a transcendent deity. Whether or not this is the case, Merton's writings express quite well the experience of hope as gift. Perhaps, like Lukács' "standpoint of totality" discussed in Chapter 2, Merton's thought can only be understood from the inside, in this case from the standpoint of Merton's Catholic faith.

FROMM'S CONCEPTS OF PROPHETIC AND CATASTROPHIC MESSIANISM

Now it is possible to thoroughly explicate Erich Fromm's prophetic messianism. It differs significantly from the perspectives examined in Chapter 2, especially the catastrophic or apocalyptic messianism of Gershom Scholem and even from the optimistic Marxist messianism of Ernst Bloch, with Bloch's stress on "rupture" and the future as absolute *Novum*. This chapter demonstrates that the dearth of scholarship on Fromm's messianism has led to an overly narrow definition of messianism that excludes Fromm's highly defensible version. I provide an overview of the main features of Fromm's prophetic messianism and look at how they differ from the account typically given of the "Frankfurt School's messianism" *in toto*.

Fromm distinguishes two kinds of messianism, one of which he sees as radical and progressive, the other as regressive and potentially reactionary. I will use the terms that he offers in a late, posthumously published manuscript: "prophetic messianism" and "catastrophic...or apocalyptic" messianism (OBH 141). These terms refer, respectively, to the pre-World War I Enlightenment-style messianism like that of Hermann Cohen, on the one hand, and to the "Gnostic" or magical attitude that awaits or induces the break-in of transcendence, on the other.

Prophetic messianism, which Fromm supports, conceives the messianic event as occurring *within history and time*[1] and not arriving through a rupture from history and time (YSB 88). According to the messianism that Fromm opposes, which he considers regressive—*catastrophic messianism*[2]—the messianic event enters history from outside, a *force majeure*, not as an outcome of human activity. While Fromm's own "prophetic messianism" is a "horizontal" longing, a longing for human-made change, catastrophic messianism is a "vertical" longing, a longing for an external, transcendent "savior" (perhaps a human leader or a deterministic law governing history) that will enter history from a realm outside of human affairs (133). Because prophetic messianism views the messianic event as the outcome of human progress, it encourages *productive and revolutionary action*, and it makes planning ("anticipatory change") possible (MMP 3). By contrast, because catastrophic messianism views the messianic event as the outcome of the transcendent entering history to rescue a fallen humanity, catastrophic messianism encourages *passive waiting* or even *destructive or unnecessarily violent action* aimed at speeding the coming of the apocalypse. Like the types of false hope that Fromm warns against, catastrophic messianism risks becoming quietism on the one hand or actively destructive nihilism on the other.

Fromm is insistent that prophetic messianism is not a version of historical determinism (unlike catastrophic messianism, which is). Fromm's prophetic-

147

messianic view acknowledges that human beings really might fail to bring about the messianic age. Although prophetic messianism involves a "certainty based on inner experience" (a certainty grounded in hope, not in empirical proof), this certainty is paradoxical and does not see the future fulfillment of its hopes as inevitable (YSB 156-7). Rather than a form of determinism, prophetic messianism is what Fromm calls an "alternativism." In *The Revolution of Hope*, Fromm contrasts the prophet's emphasis on "alternatives" with the determinist's emphasis on "prediction" (ROH 18). Given free will, it is impossible to predict the future, but it is possible to be aware of what is at stake and of the possibilities latent in the present.

Fromm's alternativism posits that freedom of the will is neither unlimited nor nonexistent. Rather, one's freedom of will is contingent upon making certain fundamental choices correctly and upon the malleability of one's character and one's awareness of the options and likely consequences of each choice (HOM 119; "Application of Humanistic Psychoanalysis" 243). Making certain choices incorrectly may lead to lack of freedom later, while choosing correctly may lead to the further expansion of one's freedom.

Fromm often states that the Hebrew prophets presented people with "alternatives" and the likely consequences of each choice (e.g., "Stop extorting widows or your city will be destroyed."). Marx, Freud, and Spinoza were likewise "alternativists," and Rosa Luxemburg, as a prophet of socialism, presented a similar "alternative" when she spoke of the need for humanity to choose between "socialism or barbarism" (HOM 119; "Application of Humanistic Psychoanalysis" 243). Acutely aware of the centrality of the question of "socialism or barbarism" for his time, Fromm writes:

> [I]n contrast to the men of the eighteenth and nineteenth centuries who had an unfailing belief in the continuity of progress, we visualize the possibility that, instead of progress, we may create barbarism or our total destruction. The alternative of socialism or barbarism has become frighteningly real today, when the forces working towards barbarism seem to be stronger than those working against it. (BC 187)

Fromm's warnings of the threat of nuclear annihilation also present a crucial alternative—disarmament or death—which was coupled towards the end of his life with an alternative between solving the ecological crisis and facing catastrophe (HOM 141; TB 7). The prophet does not force the people to pick one alternative over another—the people are free to choose—but each choice will carry certain inevitable consequences; the choice of one side of the alternative *limits* freedom and progress, while the choice of the other *enhances* freedom and progress. When faced with an alternative in this sense, there must be only two choices, because the alternative is fundamentally a choice for productivity or destructiveness, or, in similar terms, for life or for death. Practical tactical considerations come later, after this basic existential choice.

In the life of individuals, and therefore also in societies confronted with the possibility of catastrophe or progress, alternativism rather than determinism or absolute freedom is the rule (HOM 139). Fromm frequently speaks of pathological character orientations as consequences of failed choices between alternatives. For example, he considers the "destructive" character orientation (the focus of Fromm's psychoanalytic magnum opus, *The Anatomy of Human Destructiveness*) to be the result of a choice against hope and in favor of destructiveness. "Psychologically speaking, destructiveness is the alternative to hope, just as attraction to death is the alternative to the love of life, and just as joy is the alternative to boredom" (ROH 22). One does not necessarily have freedom of choice when confronted with the crucial alternative—at any rate, the difficult and transformative choice may be so dramatic in its break from the past and the future it initiates that it may be experienced almost as a miracle—but one's freedom may increase or decrease as a result of the choice (HOM 127-8, 138).

By rejecting determinism, of course, Fromm nuances the oft-oversimplified Marxist account of base and superstructure. He writes,

> If one speaks of *inner lawfulness* in individual and in social life, then there is usually no unilinear causal chain of the type "A causes B." This type of determinism is usually false. One can, however, usually say: A can lead to one, two, three or four choices, but only to these and no others. We can ascertain and determine that only a certain few choices are possible under the given conditions. Sometimes there are two, sometimes there are more. Without wanting to [prophesy] anything, I believe that today there is essentially only one choice for modern man and for the people of the earth *in toto*: the choice between barbarism and a new renaissance of humanism. (OBH 29)

Fromm's alternativist, non-determinist philosophy of history enables him to ground messianic hope on a more stable foundation than mere empirical evidence of the probability of success and the narrow conception of causality that would be required to sustain a socialist determinism. Prophetic messianism is based upon hope, which as shown in the previous chapter is based upon the slightest possibility, not probability, of success. Prophetic messianism is not a scientific conclusion about the likelihood of progress. Fromm holds that the world is teetering on the brink of catastrophe, that humanity is at great risk of being thrown into a state of barbarism, and that this is very likely to happen. Consequently, prophetic messianism has to be based upon a choice, not upon an empirical probability or certainty of success. Fromm compares prophetic messianism to a physician faced with a patient whose condition seems difficult, possibly impossible, to cure, but who nevertheless proceeds to offer care. "If a sick person has even the barest chance for survival, no responsible physician will say, 'Let's give up the effort,' or will use only palliatives"; the physician will attempt to save the life of the patient— "Certainly, a sick society cannot expect anything less" (TB 160). Attempting to avoid the collapse into barbarism is not merely optional for a moral or rational person, who is morally and rationally mandated to fight such a decline if there is the slightest chance of success.

CHAPTER 4

Fromm argues for a need to seek out empirical evidence of the attainability of the future messianic age (TB 160). There is no need to hope for the impossible and no way to rationally do so.[3] Fortunately, however, Fromm does think that there is available evidence for the possibility of the messianic age, as we noted in Chapter 3, evidence deeply rooted in human nature and life itself. The standpoint of hope enables us to see the seeds of potential that are latent in the present.

In addition to being a distinction between alternativism and determinism, the distinction between prophetic messianism and catastrophic messianism is a distinction between two historical trajectories. According to Fromm, prophetic messianism originated with the Hebrew prophets, as he outlines in *You Shall Be as Gods*, his "radical interpretation of the Old Testament." Following its origin in the prophets, the prophetic-messianic idea re-entered history on numerous occasions—in certain radical elements in early Christianity and the Middle Ages; in Renaissance humanist thinkers; in Spinoza; in Enlightenment thinkers and French revolutionaries; in the work of Lessing, Fichte, Hegel, and Goethe; in utopian socialists like Saint-Simon; in Young Hegelians Moses Hess, Heinrich Heine, and Karl Marx; and in some early socialist thinkers following Marx, including Rosa Luxemburg and Gustav Landauer (MCM 54; OBH 144-5; SS 236). The socialist movement itself was, "as Hermann Cohen, Ernst Bloch, and a number of other scholars have stated during the past decades[,]...the secular expression of prophetic Messianism" (TB 126).

Fromm believed that prophetic messianism was under threat in his times, endangered by a catastrophic messianism that had dealt it near-deadly blows in the twentieth century, through the capitulation of the Second International to nationalism before the First World War and the crushing of the 1918-1919 German uprisings, the degeneration of the Soviet experiment into bureaucratic "state capitalism," the rise of fascism, and the destructive psychological forces manifested by the nuclear arms race (SS 239; MMP *passim*). Fromm later worried, as we have seen, about a catastrophic messianism that he observed on the left in the 1960s.

In a 1961 speech Fromm expressed the same puzzlement about the First World War:

Until the First World War, European humanity was ruled by its belief in the fulfillment of these [prophetic/utopian] hopes and ideals...I have spoken of the birth process of new societies. I would almost like to say that twentieth-century man seems to be a miscarriage. What has happened, so that everything has seemed to break down at the moment when man appeared to stand at the crowning pinnacle of his historical endeavors? (OBH 21)

Before World War I, there were already cultural tendencies in Europe celebrating the creative potential of destruction and violence. Fromm's prophetic messianism stands in sharp contrast with this mentality, as well as other conceptions of messianism prevalent in the Frankfurt School, most notably Walter Benjamin's and also perhaps Herbert Marcuse's. Due to a dearth of Fromm scholarship, some characterizations of the Frankfurt School's messianism exclude Fromm's prophetic messianism and present the Frankfurt School's messianism as wholly catastrophic. One finds this in the work of Eduardo Mendieta and Anson Rabinbach (as we shall see), as well as Michael Löwy and Richard Wolin, among others (Löwy, "Jewish Messianism" 106; Wolin, *Labyrinths* 49-50). (Those who warn against this catastrophic messianism, especially Richard Wolin, perform a particularly valuable service. All of these thinkers have done important work exploring the complicated influence of Weimar thought on the Frankfurt School and Marxism.)

It is an oft-repeated claim that World War II and the Holocaust were the chief source of catastrophic messianism and of the skepticism concerning utopias, after the catastrophe of the Holocaust caused some thinkers to reject speculations about theodicy as unconscionable and to embrace difference as opposed to a unitary picture of human progress. There is some truth in the idea that this shift occurred and that it contributed to the rise of catastrophic messianism. Adorno famously asked whether poetry or even life itself was possible after Auschwitz (see *Can One Live after Auschwitz?*). Yet concerns about theodicy and utopia were already on the rise before World War II, even on the left. In fact, catastrophic messianism's pessimism, in its attempt to change the world through mere negation rather than building upon the present, may have contributed to the rise of Nazism.[4] Catastrophic messianism was reflected to an extent in the attempt at total eradication, the drive for *Lebensraum*, and widespread destructive impulses melded with a determinist fascination with destiny and fate.

In *Escape from Freedom* (1941), Fromm quotes a Nazi ideologue and draws the connection between catastrophic messianism and Nazism:

> One of the ideological fathers of Nazism, Moeller van der Bruck, expressed this feeling very clearly. He writes, "The conservative believes rather in catastrophe, in the powerlessness of man to avoid it, in its necessity, and in the terrible disappointment of the seduced optimist." In Hitler's writing we shall see more illustrations of the same spirit. (EF 194)

This insight is prefigured by Fromm's earlier work, as we saw in the first chapter, in his thinly veiled critique of his "gnostic" contemporaries in "The Dogma of Christ." Since many prominent thinkers with affinities with Nazism, including Carl Schmitt, Martin Heidegger, and Oswald Spengler, adopted the catastrophic-messianic yearning for transcendent intervention, it may be surprising that catastrophic messianism remained prominent after World War II, and even on the left. The survival of catastrophic messianism as a respectable academic and left perspective after World War II seems possible only in light of the fact that many thinkers, including Theodor Adorno, Karl Löwith, and even Heidegger[5] suggested that the catastrophe of World War II and the Holocaust had been the outcome not of apocalyptic visions and catastrophic messianism but of humanism and reason (or instrumentalized reason, which they did not always differentiate from reason as such [Wolin, *Seduction of Unreason* 159]). The prophetic messianist would likely see fascism's idolatry of leaders as one possible expression of catastrophic messianism, according to which an external "savior" would intervene into worldly affairs. According to the critics of modern reason and of prophetic messianism, however, the cause was not catastrophic messianism but rather *Enlightenment rationalism and progressivist views of history*, ideas with deep affinities to prophetic messianism.

In the 1950s, prophetic messianism and utopian hope seemed to be at an end. In the United States, the age was termed the "end of ideology," after Daniel Bell's best-seller. In Germany, the generation of German political philosophers born around 1930—Kurt Sontheimer, Niklas Luhman, Ralf Dahrendorf, and others—were termed the "skeptical generation" because of their skepticism about "utopia" after witnessing the tragedy of Nazism (Specter 5). Although to identify this skepticism with the experience of World War II might obscure the origins of this skepticism in the 1910s and 1920s, there is nevertheless some truth in the claim that 1945 marked a generation of thinkers who emerged into the intellectual world with a unique skepticism of utopian visions molded by their experience of Nazism.

Because the Cold War brought to the fore the possibility of the annihilation of civilization or even of all human life, and because neither side of the stalemate presented a viable solution to the problems facing humanity, catastrophic messianism's rejection of alternatives captured the spirit of the times. The catastrophe of Stalinism had shaken the left's prophetic hope, and the Soviet Union was (as Arthur Koestler quipped), "the god that failed," the false Messiah. In his book on foreign policy, *May Man Prevail?*, Fromm argued that "the Soviet communists, contrary to Marx, placed excessive trust, especially during the post-revolutionary and Stalinist era, in the role of creative violence applied by the noble minority in the name of the objective interests of the majority" (Chałubińksi 85).

As we have seen, Fromm saw prophetic messianism as chiefly threatened by a catastrophic messianism that was greatly strengthened and popularized by the experience of the First World War and the crushed uprisings of 1918-1919. The effects of the Holocaust, the Cold War, and subsequent events, however, did not help to revive the prophetic messianic idea, although they should not be taken as evidence for the validity of catastrophic messianism. The task is now to elucidate Fromm's messianism at length; this will be done with regard to five themes. On these five topics, we will see, Fromm differs from others in the Frankfurt School and other prominent thinkers of his time while presenting a defensible account of hope for the future.

4.1 APOCALYPTIC VS. PROPHETIC MESSIANISM: RESPONSE TO EDUARDO MENDIETA

In a recent essay (a revised version of an essay written as an introduction to Habermas's *Religion and Rationality*), Eduardo Mendieta addresses Jürgen Habermas's attempt to grapple with the tradition of "Jewish messianism," a tradition that, Mendieta writes, includes "Max Horkheimer, Theodor W. Adorno, Walter Benjamin, Herbert Marcuse—and to extend legitimately Gershom Scholem's list,[6] Erich Fromm and

Leo Lowenthal" (Mendieta 142-3). Interestingly, although Mendieta makes a point of including Fromm in his list of important Jewish messianic members of the Frankfurt School ("legitimately…Erich Fromm…"), Mendieta then proposes a list of four aspects of the Jewish messianism motivating the Frankfurt School, the first three of which clearly contradict Fromm's prophetic messianism. Mendieta's account is based upon Anson Rabinbach's account of messianism.[7] The absence of Fromm's prophetic messianism in Mendieta's account says more about the extent to which Fromm has been written out of the history of the Frankfurt School than about Mendieta's important scholarship on the Critical Theory of Religion. Fromm's legacy needs to be recuperated; when he is not written out of the history, he tends to be all too casually lumped together with others in the Frankfurt School.

Mendieta claims that the Frankfurt School's messianism is characterized by the following four elements:

1. Restoration through anamnesis, as opposed to restoration of a "Golden Age" of the past
2. An ahistorical utopianism that contradicts "Enlightenment utopianism" and views progress as "catastrophe"
3. An apocalyptic rupture with the past, leading to a future that is not even "imaginable" from the standpoint of the present
4. The view that the Messiah is not a person but consists in "messianic forces and elements" (Mendieta 143-4).

Fromm's prophetic messianism has little in common with (1) through (3) above, which in fact are mainly features of the catastrophic messianism he opposes. (Mendieta's final point I will disregard, as it has already been clarified that Jewish messianism awaits a "messianic age," not an individual human Messiah.)[8] Carefully addressing Mendieta's first three points with regard to Fromm will help to elucidate Fromm's conception of prophetic messianism and show how it differs from the catastrophic messianism adopted by others in the Frankfurt School. I will discuss Mendieta's account with regard to five themes:

1. Rupture: Fromm's prophetic messianism does not involve a dramatic "rupture" with the past and present. Instead, Fromm's messianism sees revolutionary change as an option, while not wholly repudiating the past or present.
2. Past Golden Age and Anamnesis: Fromm's messianism is not simply a return to the past, either prehistoric or historic. Rather, the messianic age is a dialectical synthesis of the prelapserian world and the achievements of human progress. Memory must be held in check, since excessive dwelling on the past can lead to psychological regression and reactionary politics.
3. The Enlightenment: Fromm's messianism consciously stands within the Enlightenment tradition and treats the Enlightenment as an unfinished project.
4. Progress and Catastrophe: Fromm's messianism chooses "progress" over "catastrophe" as a model for understanding revolutionary change.

153

5. Utopia and Imagining/Conceiving the Future: Fromm's messianism is open to the utopian imagination and to reason, seeing the future as partly understandable through the concepts and practices available to us in the present.

* * *

FROMM'S PROPHETIC MESSIANISM VS. CATASTROPHIC MESSIANISM:
FIVE KEY THEMES

1. Rupture

As already stated, Fromm's prophetic messianism sees the messianic event as occurring *within* history and time (YSB 88). This is a point on which many of his contemporaries differed, and their discussion of "rupture" and "break" was meant to emphasize that the messianic age would come about not as a result of human progress in history but as an intervention by transcendence. In this sense, then, Fromm's messianism did *not* involve a dramatic "rupture" with the present or the past. Fromm's conception of the messianic event as an outgrowth of history, not a complete break from it, differed dramatically, for example, from Walter Benjamin's assertion that "messianism demands a complete repudiation of the world as it is, placing its hope in a future whose realization can only be brought about by the destruction of the old order" (Lane 15).

Some caveats are necessary, however. Although Fromm rejected the view that the messianic age would be the result of a dramatic rupture with the present, he did not foresee a smooth and easy transition from the present to the future. Rooted in Marxism, he presumably would have agreed that revolutions may be precipitated by a "breakdown crisis," and he definitely saw the need for revolutionary change, not mere reform. Far from believing that a smooth, reformist transition would usher in the messianic age, Fromm believed that the mere survival of the human race depended upon a great deal of struggle. Nor did Fromm reject the view that the messianic future would be dramatically different from the present—he spoke of it as a time of peace, love, harmony, solidarity, knowledge, productivity, and joy, and he spoke of his present society as lacking, rent by war and plagued by a lack of love and joy.

To say that Fromm rejected a messianic "rupture" is to say that he rejected a particular revolutionary strategy, not revolution as such. Fromm did not foresee a complete break between the present and the messianic future. Although it would not arrive through a smooth, steady process of reform, neither could it arrive without *foresight and planning*. One of the chief reasons for the failure of the early socialist movement "from Marx to Lenin" was its lack of "concrete plans for a socialist or communist society" (TB 143). Planning creates the psychological conditions necessary for revolutionary action; "when people can see a vision and simultaneously see what can be done step by step in a concrete way to achieve it, they will begin to feel encouragement and enthusiasm instead of fright" (143). This does not mean that a mere utopian vision or blueprint of the society that one wants to construct is sufficient. As Fromm writes, "One cannot construct submarines by reading Jules Verne; one cannot construct a humanist society by reading the prophets" (142). Planning is slow, tedious, and entangled in specific considerations; it does not look only at the final goal but looks also at the many and painful steps between the present and the future.

Another way of saying that Fromm's messianism avoids rupture is to say that it rejects eschatology. Fromm's messianism is a *teleology*, but it is not an *eschatology*. Unlike eschatologies, which speak with certainty of events concerning an end to time, teleologies are not necessarily determinist. Although for Fromm history has a *telos*, in the sense of a proper aim or goal, humanity might not attain it. Fromm's philosophy of history is teleological in the sense that Aristotle's anthropology may be seen as teleological; although many do not attain *eudaimonia*, *eudaimonia* remains the proper aim of human life. For Fromm, history might not reach its *telos*—humanity could retreat into barbarism, or simply destroy itself—but the messianic age is the proper aim of human history.

The idea of "rupture" is linked to a specifically eschatological messianism. The *telos* of history for Fromm is not the end of *time* but if it is the end of anything, it is the end only of *history*, or in Marxist terms, the end of prehistory. In fact, Fromm thought that eschatology manifested a worrying pathology; he was attuned to unconscious desires for the end of earthly human existence. He found abhorrent and dangerous the view that one might be living in a divinely ordained eschatological time of crisis, an "end times." Like his forbear Hermann Cohen, Fromm was actively *anti*-eschatological. Later in this chapter we return to this point, in the context of a critique of Herbert Marcuse.

2. *Anamnesis and Golden Age*

The second of Mendieta's claims that needs to be addressed is the claim that Fromm rejected a "restorative" messianism that seeks to return through anamnesis to a past golden age. Although Fromm does reject restorative messianism, contra Mendieta he also rejects mythical anamnesis and the yearning for return. Before proceeding, however, we must carefully define and qualify three problematic terms that Mendieta employs in this regard: *restorative messianism*, *anamnesis*, and *golden age*. Following this initial definitional work, I then present the central allegory of Fromm's messianism (the disobedience of Adam and Eve), followed by an exploration of the question of whether Fromm's account of this myth is "gnostic." Secondly, I address the three interpretations of the allegory that would be legitimate from Fromm's standpoint: the allegory as representing the individual's birth and subsequent psychological individuation, the rebelliousness of the bourgeois revolutions, or the struggle against the temptation of fascism. Finally, I address Martin Jay's worries about melancholy, as evidence that Fromm has grasped a central concern in his rejection of both restorative messianism and mythical anamnesis.

First, prevailing definitions of *"restorative messianism"* have been shaped heavily by Gershom Scholem, who seems to use the term in more than one way. In the discussion in Chapter 2 of Scholem's delineation of three elements of messianism—restorative, utopian, and conservative—I explained that Scholem defines the restorative tendency as "directed to the return and recreation of a past condition which comes to be felt as ideal" (*The Messianic Idea* 3). This raises more questions than it answers, for it is unclear what kind of past is meant. At times, Scholem seems to speak of restorative messianism as a tendency in Orthodox Judaism to yearn for the return to the Kingdom of David, a past historical era about which there are written records. At other times, it seems that restorative messianism is a yearning to return to a primal condition pre-existing human history or even human life itself. It is not obvious whether Scholem means by restorative messianism a reactionary return to old social systems and mores or an explosive return to something primal and pre-historic.

The term *"anamnesis"* must also be clarified in this context. Historically, the term harks back to Plato (chiefly to the *Meno* and *Phaedo*) and to the recovery of the forms that are already somehow latent in the soul and need only be "remembered." The term also has a New Testament referent in Christ's Eucharistic saying, "Do this in remembrance (*anamnesis*) of me." Within the context of early twentieth century Germany, the term seems to have been deeply entwined in the *Messianismusstreit*. For Bloch, as mentioned in Chapter 2, anamnesis was not quite enough. Martin Buber's Renewal movement, Bloch argued, was severely limited by its commitment to anamnesis; by contrast, the truly radical view was that of the *Novum*, the totally new, rather than the recovery of something already present within the self, which is not truly new but "only new to the person who rediscovers it" (*Man on his Own* 80, 82).

Finally, we need to define the term *"golden age"* before we can fully understand Fromm's account of the myth of Adam and Eve. In Chapter 2, we discussed Hermann Cohen's rejection of the idea of a Golden Age. According to Cohen, Jewish messianism had to be distinguished from the idea of a golden age, which was rooted in pagan mythology and was reflected in Rousseau's account of the state of nature (*Religion of Reason* 248, 250). Cohen connects the myth of the golden age to "idolatry" and "magic" (248, 232). We also saw that Marcuse, although his reference to Heinrich von Kleist seems to suggest a return, also explicitly rejected (in *One-Dimensional Man*) any attempt to return to a past golden age. The implications of the term are plainly mythical; in rejecting the return to a lost golden age, the Frankfurt School thinkers probably sought to differentiate themselves from the plainly restorative messianism of the likes of Stefan George and Ludwig Klages. Fromm's specific rejection is rooted primarily in Hermann Cohen's rejection of myth and Cohen's interpretation of monotheism as a radical basis for international socialism and a humanist spirit of fraternity.

Having addressed the terms "restorative messianism," "anamnesis," and "golden age," I will argue that Fromm favored a carefully qualified and restricted anamnesis of the *prehistoric* past, while rejecting restorative messianism. A key distinction upon which this argument turns is the distinction between return to an historical past and return to a prehistoric past. Fromm's messianic age is not exactly a return, but to whatever extent it resembles one, it resembles a return to a prehistoric past, not an historical past. Mendieta is right about restorative messianism: Fromm categorically rejects it. There is a very limited sense in which Fromm could be understood to see the messianic age as a return to the pre-historic past, but this return is a dialectical fulfillment, not a regression.[9] Fromm differs most noticeably from Mendieta's account on anamnesis and restorative messianism on the *attitude* that one ought to have towards the past. Fromm does not try to get *behind* history to reach anamnesis of pre-historic or not-yet-human life. Rather, he integrates the strengths of prehistory and history with the openness of the future, while warning against the dangers of dwelling upon the past—he links dwelling upon the past to necrophilia, desire for regression to childhood states, and reactionary ideologies (more on that shortly).

In saying that Fromm *does not seek restoration of a lost historical golden age*, emphasis must be laid upon the word *"historical."* Fromm understands the messianic age as a dialectical synthesis of history and pre-history. Thus, the messianic age restores or renews the primordial unity between people and between people and nature, yet it is nevertheless a transformation. Fromm can be distinguished from the Zionist variant of restorative messianism and from that of reactionaries who sought a mere return to an idealized past of primordial, barbaric innocence.

Fromm rejects restorative messianism. One might find a restorative messianism more in Martin Buber and to a limited extent in Gustav Landauer, both of whom no doubt influenced the Frankfurt School; however, in speaking of the Frankfurt School's rejection of restorative messianism, Mendieta is primarily distinguishing the messianism of the Frankfurt School from religious Zionism and from German Romanticism à la Novalis. Although Romantic, backwards-looking restorative messianism may have affected other members of the Frankfurt School, such as Walter Benjamin (in which case Mendieta's claim requires qualification), Fromm remained relatively free of restorative messianism, notwithstanding his sympathy for Romantic thinkers like Landauer and Johann Gottfried Herder (BC 18). Fromm did not seek the re-enchantment of the world through some Romantic idealization of feudalism. He gradually acquired a more nuanced perception of the Middle Ages—in his early work, he underscored its authoritarianism and lack of freedom, while eventually in his later work he saw it as a time when radical Christian principles penetrated the economic system and led to a degree of spiritual progress in Europe. However, as will be addressed in the next section, Fromm was in significant respects a defender of the Enlightenment. And while Zionist messianisms viewed the coming messianic age as a restoration of the ancient Kingdom of David, Fromm was opposed to Zionism.[10] Hence, it seems that Fromm would reject any characterization of the messianic age as a restoration of a past historical Golden Age. Although I will stand by this claim, some qualification is needed to account for conflicting evidence.

Concluding, on the basis of his rejection of Zionism and Romantic nostalgia, that Fromm's messianism is not a restoration of a past historical Golden Age raises a possible complication. In *You Shall Be as Gods* and elsewhere, Fromm suggests that prophetic messianism seeks a return to the state of Paradise, a time when the contemporary alienation and fragmentation of society and of the individual were absent. There he states that messianism begins after the disobedience of Adam and Eve, an "*historical*" event in which humanity lost its original oneness with nature and its fellow humans (YSB 122). Of course, Fromm does not take the story literally, but humanity's first act of disobedience to authority, whatever form that took, was the first event of history. To speak of "history" before humanity's individuation and achievement of freedom would be nonsensical, because only free and rational beings have a history (if we mean more than a mere natural-scientific history). There is no "history of squirrels," which do the same thing from one generation to the next.

The first act of disobedience—it was not a "fall," and Fromm upholds the Jewish rejection of original sin—did not damage human dignity but was an important step in human development, a part of humanity's process of "growing up," of learning not to obey orders blindly (orders such as "don't eat from that tree"), and breaking its infantile bonds to blood and soil (122-3). Adam and Eve's disobedience was, as he states elsewhere, "the condition for man's self-awareness, for his capacity to choose... man's first step toward freedom" (HOM 20). Expelled from its original oneness with nature and with its fellow humans, humanity feels helpless and unprotected and longs for the former safety of "Paradise." Fearful of its freedom, humanity may even look to authoritarian leaders and seek to return to blind submission. Humanity has so far been unable to recognize the promise of the serpent in Genesis—"You shall be as gods"—as a blessing and not a curse. Through exercising autonomy and refusing to blindly obey authorities, humanity can indeed become god-like, as the serpent promised, but this requires developing the courage to disobey.

Despite the truth of the serpent's promise, something is lost with the act of disobedience. The fall represents, allegorically, the event of humanity's individuation. While individuation is desirable, alienation is not. Like the infant faced with the traumatic experience of birth, Adam and Eve were thrown from the comfort of Paradise into a world of suffering and loneliness. A return into this paradisiacal womb is not only undesirable from the standpoint of the psychological growth of the individual—it is also impossible (DC 166; AL 7; OBH 75). The "fall" grants individuation and self-consciousness, yet it also generates feelings of isolation and homelessness, of yearning for a union that is impossible to reclaim. Love could build a bridge that would overcome the isolation acquired by this process of individuation, yet Adam and Eve's selfishness and lovelessness are clearly conveyed in their eagerness to blame one another for the act of disobedience, rather than defending or protecting each other in the face of God's interrogation (TB 100). Human alienation must be alleviated, and the coming messianic age will be one in which the non-alienated state of Paradise is restored, but it will also be a time of new achievements.

The coming messianic age will be a dialectical sublation of both the past Paradise and the present of alienated individuation; it will incorporate elements of each and simultaneously progress beyond both. Fromm writes, "The messianic time is the time when man will have been fully born. When man was expelled from Paradise he lost his home; in the messianic time he will be at home again—in the world" (YSB 123). The messianic future envisioned by Fromm is a dialectical synthesis of, on the one hand, the primal oneness with nature and one's fellow humans experienced as the earliest stage of human life—variously characterized by Fromm as primitive communism, matriarchy (following Bachofen), and allegorically as Paradise/Eden—and the individuality and autonomy of persons advanced by humanism and the Enlightenment. Memory of humanity's early unity and non-alienation can be progressive, for Fromm, and need not result in a reactionary attempt to flee from the pressures of the present. One may conceive Fromm as standing somewhere between the two positions of Martin Buber's "renewal" and Ernst Bloch's *Novum*, rejecting both the traditionalist, utopian socialism of Buber and Landauer, and the "Total-*Futurum*" of Bloch.

Since the messianic time is a dialectical synthesis of Paradise and humanity's subsequent achievement of individuation, Fromm's philosophy of history is teleological, not cyclical. Although "paradise is the golden age of the past" and "the messianic time is the golden age of the future," these two states are quite different (YSB 123). Fromm's notion of history is not cyclical, the future is not simply a return to the past, and the origin is only half of the goal. The pre-historic golden age is defined by "man's not yet having been born" and the messianic age by "man's having been fully born" (123-4). Before the rebellion in the garden, the person is not even aware of being an individual (HOM 20). The coming messianic time is something *never before achieved* in human history, representing progress beyond both the past and the present. It sublates and fulfills all past history.

* * *

Is Fromm's account "Gnostic"? I will return to this question at the end of the chapter, but here I offer a preliminary response. The main problem here is that, for Fromm, the serpent is *right*: through disobedience, human beings could become like gods. One might worry that Fromm has made the serpent the hero of Genesis. Hans Jonas points out that the Gnostics of early Christianity employed allegories that reversed the hierarchical relations between good and evil; the reversal of these roles is supposed to demonstrate a "deeper 'knowledge'" (Jonas 92). Gnostic allegory creates a "new mythology" and rebels against established myths (94). The positive interpretation of the role of the serpent was a shining example of this and figured prominently in Gnostic thought, and, as Jonas pointed out, some Gnostic cults even named themselves after the serpent (93). But the *hero* of Fromm's account is really not the serpent but Eve. It is Eve, the first woman, who gives birth to civilization; Fromm's feminism is apparent here: "for Fromm, the archetypical act of emancipatory disobedience, indeed, the act which forced human[s] on the road to history, is one committed by a woman: Eve" (Cheliotis 2).

Is Fromm, then, standing in the tradition of Karl Kraus, Stefan George, and Heinrich von Kleist? Is Fromm quoting Kleist's allegory of sneaking into the locked Paradise, or is he referring to something else entirely? (Kleist wrote: "The gates of Eden are barred against us and the angel drives us on. We must make a journey round the world and see whether we can perhaps find another place to creep in at" (Kleist 85). Fromm wrote: "two angels with fiery swords watch the entrance and man cannot return" (OBH 75).) Our interlocutor might argue that Fromm sees the "origin" as the "goal." Like Marcuse in his more Romantic moments, one might argue, Fromm seeks to return to the primordial, to the pre-historic, to the infantile state of innocence. In that state there is no knowledge of good or evil, and the act of disobedience can be legitimately enacted and a new era begun. Sin does not exist there, so redemption through what *was* sin would now be possible—humanity would boldly disobey, eating again from the tree of knowledge. Is Fromm's praise of Adam and Eve's act of disobedience therefore a defense of Gnostic "nihilism and libertinism" (in Hans Jonas's parlance) (Jonas 270)?

A thorough examination of *You Shall Be as Gods* makes obvious which side Fromm is on, although he occasionally draws from the insights of his opponents. It becomes clear what side the book is on when Fromm writes, "There is a dialectic relationship between Paradise and the messianic time. Paradise is the golden age of the past, as many legends in other cultures see it. The messianic time is the golden age of the future" (YSB 123). This highly significant statement is central to why Fromm's messianism is *not*, and cannot be conceived as, the restoration of a Golden Age. Precisely because of this "dialectic relationship," Fromm's messianism avoids the excesses of the return to the past found in Karl Kraus, Ludwig Klages, Stefan George, Walter Benjamin, Herbert Marcuse, and others.

As seen in Chapter 1, Fromm's early work on Bachofen condemned Ludwig Klages as reactionary and denounced the rising cultural pessimism and the yearning for return to a lost primordial world. Fromm's "Dogma of Christ" also offered a pointed and thinly veiled critique of the "gnostics" of his own day, presented as a critique of ancient Christian Gnostics. There he wrote that second century Christianity had abandoned its revolutionary roots and become "revisionism" (DC 75). Against this reformist Christianity—which Fromm obviously intended to represent reformist socialism—there were the options of Gnosticism and radical Montanism. Montanism was truly radical, standing "against the conforming tendencies of Christianity" and trying to "restore the early Christian enthusiasm" (75). Then there was the Gnostic option: these members of the "well-to-do Hellenistic middle class...wanted to accomplish too quickly and too suddenly what [they] wished, since [they] announced the secret of the coming Christian development before the consciousness of the masses could accept it" (76). Despite attempting to force change, Gnosticism "rejected the real collective change and redemption of humanity, and substituted an individual ideal of knowledge"; Gnosticism endorsed social hierarchies while dividing the world into initiates and completely fallen non-initiates (77).

Raya Dunayevskaya, the founder of a "Marxist Humanist" tendency on the U.S. left and the only prominent Marxist organizer in the U.S. who took the influence of Hegel upon Marx very seriously, corresponded at length with both Fromm and Marcuse. She began her correspondence with Marcuse in 1954 in response to his *Reason and Revolution* and broke off correspondence with Marcuse for a while as she was beginning her correspondence with Fromm, initiated by Fromm's 1959 invitation to translate Marx's 1844 Manuscripts for *Marx's Concept of Man* (Anderson and Rockwell xxxv, 3, 121).

Because Fromm appears to employ allegorical imagery from both sides of the prophetic-apocalyptic divide, it might seem that he was being either obtuse or intentionally ambiguous, but neither is the case. Fromm's humanism places him in a different camp from that of Kleist's conservative admirers. The fact that Fromm makes the serpent the voice of wisdom in his account of the myth from Genesis seems puzzling, however, since this might appear to be a nod to the neo-Gnosticism that swept through Germany in the early 1920s. In the very same book he condemns the strategy of Sabbatai Zevi and the doctrine of redemption through sin and praises Rosa Luxemburg, thus opposing that wave of Gnosticism. Was Fromm just confused? No, as I will argue.

Fromm's use of symbolism from both sides of the prophetic-apocalyptic divide was not accidental, nor was he conflicted about his allegiance. As a scholar trained from youth in a multi-layered hermeneutic through his study of Jewish scriptures and tradition under Salman Rabinkow and through his study of psychoanalysis, Fromm wrote on a variety of levels to a variety of audiences. The Kabbalistic tradition teaches that there are four levels upon which a text can be read, from the more literal to the more allegorical. The Kabbalistic hermeneutic is prefigured in a less esoteric form in the tradition of *Midrash* (Gertel 437). It has been suggested that Fromm employs the tradition of *Midrash* in his hermeneutical approach to the Bible as well as in his "reading" of the individual patient (437). The method "is not only concerned with blending new insights and ancient wisdom...but must also contain *musar* (ethical teaching) and *tochachot* (criticism and reproof)" (Gertel 437, quoting Petuchowksi).

Far from any Gnostic intent and far also from the arguable obscurantism of Lurianic Kabbalah, for Fromm the disobedience of Adam and Eve serves as an allegory for three events: (1) the individual's birth and process of psychological individuation, (2) the bourgeois revolutions, and (3) the struggle against Nazism.

(1) On a psychoanalytic level, the allegory conveys the individual's discovery of individuality, when the infant realizes that it is not one with the mother. In *The Anatomy of Human Destructiveness*, Fromm writes that at birth the infant "leaves the security of the womb," but "there remains a deep craving not to sever the original ties or a deep craving to find a new situation of absolute protection and security, to return to the lost paradise" (AHD 232). Fromm continues:

But the way to paradise is blocked by man's biological, and particularly by his neurophysiological constitution. He has only one alternative: either to

161

persist in his craving to regress, and to pay for it by symbolic dependence on mother (and on symbolic substitutes, such as soil, nature, god, the nation, a bureaucracy), or to progress and find new roots in the world by his own efforts, by experiencing the brotherhood of man, and by freeing himself from the power of the past. (232-3)

Here Fromm's alternativism is brought to light. Note also the significance of the list "soil, nature, god, the nation, a bureaucracy," all dangerous idolatries critiqued by Fromm.

(2) From the perspective of political economy, the act of disobedience represents the origins of civilization, which Bachofen linked to the rise of patriarchy. The yearning for return to Paradise is thus a yearning to return to a point before human civilization. The allegory thus seems to describe the move from a society without civilization—Paradise in the allegory exists prior to organized society—to a society in which the bonds to blood and soil have been rent asunder, replaced by a hierarchal system of power in which women are vanquished. The yearning to return to pre-historical societies was intensified after the bourgeois revolutions, which re-enacted the ancient act of disobedience through overthrowing feudalism. The bourgeois revolutions produced new freedoms but also a burdensome individualism. Psychological individuation is a struggle universal to the human condition, but capitalism and the Protestant ethic increased its burdensomeness, leading to increased loneliness, despair, and fear of freedom. The fear of freedom in turn played a role in the rise of Nazism, to the attempt to renounce a higher degree of civilization that had been attained in order to regress to a pre-historic state.

(3) Fromm often consciously links his discussion to the desire for regression to the pre-historical, pre-civilizational paradise with language coded as references to Nazi propaganda: "rootedness," "blood," "soil," "nation" (AHD 232-3). More than once, he compares this desire for regression to the bizarre behavior of the "Teutonic berserkers" (HOM 120; ZB 93). Although Nazism was obviously far from being a matriarchal system, there was a common attraction to the idea of dependence associated with matriarchy. Fromm states that in the case of the Nazis (referring specifically to Himmler in this case),

[T]he need for a strong father is generated by the person's helplessness, which in turn is generated by his remaining a little boy who longs for his mother (or a mother figure) to love him, protect him, comfort him, and not to demand anything from him. Thus he feels not like a man but like a child: weak, helpless, without will or initiative. Hence he will often look for a strong leader to whom he can submit, who gives him a feeling of strength, and who—in an imitating relationship, becomes a substitute for the qualities he lacks. (AHD 304)

As we saw in Chapter 2, there were strains of proto-fascist culture in the Stefan George circle that embraced this mythos of return. We also saw in Chapter 1 how Fromm's wariness about regression was reflected in his study of Bachofen's reactionary and revolutionary admirers. Fromm's concern with the rise of Nazism is without doubt a prevailing subtext in all of his warnings against the yearning for return to the past.

* * *

Fromm's view that the messianic age would be a dialectical synthesis of the prehistoric Paradise and the historic achievements of individuality and enlightenment contrasts sharply with the restorative messianisms of the lost generation in Germany. Karl Kraus's line "origin is the goal" became the veritable slogan of a generation of messianists, while the esoteric writer Oskar Goldberg pronounced a re-enchantment of the world with his call for society to go "back to cult" (Rabinbach, "Between Enlightenment" 84; Benjamin, *Illuminations* 253; Assmann, Assmann, and Hartwich xx). The Cosmic Circle's yearning for return to Bachofen's prehistoric matriarchy found little in modernity that it wanted to appropriate for its project of aristocratic barbarism. But because Fromm's future was a dialectical synthesis, not a mere return and not a total other, Fromm's messianism required no absolute "rupture." While initiating a major change in history, the messianic age did not require absolute negation and could be envisioned and planned for to a certain extent. Wary of the yearning for return among George's circle and similar intellectual circles, Fromm saw restorative-oriented anamnesis as fundamentally dangerous.

One aspect of the dangers of memory that Fromm does not address directly needs to be dealt with here. Namely, some have suggested that a messianic future is impossible, because any bright future would still be troubled by memories of past injustice. Derrida, for example, has spoken of the way in which the past "haunts" the present, and in this he follows in the footsteps of Walter Benjamin's famous passage about the Angel of History, which looks back over its shoulder at the wreckage of progress:

> A Klee painting named "Angelus Novus" shows an angel looking as though he is about to move away from something he is fixedly contemplating. His eyes are staring, his mouth is open, his wings are spread. This is how one pictures the angel of history. His face is turned toward the past. Where we perceive a chain of events, he sees one single catastrophe which keeps piling wreckage upon wreckage and hurls it in front of his feet. The angel would like to stay, awaken the dead, and make whole what has been smashed. But a storm is blowing from paradise; it has got caught in his wings with such violence that the angel can no longer close them. This storm irresistibly propels him into the future to which his back is turned, while the pile of debris before him grows skyward. This storm is what we call progress. (*Illuminations* 257-8)

Although this is not the place to examine Derrida's or Benjamin's arguments, a possible response to the problem can be proposed briefly. If the future will be "haunted" by past victims, there are two possible reasons. First, one may feel a duty to remember past victims. If that is the case, one has little choice but to be haunted.

Although this duty of memory might dampen one's enjoyment of the messianic age, as long as the messianic age is not one of *complete* perfection and does not ground a theodicy, this poses little problem for messianism. Certainly a world in which the only burden is the memory of past suffering would be a vast advance over the present. For example, it seems almost comical that the "sermon" of the futuristic pastor in Edward Bellamy's utopian novel *Looking Backward* pertains only to how awful things used to be (Bellamy 183-194).

However, there is a second, *pathological* way in which the past can haunt the present. One could be haunted by history's victims because one is simply unable and unwilling to let go, maintaining pathological ties to the victims. One notices for example that it is common to console someone who has lost a loved one by saying that the deceased "would want you to be happy." If such advice is given too soon after the loss, one can predict that the bereaved would only become irritated and insist upon her right to mourn. But as time passes, the bereaved becomes receptive to such advice; she learns to laugh, to enjoy, and to love again, without feelings of guilt. Certainly no one who has lost someone close to them is willing to entertain the possibility of *forgetting* the lost loved one, and generally even the suggestion that the pain of the loss will someday cease is rejected by the bereaved as an impossibility or an affront. However, the one who is able to grieve in a non-pathological way will be able to experience happiness and satisfaction in life again and will not transform her grief into destructive impulses.

To employ a distinction drawn by Freud in his 1917 essay, "Mourning and Melancholia," the person who can cope well with grief *mourns* without becoming *melancholic* (Jay, *Force Fields* 90). The mourner distinguishes her own identity from that of the lost loved one. While the mourner may feel that she has "lost a piece" of herself, she acknowledges, both consciously and unconsciously, that she must live on in the face of the loss. Through "testing reality," the mourner is repeatedly reminded of the loss of the other, enabling her to "slowly and painfully withdraw [her] libido from it" (93). The melancholic, by contrast, withdraws from reality and identifies herself completely with the lost victim, experiencing a total loss of self and regressing into a childlike narcissism (rejecting a reality outside her) in a failed attempt to regain her lost identity. This narcissism expresses itself partly in a masochistic desire for punishment, which Freud considered to be the chief characteristic of the melancholic (91). Melancholy causes destructive behavior towards the self and others, either through withdrawal from the world or a manic lashing out at the world. In Martin Jay's words, melancholia results in "suicidal fantasies and deeds" and may be transformed into a destructive "mania," which "discharges a surplus of energy freed by a sudden rupture in a long-sustained condition of habitual psychic expenditure" (91).

Could there be a connection between melancholia—this memory that refuses to let go—and apocalyptic/catastrophic messianism? We have already seen that Fromm links apocalyptic messianism to despair. Martin Jay draws the connection between melancholia and apocalypticism:

There is little doubt that the symptoms of melancholy, as Freud describes them, approximate very closely those of apocalyptic thinking: deep and painful dejection, withdrawal of interest in the everyday world, diminished capacity to love, paralysis of the will, and, most important of all, radical lowering of self-esteem accompanied by fantasies of punishment for assumed moral transgressions. (*Force Fields* 92)

Jay raises this issue in the course of a critique of postmodern despair or melancholia concerning the loss of past historical ideals. He quotes Jean Baudrillard's statement that "we are all melancholic" due to the "disappearance of meaning," and Jean-François Lyotard's talk of "a kind of grieving or melancholy with respect to the idea of the modern era" (90). However, Jay notes, this problem extends beyond postmodernism to all instantiations of the apocalyptic imagination:

Such admissions [Baudrillard and Lyotard] provide us with an important clue to the apocalyptic imaginary as a whole, and not merely its postmodern variant. That is, melancholy may well be the best term to describe the underlying mental condition accompanying fantasies of termination, while mania captures the mood engendered by belief in a rebirth or redemptive unveiling after catastrophe. Although I am not usually prone to psychologizing cultural phenomena, the fit between the apocalyptic mentality and these pathologies is too striking to ignore. (90)

Jay is wise to offer the disclaimer that he does not embrace "psychologizing cultural phenomena." Psychological profiles of "The Utopian," "The Revolutionary," or "The Fanatic" are too often protean caricatures that are constantly re-adapted to meet the changing needs of the ruling class. As Alberto Toscano and William T. Cavanaugh have recently pointed out, the tendency to pathologize social movements is often employed to anti-emancipatory ends. Toscano points out, for example, that at one moment "the fanatic" or *Schwärmer* was a hot-headed religious seer, and at another, a coldly calculating, atheistic bureaucrat—all depending upon the political needs of the moment. Cavanaugh's *The Myth of Religious Violence* explores how religious sentiments have been cast in a pathological light to present all religions (or some religions, since the definition of "religion" itself is protean) as inherently violent. Although Jay wisely acknowledges the danger of political pathologizing, he recognizes a pathology of melancholia and mania within apocalyptic thought that is so conspicuous, widespread, and problematic that it must be subjected to critique.

It is unfortunate that Jay does not address Fromm in the course of these speculations, since the critique closely resembles Fromm's critique of apocalyptic/ catastrophic messianism and the false hope that forces the Messiah. It is also unfortunate that Jay does not carry his reflection on the danger of melancholy and apocalypticism further, to a critique of Adorno, Benjamin, and Horkheimer, since then he might find a worrying apocalypticism in the work of others in the Frankfurt School and rediscover Fromm as a possible corrective. (Although Jay's work builds upon Adorno's work on melancholy, it is possible that Adorno is susceptible to his own critique.) Instead, Jay leaves off with a critique of postmodernists who are convinced that philosophy or social change has ended, and a critique of "scientific apocalyptic thinking," as manifested in an unconscious yearning for environmental destruction (*Force Fields* 92-94, 84-98). If this yearning for environmental destruction seems implausible, consider for example the recent anti-technological, anti-humanist science fiction film *The Happening*, in which plants spontaneously release a toxin producing suicidal tendencies, until enough people have committed suicide for nature to flourish again; there must be some sort of market for films of that sort, which celebrate the triumph of natural forces over human civilization, since many such films have been produced lately. (I return to this theme in the Polemical Postscript below.) Jay does slip in a critique of Heidegger on technology that could potentially be expanded and employed in a critique of Heidegger's influence on Critical Theory, but Jay does not proceed in that direction either.[11]

One of the illusory forms of hope discussed in Chapter 3—inactive, passive waiting—resembles one form of the apocalyptic melancholy critiqued by Jay, that of withdrawal from the world into memory. The other form of false hope discussed in Chapter 3 is akin to "mania"; it attempts to force dramatic change through the destructive instigation of crises. Although Fromm does not offer much discussion of "melancholy," his concept of necrophilia plays a similar role, in that it can lead to either passive withdrawal or outwardly-oriented destructiveness. In his analysis of necrophilia in his antiwar pamphlet *War Within Man*, he finds internal connections between Americans' passive acceptance of possible nuclear annihilation and the coldly active destructiveness of Eichmann (J. Braune 4-5).

History cannot be retroactively corrected, nor can mere human effort eliminate all suffering. Catastrophic messianism leaves open the threat of melancholy and of regression to the infantile union with the mother, a regression that can take reactionary political forms. That is why Fromm must categorically reject restorative messianism. At the same time, however, this rejection of return—a return that is impossible and can occur only through a harmful fantasy—does not mean that there is nothing in the past, no "forgotten language" left to be redeemed. On the contrary, there remain the seeds of the non-alienated past, ready to blossom again, and which need only be watered with the rains of the struggle of present historical progress.

3.   *The Enlightenment*

Fromm saw the Enlightenment as radical for its humanism, its devotion to freedom, and its rejection of authoritarianism ("authoritarian idolatry") (SS 235). Like Jürgen Habermas, Stephen Eric Bronner, Lawrence Wilde, Richard Wolin, Kevin Anderson, Jonathan Israel, and other scholars today, Fromm saw value in the Enlightenment as a radical project, a project that remained incomplete and needed to be reclaimed. Fromm would agree with Habermas's characterization of the Enlightenment as an "unfinished project" that needs to be continued in certain respects. Further, Fromm saw that the Enlightenment's radicalism was an unconscious continuation of a radical perspective latent within Medieval religious teleology, despite the Enlightenment's surface rejection of religion. While some, like John Gray recently in the tradition of other conservatives before him, drew this connection between Enlightenment and messianism and rejected the Enlightenment because of it, Fromm did not regard the Enlightenment's secularization of messianism as something to be denounced (Gray *passim*). Fromm writes,

> The age of enlightenment was characterized by its fight against the Church, and clericalism, and the further development by a growing doubt and eventually the negation of all religious concepts. But this negation of religion was only a new form of thought expressing the old religious enthusiasm, especially as far as the meaning and purpose of history was concerned. (SS 235)

In this sense, Fromm agrees with Carl Becker, whose book *The Heavenly City of the Eighteenth-Century Philosophers* Fromm cites and recommends (MMP 11; BC 58; OBH 66). However, Becker is more pessimistic about the implications of the influence of a theological, teleological view of history on the Enlightenment. Fromm also cites Ernst Cassirer's *The Philosophy of the Enlightenment* on the humanism of the Enlightenment; Cassirer's book is much more favorable to the Enlightenment than Becker's (OBH 66).

Fromm holds that Marxism stands within the same prophetic-messianic tradition as the Enlightenment and that the Enlightenment's messianism helped give rise to Marxism. According to Fromm, "Socialism as a political movement, and at the same time as a theory dealing with the laws of society and a diagnosis of its ills, may be said to have been started in the French Revolution" (SS 249). Condorcet's radical messianism, Fromm claims, influenced Proudhon and utopian socialists Saint-Simon and Comte, and in turn Marx (SS 236). Further, Fromm writes, Marx was influenced by Lessing, Fichte, and Hegel, all of whom Fromm points out were inspired by the Enlightenment's messianism (236). Marx's own thought was "Messianic-religious, in secular language…The classless society of justice, brotherliness and reason will be the beginning of a new world, toward the formation of which all previous history was moving" (236). Of course, we know how this narrative leaves off for Fromm: this messianic spirit has suffered blows and setbacks, and the most significant one was German Social Democracy's capitulation to nationalism, marking a loss of "messianic pathos, its appeal to the deepest longings and needs of man" (Wilde, *Quest for Solidarity* 122). The subsequent murders of Luxemburg and Landauer were meant to snuff out the prophetic messianic faith in humanity (SS 239).

According to Fromm, both fascism and Stalinism were threats to prophetic messianism (SS 237-9). But Fromm sees the revival of prophetic messianism as largely dependent upon a return to *Marx's* prophetic messianism. In a footnote in *Marx's Concept of Man*, Fromm cites Georg Lukács, Karl Löwith, Paul Tillich,[12] Alfred Weber (his dissertation chair), and J. A. Schumpeter as scholars who have contributed to a rediscovery of Marx's radical messianism and "eschatology"[13] (MCM 7).

Fromm's support for the Enlightenment flowed in part from his defense of reason, although his own understanding of reason gave greater credence to imagination and affect than one might find in the most stereotypically "Enlightenment" ideal of reason. Fromm writes:

> [F]or [Freud] reason was confined to *thought*. Feelings and emotions were per se irrational, and hence inferior to thought. The enlightenment philosophers in general shared in this contempt for feelings and affect. Thought was for them the only vehicle of progress and reason [was] to be found only in thought. They did not see as Spinoza had seen, that affects, like thought, can be both rational and irrational and that the full development of man requires the rational evolution of both thought and affect. They did not see that, if man's thinking is split from his feeling, both his thinking and his feeling become distorted, and that the picture of man based on the assumption of this split is also distorted. (SFM 7)

Fromm's love of reason can hardly be understood apart from the Jewish enlightenment tradition to which he was in many respects heir, a tradition profoundly influenced by the achievement of Hermann Cohen, but which has intellectual roots in Spinoza. Fromm links Judaism and Enlightenment in his interpretation of Freud:

> Freud's Jewish background, if anything, added to his embrace of the enlightenment spirit. The Jewish tradition itself was one of reason and of intellectual discipline, and besides that, a somewhat despised minority had a strong emotional interest to defeat the powers of darkness, of irrationality, of superstition, which blocked the road to its own emancipation and progress. (SFM 3)

According to Fromm, Freud was "the last great representative of the rationalism of the Enlightenment" (PR 6). Freud's critique of religion was an Enlightenment-style critique, condemning the tendency of religion to "sanctify bad institutions" and endanger critical thinking (12). However, Freud also challenged the limits of Enlightenment rationalism, which neglected the emotions (6).

It should not be inferred from Fromm's defense of the Enlightenment as a radical and unfinished project, and from his view that the Enlightenment led to Marxism, that Fromm was an uncritical defender of the Enlightenment, and thus a defender of the Enlightenment's mechanism, scientism, sexism, racism, individualism, and bourgeois narrowness. Fromm levels a number of insightful criticisms against the Enlightenment. For example, he criticizes the Enlightenment's deterministic view that "all evil in man was nothing but the result of circumstances, hence that man [does] not really have to choose" (HOM 21). This Enlightenment determinism fueled an idolatry of "progress," "history," or the "future," an idolatry that was linked to the later destructiveness of Robespierre; in regard to this point, Fromm cites Marx's line that "history is nothing and does nothing; it is man who is and does" (ROH 8). Offering the following Robespierre quote (found in Carl Becker's book), Fromm discusses Robespierre's "idolatry" of "posterity":

> O posterity, sweet and tender hope of humanity, thou art not a stranger to us; it is for thee that we brave all the blows of tyranny; it is thy happiness which is the price of our painful struggles; often discouraged by the obstacles that surround us, we feel the need of thy consolations; it is to thee that we confide the task of completing our labors…Make haste, O posterity, to bring to pass the hour of equality, of justice, of happiness! (YSB 155; Becker 143)

Although this might seem like a mere rhetorical flourish, here Robespierre presents "posterity" as a god to which one may pray for a kind of deterministic rescue, a troubling image. Fromm might also consider it evidence of a sort of perverse attachment to memory, not to one's own memories but to the memories that the future will have of the present. Fromm warns of the danger of allowing humanism (as a major characteristic of the Enlightenment) to morph into fetishistic idolatry of humans, resulting in despise of nature (Wilde, *Quest for Solidarity* 49).

Fromm's support for the Enlightenment also did not lead him to hostility towards religion, the Medieval world, or Christianity. That Fromm's work shows the influence of various religious thinkers is plainly evident. Fromm also evolved towards a greater openness to Christianity, specifically Catholicism, over the course of his career. Especially later in his career, Fromm was in dialogue with various radical and cutting edge Christian thinkers and theologians, including Thomas Merton, Karl Rahner, Dom Helder Camara, and Ivan Illich (Funk, *Life and Ideas* 148). However, in *The Art of Loving* (1956), Fromm warns oddly that "Aristotelian logic"[14] may be a source of both the Catholic Church and the atomic bomb, and even earlier, in *Escape from Freedom* (1941), he seems to uncritically dismiss Catholicism and the Middle Ages (AL 80). Later, in a 1954 letter to Thomas Merton,[15] Fromm wrote,

> I am sure that my picture of the Middle Ages is somewhat oversimplified… Having been brought up in a Protestant country, it took some effort on my part to overcome the negative attitude toward the Middle Ages which was conveyed to me in the first 20 years of my life, and you are probably right that one can still see some of this past in my discussion in *Escape from Freedom*. (UK Special Collections Library)

Fromm also saw great potential in Renaissance humanism, and his later works in general express more optimism about a radical humanist current within Christianity. For example, he writes in *The Heart of Man* (1964), "The humanists within the Church and those outside spoke in the name of a humanism which was the fountainhead of Christianity," listing Nicholas of Cusa, Ficino, Erasmus, Pico de Mirandola and others (HOM 81). The conclusion to one of Fromm's last works, *To Have or To Be?* (1976), shows how much his attitude towards Medieval Christianity had evolved. Here he calls for a synthesis of Medieval Christian messianism and Enlightenment progress:

> Later Medieval culture flourished because people followed the vision of the *City of God*. Modern society flourished because people were energized by the

vision of the growth of the *Earthly City of Progress*. In our century, however, this vision deteriorated to that of the *Tower of Babel*, which is now beginning to collapse and will ultimately bury everybody in its ruins. If the City of God and the Earthly City were *thesis* and *antithesis*, a new *synthesis* is the only alternative to chaos: the synthesis between the spiritual core of the Late Medieval world and the development of rational thought and science since the Renaissance. This synthesis is *The City of Being*. (TB 164)

Although Fromm's support for the Enlightenment was cautious and critical, his approach differs from that of other Frankfurt School thinkers of his generation. Unlike Benjamin, Horkheimer, Adorno, and Marcuse, Fromm saw the Enlightenment as an essentially radical and progressive period of human history, leading to the development of Marxism. (Horkheimer and Adorno's critique of the Enlightenment, The Dialectic of Enlightenment, was initially supposed to be co-authored by Horkheimer and Marcuse.) Adorno, Horkheimer, and Marcuse's relationship to the Enlightenment and to the value of reason is no doubt ambiguous, and there is dispute about whether Horkheimer or Adorno is the more hostile to the Enlightenment of the pair. Horkheimer's Eclipse of Reason, with its critique of the "revolt of nature" ideology, and Adorno's scathing polemic against Heidegger in The Jargon of Authenticity might seem to place them as defenders of rationality against the partisans of irrationality, while Marcuse's fairly enduring commitment to Hegel and Marx does even more to place him in the camp of reason.

Of course, Walter Benjamin's long-time collaborator Gershom Scholem was also an intense critic of the Enlightenment, as we have seen. Scholem identifies the nihilistic messianism of false messiahs like Jacob Frank with the messianism of the Enlightenment, rather than distinguishing nihilism and Enlightenment as Fromm does (*The Messianic Idea* 84; Habermas 144; Magid 7). Significantly, Scholem also holds that both Marx and Freud—Fromm's two major intellectual influences—were dangerous heretics influenced by the same volatile spirit of the false Messiahs and of the Enlightenment (Habermas 145). In addition to the three-part distinction of messianism into restorative, conservative, and utopian tendencies, mentioned in Chapter 2, Scholem elsewhere employs a distinction between "restorative messianism" (based upon the medieval thought of Maimonides, seeking return to an historical golden age) and "apocalyptic messianism" (based upon the mysticism of the Kabbalah, advocating "rupture" from tradition and history) (Magid 7). Scholem thought that the two forms of mysticism had become hopelessly fused into a new, dangerous force once they had entered politics (7).

Although Fromm saw the prophetic-messianic spirit in the Enlightenment, he believed that the Enlightenment was ultimately undermined by its lack of true humanism. In a letter to Thomas Merton, Fromm harshly condemns the Enlightenment, here making the rare comment that the Enlightenment was a *setback* for prophetic messianism, because the Enlightenment gave rise to *nationalism* (Fromm letter to Merton, February 26, 1962). Instead of truly embracing its vision of the universal rights of humanity, the Enlightenment fell back into particularism (just as Jewish messianism later, in large part, capitulated to Zionism, a critique that surely underlies much of Fromm's concern with messianism, although he does not address it overtly in his major writings). In place of faith in "human power as its own end" (to paraphrase Marx), the Enlightenment resorted to the idolatry of mechanism, "progress," science, state, and nation.

Coming from a more "medieval" world, Fromm may have been better able to observe the limitations of the Middle Ages and the libratory elements of the Enlightenment. As noted earlier, most of those in the Frankfurt School had grown up in secular households, and to the extent that they turned to the resources of Jewish religious thought, it could be construed as a form of rebellion against their secular parents. Fromm, however, felt that he had grown up in a medieval world and had been slated to be a rabbi or Talmudic scholar. He was drawn to the circle around Rabbi Nobel and the *Lehrhaus* by a different kind of rebellion, a rebellion against Orthodox Judaism: Fromm and Nobel took long prohibited walks on the Sabbath, for example. By contrast, when Leo Löwenthal informed his enlightened secular father of his plans to keep kosher, his father burst into tears. It had been bad enough when Löwenthal married a woman from Königsberg to the east, to which his father had retorted, "You're crazy! Königsberg, that's practically in Russia!" (Hornstein 402n31). "It was a terrible disappointment for him that his son, whom he, the father, the true scion of the enlightenment, had raised so 'progressively,' was now being pulled into the 'nonsensical,' 'obscure,' and 'deceitful' clutches of a positive religion" (Löwenthal 20).

A particular dimension of Enlightenment radicalism, the idea of progress, is discussed in the next section, but with a focus not upon the Enlightenment's interpretation of the concept but Fromm's own unique interpretation.

4. Progress and Catastrophe

While Walter Benjamin, Herbert Marcuse, and others in the Frankfurt School foresaw a messianic event arriving in a time of "catastrophe," Fromm saw the messianic event as an outcome of historical progress. Fromm was living in an era which, like our own, was deeply aware of the possibility of catastrophe but (perhaps until recently) seemed unwilling to take action to avert the catastrophe. He was especially disturbed and puzzled by discussions of bomb shelters and the widespread view that American families could hide themselves below ground in the event of a nuclear catastrophe, fight off invading hordes attempting to steal their stuff, and then reemerge and rebuild civilization from the ground up. That so many people were willing to accept such a possible outcome to human history, Fromm saw as profoundly pathological. Fromm was involved in founding the anti-nuclear weapons group SANE, which he himself named and to which the title of his book *The Sane Society* is a reference (Katz 24).[16] SANE aimed at awakening Americans to the need to prevent nuclear catastrophe in an insane time of nuclear "deterrence." In a 1961 letter to Merton, Fromm wrote,

I have been thinking a good deal lately about the increasing discussion of what people will do in their fall-out shelters in case of an atomic attack. It seems that most people take it for granted that they would defend their shelters with guns against neighbors who want to intrude…this whole discussion shows what kind of life we would have, even if millions of people could stay alive by protecting themselves from fall-out in shelters. Of course big cities are written off, and those who would survive would be the part of the population in the country, removed from the cities. It would be a life of complete barbarism… Neighbor defending his life against neighbor by force, children starving, life reduced to its most primitive components of survival. Anyone who believes that in this way we can save freedom, I think, is just dishonest or cannot see clearly. (Thomas Merton Center archive)

Passages like this one clearly indicate that Fromm thought that people were *aware* of the potential for catastrophe yet unmotivated by this awareness to revolt, and if the catastrophe were actually to occur, it would probably lead to barbarism and not to socialism. In speaking of "barbarism," Fromm no doubt had in mind Luxemburg's famous speech in which she declared "socialism or barbarism!" the fundamental choice facing her times, which Fromm found to be a succinct way of formulating the fundamental alternativism posited by prophets of socialism (HOM 119).

In *May Man Prevail?*, Fromm studied the peculiar pathology that enabled Herman Kahn and other think tank pundits to "cheerfully" assure the public that society could be rebuilt in the wake of a nuclear catastrophe (MMP 194). In his 1959 testimony to the Joint Committee on Atomic Energy, Kahn urged the public to "compare the horror of war *and the horror of peace*" and to choose war against the Soviet Union (196, italics Fromm's). According to Fromm, Kahn's argument that Americans should prefer dying in a nuclear catastrophe to living in peace under Communist rule was not only a false dichotomy—evidence did not suggest that U.S. disarmament would entail annexing the United States to the Soviet Union—but also rested upon a "moral fallacy" (199). That is, although a decision to die to save another's life or to defend an ideal *can* be "one of the greatest moral achievements," it is so "only if it is the result of an *individual's decision*, a decision not motivated by vanity, depression, or masochism, but by devotion to another life or to an idea" (199, Fromm's italics). But those Americans who preferred death to surrender were propelled by unconscious or pathological motives, not the motives they professed (such as love of freedom). Furthermore, they were making this choice not only for themselves but for millions of "others, of children, of unborn generations, of nations and of the human race itself" (199).

Benjamin and Marcuse, while they surely would not have been fans of bomb shelters or nuclear destruction, took a different approach to the theme of catastrophe. As Anson Rabinbach argues in his book, *In the Shadow of Catastrophe: German Intellectuals between Apocalypse and Enlightenment*, leftists like Ernst Bloch and Walter Benjamin, on the one hand, and rightists like Carl Schmitt[17] on the other, shared an apocalyptic messianism. (We have already suggested that this characterization of Bloch may be too simplistic, although it is definitely partly correct.) Rabinbach suggests that apocalyptic messianism may have contributed to fostering fascist ideology. Rabinbach writes, linking apocalyptic messianism to fascist rhetoric, "The redemptive politics of a fallen world preferred the charismatic leader or dynamic movement to the soulless bureaucrat, prophetic speech to the 'chatter' [Walter Benjamin's term] of the parliament, and the authenticity of 'experience' to the rationality of historical progress" (*Shadow of Catastrophe* 6-7; Löwy, *Redemption and Utopia* 99). The catastrophic messianism of 1920s Germany produced both leftists and reactionaries, as we have seen.

Richard Lane points out that studies of Walter Benjamin's intellectual development usually focus on "Benjamin's shift from Messianic to Marxist thought, or...the connectivity of these phases" in light of similar messianic Marxist approaches (e.g., Lane suggests, the similar approaches of Lukács and Bloch) (Lane 9). But Benjamin's conception of messianic time as a rupture from history—a "Messianic cessation of happening"—seems an oddly undialectical approach to history for a Marxist (143). Lane argues that Benjamin's messianism was influenced by a conservative *Kulturpessimismus* like that of Spengler's *Decline of the West* (9-24). Incidentally, Fromm was highly critical of Spengler and contrasted his own philosophy of history with Spengler's in a lecture in the 1970s (ALi 84-5). Spengler held that Western culture would be destroyed "almost as a law of nature," Fromm explains, but Rosa Luxemburg formulated an "alternative" (85).

Herbert Marcuse, for his part, was influenced by Walter Benjamin in significant ways. The second to last chapter of Marcuse's *One-Dimensional Man* is titled, "The Catastrophe of Liberation." The final chapter takes up Benjamin's conception of catastrophe, worrying that now that technology has brought our imagined horrors and utopian dreams into reality, "archetypes of horror as well as of joy, war as well as of peace *lose their catastrophic character*" (Marcuse 248, italics mine). For Marcuse, this means that the revolutionary potential of utopian visions and terms like "hope" and "love" has been severely inhibited. Revolutionary activity must not (contra Fromm's assertions) build upon concepts already present under capitalism ("love," "hope," "faith," "resurrection," "progress," etc.). Rather, it must create an opening (a rupture) into which something *entirely new* can enter. The following passage, the fantasy of the destruction of the mainstream media referenced in Chapter 2, is worth quoting at length:

> To take an (unfortunately fantastic) example: the mere absence of all advertising and of all indoctrinating media of information and entertainment would plunge the individual into a traumatic void where he would have the chance to wonder and to think, to know himself (or rather the negative of himself) and his society. Deprived of his false fathers, leaders, friends, and representatives, he would have to learn his ABC's again. But the words and sentences which he would form might come out very differently, and so might his aspirations and fears.

To be sure, such a situation would be an unbearable nightmare. While the people can support the continuous creation of nuclear weapons, radioactive fallout, and questionable foodstuffs, they cannot (for this very reason!) tolerate being deprived of the entertainment and education which make them capable of reproducing the arrangements for their defense and/or destruction. The non-functioning of television and the allied media might thus begin to achieve what the inherent contradictions of capitalism did not achieve—the disintegration of the system. (245-6)

Marcuse is definitely right that many people would experience trauma if faced with the sudden absence of the advertising and entertainment industries. But Fromm would object to the tactic Marcuse proposes here and to Marcuse's Great Refusal in general. As I have pointed out elsewhere,[18] Fromm would likely object that this tactic, like the Great Refusal broadly, rests upon mere destruction, while true revolution is motivated by a radical productivity, i.e. in the sense of Marx's *Gattungswesen* (species-being), of human nature as productive. For Marcuse, it is not by building an alternative media that revolution is sparked—after all, he would point out, such a media would be forced to employ the distorted language of capitalism. Rather, the revolution would arrive through an *absence* of what has become commonplace and by an ensuing *crisis*. While Fromm attempts to *build upon the present*, Marcuse's approach depends more upon destroying and then rebuilding society on new foundations, from a *blank slate*, a view that seems odd for a philosopher who was apparently so influenced by Hegel's dialectic.[19] (This destroying-and-rebuilding resembles a left-wing version of the neoliberal "shock doctrine" implemented against planned economies by the Chicago School of Economics, addressed in Naomi Klein's book *The Shock Doctrine: The Rise of Disaster Capitalism* [Klein *passim*].) Fromm sums up Marcuse's Great Refusal in *One-Dimensional Man* as "the refusal to use concepts which bridge the gap between present and future" (CP 19). (Fromm says that this is a shift from Marcuse's earlier definition of the Great Refusal as the "refusal to accept separation from the libidinous object (or subject)" [CP 19; *Eros and Civilization* 170].)

One might object at this point that one cannot simply *assume* that it is possible to build upon the present. One could also point out that Marcuse has a good point in his analyses of popular culture and the way in which workers can be "bought off" by bread and circuses. Fromm, however, does not prefer his own "productive" approach to that of "rupture" due to a naïvely liberal wish for people to "build things up and not just tear things down," nor did he blindly assume the possibility of construction of the future upon the basis of the present. Fromm was thoroughly, painfully aware of all the social and psychological barriers to revolutionary change, but he nevertheless saw potential for it. He found elements within capitalist societies upon which it would be possible to build (love, protest movements and socialist organizing, radical education, "humanistic planning," communal and aesthetic experience, discussion groups [ROH 95]). His exploration of utopian literature likewise led him to believe that the future was imaginable from the standpoint of the present. The future would not require the absolute renunciation of the present, with all of its ideas, but could emerge through rational imagination in the present. For Fromm, reason and imagination are not at odds but rather depend upon one another.

5. Utopia: Imagining the Future

Both Fromm's critics and advocates acknowledge a utopian side to his thought, and Fromm's commitment to reason and imagination lies at the root of this utopian dimension.[20] This utopian dimension is not surprising considering that he was influenced not only by some aspects of the tradition of "utopian socialism" but also by some of his contemporaries' writings on utopia: Buber, Bloch, Karl Mannheim, and others (BC 122). Fromm's book *The Sane Society* is an interesting case in point. I begin by exploring *The Sane Society* and the mainline Trotskyist critique it garnered, followed by Fromm's writings on utopian and dystopian literature, i.e., his "Foreword" to Edward Bellamy's *Looking Backward* and his "Afterword" to George Orwell's *1984*. I then address how Fromm's utopianism can in fact be seen as his chief contribution to Critical Theory and how his related commitment to "imagining the future" (as I term it) differentiates him meaningfully from the critical-theoretic approaches of Herbert Marcuse's *One-Dimensional Man* and of Horkheimer and Adorno's *Dialectic of Enlightenment*.

The Sane Society is one of Fromm's earlier books, and it is a peculiar one in certain respects. It seems less Marxist than his later works. It repeatedly expresses admiration for Bakunin, Kropotkin, and other anarchist thinkers, and it is sharply critical of Marx, parroting typical charges: that Marx was overly optimistic about human nature (a surprising charge indeed from Fromm!), that Marx neglected the moral dimension of human existence, and that Marx was narrowly economistic in his later years (SS 264-6). Fromm would later go to great lengths to refute all of these charges in *Marx's Concept of Man* and elsewhere. (He maintained respect for Peter Kropotkin's *Mutual Aid* and the work of some other anarchist thinkers such as Landauer [TB 84].)[21]

As we have already seen, *The Sane Society* saw the utopian socialism of Saint-Simon and Comte as expressions of prophetic messianism (SS 236). The book also referenced various utopian communities and included an interesting, lengthy discussion of a contemporary workers factory cooperative. The utopian element of *The Sane Society*, not incidentally, was roundly condemned across the political spectrum. Liberal critic William Whyte criticized it in his best-seller, *The Organization Man*, while prominent U.S. Trotskyist leader Joseph Hansen snorted that the book could be easily refuted by reading *The Communist Manifesto* (Hansen 3). Hansen had chiefly three charges against the book:

1. Fromm presents too cheery a picture of capitalism in the United States (4).
2. Fromm's sources are suspect, including anarchists like Proudhon and traditional figures like Jesus and the Buddha. Hansen implies that Fromm is relying on fallacious appeals to authority (4, 6).

3. Fromm is pre-Marxist: specifically, utopian and idealist (a "disciple of the utopian cobweb spinners of pre-1848 vintage") (5).

The third of these complaints ties in most directly with our concern in this section, but a few other notes are in order. In terms of (1), one supposes that Hansen would prefer the tales of trial and travail of the working classes that filled many socialist leaflets of the day. Fromm was up to something different. He was not seeking to inspire revolt with tales of misery. He sought to present a sociological and psychological account, to provide theoretical tools to the masses. There is nothing cheery at all about the book, which regards American society in 1950s as literally insane. As for (2), it seems more like Hansen is engaging in a fallacious charge of guilt-by-association than that Fromm is fallaciously appealing to authority.

Hansen's point (3) concerns us most, since many people would, like Hansen, reject Fromm's claim to Marxism out of hand due to his utopianism and "idealism." The claim of idealism is a slippery one, since the word has more than one meaning. What Hansen means to imply is that Fromm was not a materialist, not that Fromm was an idealist in the sense of having high ideals of justice, peace, etc., although there may be a certain equivocation in his and others' presentation of this charge against Fromm. Tied to the concern about "idealism" may be a charge that Fromm is too happy-go-lucky, too sure that revolution will come almost of its own accord. Again, like the charge that Fromm's book is cheery, there is not the slightest evidence for this in the text, which is one of Fromm's darkest books. As for the traditional distinction between "idealist" and "materialist" made in Marxist circles, the philosophical approach to this question has sometimes been rather lazy. Partly due to an anti-intellectualism that is all too widespread in Marxist circles, it is often unknown or ignored to what a vast extent Marx was influenced by the idealism of Fichte and Hegel, and some would argue that Marx was not simply a materialist but was attempting to synthesize materialism and idealism. However, Fromm never claimed to be an idealist, and Hansen does not offer much in the way of support for the claim. We will move on to explore Hansen's charge of Fromm's utopianism.

Although *The Sane Society* and the response to it are instrumental in understanding Fromm's utopian commitments, a more complete understanding of this topic can be gained through the "Foreword" that he wrote for an edition of Edward Bellamy's classic socialist utopian novel *Looking Backward* and an "Afterword" that he wrote for George Orwell's dystopian classic *1984*. In the foreword, Fromm writes, "*Utopia*, in our materialistic world, means idle dreaming, instead of the ability to plan and change into a truly human world" (vi). Fromm explains:

While the word is taken from the title of Sir Thomas More's sixteenth-century *Utopia*, the more general meaning is that a 'utopia' is a society in which man has reached such perfection that he is able to build a social system based on justice, reason, and solidarity. The beginning and the basis of this vision lie in the Messianic concept of the Old Testament prophets. (vii)

Utopias not only provide a vision of the future; they are related to humanistic planning (ROH 95). They demonstrate not only the impulse to design a future but to seek ways to bridge the gap between present and future. According to Fromm, "utopia is the one element that is almost exclusively a product of the Western mind" (Foreword to Brandt vii). Fromm's "Foreword" speaks of a need for utopian literature in a time dominated by dystopian literature (*1984*, *Brave New World*). However, as he points out in the "Afterward" to *1984*, dystopian literature can serve a useful function if it presents us with alternatives and motivates us to make the right choice.

For Fromm, the achievement of a human utopia requires theory and praxis, not mere aesthetic vision or mystical inspiration (TB 142). Fromm's openness to utopias is closely connected to one of Fromm's chief contributions to Critical Theory, that of his commitment to providing not merely a critique of bourgeois society but a real alternative, not merely a negative but (to use Hegel's term) the second negation, the self-subsisting positive. Perhaps Fromm's most significant contributions to psychoanalysis lie in his attempt not merely to describe pathologies but also to give an account of psychological health, both social and individual. Similarly, while other members of the Frankfurt School tended to confine their work to critiques of presently existing social conditions, Fromm's messianism offered a positive goal for which to strive: the sane individual (the productive character) and the sane society. His commitment to advancing beyond mere negation and to offering a positive account of the future can also be seen in his defense of positive freedom, while he saw Marcuse's philosophy as a manifestation of belief in mere negative freedom. In the following subsection, I show how Fromm's utopianism is connected to his commitment to "imagining the future" and how this differentiates Fromm from Marcuse's *One-Dimensional Man* and from Horkheimer and Adorno's critique of enlightenment in *The Dialectic of Enlightenment*.

Imagining the Future   Since prophetic messianism's attitude toward the past has been addressed, it now remains to address its attitude toward the future and whether the messianic future is "imaginable." In contradistinction to Marcuse, Horkheimer, and Adorno, Fromm ascribes a high degree of rational imaginability to the messianic age from the standpoint of the present; for this reason Fromm is profoundly open to utopian thought. Although Fromm doubtless was sufficiently Hegelian to know that the Owl of Minerva only flies at dusk—Fromm would certainly consider it impossible to prescribe, like Fourier, that garbage collection would be handled by children under socialism—Fromm nevertheless saw high potential for imagining the future.

For example, according to Fromm we can legitimately say that the socialist future would be one of "love," and it is not the case that we cannot know anything about love under capitalism. Fromm writes (largely in response to Marcuse),

> [Some] share the opinion of the basic incompatibility between love and normal
> secular life within our society. They arrive at the result that to speak of love today
> means only to participate in the general fraud; they claim that only a martyr or

177

a mad person can love in the world of today, hence that all discussion of love is nothing but preaching. [In their famous debate in *Dissent* magazine, Marcuse had accused Fromm of sermonizing.[22]] This very respectable viewpoint lends itself readily to a rationalization of cynicism...This "radicalism" results in moral nihilism. (AL 131)

Fromm continues, defending his view that love is not inconceivable or impossible under capitalism:

I am of the conviction that the answer to the absolute incompatibility of love and "normal" life is correct only in an abstract sense. The *principle* underlying capitalistic society and the *principle* of love are incompatible. But modern society seen concretely is a complex phenomenon..."capitalism" is in itself a complex and constantly changing structure which still permits of a good deal of non-conformity and of personal latitude. (131-2)

It seems that Fromm is pointing out that the seeds of any new society are present in the preceding one; while the catastrophic messianism of Marcuse's "Great Refusal" suggests a radical rupture from current society, Fromm prefers to nurture the seeds of the next society that are already present within the current one. Thus, Fromm finds the future more imaginable than Marcuse does.

Marcuse presents Fromm's attempt to change individuals as regressive, as an approach that would render people content and postpone the prerequisite breaking point that would lead to the upheaval of revolution. But for Fromm, as for Hermann Cohen, the seeds of the messianic future can be seen in part in the development of personal change in the present. Fromm objects to the common claim that, "When the revolution comes, then we will have better men":

Marcuse says this, [that] before the revolution any attempt to become a better man is only reactionary. That is of course plain nonsense in my opinion because after the revolution comes and nobody has changed, the revolution will just repeat all the misery of what has happened before. Revolution will be made by people who have no idea of what a better human life could be. (ALi 163-4)

Although it might be unfair to claim that Marcuse believed that trying to become a better person under capitalism is simply reactionary, one can understand Fromm's perspective by looking at Marcuse's and Fromm's debate about psychoanalysis as it played out in *Dissent* magazine and in the pages of *Eros and Civilization* and *The Art of Loving*. For Marcuse, Fromm's attempt to restore the individual to psychological health was nothing but a psychology of adjustment that would enable the individual to function more effectively in the capitalist system and be more easily exploitable. For Fromm, of course, this was far from being the case, since Fromm interpreted the healthy, productive character as a revolutionary character, rejecting Marcuse's assertion of "the tension between health and knowledge" (*Eros and Civilization* 261).

Although Fromm may have found the future more imaginable or conceivable than did the catastrophic messianists he was confronting, there seems to be an internal tension in Fromm's thought on this point. Namely, although Fromm is drawn towards *positive*, utopian visions of the future, he also practices a *negative* political philosophy, paralleling a tendency in his work that approaches a negative theology. Wary of detailed descriptions or predictions of the future and wary of reifying concepts, turning them into "idols" by offering fixed descriptions, Fromm is tied to the Jewish tradition of the *Bilderverbot* (the ban on graven images) that Horkheimer and Adorno discuss in *The Dialectic of Enlightenment*. As we shall see momentarily, unlike Horkheimer and Adorno, Fromm embraces the *Bilderverbot* not as a restorative messianism that seeks return to the primordial past but as an ideal presenting the possibility of imagining the future.

There are multiple reasons why Fromm was attracted to the *via negativa*, including his Marxism and his Jewish background. Marx himself offered no blueprints for a socialist society and is better known for critiques of capitalism than positive descriptions of socialism.[23] Fromm writes in his posthumously published manuscript on Marx and Meister Eckhart,

[Marx] kept the purity of his vision without having to compromise it by concrete descriptions that would be obliged to anticipate developments that could not be anticipated in the old society and by the as yet unchanged man. Marx only described what communism was not. (OBH 146)

It is interesting that the above quote occurs in a document comparing Marx to, and praising the negative theology of, Eckhart and Spinoza, the great negator of all personal divine attributes. Meanwhile, the Jewish tradition in which Fromm was educated was heavily centered on negative theology. Moses Maimonides, the Medieval rationalist Jewish philosopher for whom Fromm always held such high respect, was for example a great master of negative theology. One of the central themes of Fromm's account of true spirituality is negative: the rejection of idols, which is connected in Jewish thought to the refusal to give a positive description of God. The rejection of idols is a common thread in Marxism and Judaism, according to Fromm (BF 90).

How can Fromm reconcile his atheistic *via negativa*,[24] manifested in his adamant repudiation of all "idols," with his view that the coming messianic age is imaginable and minimally describable (an age of love, peace, justice, and so on)? If Fromm believed in a God distinct from human beings, there would be no contradiction; God would be unimaginable, the human future imaginable. But since Fromm does not make such a distinction—since humanity is its own savior, is itself becoming the God it seeks—Fromm holds in tension an "atheistic religiosity" (manifesting itself politically as a radical rejection of the narrow concepts of the present) and the attempt to see the seeds of the future within the contradictions of the present age.

Fromm's and Horkheimer and Adorno's differing interpretations of the Jewish ban on idolatry have implications for the imaginability of the future. According to

Horkheimer and Adorno's *The Dialectic of Enlightenment*, the Jewish *Bilderverbot* or ban on idolatrous images was the first act of enlightenment,[25] since it curtailed the primal human desire for mimesis of nature. However, the *Bilderverbot* also dialectically counteracted enlightenment; it was a *ban on utopia*, prohibiting the Jewish people from representing, and thus *remembering*, their utopian, pre-enlightened, nomadic past, in which they had experienced oneness with nature (Horkheimer and Adorno 186). According to Horkheimer and Adorno, Judaism was able to preserve itself from totally succumbing to the Enlightenment—and thus incurred the jealous wrath of over-enlightened anti-Semites—through its prohibition upon idolatry and upon even speaking the name of God (178). In this way, by banning mimesis, Judaism preserved the experience of reality as elusive. It preserved the ancient, pre-enlightenment awe of "*mana*," of the terrifying, unexplainable force that was worshipped before the rise of mythology (i.e., before the beginning of enlightenment). Consequently, although it contributed to the rise of the Enlightenment, this prohibition was also the last bulwark against the total and final victory of enlightenment.

Fromm had an entirely different interpretation of the prohibition on idolatry and upon speaking the name of God from that of Adorno and Horkheimer, and like Fromm's allegorical account of the expulsion from Paradise, his interpretation of these prohibitions is intended to make a political point. Like Horkheimer/Adorno (and Hermann Cohen), Fromm saw the prohibition on idolatry as central to the rise of Enlightenment. However, he had a more positive view of this connection between the Enlightenment and the anti-idolatrous impulse; he held that the prohibition on speaking the name of God served the same function as the prohibition on idolatry and that both were radical and humanistic, with emancipatory intent. In refusing to tell Moses his name, and in the process uttering an expression that became honored as too sacred to be spoken, God asserted himself as a "living process, a becoming," distinguishing himself from idols, which are fixed things with names (YSB 31). In a Feuerbachian move, Fromm suggests that idols are the result of projection; humans lose their sense of self-worth through projecting onto the idol their own abilities (43-4). The idol then exerts a despotic power over its worshipper, who, though the active creator of the idol, feels passive and helpless and turns to the idol for assistance. From ancient worship of hand-made gods to modern nationalism and the fetishism of commodities, "the history of mankind up to the present time is primarily the history of idol worship" (MCM 51; YSB 43). One of the chief tasks of the prophet, from Amos to Marx, has been to speak out against such idolatry through a radical humanism that points to human beings' own capabilities and reveals the idol to be a mere product of human effort. Thus, while Horkheimer and Adorno saw the *Bilderverbot* as a necessary limit on the utopian imagination, Fromm saw the *Bilderverbot* as an engine of utopian aspiration.

In this section, we have examined Fromm's openness to utopian imagination from a number of angles. Fromm's *The Sane Society* and Joseph Hansen's critique of it, as well as Fromm's "Foreword" to *Looking Backward* and "Afterword" to *1984*, demonstrate his utopian commitments. His utopianism can in fact be seen as his chief contribution to Critical Theory, and his related commitment to "imagining the future" differentiates him from Marcuse, Horkheimer, and Adorno.

* * *

We have now pinpointed Fromm's uniqueness as a messianic thinker with regard to five themes. As we have seen, Eduardo Mendieta's (or Anson Rabinbach's) account of Jewish messianism does not accurately describe Fromm's prophetic messianism, but it may describe a catastrophic messianism in the work of other members of the Frankfurt School, such as Benjamin or Marcuse. Of course, despite the significant differences between Fromm's messianic hope and Benjamin and Marcuse's messianic hope, there remain significant and important areas of overlap in their work. Before concluding, one remaining point needs to be addressed in order to properly situate and comprehend Fromm's messianism. In the following section, I contest an interpretation given by Fromm's most established interpreter, Rainer Funk, who classified Fromm's dialectical thought as "ecstatic-cathartic."

4.2   THE ECSTATIC-CATHARTIC MODEL VS. PROPHETIC MESSIANISM: RESPONSE TO RAINER FUNK

For the young author of a dissertation on Erich Fromm to critique Rainer Funk's interpretation of Fromm might be an archetypal Oedipal fantasy. Rainer Funk's contribution to studies of Fromm is immeasurable. A scholar who knew Fromm personally, published extensively on Fromm, translated many works by Fromm, became the executor of Fromm's literary estate, the director of the Erich Fromm Dokumentationszentrum in Tübingen, Germany, the long-time leader of the International Erich Fromm Society, and the editor of its endlessly useful website, Rainer Funk is the father-figure of all things Fromm. (Fromm even cites Funk and thanks him for helping him to reach a better understanding of Christianity! [TB xx, 45n., 47, 101].) However, I prefer to think of my critique of Funk's interpretation as analogous to pushing past the gatekeeper, in the Kafka parable discussed above, not as an Oedipal rebellion.

In an otherwise very useful text surveying Fromm's thought (*Erich Fromm: The Courage to be Human*), one finds a peculiar chapter on "Forms of Fromm's Thought." The chapter argues for identifying Fromm's thought with an "ecstatic-cathartic dialectic," a term Funk draws from Ernst Topitsch (about whom more will be said shortly). According to Topitsch, the "ecstatic-cathartic dialectic" has its roots in "gnostic myths, which in turn were molded by shamanistic magic and divination" (Funk, *Courage* 223, Funk's words). "These myths were formed on the basis of experiences 'of superiority over the pressure of the environing world that occur in states of trance or under the influence of drugs...'" (223). My suggested word for describing these states of trance is *Rausch* (cf. introduction to Chapter 2 above). I have already argued that Fromm is far from the neo-Gnosticism that swept through Germany and far from its enthusiasm over magic. But Funk's equation of Fromm with the ecstatic-cathartic dialectic is flawed and poorly demonstrated, as I will show.

Funk explains, correctly, that Fromm advocates transcending Aristotelian logic through a logic of paradox (Funk, *Courage* 231). Funk also notes that Topitsch draws a connection between logics of paradox and Gnosticism, and he readily accepts Topitsch's assertion without supporting the claim in his own terms (231). And by pointing out the alliance of Fromm's thought with Marxism, Lurianic Kabbalah, and Hasidism, Funk seems to think he has made his case (229). After all, Topitsch considered all three (Marxism, Kabbalah, Hasidism) to be Gnostic and ecstatic-cathartic. Yet Funk does not point out that Topitsch's interpretation of Marx, Kabbalah, and Hasidism as gnostic is highly controversial. It seems that one of the reasons that Topitsch links Marx to Gnosticism is because he has a deterministic reading of Marx, according to which "evil and...suffering" are "necessary and destined to be abolished by man" (Funk, *Courage* 228). Yet Fromm explicitly and repeatedly rejects deterministic readings of Marx.

Although Topitsch rightly points out the connection between Gnosticism and *apocalypticism*, as Funk notes, this does not deter Funk from linking Fromm to Gnosticism (Funk, *Courage* 224, 227). Funk does not interpret Fromm's prophetic messianism as anti-apocalyptic, despite the fact that Fromm is adamantly critical of apocalypticism in *You Shall Be as Gods* and elsewhere. Nor does Funk seem to pick up on the tension between Gnosticism and rational mysticism (e.g. Spinoza) that is established in Fromm's work, in which Fromm is a partisan of the latter against the former, as we shall see. This oversight may be due to Funk's own lack of confidence in his knowledge of Spinoza, a hesitation that Funk notes in his introduction to *The Courage to Be Human* (xiii).

One can make a good argument that Fromm's philosophy shares some common features with gnostic thought. For example, as noted above, Fromm practices the introduction of new myths that reverse the hierarchical relationships of the old myths, transforming heroes into villains and villains into heroes, especially in the case of Fromm on the disobedience in the Garden of Eden, and possibly in his embrace of rebellious characters like Prometheus and Antigone (BC 180-1; Jonas 92). One also finds in Fromm the radical idea of an awareness of something divine or potentially divine within humanity, as manifested in Fromm's humanism (*Courage* 223-3). This humanistic elevation of humanity is not found solely within Gnosticism, however, but within many historical currents. Although this humanistic elevation may be a theme of Lurianic Kabbalah, it has not been adequately demonstrated that Kabbalah should be classified as gnostic and ecstatic-cathartic. Funk is correct that Fromm embraces a logic of paradox in contrast to Aristotelian logic, but this is not sufficient to classify Fromm as gnostic or "ecstatic-cathartic."

On a number of essential points, Fromm differed from Gnosticism, both new and old versions. Most importantly, Fromm rejected gnosticism's insistence upon transcendence and of the battle waged between transcendence and immanence. His stress on active hope makes it impossible for him to posit too strict a division between the sacred and the profane, a division that he is constantly dismantling. Funk clearly misses the point when he argues for preserving "archaic, mythic, and religious ideas" through which:

> [M]an attempts to make the world and his own self (the soul) comprehensible by "viewing the more remote and unknown in analogy to what is closer at hand and known, and this principally by taking certain fundamental situations of the social production and reproduction of life as models" [quoting Topitsch]. The world is thus seen in analogy to a social structure such as the family, the clan, or the state.... (*Courage* 220)

The archaic/mythic attitude as here described tries to understand the whole, the cosmic, the mysterious, by analogy to more easily understandable social structures. Although Fromm frequently does draw comparisons between the individual and the social, he is not doing precisely what Funk describes. Although Fromm writes of a human experience of transcendence, he works in the opposite direction from the direction taken by the archaic/mythic view just described. He does not start from the transcendent and work his way to the immanent—he starts from the immanent and works his way to the transcendent. For Fromm the humanist, the foundation and starting point of all true theory is humanity ("Man"). This same humanistic spirit is the basis of Fromm's rejection of the tendency to expect intervention by transcendence. He views the yearning for such intervention as both dangerous and self-destructive.

Funk rightly points out that Fromm is a dialectical thinker—one need only consider the manner in which Fromm's messianic age appropriates and negates both pre-history and history to agree about that. However, Funk is incorrect in concluding from this that Fromm was a gnostic (*Courage* 227). Topitsch's claim that dialectics is a manifestation of Gnosticism is controversial and is not a claim that Fromm would have likely accepted. The remainder of Funk's argument that Fromm is a gnostic-apocalyptic and cathartic-ecstatic seems to rest upon the influence of Lurianic Kabbalah and Hasidism on Fromm. Again, as with Marx's dialectics, Fromm was influenced by Lurianic Kabbalah and Hasidism, but Funk is too quick to agree with Topitsch's equation of these sources with Gnosticism and the ecstatic-cathartic. (Funk also fails to note that Scholem drew a strict line of division between Lurianic Kabbalah and Hasidism, seeing the former as messianic and the latter as not, while Fromm disagrees and sees unity between messianism and Hasidism.)

Funk's confusion is compounded by his misunderstanding of the role of "mysticism" in Fromm's thought. Although Fromm is open to a certain kind of "mysticism," this mysticism is far from synonymous with Gnosticism. In the rare places in the text where Funk *does* try to differentiate mysticism from Gnosticism, he does so incorrectly. For example, he writes that Fromm draws from a "gnosis that not only does without mysticism but actively combats it as irrationality" (*Courage* 230-1). What Funk should say is that Fromm combats *myth*—not mysticism. Funk's confusion is evidenced by his explanatory endnote following his statement that Fromm combats *mysticism*: "The hostility to *myth* is shared by Fromm and Cohen, who goes back to the history of the Jewish philosophy of religion and its rationalism that was influenced by the doctrine of negative attributes" (*Courage* 363n84, italics mine). Funk misses the point that "mysticism" as discussed by Fromm and numerous others precisely *is* "rationalism," "hostility to myth," and "the doctrine of negative attributes." Fromm's favorite mystic is Meister Eckhart, of whom he writes:

> The mystic Eckhart is supposed to be an opponent of rationality and of worldly activity, hence quite obviously irreconcilable with the "rationalist" and activist Marx. This misrepresentation rests upon the popular and almost universal misunderstanding of mysticism in general and Eckhart's mysticism in particular.
>
> Mysticism is more or less identified with "mystification," and it is supposed to suffer from a lack of rational clarity, to dwell in the realm of feeling and pious enchantment, and furthermore to imply flight from the social reality and consist of worldly passivity and a continuous state of mystical contemplation. To be sure, there are mystics for whom this description is more or less correct. But it is completely false as far as Eckhart and certain other mystics...[are] concerned. (OBH 159)

Here Fromm defends mysticism in so far as it contains a rational kernel.

As we have seen, Funk's argument that Fromm is ecstatic-cathartic rests chiefly upon an unconvincing equation of Marxism, dialectics, Jewish mystical traditions, and mysticism broadly, with Gnosticism, apocalypticism, and the "ecstatic-cathartic." The remaining scattered points raised by Funk—for example, the "cathartic" aspect of psychoanalysis—cannot alone provide sufficient support for the conclusion that Fromm's work fits within the ecstatic-cathartic model (*Courage* 230).

Funk's chapter on the ecstatic-cathartic is poised to fail from the outset, because it focuses more upon explicating Topitsch than defending the claim that Fromm fits the model Topitsch describes. (Topitsch himself does not appear to have mentioned Fromm in his discussion of the ecstatic-cathartic dialectic.) The closest Funk comes to quoting anything relevant by Fromm in the chapter are some references to Fromm's embrace of paradoxical logic and Fromm's description of the humanistic mystical discovery of the unity of the self and the divine through an "experience of oneness" discussed in *The Art of Loving* (*Courage* 231). But neither paradoxical logic nor mystical experience may be reduced to Gnosticism, and never does Funk actually cite Fromm saying anything that involves any of the words "Gnosticism," "ecstatic," or "cathartic."

Thus Funk fails to offer a convincing argument for identifying Fromm with the ecstatic-cathartic model. In fact, in one of the two chief areas[26] to which one would expect Funk to try to build a case that Fromm is a Gnostic, ecstatic-cathartic thinker—Fromm's *You Shall Be as Gods*, which radically rewrites the history of the Jewish religion and employs traditions of myth—Funk criticizes Fromm for *failing to be sufficiently ecstatic-cathartic*! Funk correctly states, as though it does not undermine his whole argument: "The *Urgeschichte* of religion as Fromm himself outlines it knows neither an original state that might correspond in some respects to a final one, nor such a thing as a falling out of this original state" (Courage 238). "It is precisely here that Fromm fails," Funk decides, "for he does not see man's earliest development according to the ecstatic-cathartic model..." (239). Where, then, does Funk find Fromm employing the crucial Gnostic myth of fall and return? Where, then, does Fromm's supposed Gnostic/ecstatic-cathartic orientation lie, if not in this central myth of Gnosticism? One is left only with Fromm's dialectics and his openness to mysticism, neither of which is sufficient evidence.

One final issue remains. Just as Funk appears to be naïve about Scholem, even employing Scholem's history of Judaism as an authoritative source with which to correct Fromm's definition of messianism (*Courage* 317-8n80), Funk appears terribly naïve about Topitsch in the chapter. Topitsch was a Cold Warrior who linked Marxism and Gnosticism not as a compliment but as an insult to both. Some of the ideas of Topitsch that Funk draws upon in the chapter, Topitsch in turn drew from Hans Jonas and Jacob Taubes (the apocalyptic thinker, Zionist, Heideggerian, Schmittian, and friend of Scholem and Marcuse) (*Courage* 361n28). In short, Funk is describing Fromm's thought in the chapter on the ecstatic-cathartic through the lens of Fromm's enemies, though Funk does not realize this. His only criticism of Topitsch is that Topitsch was a Neopositivist (222).

In conclusion, even Rainer Funk fails to grasp the differentiation between prophetic and apocalyptic messianism, casually lumping Fromm into the apocalyptic camp despite abundant evidence to the contrary. Until we reclaim the distinction between prophetic and apocalyptic messianism, and until we allow prophetic messianism to go by its own name (rather than "liberal progressivism," "Enlightenment optimism," or other epithets), we will not only fail to understand Fromm as a thinker, but our knowledge of fin de siècle Germany, the Frankfurt School, 1960s social movements, Jewish thought, and Marxism will continue to suffer from this devastating omission.

NOTES

[1]   One may be tempted to contrast this claim with Fromm's assertion in *To Have or To Be?* that the libratory, humanistic "being mode" *fights time*, refuses to submit to it, while the "having mode" is confined by past, present, and future (TB 103–5). Although prophetic messianism "fights" time, it does not *end* time. Although prophetic messianism posits a future that occurs *within* time, it does not *submit* to time. It is a humanistic victory over time, controlling and channeling time towards human ends.

[2]   Throughout most of this chapter, I have shortened Fromm's term "apocalyptic or catastrophic messianism" to "catastrophic messianism."

[3]   Here I am using impossible in the sense of "logically contradictory," not in Derrida's technical usage of the term.

[4]   A contribution from catastrophic messianism to the rise of Nazism was possible in the sense that catastrophic messianism is not a uniquely Jewish phenomenon but is a way of viewing history, the present, and the future that is compatible with a range of philosophical and religious worldviews; also

consider from Chapter 2 the way in which the anti-Semitic George circle manifested characteristics of catastrophic messianism and also the discussion in that same chapter of the way in which Scholem's catastrophic messianism challenged canonical accounts of Jewish history and belief.

[5] With regard to Heidegger, cf. Heidegger's infamous claim that instrumentalized Western rationality ("modern agriculture") caused the concentration camps. The "Heidegger Affair" of 1987, when new revelations of Heidegger's Nazism were published in Victor Farias' account, marked a turning point, but prior to that time and again since then, one finds that Heidegger is widely accepted by many left thinkers, although despising his political affiliations, apparently finding his philosophy extricable from them. (It will be interesting to see if a shift occurs as a result of the recent publication of Heidegger's Black Notebooks, which contain anti-Semitic comments.)

[6] Here is the passage from Gershom Scholem's *On Jews and Judaism in Crisis: Selected Essays* that Mendieta is referring to:

> The difference between the modern "theology of Revolution," as it comes to us from so many directions and the messianic idea of Judaism consists to an appreciable extent in a transposal of terminology. In its new form, history becomes prehistory; the human experience of which we have spoken turns out not to have redeemed humanity. That simplified the discussions about the value, or lack of value, of previous history (which lacked the essential element of man's freedom and autonomy), and thus placed all discussions about real, authentic human values on the plane of eschatology. That opened door after door to an uninhibitedly optimistic Utopia, one not even to be described by the concepts derived from an unredeemed state of the world. That is the attitude behind the writings of the most important ideologists of revolutionary messianism, such as Ernst Bloch, Walter Benjamin, Theodor Adorno, and Herbert Marcuse, whose acknowledged or unacknowledged ties to their Jewish heritage are evident. (287)

[7] Rabinbach's first three points are roughly identical to Mendieta's, although the fourth differs. Rabinbach's fourth point concerns the "ethical ambivalence" of (catastrophic) messianism—nihilism and quietism as two sides of the same catastrophic messianic coin (*Shadow of Catastrophe* 33–4).

[8] Presumably no one in the Frankfurt Institute anticipated the coming of a single human being as the Messiah (despite the fact that the left is sometimes tempted to venerate leaders as Messiah-figures). Lawrence Wilde points out that there is one place where Fromm seems to have faltered in his commitment to interpreting the messianic event as an outcome of united human effort. Towards the end of *The Sane Society*, Fromm suggests that a new humanistic religion must emerge, and he suggests that it might arise in the next five hundred years, perhaps spurred on by a new "great teacher" (Wilde, *Quest for Solidarity* 54). Wilde rightly points out that "there is a danger inherent in any approach that encourages us to hope for a new savior" and that this "promotes a feeling of waiting rather than acting, of being led rather than leading" (54). Fromm would share Wilde's worry, and his statement about awaiting a "great teacher" must be considered inconsistent with the general tenor of his work. Fromm does make a similar point about a future "great teacher" or religious leader elsewhere, such as in *The Revolution of Hope*, but he is careful to qualify this claim by adding that an attitude of passive waiting for the arrival of such a figure is dangerous:

> Religions are usually founded by rare and charismatic personalities of extraordinary genius. Such a personality has not appeared yet on today's horizon, although there is no reason to assume that he has not been born. But in the meantime we cannot wait for a new Moses or a new Buddha; we have to make do with what we have, and perhaps at this moment of history this is all to the good because the new religious leader might too quickly be transformed into a new idol and his religion might be transformed into idolatry before it had a chance to penetrate the hearts and minds of men. (ROH 138)

[9] Mendieta and Rabinbach may be incorrect in their assertion that *other* members of the Frankfurt School rejected such a return, in the case of Walter Benjamin, for instance, and Herbert Marcuse in his more Romantic moments, as suggested in the final section of Chapter 2. Yet Mendieta is definitely correct that Fromm rejects such a return to a past Golden Age, and this is mainly what concerns us here.

10   Fromm's outspoken opposition to Israeli government policies and his subtle digs at the idea of a Jewish state distinguished him from some other members of the Frankfurt School, apparently including Marcuse. Raya Dunayevskaya notes in a letter to Fromm that Marcuse was so hesitant to criticize Israel that he supported the Israeli military intervention over the Suez Canal (Anderson and Rockwell 207). Further, it may be unclear how much stock to put in a 1977 interview for a San Diego Jewish student publication, but there Marcuse also stated that the solution to the "Jewish problem" was a "Jewish state which can defend itself," and although he voiced opposition in the interview to Israeli arms trade with South Africa, he was also critical of a recent United Nations vote that according to the interviewer had "equated Zionism with racism" (Marcuse, The *New Left* 180-1). This way of approaching the issue of Israeli political power seems significantly different from Fromm's categorical rejection of the Zionist movement as nationalistic and an aberration from the true spirit of Judaism.

11   "It is also important to remember that the critique of technological hubris was easily appropriated by earlier thinkers like Ernst Jünger and Martin Heidegger, who had no trouble infusing their critiques with irrationalist, mythic energies" (*Force Fields* 93).

12   Paul Tillich was around the Frankfurt Psychoanalytic Institute in the late 1920s and early 30s and had influence there; at the time he was highlighting the humanism of the young Marx (Wiggershaus 55). Fromm came into contact with Tillich again in the 1940s, at meetings of Harry Stack Sullivan's "Zodiac Club" in Washington (Knapp 42-3). Fromm draws from Tillich the concepts of being "related to the world" and the courage to be related "to [oneself]," as well as Tillich's concept of "ultimate concern" (PN 46; MCM 47n1, 49; AL 126). (Fromm points out, "Socialism for Marx was, as Paul Tillich put it, 'a resistance movement against the destruction of love in social reality'" (MCM 49).)

13   This should not be taken to imply that Fromm himself viewed Marx's philosophy as eschatological; he is simply referring to a series of thinkers who cast it in those terms.

14   Fromm's account of human nature and society are in many ways Aristotelian, but like the peculiar, humanistic, atheist mystic he was, Fromm rejected the law of non-contradiction and was suspicious of categories that froze living reality into static boxes, leading to reification of historical concepts.

15   Erich Fromm exchanged roughly thirty letters with Thomas Merton over the course of fourteen years. Fromm's part of the exchange is still unpublished, but I obtained access to the correspondence between Fromm and Merton, some of which is housed in the Special Collections library at University of Kentucky and some of which is housed in the Thomas Merton Center at Bellarmine University; both archives kindly allowed me access. Some of Merton's letters to Fromm have been published in *The Hidden Ground of Love: The Letters of Thomas Merton on Religious Experience and Social Concerns* (Ed. William H. Shannon).

16   The *Sane Society* also came out in 1955, on the heels of Lewis Mumford's *In the Name of Sanity* (1954), a book Fromm later references (ROH 44). Fromm had fun with book titles. Like Marx's usage of the title, *The Poverty of Philosophy*, in response to Proudhon's *The Philosophy of Poverty*, Fromm frequently plays with the titles of popular books, titling his own as responses to them. *Man for Himself* (a presentation of the potential and goodness of human nature) was written in response to Karl Menninger's *Man Against Himself* (which argued that suicide stems from natural human impulses). Similarly, The *Art of Loving* was likely a joking jab at Norman Vincent Peale's The *Art of Living*.

17   Along with Karl Löwith, Carl Schmitt was one of the chief public defenders of the "secularization" thesis, according to which, in Schmitt's words, "all significant concepts of the modern theory of the state are secularized theological concepts" (Toscano 233). Although the defense of this thesis by reactionaries like Schmitt and conservatives like Karl Löwith might lead one to suspect that this thesis would be of little use to a radical emancipatory political program, thinkers like Fromm and Bloch also held the secularization thesis and considered it profoundly radical. For Fromm and Bloch, however, it meant that the human desire for liberation predated modernity and was fundamental to human nature. Where Schmitt and Löwith found in the secularization thesis evidence for their view that modern politics lacked a rational foundation (Schmitt celebrating this fact, Löwith lamenting it), Fromm and Bloch took the secularization thesis to mean that revolutionary change was possible and in accord with human nature or with long-held human desires.

For Schmitt, a particularist and a voluntarist (decisionist), the secularization thesis meant that politics were irrational and existed in a realm outside law. In Schmitt's words, "The exception in jurisprudence is analogous to the miracle in theology" (Toscano 233). Therefore, he held that political change occurs primarily through apocalyptic rupture, not through reason and progress. Like the miracle that breaks the laws of nature, political change occurs by breaking the laws of the state. Oddly, Schmitt's decisionism, while likely influenced even in his later years by fascist ideology, can be used not only as a defense of a politics that idolizes a leader who stands outside the law but also a brand of anarchism, in which the lawless *masses* declare the state of exception, rupturing from law and order and drawing the necessary distinction between friend and enemy about which Schmitt spoke.

Fromm was no believer in miracles, and certainly not in the political realm. Like his hero Spinoza, or Moses Maimonides (whom Fromm and Cohen, unlike Gershom Scholem's camp, admired), Fromm found radicalism in rational lawfulness. The pre-Enlightenment world was not one only of superstition and dark, mysterious forces but also a world in which human reason had grappled with perennial questions and come to solutions not wholly different from those needed today.

[18] In a paper presented at the 2008 conference of the International Herbert Marcuse Society.

[19] Marcuse presents his thought as highly dialectical and rooted in Hegel, but as Raya Dunayevskaya suggests in her correspondence with him, it may be that Marcuse is more Schellingian than Hegelian. Marcuse's capitalism is sometimes a night in which all cows are black (Anderson and Rockwell 8, 17n.17).

[20] Zilbersheid sees it as Fromm's chief strength, while Chałubiński rejects it out of hand. A better argued though highly critical interpretation of Fromm's utopianism is offered by Pietikainen.

[21] Petteri Pietikainen, one of Fromm's more astute critics, writes:

> Fromm's moral ideas tally remarkably well with those of classical anarchists, especially Kropotkin, who emphasized the innate tendency to mutual aid. One could even say that Fromm, [Otto] Gross and [Wilhelm] Reich were Kropotkin's 'spiritual sons,' since they all believed that we have an innate inclination to reciprocal altruism, solidarity, and cooperation... (Pietikainen 196).

Pietikainen's portrayal of Fromm is dangerous, because it undermines Fromm's legitimate claims to being part of the Marxist tradition. However, drawing upon anarchism for a project of socialist humanism perhaps ought not to be considered taboo, and distinctions between anarchism and socialism often come down to matters of revolutionary strategy more than to the future envisioned or the account of human nature, upon which there is more likely to be agreement.

[22] Cf. Marcuse, "Social Implications," p. 232, *Eros and Civilization* 260, and Fromm's claims about the charge of "preaching" (AL 128; WW 19). Cf. also Marcuse's claim that the goal of "optimal development of a person's potentialities and the realization of his individuality" is impossible in contemporary society and that "curing" the patient could only mean turning her into a "rebel or (which is saying the same thing) a martyr" ("Social Implications" 231).

[23] Of course, there are scattered exceptions, such as the famous passage in *The German Ideology*, in which Marx waxes utopian-poetic about a future in which humans will hunt in the morning, fish in the afternoon, and criticize after dinner. However, such descriptions are few and far between in Marx's writing and should not be taken too literally.

[24] One should be careful not to give too much weight to identifying Fromm as atheist. Although after his abandonment of Orthodox Judaism he always insisted he was not a theist, and although he was active in the American Humanist Association, an atheist organization, more than mere "secular humanism" Fromm's humanism aligns with Marx's early writings. Marx moves beyond the atheism of Feuerbach, sublating atheism by turning from an emphasis upon nature to an emphasis upon the human shaping of the world; "the criticism of heaven [in Feuerbach], is transformed into the criticism of earth" (Early Writings 44).

Additionally, Fromm was ambivalent about religion. Fromm's approach to the existence of God walks a fine line between atheism and negative theology. He was likely aware of this. Perhaps if one considers Spinoza (who profoundly influenced Fromm) as an atheist, one would consider Fromm an atheist also; if one is uncertain about whether Spinoza is an atheist, one would probably have to be uncertain about Fromm. Fromm's account of hope, of the being mode, and of the "X experience" suggest that the experience of transcendence is a genuine, mystical experience of blessedness that expresses something about the nature of reality. At the end of his life, Fromm was working on a manuscript arguing that Marx and Dominican mystic Meister Eckhart shared a "common religious concern" and were both "atheists." Fromm intentionally dances back and forth across these divides.

In "Lordship, Bondage, and the Formation of *Homo Religiosus*," Todd DuBose contrasts Fromm's conception of religious experience with French Hegelian Marxist Alexandre Kojève's, defending Fromm's against Kojève's. Kojève, DuBose argues, "confuses the *concept* of God for the *experience* to which the concept points" and consequently sees the experience of God as one of domination and submission (217-8). Fromm, by contrast, distinguishes between the concept of God and the experience of God. He holds that the experience of God is the source of our concept of God, and the attempt to reduce God to a concept, failing to understand God as a human experience, is "idolatry" (221). Consequently, "*what Kojève rejects as God, Fromm rejects as an idol*" (221, italics DuBose's). Religious experience remains nameless for Fromm, designated simply by "x," in order to avoid idolatry of it (223). DuBose's critique of Kojève is influenced by Jaspers, under whom Fromm studied (Funk, Introduction 4). Daniel Burston speaks of the similarity between Fromm and Jaspers and states that Fromm, Jaspers, and Heidegger belong to a category of phenomenological thought that is neither explicitly religious nor irreligious (Burston 201).

25 Note that by "enlightenment," Adorno and Horkheimer mean neither (only) the historical, eighteenth century "Enlightenment," nor a category existing in abstraction from history. Rather, they conceive "enlightenment" as a historical trend towards increasing instrumental reason, beginning with the creation of myths that sought to offer rational explanations of human beings' primal feelings of awe and wonder (Horkheimer and Adorno 3). Despite the obscurity of the term "enlightenment" in *The Dialectic of Enlightenment*, the book definitely expresses opposition to the historical, eighteenth century Enlightenment along with opposition to "enlightenment" in the broader sense of the term employed by Horkheimer and Adorno.

26 The other of these two areas is Fromm's book on dream interpretation, *The Forgotten Language*, which also makes significant use of myth. Although it is strongly humanistic and harshly anti-Jungian, one would expect an argument that Fromm is a mythological, Gnostic thinker to employ this text. Funk does not mention it in the chapter.

CONCLUSION

Erich Fromm's prophetic messianism constitutes an historically situated call for an active, revolutionary hope. Prophetic messianism avoids the pitfalls of quietism and nihilism. A humanistic "alternativism," it is an active orientation towards the future that seeks out the seeds of potential in the present. The potential of the present is made visible from the standpoint of the hope that prophetic messianism provides. At the same time, prophetic messianism is rooted in reality. Consequently, its hope for the future is paradoxical, simultaneously recognizing the possibility of failure. Springing into action, prophetic messianism unites theory and practice by a call for immediate involvement in transforming society and averting catastrophe. Recognizing the freedom of others, prophetic messianism does not seek to force change ("force the Messiah") but rather to liberate and rally humanity towards a future that it must create for itself, without reliance upon authorities or fate.

After a period of obscurity following his death during which Fromm was almost a "forgotten intellectual," a revival of interest in Fromm's work is finally occurring, and his contribution to Critical Theory is being rediscovered. Meanwhile, a rediscovery of the Frankfurt School's messianism is occurring. However, work on Erich Fromm's messianism has been minimal, a problem that this book has sought to remedy. As a result of the deficit of work on Fromm's messianism, the scholarly understanding of twentieth-century socialist messianism has become over-dependent upon an apocalyptic interpretation drawing heavily from Gershom Scholem, while the hopeful messianism of such thinkers as Hermann Cohen, Gustav Landauer, and Rosa Luxemburg has been almost forgotten. The time is ripe for a renewal of interest in Fromm's unique contribution to the messianism question.

To review briefly, we began by exploring Fromm's life and work through the time of his break from the Frankfurt Institute for Social Research. Some of the canonical texts on the history of the Frankfurt School, including Rolf Wiggershaus's, Martin Jay's, and David Held's, were shown to downplay or misconstrue Fromm's role. Fromm was an integral member of the early Institute, a tenured member for ten years, who joined before both Marcuse and Adorno and whose work on a synthesis of psychoanalysis and Marxism was emphasized by the Institute's early research program. Contra Wiggershaus, Held, and Jay, Fromm's work was neither marginal nor conservative, neither excessively optimistic nor flakey. Fromm not only theorized the synthesis of psychoanalysis and Marxism but put his new method to the test: in studies of criminology, the family, the German working class, the dispute between Bachofen's radical and reactionary admirers, the Soviet Union, and early Christianity. Much of his early work is united by the theme of authority, especially the way in which submission to authority generates sado-masochistic desires that the state encourages the

191

populace to satisfy through punishment and war. In addition, Fromm's important early work "The Dogma of Christ" was not only an insightful study of the way in which masochistic submission to state power dampened revolutionary sentiment in early Christianity, but also a not-so-subtle critique of the political factions of Weimar Germany, critiquing orthodox Marxists, Bernsteinian reformists, and proto-fascist "Gnostics."

Because of his studies of the authoritarian character structure of German workers, Fromm realized the magnitude of the Nazi threat early on and helped to facilitate the Institute's move to the United States. Once in America, Fromm's integral empirical and theoretical research, his public radicalism, and his broad social circle appear to have built tensions between him and the Horkheimer circle. Although the reasons for Fromm's break from the Institute are unclear—Horkheimer's desire for a close circle of followers and Adorno's hostility to Fromm no doubt played a role—Fromm neither left voluntarily to focus on clinical work nor drifted off to develop a more conservative theory, as is sometimes claimed. In fact, Fromm stated that the break was partly because Horkheimer considered his work too Marxist for publication in the United States.

Just as Horkheimer's prohibition on political involvement may also have helped spur Fromm's departure, Fromm's unwillingness to toe the line in other institutional settings and his stubborn resistance to bureaucratic, "priestly" structures fueled his involvement in channeling psychoanalysis in a more humanistic direction and supporting a "third way" humanist socialism. In these areas too, one finds a problem of "origin myths"; the history of Fromm's contributions to these areas has been greatly misunderstood and sometimes sidelined. Within the psychoanalytic community, Fromm had difficulty with regard to Freud's International Psychoanalytic Association (IPA) and lambasted its tendency towards bureaucratic control and gate-keeping; he was also suspicious of its continued operations in Berlin under the Nazi regime. Not cowed, his exclusion from the IPA as well as American psychoanalytic associations forced him to seek alternative avenues for professional collaboration and support, such as the International Federation of Psychoanalytic Societies (IFPS), which he helped to found. With regard to left politics, Fromm must be understood as a global leader and public figure in the socialist humanist movement, among whose contributions was bringing the early Marx to an American audience and organizing an important international "symposium" of socialist humanists. He joined the Socialist Party of America (SP-SDF) in the 1950s and drafted a political program for it, and he was later active in Eugene McCarthy's anti-Vietnam War presidential campaign. From Mexico he was in dialogue with Paulo Freire, Ivan Illich, Thomas Merton, D.T. Suzuki and many others. His life was one of nearly constant traveling, speaking, corresponding, and organizing. Fromm was always an activist at heart, from his early involvement in founding the *Freies Jüdisches Lehrhaus* to the 1960s and onwards, when his speeches drew thousands.

Yet Fromm's prophetic messianism was not a lone individual's invention, a cry of protest against the crowd. It emerged out of a very specific historical situation, and his defense of prophetic messianism only makes sense alongside an understanding of that context. We explored the cultural climate of Germany at the turn of the century, looking at a variety of thinkers' work on the theme of messianism, thinkers including Gustav Landauer, Hermann Cohen, Martin Buber, Gershom Scholem, Franz Rosenzweig, Ernst Bloch, Georg Lukács, and the Stefan George circle. In the historical period discussed in that chapter, Jewish cultural identity was in flux. Initially it was evolving from traditional religious practice towards a revolutionary commitment to an intentionally rootless, diasporic evangelism of the socialist or anarchist gospel of universal human emancipation. With the despair induced by World War I and the crushed revolutionary uprisings of 1918–19, however, a new generation of Jewish radicals emerged, some of whom in their rejection of Jewish "assimilation" as petit bourgeois, shunned also the tradition of the German Enlightenment and looked eastward or back into the past—anywhere but their present context in Weimar Germany—in search of alternatives to what they perceived as a hyper-rational accommodation to power. Zionism became an increasingly popular option, which Fromm joined for a short time in his youth but soon left, while various cultish, theosophical, and aesthetic rebellions also abounded. Some still held to the older messianism of Cohen and Landauer, but it was a confusing time, and threads of the new apocalypticism and mythicism can be found woven through the work of many of the thinkers of the time.

Hermann Cohen's "religion of reason" and Gustav Landauer's call to socialism constituted an era of openness to utopian ideals and a continued commitment to humanism and an optimism firmly grounded in reality, an era of future-oriented and hopeful messianism. Yet a shift began to occur away from the more "prophetic" thought of Cohen, Landauer, and Rosa Luxemburg and towards a new "apocalyptic" orientation. Martin Buber was an intermediary figure, standing between the prophetic messianism of Cohen and Landauer and the apocalyptic messianism of Gershom Scholem and Franz Rosenzweig. Buber emphasized the suddenness of the coming messianic age and its profound rupture with all that preceded it, but he also defended prophetic "alternativism" and definitely had some influence on Fromm's prophetic messianism. Buber's "renewal" movement was a spiritual utopianism which later thinkers like Bloch and Scholem would challenge as insufficiently confrontational but which nevertheless constituted a protest movement that was more rational in orientation than much of what would soon follow.

It is in the work of Gershom Scholem that a break from the old messianic model of Hermann Cohen is most plainly visible; Fromm was correct in seeing Scholem as a paradigmatic example of the catastrophic or apocalyptic model, and Scholem as among its chief defenders. For Scholem, messianism could not be conceived as an ongoing process of human progress in history but only as a "break-in of transcendence." Breaking with earlier models, Scholem defined messianism in such a way that Cohen's messianism—open to the Enlightenment, hopeful, immanent— was explicitly excluded. Likewise, Fromm's messianism did not fit under any of the three criteria that Scholem offers for messianism (the "conservative," "restorative," and "utopian" tendencies). According to Scholem, the coming messianic age would mark an absolute break from all that preceded it and would be characterized by complete otherness. The new apocalyptic, nihilistic, gnostic and antinomian worldview, reflected in Scholem's work, rejected the attempt to build support for revolution among the masses and instead awaited an intervention of transcendence that would come at a time of humanity's corruption and failure.

The apocalypticism of Scholem showed that a new option was emerging, although its contours and implications were unclear. Bloch and Lukács, however, evolved in the opposite direction, from apocalyptic messianism to prophetic messianism. For Lukács, this transition took the form of a conversion experience, a kind of Kierkegaardian leap of faith rather than the result of a philosophical argument. Lukács's "leap" enabled him to comprehend Marxism practically and theoretically, simultaneously. For Bloch, the shift was more subtle and gradual but nonetheless significant. Bloch stood in a complex network of ideas and was drawn both by the prophetic and apocalyptic tendencies, but he ended unquestionably in the socialist humanist camp, a defender of the immanent action of human beings in history, and his work on myth, at least after the 1930s, was aimed not at mystification or obscurantism but at reclaiming for the revolutionary masses the stories that had long been the property of the right-wing and finding in these stories tools for universal human emancipation. Both Bloch and Lukács evolved towards a greater emphasis upon immanence and greater wariness of transcendent interventions, although Bloch (unlike Fromm) continued to view the coming messianic age as the result of a dramatic break leading to a future of total otherness.

At the opposite end of the political spectrum, as we saw, Stefan George's circle represented a restorative messianism seeking return to a past golden age and viewing itself as the elite protectors of a mythical "sacred Germany." Like the Sabbatean doctrine of redemption through sin, the dramatic change that George's circle sought would be ushered in through ritualistic violation of social norms. Although their conservative revolution was not intended for mass consumption, this subculture in Schwabing and Heidelberg had broad appeal due to its challenge to bourgeois social norms, its exultation of the mysterious "soul" and mythical past, and its intentional distance from mainstream academic culture. This movement intrigued Walter Benjamin, and it drew the interest of the young, pre-Marxist Lukács and Bloch. Herbert Marcuse may have also felt its pull; at any rate, as we have seen, two quotations from Stefan George appear in *One-Dimensional Man*, situated in such a way as to suggest that Marcuse was intentionally bringing George and his cultural milieu back into discussion. This is further suggested by Marcuse's employment of a quotation from Heinrich von Kleist, a restorative-messianic allusion to a return to the Garden of Eden. At the conclusion of the chapter on the context of the messianism debates in Germany, we also touched upon Walter Benjamin's encounter with the George circle. At the very least Benjamin's encounter with the George circle should show us that Benjamin's shift to Marxism is not as uncomplicated as some suggest, since well into his later work, he continues to draw upon a range of sources that make it difficult to pinpoint him on the political and philosophical spectrum.

After the overview of Fromm's early work and the context of the messianism debates in Germany, we turned to a detailed explication of Fromm's philosophical account of the interconnected concepts of hope and prophetic messianism. We began by exploring Fromm's definition of hope. Fromm offers both a positive and a negative definition of hope, with the latter being more substantive. According to the negative definition, hope is not mere desiring or wishing, is not passivity or inactivity, and does not "force the Messiah." Hope is not mere desiring or wishing because hope requires faith, is active, and is not indifferent to its objects, which must not be trivial or self-destructive. Hope is not passive or inactive because its activeness is deeply rooted in human nature, and activity is nested in a philosophical tradition stretching back to Spinoza, Medieval mystics, and Aristotle, a tradition according to which activity is not the same as being busy (like a consumer satisfying impulses) but consists in being a flourishing subject. Finally, hope does not attempt to "force the Messiah"; that is, hope neither announces the arrival of messianic age before its time, nor attempts to make it come before the people are ready. "Forcing the Messiah" can take the form of uncritical endorsement of the status quo or nihilistic destructiveness. Hope is a "patience-impatience," which resists both complacency and nihilistic destructiveness. The positive definition of hope centers around the concepts of life and potential, as expressed for example in the metaphor of pregnancy. True hope is an awareness of the potential latent in all that is living or "becoming."

Hope for Fromm may be philosophically justified on the basis of an understanding of human nature. In *Man for Himself* (1947) he distinguished between "existential dichotomies" and "historical contradictions." The key to social transformation was to know the difference: to accept certain unchangeable paradoxes written into human nature, while challenging historically contingent social injustices. After Fromm's rediscovery of the early Marx and his study of the 1844 *Manuscripts* in the late 1950s and discovering the messianic element in Marx, he seemed to develop hope that even existential dichotomies might be overcome through a messianic fulfillment of human hopes. The basis for hope for Fromm became a "faith" that nonetheless requires a minimal amount of empirical evidence. This evidence need not suggest a high probability of success, but merely possibility; where there is any possibility of avoiding collapse, hope is needed to galvanize efforts for change. To sit by placidly when faced with potential catastrophe on a global scale is, for Fromm, as neurotic as waiting to be rescued from a burning building when one could escape via a stairwell.

Although Fromm's argument for hope is grounded in his account of human nature, he recognizes that philosophical arguments for hope are not the basis of hope in actual experience. Gabriel Marcel seems to be saying what Fromm was trying to say: the awareness provided by hope unveils truths that were unavailable from other standpoints. Although hope may be philosophically justified by ethical commitments and conceptions of human nature, hope is not attained as the result of being convinced by a philosophical argument but through an experience so mysterious that it seems more like a gift from life itself than a free, conscious choice. Hope often arises in response to crisis and in response to the posing of alternatives (one way leading out of the crisis, one way deeper in). The subject chooses to accept hope and thus to progress to the uniquely revelatory standpoint it provides.

After the chapter on hope, the final chapter gave a careful exegesis of Fromm's prophetic messianism, showing how it is fundamentally opposed to the picture often presented of the Frankfurt School's messianism. The messianism of the Frankfurt School, currently being rediscovered, has been misconstrued as wholly catastrophic, partly because Fromm's version has been excluded. In contrast to the prevailing model influenced by Gershom Scholem's interpretation, Fromm's messianism holds that the messianic age as the outcome of a dialectical synthesis of history and prehistory: a movement from prehistoric harmony, through disobedience and alienation in history, to the coming of the liberated humanity.

Unlike the apocalyptic or catastrophic model, Fromm's messianism did not posit an absolute rupture between the present and the future such that the future is unimaginable and not even partly constructible within the present. Fromm's messianism discouraged mystical anamnesis of the past, instead warning of the dangers of regression or melancholy. It did not reject the Enlightenment but embraced it as a radical, unfinished project, while critiquing its excesses and failures. Fromm's messianism neither feared the concept of "progress" nor reveled in visions of catastrophe. It did not envision utopia as a project that had ceased to be radical, destroyed by the relentless march of technical advance. Rather, it found in utopian thinking a tool for the creation of the future within the horizon of the present. The chapter concluded with a discussion of the ways in which Fromm's messianism differs from Rainer Funk's account of Fromm as advancing an "ecstatic-cathartic dialectic." Funk's interpretation in *The Courage to Be Human* misunderstands Fromm's messianism as gnostic, failing to see the connection of the gnostic view to the apocalyptic and catastrophic messianism Fromm adamantly rejected throughout his career. Thus, even leading Fromm scholar Rainer Funk's interpretation of Fromm's messianism relied too heavily on Gershom Scholem's apocalyptic messianism and on the Cold War interpretation of messianism as an irrational threat (as seen in his use of Ernst Topitsch). This dependence on Scholem's interpretation and on Cold War critics is often a problem in the literature on messianism.

Like Fromm's reputation broadly and the socialist humanist movement he represents, prophetic messianic must be recuperated and revivified. It is direly needed more now than ever. The prophetic messianic spirit provides the only avenue forward in a society in lock-step advance towards economic and ecological catastrophe. Now is the time to pose again a crucial alternative of life and death, hope and despair, future and melancholic attachment to the past. The way forward is not through the instigation of crises nor passive waiting for transcendence, but through hopeful, expectant, and active political programs and utopian imaginational projects.

We need a return to the ideas of immanence, progress, and planning, and a rejection of the obsession with transcendence, rupture, and suddenness. The latter set of ideas may play some philosophical or theological role of importance, but transcribed into the realm of politics they are more dangerous than helpful.

EPILOGUE (POLEMICAL POSTSCRIPT)

What is the status of the prophetic-messianic project today? Are we in a similar moment to that before or immediately following World War I, a time of despair and defeat, a moment in which apocalyptic messianism predominates? Or, are we in a new era of prophetic-messianic hope? A contribution to a 2005 book on Hermann Cohen opens thus: "Contemporary culture appears to have lost the possibility of immediate, positive access to the dimension of the future" (Fiorato 133). The writer, Pierfrancesco Fiorato, goes on to note that historical teleology faces the twin threats of a "'no future' attitude" and a "heuristics of fear." At the same time as this loss of the future, Fiorato rightly points out that there has been a "return of philosophies of history celebrating the achievement of the final goal of the historical process," yet these have by and large been "the worst mystifications and justifications of the existent," such as Francis Fukuyama's paean to post-Soviet capitalist modernity (133). Does all this mean that we are living in a post-future world, where messianic hope is no longer relevant or even possible?

Or perhaps, one might wonder whether Simon Critchley is right in saying that, "We are living through a long anti-1960s," and what the implications of this long anti-1960s might be. In an early 2011 (pre-Occupy Wall Street) essay bluntly titled "Is Utopianism Dead?", Critchley opines:

> The various experiments in communal living and collective existence that defined [the 1960s] seem to us either quaintly passé, laughably unrealistic or dangerously misguided...We now think we know better than to try to bring heaven crashing down to earth and construct concrete Utopias. To that extent, despite our occasional and transient enthusiasms and Obamaisms, we are all political realists; indeed most of us are passive nihilists or cynics. This is why we still require a belief in something like original sin... Without the conviction that the human condition is essentially flawed and dangerously rapacious, we would have no way of justifying our disappointment. ...(Critchley 1)

I suggest that the "long anti-1960s" may at last be at an end. However, we have indeed seen a predominantly catastrophic or apocalyptic worldview predominating in U.S. culture over the past few decades, which I address at greater length below.

The following polemic and political analysis was written mainly prior to Occupy Wall Street. In my view, the Occupy movement has indelibly transformed the American political climate. It has awakened new hopes of proletarian revolt long left slumbering. A crucial alternative has been posed. The people are given a choice to stand with the 99% or the 1%, with history or against it. In the words of Chris

Hedges—a pessimist who, like Marcuse changed by the New Left, had his hopes awakened by the Occupy movement:

> There are no excuses left. Either you join the revolt taking place on Wall Street and in the financial districts of other cities across the country or you stand on the wrong side of history. Either you obstruct, in the only form left to us, which is civil disobedience, the plundering by the criminal class on Wall Street and accelerated destruction of the ecosystem that sustains the human species, or become the passive enabler of a monstrous evil. Either you taste, feel and smell the intoxication of freedom and revolt or sink into the miasma of despair and apathy. Either you are a rebel or a slave. (Hedges 1)

At first, whether Occupy would lead to a rebirth of the prophetic messianic spirit or to deeper levels of despair depended in large part upon whether it would be able to embrace planning without devolving into reformism. Lack of planning seemed to be more to the point, as the fear among some left occupiers that the movement might be co-opted by the Democratic Party was rapidly nullified by events. Whether Occupy would cede to despair and desperation in the face of police violence also was a pertinent and urgent question.

Now that the Occupy movement has waned, at least in its initial form, the issue becomes whether newly formed activists radicalized by Occupy or other movements will learn that revolution requires a type of patience, not just impatient urgency. It is not enough to try and fail—we must want to win, and we must be in it for the long haul. In my view, the chances are still good that the "long anti-1960s" is finally be at an end. We may be in the midst of what the great "prophet" of socialist hope, Rosa Luxemburg, would call a "mass strike" moment: Occupy was preceded by the Arab/North African Spring, the uprising in Greece, and labor protests in Wisconsin, and Occupy's zenith was followed by upheaval in Montreal, with hundreds of thousands of students and allies protesting illegally in the streets in what may have been the largest act of civil disobedience in Canadian history, and Occupy-like resistance in Turkey beginning at Gezi Park. As new such mass movements emerge, we also face a frightening resurgence of the far right in Europe and the United States and the accelerated march of capitalist globalization, imperialism, hyper-security, and austerity measures punishing the poor. Nonetheless, great potential for resistance and transformation exists. The present moment of hope and promise for the left means that prophetic messianism is making a comeback, and it means all the more that we need to be wary of the pitfalls presented by catastrophic messianism if we want to succeed.

Before Occupy

During the 2008 U.S. Presidential campaign, the word "hope" was on the lips of millions of Americans. Liberals' outpouring of affection for Barack Obama expressed a sense of promise with regard to the future, a hope that the long Bush dynasty might finally be at an end, that the "war on terror" would not rage on indefinitely, that the U.S.'s global image might somehow be salvaged, and that the economic crisis could be remedied. It was a peculiar kind of "hope," followed by very little change, and arising in the midst of collective desperation and apocalyptic tendencies. Many Americans felt certain—and "hope" is a kind of certainty, Fromm tells us—that things would get better after Bush was out of office, but they felt certain merely because it seemed that things were not capable of getting worse.

Things were going to get better because of some basic principle of logic—the Iron Law of Worst-ness: Since nothing is worse than what is worst, anything other than the worst is better—or perhaps some fundamental law of physics: to every action, an equal and opposite reaction. The pendulum had swung so far to the right that a return to the left seemed inevitable. Without human assistance, things were about to improve. This "hope" required no action. It required no leadership. It required no protest. It required no new political party. It required no mass-mobilization, organization, education, or strategy. This hope was passive, though it bore with it a feeling of pleasure and release. As Angela Davis pointed out two days after the election at the 2008 Radical Philosophy Association conference[1] the election culminated in a cautious, "collective relief," not the full-fledged "collective joy" that the media was claiming it was. This hope lacked audacity.

The "hope" of the Obama campaign was preceded by a growing spirit of reactionary apocalypticism throughout the country. We were in an endless battle against an elusive enemy ("Terror" and "Evil"). The global economic system—apparently enduring draconian punishment from the Invisible Hand, the almighty god of the market—was rapidly speeding towards collapse. Massive pollution leading to global warming—as the polar bears devoured one another and the arctic ice-shelf was riddled by avalanches and fissures—and a growing world population, suggested to others that doom was imminent. Somewhere in the arctic, some primal, natural force, its hour having come round at last, was moving its slow, furry thighs, preparing to snuff out the progress of human civilization and reduce humanity to cave-dwelling barbarism. (It was time for the golem, our own creation, to rise up and crush us, *Battlestar Galactica*-style.) How were we suddenly so certain that things were going to improve?

Americans' hope seemed to rest upon a self-contradictory hope for catastrophe, and this was true of both much of the left-wing and much of the right-wing. The message of the day was: the worse things are now, the better the future will be. Such a message is always clearly reactionary; it makes oppression tolerable by deferring the dreams of the oppressed, who come to believe that their increasing oppression is the merely birth-pangs of a liberation that will soon descend to them from above, if they but bear their trials patiently. The right saw in catastrophe the beginning of the second coming of Christ or a New American Century. Sarah Palin, George W. Bush, and other right-wing evangelicals had preached the virtues of an apocalypse—if only things will get bad enough in the Middle East, Christ would return to save "us"—and the neo-cons in general hoped to ring in a future of unbridled U.S. hegemony on the coattails of war and destruction. The worse things get—the right-wing thought—the better they will be later.

The left also proved itself susceptible to apocalypticism, and this was particularly evident throughout the Bush administration's rule. Economic crisis is good, leftists often find themselves claiming: it means the workers will finally revolt. A military draft is what we need, some despairing activists whispered or groaned or even informed Congress: only then will Americans revolt against the Iraq war. Environmental destruction on a vast scale, others murmured, has the potential to wipe out our civilization, and then, just maybe, we could start all over with a clean slate, and evolve the right way, this time around. Nature will rise up to crush us, if we can just help it along—this seems to be the vision of some anarcho-primitivists and even somewhat of environmental theorist Derrick Jensen in his recent film *END:CIV*, the resemblances to Ludwig Klages and the era of environmentalist fascism notwithstanding. (This attitude toward environmental destruction parallels some responses to the possibility of nuclear destruction during the Cold War that Fromm critiqued.)

A deluge of Hollywood films presented the destruction of the world to audiences hungry to observe the coming apocalypse: *The Day the Earth Stood Still, 28 Weeks Later, Quarantine, Apocalypto, Eleventh Hour, 2012, The Happening*. The fall of the twin towers was only the beginning of the catastrophic destruction that lay before us. The traumatic experience of 9/11—which awakened in the American unconscious the dream of self-destruction—was a précis, we were warned, the mere beginning of the end. Films warned that New York City faced much more than a gaping hole and the deaths of some few thousand people: New York would be wiped away in a massive flood, followed by turning to ice (*The Day After Tomorrow*), would be destroyed in another terrorist attack (*Category 7*), would turn into a wilderness populated by ferocious animals and subhuman zombies (*I am Legend*), or would face terrorist attacks against the subway system before finally being annihilated by a solar flare (*Knowing*). Images abound on movie posters of the Statue of Liberty toppling or dense city blocks submerged in water or consumed by fire.

Hollywood film *Knowing* is an interesting case in point. The plot: A strange young girl begins hearing voices, apocalyptic whispers of future catastrophes. In a fit of mania, she records a series of numbers—the dates, longitudinal coordinates, and death tolls for various future catastrophes, beginning (not insignificantly) with 9/11. Fifty years later, the list falls into the hands of an astrophysicist. The astrophysicist, unrepentant atheist son of a Protestant minister (asked at the beginning of the film whether he thinks there is a plan to the universe, he replies sadly, "I think shit just happens"), discovers that he has stumbled upon a prediction that the world will end in a week. In an effort to track down the woman who received the apocalyptic revelations fifty years ago, he contacts and befriends her adult daughter (also unrepentantly atheist), whose own young daughter befriends the young son of the astrophysicist. As the two adults—caught between their parents' faith and their children's innocence and naiveté—struggle to comprehend the world's impending doom, the two children are to all appearances (and to the horror, not surprisingly, of their parents) stalked, by what appear to be either aliens or pedophiles with superpowers, who "whisper" in the children's minds and try to lure them into strange cars.

At long last the astrophysicist discovers the source of the coming catastrophe: a solar flare will soon wipe out all life on earth. His son and friend's daughter are rescued at the last minute by the aliens/pedophiles, who arrive from above in their spaceship and are revealed (so to speak) as angels, suddenly transfigured from their drab and business-like appearance into glowing, winged figures at the conclusion of the film. Then the two children, each carrying a rabbit (Noah's ark style), board the spaceship with the pedophiles/aliens/angels, who tell the astrophysicist that he can't come; "only those who heard the call" are permitted to escape. ("Those who heard the call" just happen to be two small, lily-white Protestant children from the northeastern U.S.) The now-repentant astrophysicist returns home to his minister father and family, who die in each other's arms. The two children are shown in Paradise, approaching an iconic tree. And New York—grubby, dark, anti-social, and unsaved—is annihilated in a wave of light and heat, accompanied by nuclear-like explosions.

The film abounds in symbols of apocalypticism: references to number mysticism, to the book of Ezekiel, to a new Adam and Eve. However, the most unsettling aspect of the film is the feeling one gets that the audience is supposed to experience the conclusion as a "happy ending." As he prepares to die, the astrophysicist confidently promises his family that a better life is coming. Good times ahead! Yet, jarringly, the world is to all appearances gruesomely, mercilessly annihilated. The angels (or aliens) are portrayed as cold, frightening, hurtful. They take a seemingly demonic possession of those whom they claim to help, destroying the freedom of the saved, transforming them into automatons who are forced to write lines of numbers (apocalyptic predictions), over and over again against their will. (In one of the early scenes, the young girl who received the initial prophecy is shown maniacally scratching the numbers on the inside of a door, her fingers bleeding.) The aliens/ pedophiles/angels have no compassion for the two parents, who are terrified for their lives and the lives of their children. They coldly tell the father to give up his son and that he, not having believed, is doomed. There is next to nothing here of the compassionate core of what Fromm would call "humanistic" religion. Although nearly all the apocalyptic predictions in the Bible speak of the coming of justice for the poor and oppressed, there is not even any indication that the righting of injustices will come in the future. The apocalypse in *Knowing* is joyless and fraught with terror.

As Naomi Klein has masterfully articulated in her book *The Shock Doctrine: The Rise of Disaster Capitalism*, in the 1950s the neo-conservative Chicago School of Economics began to advocate a new and oddly apocalyptic strategy for spreading neoliberalism. At a time when the majority of Western leaders supported some form of Keynesian economics, the Chicago School advocated a radical break from all state intervention in the market and the immediate establishment of completely *laissez-faire* economies. The attempt to radically and immediately wipe out all vestiges of a planned economy—especially in Chile, following Pinochet's coup, when the

Chicago School served as economic advisor to Pinochet—and to create a *laissez-faire* economy overnight on a "clean slate," struck Klein as strangely reminiscent of the CIA's MK-Ultra mind control experiments. The MK-Ultra experiments, which also began in the 1950s, attempted to make the experimental subjects into blank slates upon which the experimenters could create new personalities and beliefs. For example, the infamous Dr. Ewen Cameron's experiments with electro-shock and sensory deprivation on mental hospital patients in Canada, resulting in massive memory loss and regression, sought to erase the personality of the test subject, making it possible to completely rewrite the individual's personality. The attempt to change the personality of the subject was not to occur gradually, over a lengthy period of time, through helping the patient to re-examine her values, memories, feelings, and so on. No, through a dramatic "shock" and devastating disruption of her experience, the patient would become a helpless child, dependent upon the experimenter and a blank sheet of paper ready to take on new thoughts and behaviors.

Some left critics of Klein's theory of "shock capitalism" replied that capitalism has always employed a kind of "shock therapy" since its inception. A case in point might be Walter Benjamin's discussion of the way factory labor turned workers into automatons; the assembly-line workers experience *Chockerlebnis* (shock experience), "which causes them to react as automatons 'whose memory has been completely erased" (Löwy, Redemption and Utopia 114). However valid this point may be, it does not detract from the interesting connection between reductive behaviorist psychology or mind control approaches to psychology for the individual and the attempt to dramatically remake society from the ground up.

Were Milton Friedman (mastermind and guru of the Chicago School) and Ewen Cameron "catastrophic messianists"? What about Francis Fukuyama's theory that the post-Soviet world had reached "the end of history"? Neo-conservatives like Milton Friedman have an apocalyptic mindset but unlike Fukuyama, who believes that the end has already arrived, they would simply believe that the end is near and that it is up to them to bring it to fruition. Similarly (as Klein points out), the same catastrophic messianism or "shock doctrine" could be seen in the Bush administration's attempt to destroy and rebuild Iraq, bringing messianic "shock and awe" to the people there. A military document entitled "Shock and Awe: Achieving Rapid Dominance" frighteningly explains, in a bureaucratic and calmly didactic tone:

> Shock and Awe are actions that create fears, dangers, and destruction that are incomprehensible to the people at large, specific elements/sectors of the threat society, or the leadership. Nature in the form of tornadoes, hurricanes, earthquakes, floods, uncontrolled fires, famine, and disease can engender Shock and Awe. (Klein 3)

Throughout the course of the Bush regime, the neo-cons continued to speed the impending doom, while much of the left looked on, chanting its mournful dirge of doom. In a warped or fetishistic way, nearly everyone got their wish, though the true longings and hopes of all remain unfulfilled. While liberals gaze awestruck into the supernatural light of this apocalyptic moment of Obama's election (and re-election), their vision gradually grows dimmer and their other senses less keen; they do not observe the danger that underlies such casual reliance on the power of another. Under Bush's regime, it had become commonplace in liberal and left circles to point out the similarities between Bush's administration and Hitler's. Yet many mainstream Democratic voters now seem remarkably comfortable with ceasing being watchdogs and placidly trusting the new administration (even, we can add post-Occupy, confidently accepting massive NSA surveillance and intrusion upon personal privacy).

As Fromm pointed out, the German working class attempted to "escape" their freedom in the wake of the horrific destruction following World War I, destruction such as they had never before seen—things could not possibly be any worse!— through submission to the will of authorities. The same spirit is at work today in the American populace. Eager to escape their awesome responsibility to stop the global military, economic, and environmental catastrophe, they have consecrated the catastrophe as an act of God, and they have retreated, allowing Obama to be their decider. As Carl Schmitt pointed out, it is the role played by the decider, as someone who is appointed to tell us who our enemies are, that is primary, and the personality or values of the decider are largely irrelevant to creating the permanent crisis-mentality (the permanent "state of emergency") upon which state (and market) power rests.

The sarcastic and dark tone of this polemical postscript should not be interpreted to mean that all hope is lost. It means merely that a new kind of hope must be sought. A revival of the prophetic-messianic spirit, over against the catastrophic-messianic spirit, is the only solution to the current political crisis. Rather than relying upon crises to spark revolt, the left must appeal to the prophetic-messianic spirit still present in the working class' ("working class" broadly construed) hope and love-of-life. Our hope (politically, at any rate) lies not with an external savior who will rescue us from catastrophe by bringing an end to history, but with ourselves, who must be our own saviors. Fromm's Feuerbachian move is still the solution to the problem of our time. Religious eschatology that stands in the catastrophic tradition need not be discarded entirely, but those who still see dignity in humanity and subscribe to something like Fromm's humanism must allow orthopraxis to take precedence over orthodoxy and must choose to interpret their traditions in ways that allow for revolution and progress. Prophetic messianism remains the best engine for revolutionary praxis.

NOTE

[1] This section was inspired by the Fall 2008 Radical Philosophy Association conference in San Francisco, written largely as a response largely to (1) John Sanbonmatsu's paper on messianic time (Sanbonmatsu very kindly e-mailed me a copy of his paper at my request), (2) Angela Davis' history-

CONCLUSION

making opening plenary talk, theorizing the election of Obama as, in the long run, yet another let-down of the messianic hopes of African Americans—messianism came up in her talk, since she mentioned W. E. B. DuBois's discussion of the way that the newly emancipated ex-slaves expressed a messianic hope that in some sense "the Lord had come," only to have their hopes dashed, (3) Nick Braune's paper responding to a comment about Fromm's messianism in a *Logos* article by Kevin Anderson, and (4) Eduardo Mendieta's talk, which impressed me and led me to look up Mendieta's book on Enrique Dussel, in which I found his discussion of the Frankfurt School's messianism.

REFERENCES

Abromeit, J. (2011). *Max Horkheimer and the foundations of the Frankfurt School*. New York, NY: Cambridge University Press.

Adorno, T. (1973). *Negative dialectics* (E. B. Ashton, Trans.). New York, NY: The Seabury Press.

Adorno, T. (1974). *Minima moralia: Reflections from damaged life* (E. F. N. Jephcott, Trans.). London,UK:NLB.

Anderson, K., & Richard, Q. (Ed.). (2000). *Erich Fromm and critical criminology: Beyond the punitive society*. Urbana, IL: University of Illinois Press.

Anderson, K. B., & Russell, R. (2012). *The Dunayevskaya-Marcuse-Fromm correspondence, 1954–1978: Dialogues on Hegel, Marx, and critical theory*. Lanham, MD: Lexington Books.

Benjamin. W. (1969). Introduction (H. Zohn, Trans.). In H. Arendt (Ed.), *Illuminations: Essays and reflections* (pp. 1–55). New York, NY: Schocken Books.

Assmann, A., Jan, A., & Wolf-Daniel, H. (2010). Introduction to the German edition (W. Rauscher, Trans.). In E. Fonrobert & A. Engel (Eds.), *From cult to culture: Fragments toward a critique of historical reason*, by J. Taubes (p. 456). Stanford, CA: Stanford University Press.

Avineri, S. (1985). *Moses Hess: Prophet of communism and Zionism*. New York, NY: New York University Press.

Baeck, L. (1958). *Judaism and Christianity* (W. Kaufmann, Trans.). Philadelphia, PA: The Jewish Publication Society of America.

Becker, C. L. (2003). *The heavenly city of the seventeenth century philosophers*. New Haven, CT: Yale University Press.

Beidler, P. D. (1994). *Scriptures for a generation: What we were reading in the '60s*. Athens, GA: University of Georgia Press.

Bellamy, E. (1960). *Looking backward*. New York, NY: The New American Library.

Benjamin, W. (1969). *Illuminations: Essays and reflections* (H. Zohn, Trans. & H. Arendt, Ed.). New York, NY: Schocken Books.

Benjamin, W. (1978). *Reflections: Essays, aphorisms, autobiographical writings* (E. Jephcott, Trans.). New York, NY: Harcourt Brace Jovanovich.

Benjamin, W. (1997). Goethe's elective affinities. In M. Bullock & M. W. Jennings (Eds.), *Selected writings: Volume 1, 1913–1926* (pp. 297–360). Cambridge, MA: The Belknap Press of Harvard University Press.

Benjamin, W. (1989). Surrealism: The last snapshot of the European intelligentsia. In S. E. Bronner & D. M. Kellner (Eds.), *Critical theory and society: A reader* (pp. 172–183). New York, NY: Routledge.

Berlin, I. (1969). *Four essays on liberty*. London, UK: Oxford University Press.

Berman, R., & Tim, L. (1978). Introduction (D. J. Parent, Trans.). In *For Socialism* (pp. 1–18), by G. Landauer. St. Louis: Telos Press.

Biale, D. (1979). *Gershom Scholem: Kabbalah and counter-history*. Cambridge, MA: Harvard University Press.

Biale, D. (1992). Gershom Scholem on Jewish messianism. In M. Saperstein (Ed.), *Essential papers on messianic movements and personalities in Jewish history* (pp. 521–550). New York, NY: New York University Press.

Binswanger, H. (2009). Ayn Rand answers. *Capitalism Magazine*.

Bloch, E. (1918). *Geist der Utopie*. München, Bavaria: Verlag von Duncker & Humboldt.

Bloch, E. (1990). *Heritage of our times* (Neville & S. Plaice, Trans.). Berkeley, CA: Polity Press.

Bloch, E. (2009). *Atheism in Christianity: The religion of the exodus and the kingdom* (J. T. Swan, Trans.). London: Verso.

Bloch, E., Michael, L., & Vicki, W. H. (1966). *Man on his own: Essays in the philosophy of religion* (E. B. Ashton, Trans.). New York, NY: Herder and Herder.

Bloch, E., Michael, L., & Vicki, W. H. (1976). Interview by Ernst Bloch. *New German Critique. JSTOR*, *9*, 35–45.

REFERENCES

Bloch, E., Michael, L., & Vicki, W. H. (2000). *The spirit of utopia* (A. A. Nassar, Trans.). Stanford, CA: Stanford University Press.

Bloom, H. (1975). *Kabbalah and criticism*. New York, NY: The Seabury Press.

Bloom, H. (1987). Scholem: Unhistorical or Jewish gnosticism. In H. Bloom (Ed.), *Gershom Scholem* (pp. 207–220). New York, NY: Chelsea House Publishers.

Blumenthal, M. (2009). *Republican Gomorrah: Inside the movement that shattered the party*. New York, NY: Nation Books.

Bouretz, P. (2010). *Witnesses for the future: Philosophy and messianism* (M. B. Smith, Trans.). Baltimore, MD: Johns Hopkins University Press.

Brandt, H. (1970). *The search for a third way: My path between east and west* (A. Salvator, Trans.). Garden City, NY: Doubleday and Company, Inc.

Braune, J., Erich, F., & Thomas, M. (2011). Biophilia, necrophilia, and messianism. *Fromm Forum, 15*, 1–7.

Braune, N. (2011). Fromm's biophilia: Insights from Sigmund Freud's mission. *Fromm Forum, 15, 1–7.*

Braune, N., & Joan, B. (2009). Erich Fromm's socialist program and prophetic messianism. *Radical Philosophy Review, 12*(1–2), 355–389.

Bronner, S. (2002). *Of critical theory and its theorists* (2nd ed.). New York, NY: Routledge.

Buber, M. (1949). *Paths in Utopia* (R. F. C. Hull, Trans.). London: Routledge & Kegan Paul.

Buck-Morss, S. (1989). *The dialectics of seeing: Walter Benjamin and the arcades project*. Cambridge, MA: The MIT Press.

Buck-Morss, S., & Walter, B. (1984). An aesthetic of redemption. Rev. of Walter Benjamin: An Aesthetic of Redemption, by R. Wolin. *Theory and Society, 13*, 743–748.

Bucke, R. M. (1940). *Cosmic consciousness: A study in the evolution of the human mind*. New York, NY: E. P. Dutton.

Burston, D. (2007). Reply to Pnina Shinebourne's essay review in existential analysis 17.2 on 'The art of loving' by Erich Fromm. Existential Analysis 18(1), 198–201.

Butler, J. (2010). Introduction (A. Bostock, Trans.). In J. T. Sanders, & K. Terezakis, *Soul and form* (pp. 1–15) by G. Lukács. New York: Columbia University Press.

Cartwright, J. (2012). Prophet of doom. *The Guardian*, 1–5.

Cassirer, E. (2009). *The philosophy of the enlightenment* (F. C. A. Koelln & J. P. Pettegrove, Trans.). Princeton, NJ: Princeton University Press.

Cavanaugh, W. T. (2009). *The myth of religious violence: Secular ideology and the roots of modern conflict*. New York, NY: Oxford University Press.

Chalubiński, M. (2001). The sane society: Remarks on Utopianism by Erich Fromm (A. Rodzińska-Chojnowska, Trans.). *Dialogue and Universalism, 7*, 77–104.

Cheliotis, L. K. (2010). Naricissism, humanism and the revolutionary character in Erich Fromm's work. In L. K. Cheliotis (Ed.), *Roots, rites and sites of resistance: The banality of good*. Basingstoke, Hampshire: Palgrave Macmillan.

Cocalis, S. L. (1978). The transformation of 'Bildung' from an image to an ideal. *Monatshefte, 70*, 399–414.

Cohen, H. (1971). *Reason and hope: Selections from the Jewish writings of Hermann Cohen* (E. Jospe, Trans.). Cincinnati, OH: Hebrew Union College Press.

Cohen, H. (1995). *Religion of reason out of the sources of Judaism* (S. Kaplan, Trans.). Atlanta, GA: Scholars Press.

Colman, A. M. (2001). *A dictionary of psychology*. Oxford, UK: Oxford University Press.

Critchley, S. (2011). Is utopianism dead? *The Harvard Advocate*, Winter, 1–8.

De, M., & Sonja, G. The history of the International Federation of Psychoanalytic Societies. *Internationalen Erich Fromm Gessellschaft*.

Derrida, J. (1994). *Specters of Marx: The state of the debt, the work of mourning, and the new International* (P. Kamuf, Trans.). New York, NY: Routledge.

Deuber-Mankowsky, A. (2005). Hanging over the abyss: On the relation between knowledge and experience in Hermann Cohen and Walter Benjamin. In R. Munk (Ed.), *Hermann Cohen's critical idealism*. Dordrecht, Netherlands: Springer.

Deutscher, I. (1968). *The non-Jewish Jew and other essays*. London, UK: Oxford University Press.

DuBose, T. (2000). Lordship, bondage, and the formation of the homo religiosus. *Journal of Religion and Health, 39*(3), 217–226.

Dubnov, A. (2008). Priest or jester? Jacob L. Talmon (1916–1980) on history and intellectual engagement. *History of European Ideas, 34*, 133–145.

𝄐 Dunham, K. (1969). *Island possessed*. Garden City, NY: Doubleday and Company, Inc.

Erich Fromm: The Mike Wallace interview. Retrieved from http://www.hrc.utexas.edu/multimedia/video/2008/wallace/fromm_erich_t.html

Erös, F. (1992). *Wilhelm Reich, Erich Fromm, and the analytical social psychology of the Frankfurt School.* Retrieved from http://www.erich-fromm.de/biophil/en/images/stories/pdf-Dateien/Eroes_F_1992.pdf

Farr, A. L. (2009). *Critical theory and democratic vision: Herbert Marcuse and recent liberation philosophies*. Lanham, MD: Rowman and Littlefield.

Fedderson, J. (2007). Erich Fromm: Die Kunst der Abfuhr. *Die Tageszeitung*. Retrieved September 10, 2007 from http://www.taz.de/?id=start&art=4394&id=theorie-artikel&cHash=c1595411ff

Fiorato, P. (2005). Notes on future and history in Hermann Cohen's anti-eschatological messianism. In M. Reinier (Ed.), *Hermann Cohen's critical idealism* (pp. 133–160). Netherlands: Springer.

Fishman, S. M., & McCarthy. L. (2007). *John Dewey and the philosophy and practice of hope*. Urbana, IL: University of Illinois Press.

Fleming, P. (2004). The secret Adorno. *Qui Parle, 15*(1), 97–114.

Foa, R., & Meaney, T. (2011). The last word. *The Utopian*. Retrieved February 22, 2011 from http://www.the-utopian.org/post/3217295807/the-last-word

Freire, P. (2006). *Pedagogy of hope: Reliving pedagogy of the oppressed* (R.R. Barr, Trans., & A. Maria & A. Freire, Eds.). London: Continuum,

Friedman, L. J. (2013). *The lives of Erich Fromm: Love's prophet*. New York, NY: Columbia University Press.

Fromm, E. (1951). *The forgotten language: An introduction to the understanding of dreams, fairy tales, and myths*. New York, NY: Grove Press, Inc.

Fromm, E. (1955). The human implications of instinctivistic 'radicalism'. *Dissent, 2*(4), 342–349.

Fromm, E. (1955). *The sane society*. New York, NY: Rinehart and Company.

Fromm, E. (1956). *The art of loving*. New York, NY: Harper & Row.

Fromm, E. (1959). *Sigmund Freud's mission: An analysis of his personality and influence*. New York, NY: Harper & Brothers Publishers.

Fromm, E. (1960). A foreword by Erich Fromm. In A.S. Neill (Ed.), *Summerhill: A radical approach to child rearing*. New York, NY: Hart Publishing Company.

Fromm, E. (1960). Foreword. In E. Bellamy (Ed.), *Looking backward* (pp. 5–20). New York, NY: The New American Library of World Literature, Inc.

Fromm, E. (1961). *May man prevail?: An inquiry into the facts and fictions of foreign policy*. Garden City, NY: Doubleday and Co.

Fromm, E. (1963). *Beyond the chains of illusion: My encounter with Marx and Freud*. New York, NY: Pocket Books, Inc.

Fromm, E. (1963) . *War within man: A psychological enquiry into the roots of destructiveness*. Philadelphia, PA: American Friends Service Committee.

Fromm, E. (1964). *The heart of man: Its genius for good and evil*. New York, NY: Harper & Row.

Fromm, E. (1966). *The dogma of Christ: And other essays on religion, psychology, and culture*. Garden City, NY: Anchor Books, Doubleday & Company.

Fromm, E. (1966). *You shall be as gods: A radical interpretation of the old testament and its tradition*. New York, NY: Holt, Rinehart, and Winston.

Fromm, E. (1967) . *Martyrs and heroes*. Retrieved from http://www.erich-fromm.de/data/pdf/1990s-e.pdf

Fromm, E. (1968). *The revolution of hope: Towards a humanized technology*. New York, NY: Harper & Row.

Fromm, E. (1970). Foreword (H. Brandt, Trans.). In S. Attanasio (Ed.), *The search for a third way: My path between east and west*. Garden City, NY: Doubleday.

Fromm, E. (1968). Marx's contribution to the knowledge of man. In E. Fromm (Ed.), *The crisis of psychoanalysis: Essays on Freud, Marx, and social psychology* (pp. 62–76). New York, NY: Henry Holt and Company.

Fromm, E. (1970). *The crisis of psychoanalysis: Essays on Freud, Marx, and social psychology*. New York, NY: Henry Holt and Company.

Fromm, E. (1974). *The anatomy of human destructiveness*. New York, NY: Holt, Rinehart, and Winston.

Fromm, E. (1978). *Psychoanalysis and religion*. New Haven, CT: Yale University Press.

Fromm, E. (1980). *Greatness and limitations of Freud's thought*. New York, NY: Harper & Row.

Fromm, E. (1981). *On disobedience and other essays*. New York, NY: The Seabury Press.

Fromm, E. (1984). Afterword (pp. 257–267) by G. Orwell.

Fromm, E. (1989). Politics and psychoanalysis. In S. E. Bronner & D. M. Kellner (Eds.), *Critical theory and society: A reader* (pp. 213–218). New York, NY: Routledge.

Fromm, E. (1989). *Das jüdische Gesetz: Zur Soziologie des Diaspora-Judentums: Dissertation von 1922*. Weinheim, Germany: Beltz Verlag.

Fromm, E. (1990). *Man for himself: An inquiry into the psychology of ethics*. New York, NY: Henry Holt and Company.

Fromm, E. (1994). *On being human*. New York, NY: Continuum Publishing Company.

Fromm, E. (1994). *The art of listening*. New York, NY: Continuum.

Fromm, E. (2000). Autobiographical sidelights. *International Forum of Psychoanalysis, 9*, 251–253.

Fromm, E. (2000). The social determinants of psychoanalytic therapy. *International Forum of Psychoanalysis, 9*(3–4), 149–165.

Fromm, E. (2004). *Marx's concept of man*. London, UK: Continuum.

Fromm, E. (2004). *The art of being*. New York, NY: Continuum.

Fromm, E. (2009). Being centrally related to the patient. In R. Funk (Ed.), *The clinical Erich Fromm: Personal accounts and papers on therapeutic technique*. Amsterdam, Netherland: Rodopi.

Fromm, E. (2009). *To have or to be?* New York, NY: Continuum.

Fromm, E. (2010). *Beyond Freud: From individual to social psychoanalysis*. Riverdale, NY: American Mental Health Foundation Inc.

Fromm, E. (2010). *The pathology of normalcy* (American Mental Health Foundation, Inc., Trans.). Riverdale, NY: American Mental Health Foundation, Inc.

Fromm, E. (2012). *Psychoanalysis and sociology*. Retrieved February 18, 2012 from http://www.philosophy.ru/upload/1158745816_file.pdf

Fromm, E. (Ed.) (1965). The application of humanist psychoanalysis to Marx's theory. *Socialist Humanism: An International Symposium*. Garden City, NY.

Fromm, E. (2000). A letter from Erich Fromm to Jan Strezelecki. *Dialogue and Universalism, 10*(5/6), 175.

Fromm, E. (1972). *Escape from freedom*. New York, NY: Avon Books.

Fromm, E . The social philosophy of 'will therapy'. Retrieved from http://www.erich-fromm.de/data/pdf/1939a-e.pdf

Fromm, E., Hart, W. O., Davidson, W. C., Valentine, B., & Kempton, M. (1960). *We have a vision...a deep faith: 5 statements on why join the Socialist Party-Social Democratic Federation*. New York, NY: Socialist Party-Social Democratic Federation.

Funk, R. (1982). *Erich Fromm: The courage to be human* (M. Shaw, Trans.). New York, NY: Continuum.

Funk, R. (1999). Introduction. In A. Kevin (Ed.), *Erich Fromm and critical criminology: Beyond the punitive society*. Urbana, IL: University of Illinois Press.

Funk, R. (2000). *Erich Fromm: His life and ideas: An illustrated biography*. New York, NY: Continuum.

Funk, R. (2003). *Major points in Erich Fromm's thought* (originally a talk at 1975 conference, Possibilities of psychoanalysis: Retrospect and prospects in honor of Erich Fromm's 75th birthday). Retrieved July 3, 2011 from http://www.erich-fromm.de/data/pdf/Funk,%20R.,%201975a.pdf

Funk, R. (2003). *The Jewish roots of Erich Fromm's humanistic thinking*. Retrieved from http://www.erich-fromm.de/data/pdf/Funk,%20R.,%201988f.pdf

Galli, B. E. (1999). Introduction. In A. Udoff & B. E. Galli. (Eds. & Trans.), *Franz Rosenzweig's The new thinking* (pp. 1–41). New York, NY: Syracuse University Press.

Gay, P. (2001). *Weimar culture: The outsider as insider.* New York, NY: W. W. Norton & Company.

Gertel, E. B. (1999). Judaism: Fromm, Freud, and Midrash. *EBSCOHost, 48(4),* 429–439.

Geuss, R. (2004). Dialectics and the revolutionary impulse. In F. Rush (Ed.), *The Cambridge companion to critical theory* (pp. 103–138). Cambridge, UK: Cambridge University Press.

Goggin, J. E., & Eileen, B. G. (2001). *Death of a "Jewish science": Psychoanalysis in the third Reich.* Bloomington, IN: Purdue University Press.

Gray, J. (2007). *Black mass: Apocalyptic religion and the death of utopia.* New York, NY: Farrar, Straus and Giroux.

Groiser, D. (2005). Jewish law and tradition in the early work of Erich Fromm. In M. Kohlenbach & R. Guess (Eds.), *The early Frankfurt School and religion.* New York, NY: Palgrave Macmillan.

Gutierrez, G. (1991). *A theology of liberation: History, politics, and salvation* (S. C. Inda & J. E. Maryknoll, Trans. & Eds.). New York, NY: Orbis Books.

Habermas, J. (2002). *Religion and rationality: Essays on reason, religion, and modernity.* Cambridge, MA: MIT Press.

Hansen, J. (1956). A psychoanalyst looks for a sane society. *Fourth International, 17(2),* 65–69. Retrieved May 18, 2009 from http://www.marxists.org/archive/hansen/1956/xx/psych.htm

Hartman, D. (2011). Sinai and Exodus: Two grounds for hope in the Jewish tradition. *Religious Studies, 14(3),* 373–387. Retrieved February 10, 2011 from http://www.jstor.org/stable/pdfplus/20005502. pdf?acceptTC=true

Hausdorff, D. (1972). *Erich Fromm.* New York, NY: Twayne Publishers.

Held, D. (1980). *Introduction to critical theory: Horkheimer to Habermas.* Berkeley, CA: University of California Press.

Hooks, B. (2000). *All about love: New visions.* New York, NY: Harper Perennial.

Hooks, B. (2010). *Surrendered to love: Martin Luther King's legacy.* Retrieved from http://mindful.org/the-mindful-society/activism/surrendered-to-love-martin-luther-king%E2%80%99s-legacy

Horkheimer, M., & Adorno, T. W. (2002). *Dialectic of enlightenment: Philosophical fragments* (G. S. Noerr Ed., & E. Jephcott, Trans.). Stanford, CA: Stanford University Press.

Hornstein, G. A. *To redeem one person is to redeem the world: The life of Frieda Fromm-Reichmann.* New York, NY: The Free Press.

Hudson, W. (1982). *The Marxist philosophy of Ernst Bloch.* New York, NY: St. Martin's Press.

Huffman, R. (2009). *The gun speaks: The Baader-Meinhof at the dawn of terror.* Retrieved August 29, 2009 from http://www.baader-meinhof.com/gunspeaks/gunintrochapter.html

Idel, M. (1988). *Messianic mystics.* New Haven, CT: Yale University Press.

International Federation of Psychoanalytic Societies (IFPS). (2011). Retrieved December 17, 2011 from http://www.ifps-online.com/index.html

International Federation of Psychoanalytic Societies (IFPS). (2013). Retrieved August 10, 2013 from http://www.ifp-s.org/

Jamison, A. (1994). *Seeds of the sixties.* Berkeley, CA: University of California Press.

Janaway, C. (2002). *Schopenhauer: A very short introduction.* Oxford, UK: Oxford University Press.

Janik, A. (1973). *Wittgenstein's Vienna.* New York, NY: Simon and Schuster.

Jay, M. (1973). *The dialectical imagination: A history of the Frankfurt School and the Institute of Social Research, 1923-1950.* Boston, MA: Little, Brown and Company.

Jay, M. (1984). *Marxism and totality: The adventures of a concept from Lukács to Habermas.* Berkeley, CA: University of California Press.

Jay, M. (1993). *Force fields: Between intellectual history and cultural critique.* New York, NY: Routledge

Jay, M. (2009). *Walter Benjamin, remembrance, and the First World War.* Retrieved July 13, 2009 from http://www.march.es/ceacs/publicaciones/working/archivos/1996_87.pdf

Johnston, C. (2012). *Starvation of a witness.* Retrieved February 2012 from http://www.southerncrossreview.org/15/weil.htm#ref10

Jonas, H. (1963). *The gnostic religion: The message of the alien god and the beginnings of Christianity* (2nd ed.). Boston, MA: Beacon Press.

Kant, I. (1999). On the common saying: That may be correct in theory, but it is of no use in practice. In M.J. Gregor (Ed. & Trans.), *Practical Philosophy* (pp. 273–310). Cambridge: Cambridge University Press.

REFERENCES

Katz, M. S. (1987). *Ban the bomb: A history of SANE, the committee for a sane nuclear policy*. New York, NY: Praeger.
Kellner, D. (n.d.). *Erich Fromm, Judaism, and the Frankfurt School*. Retrieved from http://www.gseis. ucla.edu/faculty/kellner/essays/erichfrommjudaism.pdf
Kellner, D. (1984). *Herbert Marcuse and the crisis of Marxism*. Houndmills, UK: MacMillan.
Kellner, D. (1991). Introduction to the second edition. *One-dimensional man: Studies in the ideology of advanced industrial society* by H. Marcuse. Boston, MA: Beacon Press.
Klein, N. (2007). *The shock doctrine: The rise of disaster capitalism*. New York, NY: Henry Holt and Company.
Kleist, H. (1976). Puppet theatre. *Salmagundi, 33/34*, 83–88.
Knapp, G. P. (1989). *The art of living: Erich Fromm's life and works*. New York, NY: Peter Lang.
Kohlenbach, M., & Guess, R. (Eds.). (2005). *The early Frankfurt School and religion*. Houndmills, Basingstoke, Hampshire, UK: Palgrave MacMillan.
Kolakowski, L. (1968). *Towards a Marxist humanism: Essays on the left today* (J. Z. Peel, Trans.). New York, NY: Grove Press, Inc.
Kolakowski, L. (2005). *Main currents of Marxism* (P. S. Falla, Trans.). New York, NY: W. W. Norton & Company.
Koltun-Fromm, K. (2010). *Material culture and Jewish thought in America*. Bloomington, IN: Indiana University Press.
Kouvelakis, S. (2003). *Philosophy and revolution: Philosophy and revolution from Kant to Marx* (G. M. Goshgarian, Trans.). London: Verso.
La Vopa, A. (1997). The philosopher and the Schwärmer : On the career of a German epithet from Luther to Kant. *The Huntington Library Quarterly, 60*(1/2), *Enthusiasm and Enlightenment in Europe, 1650–1850*, 85–115.
Landauer, G. *Aufruf zum Socialismus*. Retrieved from http://www.anarchismus.at/anarchistische-klassiker/gustav-landauer/108-gustav-landauer-aufruf-zum-sozialismus-teil-1 3/4/12
Landauer, G. *Anarchism in Germany and other essays*. Oakland, CA: AK Press.
Landauer, G. (1978). *For socialism* (D. J. Parent, Trans.). St. Louis, MO: Telos Press.
Landauer, G. (2010). *Revolution and other writings: A political reader* (G. Kuhn, Ed. & Trans.). Oakland, CA: PM Press.
Lane, R. (2005). *Reading Walter Benjamin: Writing through the catastrophe*. Manchester, NY: Manchester University Press.
Large, W. (2010). *Time & money: Philosophy of religion and the critique of capital*. Retrieved from http://www.jcrt.org/archives/09.1/Large.pdf
Lazier, B. (2008). *God interrupted: Heresy and the European imagination between the world wars*. Princeton, NJ: Princeton University Press.
Leaman, O. (2003). Jewish existentialism: Rosenzweig, Buber, and Soloveitchik. In D. H. Frank & O. Leaman (Eds.), *History of Jewish philosophy*. London: Routledge.
Lebovic, N. (2006). The beauty and terror of *Lebensphilosophie*: Ludwig Klages, Walter Benjamin, and Alfred Baeumler. *South Central Review, 23*, 23–39.
Lebovic, N. (2004). *Dionysian politics and the discourse of Rausch* (pp. 1–9). Working Papers, UCLA Center for European and Eurasian Studies.
Lebovic, N. (2008). The Jerusalem school: The theopolitical hour. *New German Critique*, 97–120.
Lefebvre, H. (2008). *Critique of everyday life*. (Vol. 1). (J. Moore, Trans.). London: Verso.
Lilla, M. (2007). *The stillborn God: Religion, politics, and the modern West*. New York, NY: Alfred A. Knopf.
Lilley, S., McNalley, D., Yuen, E., & Davis, J. (2012). *Catastrophism: The apocalyptic politics of collapse and rebirth*. Oakland, CA: PM Press.
Löwenthal, L. (1987). *An unmastered past: The autobiographical reflections of Leo Lowenthal*. Berkeley, CA: University of California Press, Ltd.
Löwith, K. (1949). *Meaning in history*. Chicago, IL: University of Chicago Press.
Lowy, M. (1980). Jewish messianism and libertarian utopia in central Europe (1900–1933). *New German Critique, 20*, 105–115.

Lowy, M. (1992). *Redemption and utopia: Jewish libertarian thought in central Europe: A study in elective affinity* (H. Heaney, Trans.). Stanford, CA: Stanford University Press.

Lowy, M. (2001). Messianism in the early work of Gershom Scholem. *New German Critique, 83*, 177–191.

Lowy, M. (2009). Capitalism as religion: Benjamin and Weber. *Historical Materialism, 17,* 60–73.

Lowy, M. (2012) Anticapitalist readings of Weber's Protestant ethic: Ernst Bloch, Walter Benjamin, Georg Lukacs, Erich Fromm. *Logos Journal, 9*(1) . Retrieved January 26, 2012 from http://logosjournal.com/2010/lowy/

Lukács, G. (1971). *History and class consciousness: Studies in Marxist dialectics* (R. Livingstone, Trans.). Cambridge, MA: MIT Press.

Lukács, G. (1971). *The theory of the novel: A historico-philosophical essay on the forms of great epic literature* (A. Bostok, Trans.). Cambridge, MA: The M.I.T. Press.

Lukács, G. (1980). *The destruction of reason* (P. Palmer, Trans.). London: The Merlin Press.

Lukács, G. (2010). *Soul and form* (A. Bostock, Trans.). J. T. Sanders & K. Terezakis, (Eds.). Introduction. Judith Butler. New York, NY: Columbia University Press.

Lundgren, S. (1999). *The fight against idols: Erich fromm on religion, Judaism, and the Bible.* Frankfurt am Main: Peter Lang.

Luxemburg, R. (1979). Socialism and the churches. *Marxist internet archive.* Retrieved March 3, 2009 from http://www.marxists.org/archive/luxemburg/1905/misc/socialism-churches.htm

Luxemburg, R. (1980). Theory & practice. *Marxist internet archive.* Retrieved February 1, 2011 from http://www.marxists.org/archive/luxemburg/1910/theory-practice/ch05.htm

MacIntyre, A. (2006). *Edith Stein: A philosophical prologue: 1913–1922.* Lanham, MD: Rowman & Littlefield Publishers, Inc.

Magid, S. (2008). Gershom scholem. In E. Zalta (Ed.), *The Stanford encyclopedia of philosophy* (Fall ed.). Retrieved from http://plato.stanford.edu/archives/fall2008/entries/scholem/

Marcel, G. (1951). *Homo viator: Introduction to a metaphysic of hope* (E. Crauford, Trans.). Chicago, IL: Henry Regnery Company.

Marcuse, H. (1955). The social implications of Freudian 'revisionism'. *Dissent, 2*(3), 221–240.

Marcuse, H. (1965). Socialist humanism? In E. Fromm (Ed.), *Socialist humanism: An international symposium.* Garden City, NY: Doubleday & Company, Inc.

Marcuse, H. (1966). *Eros and civilization: A philosophical inquiry into Freud.* Boston, MA: Beacon Press.

Marcuse, H. (1969). *An essay on liberation.* Boston, MA: Beacon Press.

Marcuse, H. (1991). *One-dimensional man: Studies in the ideology of advanced industrial society.* Boston, MA: Beacon Press.

Marcuse, H. (1999). *Reason and revolution: Hegel and the rise of social theory.* Amherst, NY: Prometheus Books.

Marcuse, H. (2005). The new left and the 1960s. In D. Kellner (Ed.), *Collected papers of Herbert Marcuse* (Vol. 3). London: Routledge.

Marx, K. (1965). *Early writings* (T. B. Bottomore, Ed. & Trans.). New York, NY: McGraw-Hill.

Marx, K. (1977). In D. McLellan (Ed.), *Karl Marx: Selected Writings.* Oxford, UK: Oxford University Press.

Marx, K. (2007). Introduction to the contribution to a critique of Hegel's philosophy of right. *Marxist Internet Archive.* Retrieved April 22, 2007 from http://www.marxists.org/archive/marx/works/1843/critique-hpr/index.htm

Marx, K. (2011). Theses on Feuerbach. *Marxist internet archive,* 1–4. Retrieved July 14, 2011 from http://www.marxists.org/archive/marx/works/1845/theses/index.htm

McLaughlin, N. (2012). Critical theory meets America: Riesman, Fromm, and the lonely crowd. Retrieved January 23, 2012 from http://tucnak.fsv.cuni.cz/~hajek/ModerniSgTeorie/literatura/kritickateorie/krit_teorie1.pdf

McLaughlin, N. (1998). How to become a forgotten intellectual: Intellectual movements and the rise and fall of Erich Fromm. *Sociological Forum, 13,* 215–246.

McLaughlin, N. (1999). *Origin myths in the social sciences: Fromm, the Frankfurt School and the emergence of critical theory.* Retrieved July 6, 2009 from http://www.ualberta.ca/~cjscopy/articles/mclaughlin.html

REFERENCES

Mendieta, E. (2007). *Global fragments: Globalizations, Latinamericanisms, and critical theory*. Albany, NY: State University of New York Press.

Merleau-Ponty, M. (2003). *Nature: Course notes from the Collège of France*. Evanston, IL: Northwestern University Press.

Merton, T. (1968). The answer of Minerva: Pacifism and resistance in Simone Weil. Retrieved February 12, 2011 from http://www.dartmouth.edu/~engl5vr/Merton.html

Merton, T., & Erich, F . Fromm/Merton letters. Archives at Bellarmine University, LA and at University of Kentucky, KY.

Merton, T. (1988). *A vow of conversation: Journals, 1964-1965*. N. B. Stone (Ed). New York, NY: Farrar, Straus, Giroux.

Millán, S., & Gojman, S. (2000). The legacy of Fromm in Mexico. *International Forum of Psychoanalysis, 9*, 207–215.

Miri, S. J. (2010). Religion and social theory in the frommesque discourse. *Islamic perspective, 4*. Retrieved January 26, 2012 from http://iranianstudies.org/wp-content/uploads/2010/12/Ipcss4-LAIS. pdf

Miri, S. J. (2010) . Rereading Fromm's conditions of the human situation. *Transcendent Philosophy: An International Journal for Comparative Philosophy and Mysticism. 11*, 233. Retrieved January 26, 2012 from http://iranianstudies.org/wp-content/uploads/2010/04/Trans-Phil-Vol11-e3-Web.pdf

Mittelman, A. (2009). *Hope in a democratic age: Philosophy, religion, and political theory*. Oxford, UK: Oxford University Press.

Morgan, M. (2001). *Interim Judaism: Jewish thought in a century of crisis*. Bloomington, IN: Indiana University Press.

Moltmann, J. (1996). *The coming of God: Christian eschatology* (M. Kohl, Trans.). Minneapolis, MN: Fortress Press.

Neumann, B. (2000). The National Socialist politics of life. *New German Critique, 85*, 107–130.

Noll, R. (1994). *The Jung cult: Origins of a charismatic movement*. Princeton, NJ: Princeton University Press.

Norton, R. E. (2002). *Secret Germany: Stefan George and his circle*. Ithaca, NY: Cornell University Press.

Novalis. (1997). *Philosophical writings* (M. M. Stoljar, Trans.). Albany, NY: State University of New York Press.

Ohana, D. (2010). *Political theologies in the holy land: Israeli messianism and its critics*. London: Routledge.

Osborne, P., & Matthew, C. (2011). Walter Benjamin. In E. N. Zalta (Ed.), *The Stanford encyclopedia of philosophy* (Spring ed.). Retrieved from http://plato.stanford.edu/archives/spr2011/entries/benjamin

Pangilinan, R. (2009). Against alienation: The emancipative potential of critical pedagogy in Erich Fromm. *Kritike, 3*(2), 21–29. Retrieved from http://www.kritike.org/journal/issue_6/pangilinan_december2009.pdf

Pietikainen, P. (2007). *Alchemists of human nature: Psychological utopianism in Gross, Jung, Reich. and Fromm*. London: Pickering & Chatto.

Pollock, B. (2009). Franz Rosenzweig. In E. N. Zalta (Ed.), *The Stanford encyclopedia of philosophy* (Fall ed.). Retrieved from http://plato.stanford.edu/archives/fall2009/entries/rosenzweig/

Poma, A. (1997). *The critical philosophy of Hermann Cohen* (J. Denton, Trans.). New York, NY: State University of New York Press.

Rabinbach, A. (1997). *In the shadow of catastrophe: German intellectuals between apocalypse and enlightenment*. Berkeley, CA: University of California Press.

Rabinbach, A. (1985). Between enlightenment and apocalypse: Benjamin, Bloch and modern Jewish messianism. *New German Critique, 34*, 103.

Rabinkow, S. B. (1987). The individual and society in Judaism. In L. Jung (Ed.), *Sages and Saints* (pp. 133–155). Hoboken, NJ: The Jewish library, Vol. X. Ktav Publishing House, Inc.

Rand, A. (1966). *Capitalism: The unknown ideal*. New York, NY: The New American Library, Inc.

Rickert, J. (1986). The Fromm-Marcuse Debate Revisited. *Theory and Society, 15*, 351–400. Dordrecht, Netherlands: Martinus Nijhoff Publishers. Retrieved February 11, 2012 from http://www.erich-fromm.de/biophil/joomla/images/stories/pdf-Dateien/Rickert_J_1986.pdf

Roazen, P. (2001). The exclusion of Erich Fromm from the IPA. *Contemporary Psychoanalysis, 37*(1), 5–42. Retrieved June 26, 2011 from http://www.erich-fromm.de/data/pdf/Roazen,%20P.,%202001.pdf

Roazen, P. (2000). Fromm's 'Escape from freedom' and his standing today. *International Forum of Psychoanalysis, 9*(3/4), 239–240.

Rockmore, T. (1980). *Fichte, Marx, and the German philosophical tradition.* Carbondale, IL: Southern Illinois University Press.

Rosenzweig, F. (1971). *The star of redemption* (W. W. Hallo, Trans). Boston, MA: Beacon Press.

Rothstein, E., Muschamp, H., & Marty, M. E. (2003). *Visions of utopia.* Oxford, UK: Oxford University Press. Retrieved December 14, 2009 from http://www.scribd.com/doc/22472651/rothstein-et-al-visions-of-utopia-2003

Saperstein, M. (Ed.). (1992). *Essential papers on messianic movements and personalities in Jewish history.* New York, NY: New York University Press.

Saunders, F. S. (1999). *The cultural cold war: The CIA and the world of arts and letters.* New York, NY: The New Press.

Schacter, J. J. (Ed.). (1987). Reminiscences of Shlomo Barukh Rabinkow. In L. Jung (Ed.), *Sages and saints* (Vol. X, pp. 93–132). Hoboken, NJ: The Jewish library, Ktav Publishing House, Inc.

Schaeder, G. (1996). Martin Buber: A biographical sketch (R. C. Winston & H. Zohn, Trans.). In N. M. Glatzer & P. Mendes-Flohr (Eds.), *The letter of Martin Buber: A life of dialogue* (pp. 1–62). Syracuse, NY: Syracuse University Press.

Scholem, G. (1954). *Major trends in Jewish mysticism.* New York, NY: Schocken Books.

Scholem, G. (1971). *The messianic idea in Judaism and other essays on Jewish spirituality.* New York, NY: Schocken Books.

Scholem, G. (1973). *Sabbatai Sevi: The mystical messiah (1626–1676).* Princeton, NJ: Princeton University Press.

Scholem, G. (1976). *On Jews and Judaism in crisis: Selected essays* (W. J. Dannhauser, Ed.). New York, NY: Schocken.

Scholem, G. (1980). *From Berlin to Jerusalem: Memories of my youth* (H. Zohn, Trans.). New York, NY: Schocken Books.

Schroyer, T. (1973). *The critique of domination: The origins and development of critical theory.* Boston, MA: Beacon Press.

Shannon, W. H. (2003). Thomas Merton and Judaism. In B. Bruteau (Ed.), *Merton & Judaism: Recognition, repentance, and renewal: Holiness in words.* Louisville, KY: Fons Vitae.

Shell, S. (2009), 'To spare the vanquished and crush the arrogant': Leo Strauss' lecture on 'German Nihilism.' In S. B. Smith (Ed.), *The Cambridge companion to Leo Strauss* (pp. 171–192). Cambridge: Cambridge University Press.

Siebert, R. J. (1985). *The critical theory of religion: The Frankfurt School from universal pragmatic to political theology.* Berlin: Walter de Gruyter & Co.

Silver, A. S. (1999). Frieda Fromm-Reichmann and Erich Fromm. *International Forum of Psychoanalysis, 8*, 19–23.

Specter, M. G. (2010). *Habermas: An intellectual biography.* Cambridge: Cambridge University Press.

Spirer, E. (2010). Candidates for survival: A talk with Harold Bloom. *Boston Review*, 1–5. Retrieved September 13, 2010 from http://bostonreview.net/BR11.1/bloom.html

Susman, M. (1999). The exodus from philosophy. In A. Udoff & B. E. Galli (Ed. & Trans.), *Franz Rosenzweig's "The New Thinking"* (pp. 105–111). Syracuse, NY: Syracuse University Press.

Suzuki, D. T., Fromm, E., & De Martino, R. (1963). *Zen Buddhism and psychoanalysis.* New York, NY: Grove Press, Inc.

Swedberg, R., & Reich, W. Georg Simmel's aphorisms. *Theory, culture, and society*, 24–51. Retrieved March 3, 2012 from http://www.soc.cornell.edu/faculty/swedberg/Georg%20Simmels%20Aphorisms.pdf

Tar, Z. (1977). *The Frankfurt School: The critical theories of Max Horkheimer and Theodor W. Adorno.* New York, NY: John Wiley and Sons.

Taubes, J. (2010). *From cult to culture: Fragments toward a critique of historical reason* (E. Fonrobert & A. Engel, Ed.). Stanford, CA: Stanford University Press.

Taubes, J. (2009). *Occidental eschatology* (D. Ratmoko, Trans.). Stanford, CA: Stanford University Press.

Taubes, S. A. (1967). Simone Weil: The absent God. In T. J. J. Altizer (Ed.), *Toward a new Christianity: Readings in the death of God theology* (pp.107–119). New York, NY: Harcourt, Brace & World, Inc.

Thomson, A. (2009). *Erich Fromm: Explorer of the human condition.* Houndmills, Basingstroke, UK: Palgrave MacMillan.

Toscano, A. (2010). *Fanaticism: On the uses of an idea.* London: Verso.

Treanor, B. (2010). Gabriel (-Honoré) Marcel. In E. N. Zalta (Ed.), *The Stanford encyclopedia of philosophy* (Fall ed.). Retrieved from http://plato.stanford.edu/archives/fall2010/entries/marcel/

Vickrey, D. (2010). Erich Fromm and the Baader-Meinhof. *Dialog International.* Retrieved August 28, 2010 from http://www.dialoginternational.com/dialog_international/2007/09/erich-fromm-and.html

Viviano, B. T. (1980). The kingdom of God in Albert the Great and Thomas Aquinas. *Thomist: A Speculative Quarterly Review, 44*(4), 502–522.

Waggoner, M. (2006). The Frankfurt School on religion. *Journal of Cultural and Religious Theory.* Retrieved March 3, 2010 from http://www.jcrt.org/archives/08.1/waggoner.pdf

Watkins, M., & Shulman, H. (2008). *Towards psychologies of liberation.* Houndmills, UK: Palgrave MacMillan.

Weil, S. (1986). *Simone Weil: An anthology* (S. Miles, Ed. & Trans.). New York, NY: Grove Press.

Whitebook, J. (2004). The marriage of Marx and Freud: Critical theory and psychoanalysis. In F. Rush (Ed.), *The Cambridge companion to critical theory* (pp. 74–102). Cambridge, UK: Cambridge University Press.

Wheatland, T. (2009). *The Frankfurt School in exile.* Minneapolis, MN: University of Minnesota Press.

Whyte, W. H. Jr. (1956). *The organization man.* New York, NY: Simon and Schuster.

Wiggershaus, R. (1994). *The Frankfurt School: Its history, theories, and political significance* (M.Robertson, Trans.). Cambridge, MA: MIT Press.

Wilde, L. (2001). Against idolatry: The humanistic ethics of Erich Fromm. *Marxism's Ethical Thinkers.* L. Wilde. (Ed.), Houndmills, U.K.: Palgrave.

Wilde, L. (2004). *Erich Fromm and the quest for solidarity.* New York, NY: Palgrave MacMillan.

Wolin, R. (n.d.). *Benjamin meets the cosmics.* Retrieved from www.law.wisc.edu/.../wolin...benjamin_meets_the_cosmics.doc

Wolin, R. (2006). *The Frankfurt School revisited and other essays on politics and society.* New York, NY: Routledge.

Wolin, R. (2001). *Heidegger's children: Hannah Arendt, Karl Löwith, Hans Jonas, and Herbert Marcuse.* Princeton, NJ: Princeton University Press.

Wolin, R. (1995). *Labyrinths: Explorations in the critical history of ideas.* Amherst, MA: University of Massachusetts Press.

Wolin, R. (2004). *The seduction of unreason: The intellectual romance with fascism from Nietzsche to postmodernism.* Princeton, NJ: Princeton University Press.

Wolin, R. (1992). *The terms of cultural criticism: The Frankfurt School, existentialism, poststructuralism.* New York, NY: Columbia University Press.

Wolin, R. (1994). *Walter Benjamin: An aesthetic of redemption.* Berkeley, CA: University of California Press.

Zilbersheid, U. (2002). The idea of abolition of labor in socialist utopian thought. *Utopian Studies, 13,* 21–42.

ABBREVIATIONS*

AB: *The Art of Being*
AHD: *Anatomy of Human Destructiveness*
AL: *The Art of Loving*
Ali : *The Art of Listening*
AS: "Autobiographical Sidelights by Erich Fromm"
BC: *Beyond the Chains of Illusion: My Encounter with Marx and Freud*
BF: *Beyond Freud*
CP: *The Crisis of Psychoanalysis*
DC: *The Dogma of Christ: And Other Essays on Religion, Psychology, and Culture*
EF: *Escape from Freedom*
FL: *The Forgotten Language*
GL: *Greatness and Limitations of Freud's Thought*
JG: *Das jüdische Gesetz*
MFH: *Man for Himself*
MMP: *May Man Prevail?*
MCM: *Marx's Concept of Man*
OBH: *On Being Human*
OD: *On Disobedience*
PN: *Pathology of Normalcy*
PP: "Politics and Psychoanalysis"
PR: *Psychoanalysis and Religion*
ROH: *Revolution of Hope*
SFM: *Sigmund Freud's Mission*
SS: *The Sane Society*
TB: *To Have or To Be?*
WW: *War Within Man*
YSB: *You Shall Be as Gods*
ZB: *Zen Buddhism and Psychoanalysis*

* All titles are by Erich Fromm.

NAME INDEX

217

Wheatland, Thomas, xxi, 4, 8, 29–31, 41–43
Whitman, Walt, 50, 60, 61, 133
Whyte, William, 175
Wilde, Lawrence, xx, xxv, 4, 133, 135, 140, 166, 167, 169, 186
Wolfskehl, Karl, 94
Wolin, Richard, xxi, xxv, 28, 55, 63, 68, 77, 96, 98, 103–105, 110, 151, 166

Z
Zevi (Sevi), Sabbatai, 45, 75–77, 90, 126, 161
Zilbersheid, Uri, 16, 45, 188
Žižek, Slavoj, xx, xxv

CPSIA information can be obtained at www.ICGtesting.com
Printed in the USA
LVOW11s0603271014

410596LV00005B/12/P